# THE RIDDLE
# OF THE
# SCROLLS

Reading like a detective thriller involving the highest of stakes, this is the story of a discovery that is still to be fully revealed, one that has split the scholarly community worldwide, and which may yet transform our understanding of two of the world's religious faiths. The manuscripts known collectively as the Dead Sea Scrolls have been the subject of controversy ever since the discovery of the first texts in a cave in the Judean Desert at Khirbet Qumrân in 1947. The precise details of this find, and the story of what happened to these manuscripts and the many others found subsequently on other sites are shrouded in mystery, partly because some were uncovered during illegal explorations which destroyed important evidence of provenance, and partly because it soon became apparent that the contents of the scrolls themselves were highly sensitive, consisting of religious texts, many previously unknown. The first Qumrân finds took place during the pivotal period when the new Zionist nation of Israel was in its infancy, and any discoveries bearing on the early history and identity of the Jews in the region took on added significance. Even more important, the new texts had and still have the potential to radically change our perception of early Judaism, the birth of Christianity and the nature of Judaeo-Christian religious belief itself. Beginning with an account of the discovery of the first scrolls, Del Medico deals with possible authorship and translation before presenting translations of the seven non-Biblical texts from Cave 1 including the much-debated Book of the War of the Sons of Light against the Sons of Darkness. Who wrote these manuscripts; when, where and why were they written; were they really sacred writings; who was the mysterious Teacher of Righteousness; what do the scrolls tell us about the past and the present? Today, there are several hundred documents and fragments that are considered Dead Sea Scrolls, but these fundamental questions are not fully resolved, and Del Medico's classic work provides the best and clearest background to the continuing riddle of the scrolls.

**www.keganpaul.com**

# THE KEGAN PAUL LIBRARY OF ARCANA

# THE RIDDLE OF THE SCROLLS

## H. E. DEL MEDICO

Kegan Paul
London · New York · Bahrain

First published in 2007 by
Kegan Paul Limited
UK: P.O. Box 256, London WC1B 3SW, England
Tel: 020 7580 5511 Fax: 020 7436 0899
E-Mail: books@keganpaul.com
Internet: http://www.keganpaul.com
USA: 61 West 62nd Street, New York, NY 10023
Tel: (212) 459 0600 Fax: (212) 459 3678
Internet: http://www.columbia.edu/cu/cup
BAHRAIN: bahrain@keganpaul.com

Distributed by:
Marston Book Services Ltd
160 Milton Park
Abingdon
Oxfordshire OX14 4SD
United Kingdom
Tel: (01235) 465500 Fax: (01235) 465555
Email: direct.orders@marston.co.uk

Columbia University Press
61 West 62nd Street, New York, NY 10023
Tel: (212) 459 0600 Fax: (212) 459 3678
Internet: http://www.columbia.edu/cu/cup

ISBN: 0-7103-1050-1

**British Library Cataloguing in Publication Data**
Medico, H. E. Del
The riddle of the scrolls. – (Library of Arcana)
1.Dead Sea scrolls
I.Title
296.1'55
ISBN 0710310501

# CONTENTS

# ACKNOWLEDGEMENTS

The Author and the Publishers wish to thank Professor H. H. Rowley for reading the proofs of this work and for his help in an advisory capacity during the production of the book.

They also wish to thank Helene Bieberkraut for permission to reproduce the photographs which appear facing pages 192, 193 and 224.

# ILLUSTRATIONS

# Author's Preface

Since the discovery of Hebrew manuscripts in a cave in the Judean Desert close to the Dead Sea, more than a thousand studies have been published on them, and fresh studies continue to appear almost every day. In some works attempts have been made to present general conclusions, but they have immediately been outdated by fresh facts, new theories, or the results of research, often on some point of detail. Works of a general nature aim at putting the manuscripts in their setting; and what is read in the texts is interpreted in accordance with the date assigned to them, and the environment in which their authors are placed. One has to start with assumptions based on what are considered assured facts, but since the discovery of the first manuscripts, many published items of information have been found to be incorrect. Some have since been corrected, but such corrections, being published in specialist reviews, are often not noticed or are passed over in silence. In considering these Dead Sea Scrolls, theories are sometimes based on fresh data which are open to question. In a word, it is the texts, and the texts alone, which can tell us their history.

At the time when I wrote my first article on the manuscripts from the Judean Desert[1] I had recognised that the writings, a few samples of which had just been published, could not be earlier than the first century A.D. I said that these writings could only have come from a *geniza* (depository for unusable sacred books, etc.), a cemetery for books, not from a hidden library as has been claimed for them since then. For a long time it was insisted that these manuscripts dated from the second century B.C., but in the end the first conclusion to which I had come was admitted to be correct. As regards the non-Biblical writings, a number of scholars still talk about ancient texts having been recopied, and want to date the composition of them in the Maccabean period. The majority of scholars, however, agree in assigning them to a later date. My second conclusion

[1] *Recherches de Science Religieuse*, XXXV (1948) pp. 589–92.

is still rejected. These Dead Sea manuscripts are often attributed to the Essenes: there is always the desire to see in these rolls and fragments the remains of a precious library buried, at a time when war was raging, by Jewish monks, who hoped one day to recover them intact.

It is with this assumption as a starting-point that all these texts are read and interpreted. It is in this hypothetic monastic environment that is placed the drawing up of all the manuscripts found in the caves of Qumrân, and everything that is read in them is considered to be part of the customs, beliefs and manners of the Essenes.[1]

Nothing that has been published up to the present has allowed me to modify my first impression. On the contrary, many new details have confirmed my opinion that the Dead Sea Scrolls do not form a homogeneous whole, a library, but a heap of various writings and fragments which rabbinic authority consigned to *genizoth* because it was necessary for some reason or other to withdraw them from circulation, and yet not destroy them, the Jews' bibliolatry forbidding the destruction of any writing in which the name of God occurred. I still hold that each text should be considered as a separate document, standing by itself. The only point in common in all these manuscripts is that from the rabbinic point of view they were "apocryphal"—that is to say, unorthodox, irregular, imperfect, defective or fragmentary.

This book does not claim to be written for the specialist. Notes are reduced to the minimum. The opinions of different scholars who have gone into the problem of these manuscripts have not all been quoted or discussed. It seemed useful to recount what are believed to be the facts of the first discovery, and what later discoveries have brought to light. It seemed equally necessary to recall the state in which these manuscripts and fragments were found, details which are too often left unmentioned. As a great deal has been made of the Essenes and a supposed Jewish monasticism lasting from the third century B.C. to the middle of the first century A.D., I considered it necessary to give a brief summary of the results of my research on the sources of our knowledge concerning the Essenes. A number of pages have been devoted to the ruins at Qumrân,

---

[1] Even for the study of variants between the current Hebrew version (the Massoretic text) of the canonical books and manuscripts from the Judean Desert, it is most important to know if what has been discovered, the different readings, the omissions, the additions, etc., belonged to a well-established tradition, or if it was the very fact of these variations that caused the manuscripts to be judged defective and thrown aside. The writing of a master found in a library has a very different value from that of a bad copy made by a pupil and thrown into the dustbin.

which some would identify with an Essenian monastery. Another chapter gives some information concerning the Qaraite movement, which some people regard as a survival of Essenism, and concerning a medieval writing of that Jewish sect found in Cairo and often associated with the Dead Sea Scrolls.

In another chapter, an analysis is made of the texts and fragments found in Cave I at Qumrân. It also appeared useful to give a short résumé of what is known concerning movements within Judaism from the Hellenistic period down to the first centuries A.D. The leading lines of thought in each text should make it possible to some extent to attribute it to the sect within which it was drawn up. The study of the manuscripts, however, leads to the conclusion that many works are as a matter of fact of a composite nature, different fragments being put together. Thus in addition to the problem of the date and place of origin of each constituent part of a manuscript, there is that of its compilation. Finally, as far as the scanty information on Jewish ecclesiastical history permits, an attempt has been made to find out at what time and under what circumstances each of the manuscripts under study could have been seized by rabbinic authorities and consigned to the *geniza*.

In Part II will be found translations of the texts and principal fragments found in Cave I, accompanied by brief commentaries. In Part III is given a translation and commentary of the Qaraite fragments found in Cairo. The limits as to what a publication of this kind may contain have forced me to renounce linguistic notes. I have also had to abandon any systematic comparison between the Old Testament and the phrases used by the different authors. In the first centuries A.D., Hebrew was certainly spoken and written in Palestine, but the literary style had become rigid, ready-made forms of expression borrowed from the Bible being employed. These expressions no longer had the value of quotations, being merely part of the current phraseology. When other texts of the same period are better known, it will be possible to think of making a dictionary of phrases used in Hebrew literature of that time. It would not fail to supply some surprising and unsuspected items of information.

As far as possible, the translations are word for word.[1] At times it has seemed necessary to break up sentences which were very long. Necessary complements have been added in parentheses ( ). Some gaps in the text

---

[1] This English translation follows the original text as closely as possible without being word for word. That would have necessitated unusual forms of sentences which would have been difficult to read, and might not have given the proper meaning. (*Translator's note.*)

have been filled in, but as sparingly as possible. These additions are enclosed in brackets [ ].

It has not been possible for me to give all the varying readings to which some passages lend themselves. I have been content to give those which seemed the most likely, and where the manuscripts have already been translated differently, as a rule I have refrained from any discussion of the other proposed versions. I should like to thank all those who by their constructive criticisms have enabled me to correct some of my earlier translations.

★        ★        ★

This book was completed in June 1955, but it was not till December 1956, that it could be given to the printer. The manuscript had been revised so as to take account of the latest developments of the problem of the Dead Sea Scrolls. Even so, it was necessary to add to it a final detail, for at the moment when the Sinai campaign was completed, the Israel Radio announced that, in collaboration with Professor Nahman Avigad, Professor Yigael Yadin, a general in the Israeli Army, had just published a translation of the last remaining unpublished roll from Cave I. Account has been taken as far as possible of this publication, which has only just reached France.[1] It is a preliminary report, only a few pages of the manuscript being given in photographic reproduction with transcription and translation into Hebrew and English. Doubtless a considerable time must elapse before the publication of the definite edition of the text, which is very fragmentary, while the unrolling and reading present great difficulties. This accounts for a gap in the list of manuscripts which ought to be dealt with here. I have tried to compensate for this by occasional references to manuscripts found in other caves in the region of Qumrân, which in my original scheme were not to have been included in this present study.

PARIS,
*March, 1957.*

[1] Nahman Avigad and Yigael Yadin, *A Genesis Aprocryphon,* Jerusalem, 1956.

# PART ONE

# The Riddle and Its Solution

# I

# A Sensational Discovery

During the spring of 1948, the Press throughout the world announced a sensational discovery which had just been made in Palestine. Some manuscripts of books from the Old Testament, much older than any known before, along with some other Hebrew writings not included in the Canon, had come to light. The British mandate for Palestine had come to an end. Not only on all its frontiers, but also in the heart of the country created by the fierce determination of the Zionist pioneers, the small nation of Israel was engaged in a heroic struggle against the coalition of Arab nations who denied it the right to exist. News of the fighting passed into the background. Public opinion was wild for information about the manuscripts and was eager to know the details of the discovery. Every newspaper, every Press agency wished to surpass its rivals in the sensationalism of its news. Scholars were interviewed, and often were caught unprepared, so that more than one voiced opinions which could not be sustained.

The prologue to this drama of several acts is set in Bethlehem a year earlier. In the spring of 1947, whilst seeking a straying sheep, some Bedouin of the Ta'amireh tribe had found some old rolls of leather in a cave of the Judean Desert. By hearsay, they knew that such antique objects might be of value. They offered them to a Mohammedan of Bethlehem, asking twenty or twenty-five Palestinian pounds for the whole collection. He refused to pay this sum, and the Bedouin offered them to another dealer in the same town, a Syrian Christian. This shopkeeper would not himself buy them, but passed on the information to a fellow Syrian Christian named Kiraz. He in turn spoke about this offer to the Syrian Metropolitan, Mar Athanasius Samuel, at St. Mark's Monastery. Finally, in association with this Anthony Kiraz, the Metropolitan bought the collection, after having received all sorts of guarantees as to its genuineness. The Bedouin said that the manuscripts had been found by them in a cave near to the Dead Sea. They agreed to take there two of the Metropolitan's personnel. In the course of this visit to the cave, pieces of fabric, fragments of pottery, and a jar still intact were found. The last object was of great interest to the visitors, but they could not take it away with them, for the cave was difficult to reach, and the tropical heat which reigns there during the summer months made all physical effort painful.

The Bedouin therefore had not been mistaken: they had really discovered some antiquities, and had even managed to sell them. Nearly six months later, so it is said, they came again to the Bethlehem shopkeeper with another collection of manuscripts and two jars. This time the dealer did not let the chance go by. He sent a "sample" to an antique dealer in Jerusalem with whom he had business relations, and on 25th November 1947 the latter offered this fragment to Professor Sukenik of the Hebrew University, giving him guarantees as to its place of origin. Professor Sukenik arranged to meet the Bethlehemite trader on 29th November, and that afternoon, after the customary bargaining, he bought this second collection of manuscripts and two jars. The return journey to Jerusalem with his precious burden was a perilous business. Fighting had just broken out, and it was only with great difficulty that the Professor was able to get back to his home at Rehavia in the modern Jewish quarter of Jerusalem.

Have we here the true account of the discovery? There is room for doubt. Years have passed since the different versions came to the knowledge of Professor Walter Baumgartner, who gave a detailed account of them.[1] Reasons for treating the susceptibilities of certain persons with great caution no longer seem to exist.

According to the account of the discovery which the Director of the Jordanian Department of Antiquities, Mr. G. Lankester Harding, now gives,[2] the Bedouin who entered the cave brought out only three rolls, a large roll which may have been *Isaiah "A"*, and two smaller ones which seem to have been the *Manual of Discipline* and the *Habakkuk Commentary*. After having been offered to the antique dealer in Bethlehem, these rolls were bought by Mar Athanasius Samuel and Anthony Kiraz. We are now told that the Bedouin played no part in the subsequent discoveries in the

[1] *Theologische Rundschau*, XIX (1951), pp. 101-6. There are many and very varying accounts of this discovery. See the Bibliography in H. H. Rowley, *The Zadokite Fragments and the Dead Sea Scrolls*, Oxford, 1952, pp. 3ff. and note 6.
[2] *Discoveries in the Judean Desert, I: Qumrân Cave I*, Oxford, 1955, p.5.

cave. All the other manuscripts which became the subject of transactions came directly from destructive excavations when, "during the next few months, people from the monastery made frequent visits there, enlarging a lower entrance, and excavating it very thoroughly. In the course of this work they must have recovered all the rest of the known manuscripts and large fragments, some of which were eventually acquired by the Hebrew University." Thus, if we are to trust the results of a very thorough investigation, made, it is true, a little late, the Bethlehemite dealer from whom Professor Sukenik bought a collection of manuscripts on behalf of the Hebrew University of Jerusalem was only an intermediary through whom the Metropolitan and his partner tried to dispose of their goods. The fourth roll and some fragments of the Book of Daniel in the possession of the Syrian Metropolitan came from clandestine digging carried out by the personnel belonging to the monastery.

This very late version, only made public after Athanasius Samuel found himself prohibited from returning to Jordan, and therefore no longer in danger of even slight punishment, is now left behind by two further versions.

We must go back and, as far as frequently contradictory statements allow, follow the fortunes of the manuscripts bought by the Syrian Metropolitan and his associate, A. Kiraz. It was necessary first of all to be sure of their monetary value, and that, of course, depended upon the age and rarity of the rolls. During the month of July 1947, Kiraz tried to obtain the opinion of experts. The manuscripts were shown to a specialist of the Archaeological Museum in Jerusalem and to the Fathers of the Ecole Biblique, and to each a different story was told about the origin of the rolls and how they came to be at St. Mark's Monastery. All who saw them were unanimous in declaring that the manuscripts were of no interest and of no value. Somewhat doubtful, perhaps, as to the importance of their acquisition, the Syrians had already sought the opinion of a Jew. A journalist, Mr. Wechsler, thought he recognised in one of the rolls shown to him a collection of *Haphtaroth*—extracts from the books of the Prophets which are read during the service in the synagogue on Sabbaths and Festivals. This opinion, given on the spur of the moment, and probably influenced by the story told him in explanation of how the rolls came to be in St. Mark's Monastery, became the cause of much confusion. We are told that Mr. Wechsler wanted to find confirmation for his first impression. Even if the rolls were only four or five centuries old, they might have a certain value for Jewish studies. He spoke about them, therefore, to one of the librarians of the Hebrew University of Jerusalem, and the latter at the beginning of the month of December 1947 informed Professor Sukenik of what he had been told.

In the meantime, thanks to the help given by Professor Biberkraut, the rolls acquired by the Hebrew University had been partly unrolled and studied. Professor Sukenik immediately saw a connection between these manuscripts and those at the Syrian monastery, and when, towards the middle of January 1948, he received a letter from Kiraz asking him his opinion upon the rolls which he had helped to purchase, Professor Sukenik was practically sure where they had come from. The Battle of Jerusalem was already raging, and St. Mark's Monastery was situated in the old city, which was in the hands of the Arabs. Professor Sukenik was living in the modern, Israeli, part of the town, so a meeting was arranged within the neutral zone at the Y.M.C.A. building.

This time Kiraz could not tell his fable about a Syrian monastery near to the Dead Sea, and of the remains of its former library. He had to admit to Professor Sukenik that the rolls had been bought from some Bedouin and that they had found them in a cave which he himself had since visited and where he had seen evidence confirming what the Bedouin had said. Professor Sukenik declared that he was prepared to purchase the manuscripts, but Kiraz protested that it was necessary to consult with his partner, and he was unwilling to indicate his price. All the same, he entrusted three rolls to the Israeli professor so that he might study them, and a further meeting was fixed for 6th February.

On the day arranged, Professor Sukenik took the manuscripts back to Kiraz and offered to buy them, but the latter, like a true son of the Orient, showed himself more cunning. Still refusing to state a price, he insisted on an offer which he could transmit to his partner, the Metropolitan. During the same interview, Professor Sukenik also saw two other rolls belonging to Mar Athanasius, and these brought the number of rolls offered for sale up to five. It was agreed that a further meeting would bring the transactions to an end with the payment of an agreed price.

Having received an offer from the Hebrew University, the Syrian Metropolitan set out to find a higher bidder. On 19th February, Father Butros Sowmy—who afterwards, on 16th May, met his death during the bombardment of Jerusalem by the guns of the Arab Legion—arranged to meet J. C. Trever, the acting Director of the American School of Oriental Research. He showed him the rolls, telling him all the time that they were part of the library of St. Mark's Monastery. J. C. Trever did not buy the manuscripts, but he obtained permission to photograph them, and as he had made no attempt to conceal the value he attributed to them, it is not surprising that the negotiations between A. Kiraz and Professor Sukenik did not mature.[1] Towards the end of February 1948, the latter received a letter in which Kiraz informed him that the sale of the manuscripts had been put off to a later date when, relations with the outside world having been re-established, it would be possible to assess their value in the world market. As a matter of fact, J. C. Trever had advised Father Sowmy to send the manuscripts out of the country. The St. Mark's Monastery rolls were therefore taken to the United States, where they were offered to potential buyers at the price of a million dollars.

Thinking that offers would flow in as soon as the contents of the rolls were better known, Mar Athanasius Samuel had authorised the American School of Oriental Research to publish the photographs of these manuscripts, reserving for himself half the profits of this publication. His hope was not realised, and thus it came about that the so-called St. Mark's Monastery manuscripts were exhibited in a number of towns in the United States without finding a purchaser. They were eventually bought by the Hebrew University of Jerusalem at a more reasonable figure than that first proposed.

★      ★      ★

During the month of September 1948, and in spite of the fighting which was raging in the country, Professor Sukenik succeeded, with the help of the Bialik Foundation, in publishing the first preliminary report on these manuscripts. In 1950, his second preliminary report appeared, and at the same time Millar Burrows, Professor at Yale University, published the manuscript of Isaiah "A" and that of the Habakkuk Commentary, two of the rolls from St. Mark's Monastery. Meanwhile, the interest aroused by the discovery of these manuscripts had had far-reaching effects, even in Palestine itself. There was the desire to see the cave from which the manuscripts had come, to make sure that there were not other fragments still there. There was the wish to retrieve what might still be in the hands of the Bedouin or of dealers. Thus at the time that texts were beginning to be published there also began a campaign of excavations which were quite as "Oriental" as the bargaining over the purchase price of the rolls.

J. M. Allegro of the University of Manchester has recently given an account of the preliminaries which led up to the archaeological campaign in the region of the Dead Sea.[2] It was not till December 1948, and under

[1] A detailed account of the visits paid by Father Butros Sowmy to the American School of Oriental Research is given by Millar Burrows in his The Dead Sea Scrolls, New York, 1955.
[2] J. M. Allegro, The Dead Sea Scrolls, Harmondsworth, 1956 (Pelican Books, A 376).

the pressure of world-wide public opinion, that Mr. G. Lankester Harding, Director of the Jordanian Department of Antiquities, instructed Joseph Saad, belonging to the Palestine Archaeological Museum, to find out at all cost the position of the treasure cave. What is now related reminds one of a detective thriller with its many unexpected turns and changes. On that ground alone, it would merit the honour of a film.

ii

## THE FIRST EXCAVATIONS

Setting out from Jerusalem, more than 2,500 feet above sea-level, by a road which winds across the barren and inhospitable Judean Desert, one comes to a point where a post bears the legend *Sea-level*. After descending another 650 feet, there is a fork in the road. To the left, the way leads to Jericho; to the right, to the installations of the Company extracting salts of potash from the Dead Sea, 1,292 feet below sea-level. Not far from there was formerly a restaurant called Kallia, offering refreshment to those tourists who wanted to plunge into the Dead Sea, whose waters are so dense that no one can sink in them. Since the fighting, the place is in ruins. From its terrace at the edge of the Dead Sea, one looked across to the other side, with its bare, steep slopes, which border the plateau of Trans-jordania. To the south one saw the profile of Ras Feshkha where the cliffs of the Palestinian side fall almost perpendicularly to the Dead Sea. But a stay at Kallia was by no means enchanting. The tropical heat and the barometric pressure soon becomes trying. Countless insects flit around undisturbed—for no bird can bear the heavy pressure which reigns here—and they are a veritable plague. The air too is difficult to breathe.

In this north-east corner of the Dead Sea the fertile plain of Jordan continues as a level desert, where in a few rare places a scanty scrub grows. Any moisture is immediately absorbed by the dry soil, though at the time of subtropical rains the *wadis* pour down torrents of yellowish water from the neighbouring ridges, carrying down to the sea the rare traces of humus which the winds have deposited as dust on the rocks of the Judean Desert.

About three miles south-west of Kallia, where the edge of the plateau, here about 650 feet in height, is only three-quarters of a mile from the shore, a promontory may be noticed, one similar to many others. It is there that the ruins and cemetery of Khirbet Qumrân are found, and in the steep and broken face of the neighbouring cliff are the caves, one of which became so suddenly famous. What name was to be given to this cave situated in an uninhabited and uninhabitable region? Was it to be named after the Jewish restaurant, Kallia, or should it be named Gomorrah —Qumrân in Arabic? There was hesitation. It was quite understandable that the story of the destroyed town should be played here where the broken rocks looked like ruins, and everything had the air of infinite waste and desolation. Preference was given to the name of a spring a couple of miles further south. Its water is not good for drinking, but for the Bedouin who wander about this region it forms an ideal landmark. It is less than two miles from Ras Feshkha, where the cliff projects into the sea, and has therefore been called 'Ain Feshkha ('ain=spring). The cave was therefore called the Cave of 'Ain Feshkha, but afterwards this name was abandoned in favour of Qumrân I. It is upon this area that the interest of scholars became concentrated.

Though J. C. Trever had obtained from Father Butros Sowmy some information concerning the cave of the manuscripts, yet, in view of the fighting and the insecurity of the region, he had not dared to think of the possibility of a visit to it. His interest having been aroused by the news which reached him from Europe, Captain Ph. Lippens of the Belgian Army, a United Nations observer in Jordan, took the initiative and spoke to Major-General Lash, one of the British officers attached to the Jordanian Arab Legion. The latter instructed an Arab Captain to reconnoitre the region, and at the end of two days the cave was identified. On the 8th February, nearly two years after the discovery, Mr. G. Lankester Harding, Director of the Jordanian Department of Antiquities, went there himself, and a week later, on the 15th, returned there accompanied by Father R. de Vaux, Director of the Ecole Biblique et Archéologique Française of Jerusalem.

When they arrived at the place, the members of this scientific expedition could only confirm the statement made by the Arab Captain. Clandestine diggers had turned all the soil of the cave upside down. Heaps of broken pottery and scraps of fabric lay in the entrance to the cave which had been enlarged to facilitate the work of the plunderers.

Access to the cave is difficult. There is now at floor-level an opening about 30 inches high. The cave is about 25 feet in depth, and its maximum height is nearly 10 feet. It was easy to identify the clandestine diggers, as in the course of their visits they had left behind them a few personal objects. Afterwards, as a result of tiresome efforts and tortuous bargaining, it was possible to buy back from them a few detached pages of manuscript.

The visit to the cave was a revelation of the vandalism of the first explorers. The Bedouin who had found the cave admitted that they had seen there eight jars still intact, five on one side and three on the other. According to their account, they were all empty except the one which contained the three manuscripts bought by the Syrian Metropolitan. We know that subsequently two jars were bought by Professor Sukenik, but when the archaeologists visited the cave all they found were fragments of pottery, many of them showing fresh breakages made "in the course of the modern pillage".[1]

Part of the evidence has been irreparably destroyed. As a result of these first excavations, lasting from 15th February to 5th March 1949, the archaeologists were nevertheless able to bring away about 600 fragments of manuscripts, though some were minute and bore only a few letters or parts of letters. Besides these fragments which will be considered later and which form the subject of a fine publication,[2] they had a rich harvest of pottery fragments and of scraps of fabric, all of which were carefully studied later.

As these results became known, theories began to pile up. Professor Sukenik had spoken of "apocryphal works" (*Megilloth Genuzoth*) and of a Jewish *geniza*. He had seen, and quite rightly, that these were only discarded rolls, and he had the proof of it. Others wanted to show that he was mistaken. Every detail therefore was so interpreted as to prove that the cave could not have been a *geniza*, but that it had harboured the rich library of a Jewish monastery of the Maccabean period. We shall see later what must be thought about a Jewish monasticism, but first let us see what information some people deduced from the archaeological finds.

The pottery fragments collected from within the cave or from the entrance were divided into "Hellenistic" and "Roman". The two intact jars which were held to have come from this cave had already been styled "Hellenistic" and as the fragments in the first category seemed to be the débris of fifty or so similar jars, the conclusion was arrived at that the manuscripts must have been carried to the cave in these jars during the third century B.C. or that, in any case, their internment could not have been later than the end of the second century B.C. As to the Roman fragments, they merely showed that the cave had been violated during the Roman period. This deduction did not take into account the average length of

[1] Father R. de Vaux in *Qumrân Cave I*, p. 8.
[2] Fathers D. Barthélemy and J. T. Milik in *Qumrân Cave I*, pp. 43-165.

life for a jar,[1] nor of the persistence of technical processes, a fact which helps considerably in the production of forgeries! Nor did it pay attention to the fact that among the fragments of texts were some which certainly seem to have come from codices.[2]

A little later, it was stated that the minute pieces of manuscript written on both sides did not come from books, but from "re-used rolls". The proof of this was that the writing on the back was not the same as that on the front. No one thought of remarking that there was no known precedent for a papyrus roll to have been used in this way, nor did anyone point out that the presence of different handwritings in a manuscript proved nothing, a number of rolls coming from the same cave, as a matter of fact, having been written by two, or even three, different hands. However that may be, many recent publications still systematically avoid all mention of the existence of these fragments of codices.

For a long time, conscientious scholars were led into error, believing rightly that "too much importance can never be given to archaeological criteria". Then this dating, with the conclusions drawn from it, described as a "pious untruth",[3] was retracted in a resounding declaration with which there was a desire to associate "all competent archaeologists".[4] There was then a tendency to go too far in the opposite direction. In spite of the presence in the Turin Museum of two similar jars found in Egypt, where they had contained papyri written in demotic or in Greek; in spite of the existence of a letter in Arabic of the eighth or ninth century A.D. giving the price of jars to be used for holding writings;[5] in spite of the fact that

---

[1] Who does not have some plate or other piece of china in his home which belonged to his grandparents? The two jars bought by Professor Sukenik, and which are supposed to come from the same cave, had been used by the Bedouin for carrying water until the moment of their purchase. In 1953, John Allegro bought a similar jar which had been put to domestic uses by the Bedouin for a long time. This will be referred to later. The present writer has himself seen semi-nomads near to Kültépé in Cappadocia using Hittite pottery found almost intact in some neighbouring *hüyük*.

[2] Rolls (*rotuli*) were only written on on one side, whilst books (*codices*) which only appear in the second century A.D. were composed of pages written on both sides.

[3] G. Etiemble in *Les Temps Modernes*, January 1951.

[4] "I was mistaken . . . in attributing the manuscript jars to the pre-Roman period. They are quite a century later, and prove that within a restricted environment, ancient techniques may survive. I was mistaken also in saying that the jars had been fabricated for the purpose of holding manuscripts; they were an everyday type of domestic pottery. I was mistaken in assigning to a later violation the fragments of a pot, a pitcher and of lamps which were found in the cave . . ." *Comptes Rendus de l'Academie des Inscriptions et Belles Lettres*, 1952, p. 174.

[5] R. de Vaux in *Qumrân Cave I*, pp. 9, 12 (also B. Couroyer, in *Revue Biblique*, LXII, 1955, pp. 76-81).

pieces of rolls had been found adhering to fragments of pottery in Qumrân Cave 1,[1] the conclusion was made that these jars "could have served other purposes: they are a domestic type of vessel".[2] As a matter of fact, not one but many types of jars have been identified at Qumrân, and probably they corresponded to different purposes. All the same, we are asked to recognise that "the difference in the clay and in the baking make it hardly likely that the jars found in the cave at Qumrân should have been imported from the Valley of the Nile".[3]

This last deduction seems superfluous. In fact it is difficult to see how a trade in jars said to be of an everyday type should be set up between the valley of the Nile and the depression of the Dead Sea. But from this declaration a conclusion was going to be drawn in support of a new theory, more enticing than that of the Maccabean origin of the deposit in the cave.

A number of hypotheses had been put forward by those who had not wished to take account of the "archaeological criteria". One of these, which attributes the buried library to the Essenes, appeared especially attractive. It gave a new turn to the excavations and a new orientation to their interpretation.

After having underlined that (1) the fragments of papyrus written on both sides must have come from codices (which were not in use in the Orient before the end of the first century A.D. or the beginning of the second century), and that (2) the corrections in the roll *Isaiah "A"* could only have been made after the definite fixing of the text of the Old Testament which served as foundation for the Massoretic Text, Professor Kahle of Oxford[4] made the suggestion that there could easily have been a connection between the cave of the manuscript and the ruins of a building about half a mile away, called Khirbet Qumrân.

A preliminary excavation made at Khirbet Qumrân had shown that this site was inhabited at the end of the third or the beginning of the fourth century A.D. This point was made in spite of the disturbing observation made by Harding that the fragments of pottery found on this site were of the same period as those of the cave which had already been described as "Hellenistic".

Professor Kahle did not believe that the cave of the manuscripts could

---

[1] p. 12 and Plate 1, 8–10.
[2] *Ibid.*, R. de Vaux in *Qumrân Cave, I*, p. 13.
[3] *Ibid.*, p. 9.
[4] "The Age of the Scrolls," in *Vetus Testamentum*, I (1951), pp. 40-1.

have been a *geniza*.[1] He leaned towards the theory of an Essene library, and he supported it by a rather specious argument.[2] His idea was immediately taken up. The rolls and other fragments of manuscripts found in the cave were attributed to the Essenes: the ruins of Khirbet Qumrân were connected with the cave called that of 'Ain Feshkha, which was renamed the "Qumrân Cave". On the other hand, the more solid part of Professor Kahle's argument, that of the dating of the manuscripts, was passed by without discussion. New excavations were carried out at Khirbet Qumrân, and this time everyone knew what they wanted to find. All the results of the excavation, however contradictory, were interpreted so as to prove that an important community of Jewish monks, the Essenes, had had their monastery there until the first century A.D.

This matter of associating the ruins of Khirbet Qumrân with the caves and their manuscripts will be discussed later, as will also the discovery of seats and desks of the *scriptorium* of the monks of Qumrân, now set up on wooden stands in the Palestine Archaeological Museum,[3] and the identification of inkwells used by the monks in writing the rolls, found in the cliff a little distance from the ruins.

★     ★     ★

The cave of the manuscripts visited in August 1947 by Father Joseph and A. Kiraz was the scene of many clandestine excavations before November 1948. Newspapers accidently left behind by these visitors supply the date of one of these excavations. One of the searchers, whose name has only recently been divulged, could be identified by his tobacco pouch, which

---

[1] *Ibid.*, p.38. Professor Kahle states that a *geniza* is either joined to a synagogue or in its immediate neighbourhood. But this is not the case. A *geniza* of orthodox Jews is always connected with a cemetery, and in the East a cemetery is never found in the vicinity of a synagogue.

[2] *Ibid.*, pp. 46-7. In what is called the Cairo *geniza*, three manuscript fragments have been found of a Hebrew version of *Ecclesiasticus*, or *Ben Sirach*, hitherto only known in Greek or derived versions. The manuscripts were of the ninth to the twelfth centuries A.D., but as they are copies of older texts, Professor Kahle supposes that the Qaraites to whom the *geniza* belonged had formerly been acquainted with certain manuscripts found in a cave. In his opinion, there can be no doubt (1) that the cave from which the originals copied by the Qaraites of Cairo came was that of 'Ain Feshkha, (2) that this cave must have contained at least three manuscripts of *Ecclesiasticus* in Hebrew (actually no fragment of this book has so far been found there), and (3) that the library must have been of the Essenes, because "it is more than seventy years ago that J. Reifmann pointed out that the Essenes had a special regard for the *Book of Ecclesiasticus*, and tried to show that Ben Sirach belonged himself to the Community of the Essenes". Fragments of *Ecclesiasticus* have since been found in other caves at Qumrân; nevertheless, it would seem that the *Ben Sirach* in Cairo was a re-translation of the book back into Hebrew, and not a copy of an ancient Hebrew manuscript.

[3] For photographs, see J. M. Allegro *The Dead Sea Scrolls* (Pelican A 376) Plates 33 and 34.

he lost in the cave. It is said that a not-unimportant person attached to the Syrian monastery had taken part in this expedition.[1]

Kiraz had declared to Professor Sukenik that he had seen in the cave a single intact jar, but that he had not been able to carry it away on the occasion of his first visit. Is this really true? Were there not a number of others in good condition? When Captain Lippens asked the British officer commanding the Arab Legion to have the area explored, no long search was necessary to identify the cave of the manuscripts. A heap of potsherds on the slope of the rock made it easy to recognise the entrance to the treasure cave. Will it ever be known what these clandestine diggers really found in the cave, and what they took away? If their harvest had been poor, they would certainly have loaded themselves with jars and various kinds of débris. But such was not the case. One gets the impression that these diggings were carried out with the vandalism characteristic of the greed of those who find themselves faced with a treasure too rich to be all carried away. Thus, contrary to current opinion, it may be supposed that numerous manuscripts found in the cave are still in the hands of speculators who are waiting till the prescriptive right of long possession allows them to offer them for sale in the antiquity market, perhaps in single sheets and as having come from other sources. Already a price list has been fixed for the manuscript fragments which give rise to a kind of speculation, against which the Jordan Government, which occupies this part of Palestine, says it is not in a position to take severe measures.[2]

The market price for Hebrew manuscripts, fixed at £1 sterling per square centimetre, naturally excited the envy and spite of the Bedouin, who, after all, were the prime cause of the discovery. They therefore carried out an exploration of the region, and a short time after the first digging expedition at Khirbet Qumrân had ended they offered manuscript fragments for sale without revealing where they had been found. A methodical exploration of the cliffs which border the north-west corner of the Dead Sea was organised. Great was the surprise when some thirty caves were found in which were pottery fragments of the same type as those recovered in the cave of the manuscripts. All the caves had been visited by clandestine

---

[1] W. Baumgartner, in *Theologische Rundschau*, XIX (1951), p. 108.

[2] After having devoted £15,000 sterling to the purchase of manuscript fragments in the possession of dealers, the Jordan Government had to resolve to allow certain learned institutions, such as universities, to buy and export fragments which were being offered for sale. Announcements have been made of purchases by McGill University ($15,000), University of Manchester (£2,000), the Vatican Library, and other institutions (H. H. Rowley, *The Dead Sea Scrolls and Their Significance*, London, 1955, p. 7).

diggers except one, in which a few fragments of manuscripts and two copper rolls were found, one consisting of two sheets joined together, and the other of one sheet. It could be seen that these copper sheets were inscribed, the traces of the letters showing through to the reverse side. The rolls were too oxidised to unroll. None of the suggested chemical processes seemed very safe, and these relics of the past could not be exposed to dangerous treatment. For a long time they still kept their secret.

The other caves yielded a less important collection of manuscript fragments, some of the canonical books, and some of the Apocrypha. "The" cave from which came the rolls in 1947 was not therefore unique. Hypotheses had been piled up on this first cave and on the succession of visits it must have received since the beginning of the third century A.D. Everything that could possibly be connected with writings coming from a cave, from the fifth column of Origen's *Hexapla* to the Qaraite writings in Cairo, had been credited to the account of "the" cave of the manuscripts, as the cave of 'Ain Feshkha had been called. Now more than twenty-five similar caves had come to light, and all had been more or less systematically excavated in ancient or in modern times. And still more were going to be found later.

At present, the manuscript fragments recovered from the caves number several thousands. No one knows how many are still in the hands of dealers. Surely it is only logic that one should expect now another striking confession, the formal renunciation of the theory of a buried library. It is quite clear that a large number of caves in the cliffs near Khirbet Qumrân have been used to inter works which for one reason or another had to be "hidden" (Greek, *kryphô*) and become "apocrypha". This renunciation is not forthcoming. On the contrary, the theory of the Essene library is held in greater honour than ever. There is a categorical refusal to admit that it may be a question of *genizoth*.

However, a few reservations begin to be expressed. It is acknowledged that the manuscripts mentioned by Origen and by Bishop Timothy could have been found in any one of the manuscript caves in the region of Qumrân. It is recognised that the jars found in the caves, whether intact or broken, had not all contained manuscripts. And it is admitted that many manuscripts were placed in the caves without being enclosed in jars.[1] Yet all the manuscripts from the caves continue to be attributed to the library of the Essenes or monks of Qumrân.[2]

[1] G. L. Harding and R. de Vaux, *Qumrân Cave I*, pp. 3, 13.
[2] G. L. Harding and J. T. Milik, *ibid.*, pp. 4, 88, 103 *et passim*.

iii

## WHAT IS A *GENIZA*?

The name *geniza* acquired its present meaning at the beginning of the first century A.D., when Rabbi Simon ben Gamaliel I, engaged in fixing the canon of the Old Testament, ruled that certain books of doubtful authenticity ought to be "hidden" in some secret place. The books which it was necessary to put away in this manner were called *genuzim,* or, in translation, "apocrypha", things hidden away. The place where they were to be taken was called a *geniza.*

Originally, therefore, a *geniza* was merely for "apocryphal" books. It was, then, neither a depository nor a cemetery, but a secret hiding-place in which to enclose certain writings which were not accepted as canonical in Palestine, although they formed part of the Greek Bible of Alexandria: *Maccabees I and II, Ecclesiasticus, Enoch, Judith, Tobit, Wisdom of Solomon, Baruch,* etc. There was long discussion as to whether Ecclesiastes ought not also to be considered apocryphal. Some rabbis wished to consign the Book of Proverbs to the *geniza*, and even the Book of Ezekiel only just escaped exclusion from the canon.

Soon a *ne varietur* text was established for the Hebrew Bible. All manuscripts of Biblical books which were defective—that is to say, needed more than five corrections on the same page—were declared *pesûlîm* and had to be taken to the *geniza*. The rule was soon extended to include certain translations of the canonical books which did not follow the official version word for word. The ancient Greek version of the Bible, the Septuagint, was declared "apocryphal", although it was in current use in the synagogues in Egypt. A Greek from Pontus, Aquila, who was a recent convert to Judaism, was instructed to make a new translation of the sacred text, observing even the smallest niceties of Hebrew syntax.

Jewish bibliolatry received further sustenance in all these regulations. The most detailed directions were drawn up for the copying of the sacred books. Nothing was to be written from memory. Everything had to be copied faithfully, even the spelling mistakes of the prototype. Severe rules were invented for the scribes. Even in the Middle Ages they had to purify themselves before writing the name of God. The custom grew of leaving the NAME blank. The scribe was to write it later, with another pen, in perfectly pure ink, and after he had plunged himself into the waters of cleansing.

The prohibition against touching the sacred books was naturally accompanied by a severe taboo, but it is easy to understand that this was difficult to formulate. In the time of Rabbi Simon ben Gamaliel I, it went no further than saying, what at first sight seems somewhat contradictory, that "the sacred books defile the hands" as soon as they are taken outside the synagogue. An exception was made for the Book of Esther, as the reading of this in the family circle during the Feast of Purim had become traditional. Contact with any other canonical roll outside the synagogue involved the most serious of defilements: that which is contracted by touching a corpse. Of all the Jewish canonical books, the roll of Esther is the only one that may be kept in a secular building: it is the only one that does not "defile the hands". As it can never become impure, it need never be consigned to a *geniza*.

Before very long, the obligation to consign apocryphal books to the *geniza* was extended to all heretical or subversive writings which made mention of the name of God, and which for this reason could not be burnt. An exception was made for books found in the hands of un-believers: those could be destroyed. At any rate, they ought to be passed through the flames if there was any doubt about the scribe. On the other hand, if one was sure that a roll found in heathen hands had been written by an orthodox Jew, then it should be carried to the *geniza*. In addition to subversive and unorthodox writings, a number of other documents were declared taboo, and their transfer to the *geniza* was made compulsory. Thus a marriage deed or an act of divorce, if dated by the reign of the Roman sovereign and not by the Mosaic era, was *pasûl*. It was the same if one of the witnesses had signed his name in its Greek form or in Greek characters, because of the phrase "according to the law of Moses" which it was compulsory to introduce into these documents. It would be fastidious to give here the long list of writings which for one reason or another had become taboo, and had to be consigned to the *geniza*. It may be sufficient to recall that many times between the first and third centuries A.D. the rabbinic authorities, fearing a rising by the people against the Roman oppressor, made a clean sweep through the country of all subversive writings and had them taken to the *geniza*.

It remained to draw up the rules concerning the *genizoth*.[1] The regu-

---

[1] It is difficult to establish the dates at which different rabbinic regulations were formulated and put into writing. Generally, they took into account local customs which were older and often divergent. Even when a regulation has been codified at a relatively late date, it should not be forgotten that often it goes back to an ancient tradition, long observed in certain communities before becoming general. It is also necessary to take into account the fact that the central authority had not always the power to impose its decisions everywhere. Some local customs have survived to our own time, in spite of being contrary to rabbinic regulations.

lations were numerous, detailed, and varied, as is proper when it is a question of taboo. One rule stipulated that the *geniza* of a book of the Law, partly destroyed or defective, ought to be situated near the tomb of a scholar or that of a pupil of a scholar. In accordance with an interpretation of Jer. 32.14, the roll was to be placed in a baked earthen pot. Even in our days, the rolls of the Law can become *pasûl* accidentally. A letter written in thick ink may come away and stick to the back of the parchment roll. If the accident is considered serious, the roll is immediately folded up again, and carried to a subsidiary part of the synagogue. In certain Eastern communities it is wrapped up in pure linen and then carried to the *geniza* at the cemetery. In other communities, one waits till a pilgrim undertakes to take the package to Jerusalem, so that it may be buried in the Holy Land, near to the tomb of some learned rabbi. In the countries of Central Europe, the *genizoth* are often so arranged as to hasten the decomposition of the rolls placed in them.

Other rules were laid down for marriage contracts which became *pasûl*. But there is one fact that is common to all *genizoth*. They are unclean to the highest degree, and that which is placed in them should never be touched by the hand of man. In the first centuries of our era, Jews arranged to be buried in caverns in the rock, and in sarcophagi. In the same way, they buried defective rolls of the canonical books in sarcophagus jars. Later, the *genizoth* were established in cemeteries. The Qaraites of Cairo seem to have interpreted the laws as to uncleanness in their own way, and had their *geniza* close to their synagogue, but they were Qaraites, a sect held to be heretical by the rabbinic Jews. The precedent of what is called "the Cairo *geniza*"[1] has prevented scholars from recognising the real nature of the caves near to Qumrân.

iv

## THE WRAPPINGS OF THE ROLLS AND THE OTHER FINDS IN CAVE I

In spite of the discovery of further caves, and in spite of the often-quoted rabbinic laws concerning *genizoth*, there is no sign that the manifestly false theory of the buried library is being abandoned. Yet it was Cave I itself that was to produce a new piece of evidence testifying to its character as a *geniza*.

Reference has already been made to the numerous pieces of fabric

---

[1] See *Jewish Encyclopedia*, V (1907) 613, article, *geniza*.

which were gathered from the floor of the cave by the archaeological mission which visited it in February 1949. These have been thoroughly studied by Mrs. G. M. Crowfoot, and her detailed report has now been published.[1] These squares of material, we are told, were specially woven for certain uses. Some, the finest, were often found decorated with simple, inwoven lines of blue thread, and had fringes. Their one purpose was to wrap up the sacred rolls. The name given to this kind of pieces of fabric was *miṭpaḥat,* and they are often mentioned in rabbinic literature. These serviettes for liturgical use had to be of pure linen and contain no wool. Actually the fabrics found in this cave do not have in them a single woollen thread, which is not the case with similar fabrics of the same period found at Palmyra, Dura-Europos, and elsewhere.

One serviette was found neatly folded, and there were other pieces of material which obviously were not wrapping up rolls. On this point, Mrs. Crowfoot recalls a resolution of the Talmud which lays down that old coverings for rolls which were torn or damaged were to be consigned to the *geniza.* In exceptional cases, they could be used to make shrouds for corpses which had been found by accident, but they could be put to no other kind of use. Mrs. Crowfoot has also pointed out that, except in about two cases, the seventy-seven pieces of fabric which had been sent to her all bore signs of wear, of darning, or of some other kind of repair. Since it cannot be supposed that anyone would carefully hide unusable rags, there is one conclusion that must be drawn: that the cave can only have been a *geniza.*

A piece of fabric was studied by Dr. W. F. Libby of the University of Chicago to establish its age through the radiations of carbon 14 found in all organic matter. It is known that this element loses a half of its mass in the space of about 1,000 years. By comparing the amount of radiation sent out from a fibre of newly gathered flax with that sent out by the linen to be reported on, it is possible to determine approximately the date when the woven fibre ceased to be living. Naturally, a margin of uncertainty has to be allowed, and in this kind of case it is about 20 per cent. It is not necessary here to enter into the technical details of the analysis of carbon 14 by radioactivity. It is enough to know that the method makes possible the calculation of approximate limits within which the age of the submitted sample must fall. The case may be compared with that of a coin bearing no date, when we know the year when this type of coin was first struck and the year also when it ceased to be struck. The coin can be of

---

[1] *Qumrân Cave I,* pp. 18-38.

any year between those two limits, and there is nothing to give preference for one year as against another.

As regards the linen studied at Chicago, and upon which we do not know the number of tests made, the limiting dates have been worked out as 167 B.C. and A.D. 233. The flax therefore which was woven into this piece of fabric can have been gathered at any time between these two approximate limits. Yet the archaeologists have decided otherwise. They have taken the arithmetical mean between these two dates and have fixed A.D. 33 as the year when the flax was cut. Naturally, that is held to be a confirmation for the theory according to which the pieces of fabric were placed in the cave during the second half of the first century A.D.

This conclusion is rather surprising. Let us remember that, taking the radioactivity of carbon 14 by itself, there is nothing to say that the flax was not cut in the year A.D. 233. Moreover, this form of test cannot say when the linen ceased to be used, nor when it was placed in the cave. Other finds from Cave I could have given more precise information on this point. They have not been analysed by the method of the radio-activity of carbon 14.

Mrs. Crowfoot's report was made known in 1951, and it was not given the importance that it deserved. And so it has come about that still no question has been raised as to whether there were not other articles which had had to be consigned to the *geniza* because they had been in contact with sacred books. The presence of apparently empty jars, of five lamps, three basins, a cooking-pot, a small jug, etc., in a cave difficult to get into and quite uninhabitable has not appeared to be remarkable. While it was still maintained that the cave was the shelter for the valuable library of the monks of Qumrân, it was supposed that "it was also able to serve as a store or hiding-place for people who lived close at hand, in tents or in huts".[1] That does not seem to be very possible.

The whole of one tractate of the Talmud, the tractate *Kelim* (vessels), is practically taken up merely with the purity of utensils and receptacles, but it does not cover everything. In any case, the possibility is not excluded that in certain cases, the rabbinic authorities may have insisted on the transfer to the *geniza* of receptacles that had been in contact with the holy books, of the lamps which had burned in front of the Ark containing the sacred rolls. For the moment it is only a hypothesis. But it is well known, on the other hand, that both orthodox and unorthodox rabbis have at

[1] R. de Vaux, *Qumrân Cave I*, p. 13.

times kept in the Ark of the Holy Books articles of food which came from their *terumah,* or cult contribution received in kind. As this practice might attract mice into the synagogue, a decision in another tractate laid down that the Roll of the Pentateuch made unclean "all the articles of food" that came into contact with it. It is a logical sequence that a jar that had held the articles of food, or any other secular utensil found near the Holy Books, must have been taken to the *geniza* in the same way as the cloths which had enclosed the rolls of the canonical books. We shall have to come back to this point later.

Among the lamps found in the cave, it is announced that the fragments of two of them "are characteristic of a series whose extreme dates seem to be 100 B.C. and A.D. 300". As has been said earlier, whilst it is possible at times to fix the date at which a type of pottery came into being, it is impossible, on the other hand, to determine when an object ceased to be used. Yet here again the arithmetical mean between two extreme dates has been taken as a basis for calculation, and date of the placing of the lamps in the cave has been fixed as the first century A.D. or, "more precisely, before A.D. 70".

v

## FURTHER DISCOVERIES OF CAVES

After the excavations at Khirbet Qumrân and the discovery in 1949 of numerous caves in the cliffs which had contained manuscripts, a guard-post was set up near to the ruins of Qumrân to prevent the clandestine diggers from overrunning the region. However, in the autumn of 1951, the Bedouin once again offered Hebrew manuscripts for sale. Negotiations were begun with the purpose of getting the diggers to reveal the source of their riches. Led by some Bedouin, an archaeological mission on the 21st January 1952 visited the region of the Wadi Murabba'at, also on the western side of the Dead Sea, but six or seven miles south of Qumrân and at a much higher altitude. It ran up against the hostility of other Bedouin, and for the time being had to abandon the project.

If we are to believe the account published by J. M. Allegro, the second expedition into the region of the Wadi Murabba'at tested severely the alpinist and speleological talents of its members. Here the summit of the cliff is practically at sea-level. Birds therefore can nest here, and for many years the Bedouin of the Ta'amireh tribe came to gather the guano, which they sold to agriculturists. The caves which the mission explored gave

B

evidence of human occupation going back to the fourth millennium B.C. Flint arrow-heads and worked pieces of bone, bronze pins and a scarab of the Hyksos Age were picked up. Pre-exilic Judean pottery was found, and also objects and weapons of the Roman period, to which belonged a score of coins dating from the reign of Nero (A.D. 54-68) to the time of Bar Kochba.

The manuscripts fragments which were found in these caves, at first sight, seemed to have been placed there at very different dates. A papyrus palimpsest[1] was found with both texts written in archaic characters, and only a very close study will make it possible to decide if the list of names to be read on it really goes back to the seventh or eighth century B.C., as one is inclined to believe. The other fragments are almost all of the first and second centuries A.D.: Biblical fragments in Hebrew; complete phylacteries; a papyrus dating from the brief reign of Bar Kochba (A.D. 132-5), whose real name of Simon Ben Kosibah comes to light for the first time; letters and deeds written in a running hand which has not yet been entirely deciphered, though the language seems to be Hebrew; marriage contracts and acknowledgements of debt written in Greek and dating from A.D. 124 and A.D. 171 and even from the reign of Commodus (A.D. 180-92); literary fragments in Hebrew, one of which seems to be a page from the *Chronicles of the Second Temple* (*dibre-hayamim bayit haśeni*), a composition made use of by Josephus and taken over in the Hebrew version of his work known under the name of *Yossipon*. There is even a fragment in Latin from the second century.

These caves are of considerable size, containing chambers connecting with each other by wells and by galleries, or arranged one behind another. They were inhabited in chalcolithic times, and probably gave temporary shelter to Judeans in the Assyro-Babylonian period. Later they must have sheltered Jewish guerrillas in the time of the Second Revolt. Before that time, and still more afterwards, these caves must have been used as *genizoth,* as is shown clearly by the kind of fragments which have been found in them. A Jewish deed of registration, written in Greek and dated by the reign of the ruling power can only be found in one place—a *geniza*.[2] But once again, as though that word were unpronounceable, everything is spoken of except that! Out of a score of coins found in these caves, three

---

[1] Manuscript from which original writing has been effaced to give room for a new inscription.

[2] The rabbis had declared absolutely null and void all Jewish deeds, etc., dated by the Roman era. See p. 29 above. All deeds and contracts drawn up irregularly were to be interred in a *geniza*. It is exactly documents of this type which have been found at Wadi Murabba'at.

only date from the reign of Nero. The rest are all later than the destruction of the Temple in A.D. 70, while nine certainly belong to the reign of Bar Kochba. Yet the conclusion has been drawn that these caves were inhabited in the first century A.D. by the Zealots of the First Revolt, to whom there is now the desire to join the Essenes.[1]

It is agreed that the discoveries at the Wadi Murabba'at have no direct connection with the "Essene library" with which the finds of the Qumrân area are obstinately identified, but no admission has been made that here at any rate one is dealing with caves which were *genizoth* though they had served as temporary refuges in times of war. It has been preferred to let it be understood that the Zealots too had been able to hide away in caves the books of their "sect", their official deeds and other writings.

Like the site of Qumrân, the caves of the Wadi Murabba'at were occupied by the Arabs in the thirteenth century. Coins, Arabic texts written on paper, and fragments of pottery prove that the site was known in the Middle Ages, and doubtless dug over. We shall have to come back to these ancient excavations. What is of importance here is the fact of the great multiplicity of caves with manuscripts in the Judean Desert, near to the Dead Sea, on a strip of country several miles along.

★     ★     ★

The chapter of discoveries seemed closed when in September 1952 Father de Vaux, the head of the Ecole Biblique in Jerusalem, found himself offered an enormous quantity of Hebrew manuscripts by the Bedouin. There could be no doubt but that these came from yet another source. Enquiries this time led to a very disturbing fact. These manuscripts had come from the very site of Khirbet Qumrân where methodical excavations had been carried out eighteen months before. A guard-post had even been established in the midst of the ruins to prevent the destruction of remains laid open to view. It seems that the attention of the guards or of Bedouin who visited them had been drawn to a hole at

[1] A. Dupont-Sommer, *Nouveaux Aperçus sur les Manuscrits de la Mer Morte*, Paris, 1953 (English translation by R. D. Barnett, *The Jewish Sect of Qumrân*, Second Edition, London, 1955, p. 11, note 16): "Hippolytus (*Elenchos, IX, 26*) links the Zealots directly with the Essene sect, though representing them apparently as heterodox persons distinguished by their fanaticism and extremism." Hippolytus certainly had never seen an Essene. As to the Zealots, if he was referring to a political movement of the first century A.D., he could only speak about them by hearsay. On the other hand, if by Zealots he meant those who in the second and third centuries styled themselves the zealous, he had in mind country people ready to accept any belief or superstition, and certainly not a Jewish monastic order.

the edge of the terrace which supports the cemetery of 1,100 tombs. They had entered and gathered a harvest of manuscripts which proved to be more important than anything which had been found up till then. Obsessed by the idea that they must find the monastery of the Essenes in the ruins which crowned this plateau, the archaeologists had not even thought that a *geniza,* of a different type from those set up in caves, could, and even ought to be found near to a cemetery. On principle, they had put aside any idea of a *geniza,* and so once more the honour, and still more the profit, of a discovery fell to obscure Bedouin. Once more an archaeological expedition arrived, and below the level of the ruins and tombs explored what is now called the Fourth Cave of Qumrân, designated by the *siglum* 4Q. Thousands of written fragments came to light: fragments from the Old Testament, from the Apocrypha, from the Pseudepigrapha, and from other writings. Texts in Hebrew, in Greek, and in Aramaic were found. This harvest, which exceeds all that the 1947 cave had yielded, must now be bought from the Bedouin, and it will never be known how many documents will have been lost to science in the meantime.

On the plateau, the expedition found a second cave (5Q), and a small hiding-place in 4Q overlooked by the Bedouin. It learned that clandestine digging had led to the discovery of a further cave situated in the cliff a little to the south of Qumrân. This cave (6Q) was visited, and what had been missed by the diggers was carefully collected.

Although the caves 4Q and 5Q had been artificially hollowed out in the little plateau of marl on which stand the ruins of Qumrân and the cemetery which is considered now as being Jewish, yet there is still the refusal to admit that it is a question of *genizoth.* More than ever there is talk about "the books belonging to the sect" found in a hiding-place, this time quite close to the "monastery", only a few yards from the *scriptorium* where these writings were composed or copied. Unfortunately, one is nowhere near finding out "all" that these cavities may have received. Long negotiations and much money will be necessary before the Bedouin restore what they have taken from them. Foreign institutions have placed considerable sums of money at the disposal of those who act as go-between so that at least a few manuscripts may be known before they get scattered.

★          ★          ★

It remains to write a last chapter of what has been called "a phenomenal discovery", and once again it is the Bedouin who play the principal part.

In the summer of 1952, new manuscripts appeared on the antiquity market in Jerusalem. This time they were not in Hebrew, but in Palestinian Syriac. The Bedouin stated that they had been found in a cave in the Kedron Valley halfway between Jerusalem and Qumrân. A Belgian archaeological mission led by Canon Robert de Langhe succeeded in identifying the scene of their finds. It was not a cave, but the ruins of the Byzantine monastery of Castellion, founded by St. Sabas at the end of the fifth century. Numerous fragments in uncial and cursive Greek, in Palestinian Syriac and in Arabic were found there. They came from books of the Old and the New Testament, from the Apocrypha and from the Pseudepigrapha (*Jubilees* and *Enoch*). This time remains of an important monastic library had indeed come to light. The monks of Mird were not hypothetical Essenes, but good Christian monks for whose existence there is complete evidence. So is it to be wondered at if the discoveries of Khirbet Mird have not called forth the same amount of public interest as the manuscripts of Qumrân, upon which scholars can base all sorts of theories? And yet who knows what surprises may not be in store among these beautifully written texts, where already a fragment of Euripides' *Andromache* has been identified. Granted that it is of the sixth century A.D., but that is quite 1,000 years earlier than the earliest recension known today, one dating from the Renaissance.

*     *     *

But the series of discoveries was not yet ended. Not far from the cave called 4Q four further caves were found in 1953 (7Q to 10Q). They held only a few manuscript fragments of little importance. In the cliff which overlooks the cave 1Q—that which is the foundation of the whole controversy—in the spring of 1956 Bedouin found a fresh cave (11Q) which seems to have contained many important manuscripts. There again we shall never know the state of the cave before it was violated. For the moment, all that can be done is to appeal to universities and academies to collect funds which will make it possible to buy from the diggers the documents which they will wish to sell piece by piece.

The exact source of a number of manuscripts bought in July 1953 by the Palestine Archaeological Museum still remains unknown, and, in spite of all the assurances given to the authorities, one can never be sure that a number of unknown caves are not being emptied of their contents by the Bedouin even now.

vi

## VIOLATIONS OF *GENIZOTH* IN PAST DAYS

The discovery of caves with manuscripts near to the Dead Sea seems to have surprised the learned world. As a matter of fact, such caves have been known to history since the third century A.D. They had been visited and emptied of their contents.

So long as it was thought that Cave I of Qumrân was unique, it was possible to talk about successive visits to this buried library; it could be claimed that this cave, discovered in 1947, had been visited at the beginning of the third century, and that from it had come the manuscripts used by Origen for the fifth column of his *Hexapla,* and perhaps also for the sixth. According to an ancient tradition, Origen made use of Hebrew and Greek manuscripts which had been found in a jar near to Jericho.[1] Today, if one thinks that this jar was discovered in a cave used as a *geniza,* perhaps one of the thirty odd which have been identified, it is surely not that one which in 1947 still contained the rolls found by the Bedouin. One can equally well imagine that this "discovery" was made by a non-Jew. In A.D. 217 the Jews were still carrying rolls to these *genizoth,* and it was surely not to put them at the disposal of an Origen. The discovery could be attributed to a Gentile, perhaps an eyewitness of the interment of the jar. In any case, it is necessary to dismiss completely the idea that a digger in ancient times would have left a number of manuscripts almost intact in a cave which he visited, for them to be discovered seventeen centuries later.

Otto Eissfeldt has drawn attention to a letter of the Nestorian Patriarch, Timothy, who, about 800, informed Sergius, the Metropolitan of Elam, that a sensational discovery had taken place ten years earlier.[2] Running after a stray sheep, a Bedouin's dog had fallen through into a cave, and as it did not come out the master followed it. Great was his surprise to find Hebrew manuscripts there. In that age, no one dreamed about the market value of such manuscripts, and we do not know if the rolls were sold, nor at what price. Timothy tried to find out if these books were "apocryphal". Doubtless he thought that they had come from a *geniza,* for he had obtained very precise information on some points. His information came from a Jew recently converted to Christianity, and he asked him if these Biblical manuscripts contained certain phrases which figured as quotations in the current version of the New Testament, but which did not appear

[1] P. Kahle, *The Cairo Geniza,* London, 1947, pp. 161-2, 284.
[2] *Theologische Literaturzeitung,* LXXIV (1949), cols. 597-600.

in the Jewish version of the Hebrew Bible. He was particularly interested in Matt. 2.23, "He shall be called a Nazarene"; in 1 Cor. 2.9, "Things which eye saw not, and ear heard not"; and in Gal. 3.13, "Cursed is everyone that hangeth on a tree". His Hebrew-speaking informant gave him an affirmative answer, but the Patriarch showed that he was not satisfied: he wanted confirmation of these oral statements, but could not get it.

There has been a desire to draw a number of conclusions from this letter. From the reply which his informant gave to the Patriarch on the spur of the moment, the deduction has been made that the manuscripts came from the library of a Judeo-Christian sect. And as it was supposed that they had been found in "the" cave like the rolls sold in 1947—it was the only cave known at the time—the further deduction was made that the manuscripts bought by Mar Athanasius Samuel and Professor Sukenik were also Judeo-Christian. At the present day, it has to be admitted that that second discovery of manuscripts was made in one of the many other caves which in 1951 contained nothing, or merely a few potsherds. We should remember that the cave discovered at the end of the eighth century was visited by Jews from Jerusalem, who took away "all" the manuscripts and carefully studied them. From this we can conclude (1) that the cave was emptied entirely of its contents, and (2) that the Jewish visitors never dreamed that it could be a *geniza*. If they had, they would certainly never have taken these rolls in their hands.

Another comparison has been made[1] with a passage of a treatise in Arabic, the work of a Qaraite author of the tenth century, Qirqisâni. Speaking of the ancient sects in Judaism, Qirqisâni mentions that of the Maghâriya (the cave-men), so called because their books had been found in a cave (*maghâr*). Had that discovery taken place in the lifetime of Qirqisâni? Was it older? Had there been several discoveries of manuscripts in a comparatively short space of time? We do not know. The fact is that Qirqisâni had not invented the name of the Maghâriya. It is said that Benjamin al-Nihâwendi (about A.D. 850), the first Qaraite author to use Hebrew, borrowed the allegorical method of interpreting the Scripture from the "cave-men". But that does not resolve the problem as to how many discoveries took place between the eighth and the tenth centuries. In any case, Qirqisâni seems to have been well informed about the rolls which had come to light. He said that one comprised the *Alexandrian* writing—the Bible as used in Alexandria? Another was a *Book of Knowledge*. The rest was mere verbiage, of no value. However, among those remaining

[1] P. Kahle, "The Age of the Scrolls", in *Vetus Testamentum*, I (1951), p. 44.

rolls must have been a copy of the *Book of Jubilees*. The celebrated Arab historian Al-Birûni (973-1048) in fact mentions the calendar of the Maghâriya. It is generally held that his source of information was the Islamic writer of the ninth century, Issâ Al-Warâq, who was also used by Shahrastâni (1071-1153). The last-named records some information from which some scholars would like to deduce a fixed point for their calculations. He said that the Maghâriya had influenced the teaching of Arius, the founder of Arianism, who died in A.D. 336, and that this sect had flourished "four hundred years" before Arius. Is there any need to give the reminder that "four hundred" merely signifies "many", in the same way that "forty" does in many place-names and in the folk-lore of the East?[1] To be willing in this twentieth century to give credence to the Maghâriya and to fix the founding of their sect in 80 B.C. is, to say the least, an anachronism.

However, some would go even further. It has been claimed that the real name for the Maghâriya was "Essenes". From what we learn, Qirqisâni placed the teaching of the Maghâriya halfway between that of the Zadokites and that of the Christians. There is no mention of date, any more than with Shahrastâni. It is a simple indication of doctrine as far as Qirqisâni was able to recognise it in the manuscripts. For the most part, these must have been composite, reflecting at times tendencies which were definitely Zadokite, and at other times beliefs which were almost Christian. It is almost the same thing today, and must be so long as one believes in a library, and seeks a unity where there is merely the juxtaposition of incongruous fragments.

To what extent was later Qaraite literature influenced by the manuscripts which came from one or from several of the caves of the Judean Desert? It is hard to say. An anti-Qaraite polemic writer of the thirteenth century reproached this Jewish sect for having accepted as authoritative books found buried in the ground. This reproach seems to be justified. It was in buildings belonging to the Qaraite synagogue at Cairo that the medieval fragments of a Hebrew version of *Ecclesiasticus* were found along with other apocryphal writings. It cannot therefore be ruled out that, in a desire to carry back to a high antiquity the origins of their movement, the Qaraites might not to some extent adopt ancient apocryphal works,

[1] There are many such place-names as "Forty Churches", "Forty Towers", "Forty Springs", etc. One recalls Ali Baba and his forty thieves. In the Bible we find mention of "four hundred men" and the very frequent use of the number "forty". The mention of four and its multiples, like that of seven and its multiples, often makes it possible to mark off one group of fragments from the others in a composite text.

never dreaming that they came from a *geniza*. Many Qaraites who came from Persia and Mesopotamia picked up Hebrew phraseology from these unorthodox books. This will have to be considered later when dealing with the so-called "Zadokite Fragments" or "Damascus Document" found in the Qaraite *geniza* at Cairo.

It remains to mention the Jericho Pentateuch, of which the Massoretes of the ninth century made a great deal. It is well known that the linguistic study of the text of the Bible—*Massorah*—had been especially the work of the Qaraites, who, moreover, introduced the Tiberian vocalisation into Palestine. The Massoretes perhaps made use of an old Pentateuch which came from Jericho, perhaps even a manuscript found in some *geniza* of that region. However that may be, at that period rabbinic Jews raised no objection on this point, and that seems to indicate that they had preserved no memory of *genizoth* in the caves near to the Dead Sea—if it was from there that the Jericho Pentateuch came.

It is also fitting to recall here a sad story which has to do with the discovery of manuscripts in a cave, this time in the valley of the Arnon, on the eastern side of the Dead Sea. It goes back to 1878. An antiquary of Jerusalem, W. Shapira, had bought from some Bedouin a curious manuscript on leather containing the Book of Deuteronomy written in the ancient characters called "Phoenician". His agents had told him that they thought that the rolls found in the cave had contained precious objects. They had torn up the linen covers and the sheets of leather and had found nothing inside. Not having found anyone who believed that this roll was ancient, Shapira set out to London in July 1883, where he submitted the manuscript to the judgement of experts. Clermont Ganneau, who was about to specialise in the denunciation of "archaeological frauds", notably that of the tiara of Saitapharnes, went to see the fragments, and declared immediately that they could only be counterfeits. The whole world of learning immediately followed his lead, and, overcome with vexation, Shapira committed suicide in Rotterdam in 1884. He left behind him a small daughter, who, under the name of Myriam Harry, was to become celebrated by the account of her father's misfortunes, which she published as a novel in 1914 with the title of *La Petite Fille de Jérusalem*.

Quite recently, Professor Samuel Yeivin, Director of the Department of Antiquities in Israel, has asked for a fresh investigation on this roll, which he thought should still be found in one of the *oubliettes* of the British Museum. There are now serious reasons for believing that Shapira's Deuteronomy was no more a forgery than the manuscripts of Qumrân,

B*

the authenticity of which was denied by the specialists who examined them in 1947.

More recently still, J. L. Teicher announced[1] the coming publication of *The Shapira Deuteronomy,* not from the original, which has unfortunately got lost, but from facsimile photographs which are found in the British Museum. After having given a detailed account of the collusion of the scholars who declared that they unanimously held the manuscript to be a forgery, Teicher shows the marked resemblance of the writing with that of fragments which have come from Cave I of Qumrân. A fact of first importance concerning this roll is that there are significant omissions and additions. In particular, there are certain phrases which were obviously inspired by the Gospels. Whilst awaiting the appearance of his book, which will comprise an edition of the text, Teicher announces that the date of the manuscript probably falls in the second or third century A.D., and that this revised version of Deuteronomy may have been the work of Jewish-Christians. He is of the opinion that a systematic exploration of the caves on the eastern side of the Dead Sea would result in the discovery of more rolls of the same kind in the neighbourhood of the place where in 1878 the Shapira Deuteronomy was found. It is to be hoped that these researches will be carried out by experts and not by the Bedouin.

Unfortunately, the visits to caves of which the echoes have been preserved are not the only violations of *genizoth.* The caves of Murabba'at were inhabited by Arabs, and it may be presumed that the leather of rolls found there has been put to all sorts of uses. If one can regret that a number of very small fragments of manuscripts, decomposed by the droppings of pigeons, have been mixed with the guano and sold by the Bedouin to Jewish colonies in Bethlehem, and so have come "to manure the orange groves",[2] is it not surprising that not a word of regret has been expressed concerning the most profane uses to which the Bedouin put any leather that they could employ? Was there not found in a cave at Murabba'at "the traces almost entirely obliterated of a long text . . . on the inside of a sack made by sewing two skins together"?

The exploration of caves by the Bedouin and the sale of Jewish antiquities found in them is a very old industry in Palestine. Anybody who has lived in the country can say much on that subject. At the present time it is carried on systematically by the Ta'amireh tribe, and it is estimated that in

[1] *The Times Literary Supplement,* 22nd March 1957, p. 184.
[2] These "regrets" have been often expressed. See Vermès, *Les Manuscrits du Désert de Juda,* Tournai, 1953, p. 26 and note 48.

five years it has brought in to these nomads more than 30 million francs, which have been paid them officially for fragments of manuscripts. Is it necessary to talk about "Jewish" orange groves—which do not exist at Bethlehem—to account for the loss of ancient manuscripts? Political considerations sometimes force statesmen to make certain accommodations. One could have hoped for more impartiality and frankness on the part of men of learning when the only matter at issue is to establish facts which may lead to the knowledge of the truth.

vii

## THE STATE OF THE MANUSCRIPTS

Many years will have gone by before it will be possible to have a comprehensive view of *all* the manuscripts found in the Judean Desert. Provisionally, the finds have been separated into three groups, according to the area from which they come. Many pieces, however, bought from clandestine diggers are of uncertain origin, and it is to be feared that market prices and other considerations have sometimes led the holders to make false declarations as to the place where they were found.

At present, in spite of the distance between some of the caves, all objects from the Qumrân area form one group, whether coming from the caves in the cliff or from cavities made in the marl of the plateau on which stand the ruins of Khirbet Qumrân. Objects from the Wadi Murabba'at form a second group, and those from the ruins of Khirbet Mird form the third.

From the fact that the caves of the Wadi Murabba'at have yielded evidence spread over 4,000 years, the study of this will demand long preparation. Certain theories have been put forward upon the occupation of these caves during the Second Jewish Revolt (A.D. 132-5). There was talk of the Zealots and their affinity with the Essenes of Qumrân even before all the documents had been made public. For the moment it would seem premature to discuss pieces of evidence imperfectly known and from a file which is far from complete.

The fragments coming from Khirbet Mird belonged to the library of a Christian monastery well known to history. They date from the fifth to the ninth centuries A.D., and for the present should be studied quite apart from those manuscripts termed the Dead Sea Scrolls.

As regards the documents coming from Qumrân, still looked upon as having formed the library of the Essene monastery, it will be necessary to wait a long time before their publication is complete. The contents of just

the first cave, the one found in 1947, are almost entirely known, and it
is on the manuscripts from this cave that all the theories at present maintained have been built. It is always the rolls bought by Mar Athanasius
Samuel and Professor Sukenik that are quoted in speaking of the Dead
Sea Scrolls. Evidently, finds coming from the other caves will bring much
that is new. Perhaps they will compel the holders of the theory of the
Essene library to modify their opinion somewhat. Already some writers
are showing a little more reserve. According to some of them, it was
only the other caves in the area that contained later documents, so that
Cave I should be considered as a case apart, and not connected with
other hiding-places in the same area. We must therefore for the present
devote our attention to the manuscripts coming from Cave I of Qumrân.

Unless we suppose that the rolls had been fabricated simply for a
commercial purpose and placed in the cave so as to deceive the eventual
purchaser, it is clear that we cannot talk about forgeries. We can discuss
their date, but not their authenticity.[1] Putting aside the theory of
"forgeries", we are faced with two sets of hypotheses as regards the use of
the caves. Either they and the artificial cavities were hiding-places for
manuscripts which it was hoped to preserve so that later they could be
recovered in a complete state, or these places were just *genizoth*. Therefore,
in the last analysis, it is the state of the manuscripts at the time of their
recovery, together with their contents, which should make it possible for
us to decide whether we may talk about hiding-places or whether we
should consider these caves as cemeteries for books.

Whatever the circumstances may be which lead a person or group of
persons to remove writings or objects to a place of safety, steps are taken
to prevent their deterioration by the effects of time. It is true that complete
jars have been found in these Dead Sea caves, and it is admitted that one
at least of them had contained some rolls. There was also found, sticking
to the broken lid of a jar, a small lump of matter which seemed to have
been part of a manuscript, though we shall never know what it was about,
for it is impossible to recover the text.[2] But it is equally true that many
manuscripts were placed in the caves and hollowed-out places without any

---

[1] S. Zeitlin, in several articles published in *The Jewish Quarterly Review*, maintains the opinion
that the manuscripts are medieval. The Middle Ages are from A.D. 395-1453. It is rather vague.
Even as a hypothesis, it would be interesting to know what are the reasons which are supposed
to tell against a closer dating. In any case, the author's linguistic study deserves to be carefully
taken into consideration. It absolutely excludes the possibility that the manuscripts go back to
the second century B.C., but leaves plenty of margin for placing them in the second century A.D.

[2] D. Barthélémy and J. T. Milik, *Qumrân Cave I*, Plate 1, 8-10.

steps being taken to preserve them. What is more, it is certain that many jars never contained manuscripts, and that the greater part of the pottery fragments found in the caves come from vessels broken before, or at the moment of, their being deposited there.

Let us make a rapid study of the condition of the manuscripts and manuscript fragments obtained from Cave I of Qumrân.[1]

The rolls of Isaiah "A" and the Habakkuk Commentary were published in 1950,[2] followed by the Manual of Discipline in 1951.[3] The three manuscripts acquired in 1947 by the Hebrew University of Jerusalem were in their turn presented to the world of learning in 1954.[4] Through the co-operation of the Jordanian Department of Antiquities, the Ecole Biblique et Archéologique of Jerusalem, and the Palestine Archaeological Museum, an extremely fine publication gives the reproduction and transcription of most of the fragments recovered from Cave I,[5] along with those obtained by purchase and believed to come from the same cave. It is impossible to admire too greatly the patient toil which has been put into this work. Fragments, often extremely small, have been fitted together and their place found in texts, some already known and others not known. They have been translated and supplied with scholarly notes.

Alas, it is necessary here to call to mind the axiom, "Archaeological excavation is always destructive, in spite of the most scrupulous care". The layers which cover a buried site are cleared away and, in general, all that they would have been able to teach us about the history of the site is irreparably lost. Often the bringing to light of an ancient building involves the destruction of later constructions which cover it. Objects which are found frequently undergo change when transferred to museums and collections through being handled, and as a result of the steps taken to preserve them. This remark is applicable to the manuscripts found in the Dead Sea caves. Had the rolls been found in the course of a scientific expedition, it is to be supposed that photographs would have been taken

[1] See present writer's article in Vetus Testamentum, VII (1957), pp. 127-38.

[2] The Dead Sea Scrolls of St. Mark's Monastery, Vol. I, edited by Millar Burrows, with the assistance of John C. Trever and William H. Brownlee, New Haven, 1950.

[3] Ibid., Vol. II, fasc.2, New Haven, 1951.

[4] 'Ôṣar ham-Megillôth hag-Genûzôth, Jerusalem, 1954, a publication by the Hebrew University of Jerusalem and bearing the name of Professor E. L. Sukenik, who died 28th February 1953. English edition under the name of The Dead Sea Scrolls of the Hebrew University, published in 1955.

[5] Discoveries of the Judean Desert, I: Qumrân Cave I, by D. Barthélémy and J. T. Milik, with contributions by R. de Vaux, G. M. Crowfoot, H. J. Plenderleith, G. L. Harding, Oxford, 1955. (This work has already been frequently referred to as Qumrân Cave I.)

of them *in situ,* and also in the different stages of being unrolled. Unfortunately, they were discovered by accident and they have passed through too many hands for any precise knowledge now as to their condition at the moment of discovery.

There are points which have not been noted even concerning the fragments brought back by the archaeological expedition of February 1949 and those afterwards purchased from the Bethlehemite dealer. The following points, however, deserve attention:

(*a*) Several fairly large pieces of leather which bore no writing and which therefore had not come from some manuscript were found crumpled up or folded one into another.

(*b*) The fragments of canonical books which were found in the cave are not distributed evenly through a complete roll, but generally come from one or two pages only, these being neither the beginning nor the ending of a roll.

(*c*) Some fragments from the Book of Samuel belonged to three successive sheets of a roll and "were found in the form of a strip which had been rolled up, crushed together, folded back, and partly eaten away". The published photograph shows a little ball, like that of torn-up papers which are tossed into the waste-paper basket.

(*d*) A phylactery (?), rolled up into a ball, had to be partly sacrificed in the process of unrolling. From the fragments which remained, it can be inferred that the beginning of the text was in the middle of the little ball, and that this phylactery was taken to the cave rolled back to front.

(*e*) A *Commentary on the Psalms* must have been rolled correctly, with the beginning on the outside, but a similar text has been found in another cave rolled back to front.

(*f*) The fragments of the *Sayings of Moses* were rolled backwards, with the beginning of the passage in the interior of the roll.

(*g*) A large fragment of *The Book of Mysteries,* coming from the bottom part of two sheets, was found in a roll which had been pressed flat. Other parts of the same book were found scattered about the cave.

(*h*) A few columns, said to have been detached from the *Manual of Discipline,* and a fragment of the title-page of the roll were bought from the Bethlehemite dealer. The publication of these texts reveal that these columns had nothing to do with the *Manual of Discipline,* and that they could not have been sewn either to the beginning or the end of that roll. If the dealer is to be believed, these columns, separated from some other work, had been rolled round the *Manual of Discipline.*

The state of those manuscripts which were the object of the 1947 transactions is also very significant.

(1) *The Isaiah "A" Roll.* This is the very type of roll which was *pasûl*: several torn sheets had been patched and re-sewn, but other tears had not been repaired, and they left gaps in the text. Moreover, the book did not conform to rabbinic tradition, which is represented in the roll *Isaiah "B"* (see p. 50). It had been inspected by rabbis whose initials may be seen in the margins: attempts had been made to correct the roll by erasures, over-writing, and by additions, but these corrections were imperfect and too numerous. There was only one thing to do—consign it to the *geniza*. In any case, its place was not in a library, as only a synagogue could keep a canonical book. The roll is fairly well preserved, and has not suffered too much from the ravages of time since it was interred. It should be noticed, however, that the fly-leaf, which had not been written on, has been cut off with a knife approximately along the line of the stitching which attached this sheet to the rest of the manuscript. As this mutilation is ancient, one is driven to the conclusion that the owners of the roll were allowed to retain a sheet of unwritten leather when the roll was seized by the rabbinic authorities as an "apocryphon". Nobody cuts off a blank sheet from a book that he is wanting to put into a safe place. If the *Isaiah "A"* roll was in fact discovered in a jar, rolled up in a piece of linen and deprived of its fly-leaf, it should be considered a dead book which was interred ritually with all the ceremonial belonging to the depositing of canonical rolls in a *geniza*.[1]

(2) *The Habakkuk Commentary.* This roll has a peculiarity which up to now does not seem to have been noticed. The upper margin is almost intact, while the lower part of the columns is missing, but not in a uniform manner. Photographs show that the partial destruction has been rather regularly done, following a wavy line, the crests of which are more sharply pointed at the beginning (columns III–IV) than towards the end (columns IX–XIII), where the curve is less marked and almost approaches a straight line. What has befallen this roll cannot be attributed to the effects of time nor the ravages of insects. For this phenomenon there

[1] It should be remembered that in synagogues rolls were not kept in jars, but in a cupboard or chest, called the Ark (*'rwn*). Each roll was wrapped up in a linen cloth (*mtpht*), contact with which outside the synagogue "defiled the hands". To touch the covering of a sacred book defiled in the same way as touching a corpse (*Kelim*, 24.14). As to the jars which have been discovered, a few were a kind of sarcophagus for rolls taken to the *geniza*. Professor E. L. Sukenik, in *Megilloth Genuzoth*, II (1950), p. 21, quotes the Babylonian Talmud on this subject: "A defective book of the Law is taken to the *geniza*, near to the tomb of a disciple of a man of learning . . . and it is put into an earthen pot so as to be preserved a long time" (Jer. 32.14).

is only one possible explanation—the roll had been partly burnt before being carried away to the *geniza*. In fact, if the experiment is made with a roll of packing paper for want of leather, it will be seen that only fire can leave such an effect as that found on this manuscript. If the photographs of the roll are carefully studied, it will also be seen that in places the leather seems to be scorched, especially at the bottom of columns I-IV. This cannot be the result of an accident, because the marks left by burning cannot be so regular unless the roll is held horizontally with the bottom edge in the flame. What then, is the explanation of this roll being partly burnt, and nowhere except in its bottom part? What interpretation is to be given to the fact that this beginning of destruction took place immediately before the roll was taken to the *geniza*?

We know that unorthodox writing had to be entirely burnt if it had been written by the hand of an unbeliever, but consigned to the *geniza* if it had been written by a Jew. But what was to be done if there was any doubt, or if the roll had been partly written by an orthodox Jew and partly by a Gentile or a schismatic? In this present case we have two different handwritings. Corrections have been made to the text, and a second hand wrote the end of column XII and the whole of column XIII. A well-known rabbinic rule applies in such a case! "Where there is doubt, sacrifice a half!" That is the rule of the *meḥeṣeh*. It is applied to foodstuffs the purity of which is in doubt, and in many other cases. Perhaps this rule has been somewhat abused. Many stories about *meḥeṣeh,* and of a rather Rabelaisian character, are found in Jewish folklore. One fact seems certain: this rule must have been applied to the *Habakkuk Commentary*. By burning a part, theoretically a half, of this writing, what remained could be considered as an unorthodox or subversive work written by the hand of an orthodox Jew. Thus, even though its origin was not exactly known, the remaining half of this roll could be, and had to be, consigned to the *geniza*.

(3) *The Manual of Discipline.* When this roll was shown to the American School of Oriental Research in Jerusalem, it was in two pieces, but the break seemed to be of recent date. It was put down to the frequent handling that this brittle roll had had. In fact, the two pieces fitted together perfectly.

The manuscript includes a bit of everything. Fragments from the rules of Zadokite societies lie side by side with others coming from rabbinic schools, etc. Four non-Biblical psalms complete this incongruous manuscript. In all probability, the roll belonged to some Jews who had not been regarded as schismatics. The initials of rabbis in the margins, in any case, prove that it had been inspected and censored. After this inspection, the manuscript was passed through the flames: witness the characteristic wavy line at the bottom of the columns. This condemnation, however, was only symbolic: merely a little part of the text suffered from this treatment. Found in the hands of Jews, and written by Jews, this roll need not even have been "half-burnt", although a great deal of its contents was unorthodox, and even seditious. After having been simply passed through the flames, which did no more than slightly scorch the lower part of the columns, the roll called the *Manual of Discipline* had to finish up in a *geniza*.

(4) *The Aramaic Genesis Apocryphon.* The unrolling of this manuscript, which formed part of the collection in the possession of Mar Athanasius Samuel, has not yet been completed. A preliminary report has been published.[1] It brings out the fact that this roll has suffered greatly from its long burial in conditions which only very difficult chemical analysis will be able to elucidate. The published photographs lead one to presume that the roll must have remained in a lying-down position, and been subjected to the influence of some liquid with which the leather is impregnated. As a result, all one side of the roll is corroded and a part of it irreparably lost. The other side, however, impregnated by diffusion or by the capillary action of the leather, has literally drunk up the ink which has run "as if on blotting-paper". In places a rather curious thing has happened. Under the influence of the liquid which the roll has absorbed, the ink has decomposed and eaten into the leather, in places leaving only narrow strips between the lines. The three last columns are the only ones which have not been affected by this chemical agent, which enters into composition with the ink. Apart from a few very small irregularities, they are practically intact.

The roll was found correctly rolled up. From the effects of time, and probably also from inexpert handling during seven years, all the beginning is lost, and it will never be known how much is missing. Another peculiarity of this roll is that the lower part of columns X-XV was found covered with some substance which looks like "a very smooth, white sheet". In places it sticks firmly to the leather, and only with most delicate manipulation can it be detached. Fragments of this substance are going to be analysed, and perhaps we shall know of what it consists.

The last three columns are fairly well preserved, but the text comes to an end in the middle of a sentence. To the left there is stitching and a narrow strip of leather. This shows that the conclusion of the manuscript— exactly how many columns one cannot say—was cut off with a knife.

[1] N. Avigad and Y. Yadin, *A Genesis Apocryphon*, Jerusalem, 1956.

The look of this roll sufficiently indicates that it was not a manuscript put into a safe place so as to be found intact at some later date, but one which had met with an accident and been deliberately mutilated before being taken to the *geniza*. Obviously, any explanations as to what may have happened belong to the realm of pure hypothesis, but it may be well to state them if only to be assured of their being sound. Experiments might be attempted to reproduce those reactions which resulted in so curious a decomposition of this roll.

The first idea that comes to mind is that an accident must have damaged the lower part of columns X-XV. A reader may have accidentally knocked over a glass of wine, and, after having dried the roll as well as he could, folded it up with the mysterious sheet put inside to prevent the roll from sticking together. The steps he took proved of little use. The leather continued to soak up the acid liquid, the ink ran and began to eat into the leather, both towards the centre of the roll and towards the outside, but mostly towards the side on which the roll was lying. When the roll was opened out later, it was seen that it was not worth preserving. The conclusion of the manuscript which had not been affected was cut off with a knife, and the rest was taken to the *geniza*.

\*          \*          \*

Unlike the rolls acquired by Mar Athanasius Samuel, those of the Hebrew University collection were not handled very much. There is a simple reason for this. Only one manuscript was in the form of a scroll easy to unroll. For the others, three rather shapeless bundles, much work was necessary before their contents could be exactly known. Thus it was that for a long time there was talk of four manuscripts, whilst in reality there were only three, one of these being divided between two bundles. Photographs were taken before and during the process of unrolling. Observations were carefully noted, and today it is possible to get an idea of the state of the manuscripts at the moment of their discovery, since it is difficult to imagine deliberate mutilation of the rolls by persons wanting to sell them.

(5) *The Isaiah "B" Roll.* At the time that it was acquired, this manu-script looked like a rather shapeless roll or twist of unequal thickness.[1] The leather sheets were almost inextricably stuck together, and the un-rolling had to be given over to specialists. In the course of this work, it was possible to retrieve a few columns at the end of the book. The writing

---

[1] For all these observations, see E. L. Sukenik, *The Dead Sea Scrolls,* Figs. 18-24, Plates 1-15.

has lost its colour, and can only be read in infra-red photographs. One large piece seems to be made up of five strips running obliquely from left to right and from the bottom edge to the upper one. On all the photographs it may be noticed that the writing is better preserved along what seem to be lines going in the same direction.

The text of the manuscript, at least in those parts which have been retrieved, appears to conform entirely with rabbinic tradition. The writing is carefully done, and the number of corrections that could be noticed are very few. This therefore is not a roll that was held to be an *apocryphon* or defective. It was probably a roll which had met with a mishap. Before being unrolled, it looked like a twisted linen rag with the two ends most tightly wound. Linen fibres stuck to the leather clearly reveal that the roll had been twisted in a wet state while wrapped round in its linen cover. The shape of the recovered fragments, the state of the writing, and above all the detached pieces found in the cave suggest that the roll had probably been taken out of water before being taken to the Qumrân cave. It is therefore certain that the roll did not meet with misfortune after being discovered. Besides, the condition of other manuscripts from the same cave, and above all the dryness of the region, exclude the possibility of attributing the condition of the roll to infiltrations, to the humidity of the air, or to a spontaneous decomposition of the leather. To all appearances, the *Isaiah "B"* roll was deposited in the cave in very much the same condition as that in which it was found.

(6) *The Roll of the War of the Sons of Light against the Sons of Darkness.* This is the best preserved of the three manuscripts. Photography shows that it was rolled backwards—that is to say, with the beginning of the text in the interior and the end of it on the outside. The lower part of all the columns has been destroyed, following a fairly regular wavy line, blackened here and there. The upper part is only very slightly damaged, and very irregularly. The impression is clearly given that the roll was deliberately burnt and that the fire consumed only the lower part. In a word, it is a roll to which the rule of the *meḥeṣeh* has been applied, as in the case of the *Habakkuk Commentary.* It should be noted that those who had been the last to read it had not thought it worthwhile to re-roll it properly. The leather strap which was used to keep the roll together was found in the middle.

(7) *The Collection of Thanksgiving Hymns.* This manuscript was not found in the form of a roll made of leather sheets sewn one to another, but in two separate bundles. When unrolled, the first bundle yielded first

of all a sheet of four columns, the last one coming into view first. Inside this roll were two sheets rolled together one upon the other, and in this case rolled in the right direction. The outside sheet, however, had been torn in two, and it was the second half, the left part, which was seen first. The inmost sheet was also of four columns, but the last column, with half of the last but one, was in a different handwriting. There can be no question but that these sheets had formerly been sewn together to form a single roll. In places the holes made by a needle still remained. It was therefore a torn-up roll that had been thus taken to the cave. And this was not the only mutilation that this roll had suffered. From the photographs, the impression is also given that these sheets had been pierced by a red-hot iron, and had been passed through flames as well.

The state of the second bundle is even more significant. A single sheet in the handwriting of the first scribe has been used to wrap up a number of fragments rolled into a ball. Some of these are in the handwriting of the first scribe and some in that of the second. We are told that the packet also contained very small fragments of other manuscripts.

★        ★        ★

If a summary is made of what is known up to the present about the state of the manuscripts which were the subject of the 1947 transactions, it will be found:

(1) *Isaiah "A"*: complete roll in fairly good state of preservation, found rolled up in the right direction; fly-leaf cut off with a knife.

(2) *Habakkuk Commentary*: complete roll found rolled in right direction. Upper part of the sheets hardly affected by time, but, on the other hand, the lower part is missing and presents the characteristic line of a roll passed through flames.

(3) *Manual of Discipline*: roll found correctly rolled, but deprived of its fly-leaf, a single piece of which was found elsewhere. A little damage here and there in the upper part of the first columns; all the lower part of the columns attacked along a wavy line similar to that of the preceding roll.

(4) *Isaiah "B"*: roll greatly damaged; seems to have been twisted while damp and before being carried to the cave.

(5) *The War of the Sons of Light against the Sons of Darkness*: found rolled inside out, all the lower part of the sheets destroyed in a regular manner, following a wavy line, the edges of which are scorched. Signs of damage on upper part are rare and not regular.

(6) *Thanksgiving Hymns*: found in two bundles. Originally a single

roll in two different handwritings, but found separated into sheets, some of which had been irregularly rolled together; others had been torn into shreds and wrapped up in a leather sheet coming from the middle of the same manuscript.

(7) *Genesis Apocryphon*: an Aramaic manuscript found damaged, with a sheet inserted where mishap had occurred. The end columns of the roll had been separated by a knife before the remainder of the partly-destroyed manuscript was carried off to the cave. Here chemical action, which had already begun, continued on what must have been the lowest part of the roll.

Reference has been made already to the different fragments rolled into a ball, reduced to bits, folded one into another, torn, etc., which have been collected in Qumrân Cave I.

Not only is it a fact that not one of these manuscripts looks as if it was preserved so that some day it might be recovered intact, but five of them give a definite impression of having been deliberately mutilated, passed through flames, torn, etc., before being taken to the cave. One cannot therefore talk about a buried library, and about precious manuscripts which, for some reason or other, it was desired to put in a place of safety. This conclusion is arrived at from the appearance of the manuscripts and from the state in which they were discovered.

★     ★     ★

We may now pass on to the nature of the rolls. Two of them reproduce a canonical text, the Book of Isaiah. What reasons can be invoked to explain why two copies of this widely circulated work should be put into hiding? It cannot have been to save the "text", for that had a wide distribution and had been known in the whole Jewish world since the fifth century B.C., and had been translated into Greek in the third century. Nor can it be held that the copies discovered here could have had a special value as prototypes, rare manuscripts, works of art, etc., for even in the case of *Isaiah* "*A*", the better preserved of the two rolls, the handwriting shows little sign of care, and in many places the text has been erased and written over. In brief, there is no sign of any special reason for its preservation. The fragments of other canonical books can hardly be said to be remarkable either on grounds of rarity or of penmanship. One handwriting is referred to as "very typical, a mere scrawl, and badly formed" and another as "somewhat odd", while as to the text, in 2 Sam. 20.8 there is "a long omission which destroys the sense".

As to the other writings, the *Habakkuk Commentary* and the *War of the*

*Sons of Light against the Sons of Darkness* are in good, careful handwriting, but that of the *Manual of Discipline* and the *Thanksgiving Hymns*, especially in the case of the second scribe of the latter work, is just slovenly. As no other copies of these works are known, it might have been supposed that these were prototypes, perhaps unique copies, but that is not the case. Three of these writings are in fact only compilations of fragments from other works, and similar compilations were later found in other caves at Qumrân. It cannot therefore be supposed that the motive for putting them in safety was that these writings were rare, original, or valuable in the eyes of their owners. And the other non-Biblical texts of which fragments have been found do not merit being put in a library any more than these do.

In spite of this, it is the theory of a buried library which is accepted by most of those who study this subject.[1] It is the basis of every deduction that they draw from the manuscripts found near the Dead Sea: the whole problem of these manuscripts is made to depend upon that premise.

Before going on to analyse the contents of these manuscripts, it will be well to state (1) that they were not put into a safe place in order to be preserved, and (2) that they did not come from a library. With these two points established, there is no longer any reason for all the discussions about the Essene sect to which they are attributed. All the same, it will be necessary to devote a long chapter to that subject. Before that, however, attention should be drawn to the results of some recent research into the discovery of the first cave at Qumrân in 1947 and into a few questions which still remain unanswered.

viii

## EPILOGUE

From the beginning, the problem of the Dead Sea manuscripts has been put in such a way that its solution must present great difficulties. Essential facts were not made public and, worse still, what was said was not always true. Nor must it be forgotten that in this affair everybody was acting at the extreme limit of what was lawful. The law of the Kingdom of Jordan forbade clandestine digging. All dealings with the Bedouin and

---

[1] See Géza Vermès, *Les Manuscrits du Désert de Juda*, Second Edition, Tournai, 1954, where he maintains this theory and quotes the opinion of a large number of scholars (English Edition, *Discovery in the Judean Desert*, New York, 1956). For a more detailed account, see H. H. Rowley, *The Zadokite Fragments and the Dead Sea Scrolls*, Oxford, 1952 (with bibliography); John M. Allegro, *The Dead Sea Scrolls*, Harmondsworth, 1956 (Penguin Books Ltd.) (also with bibliography).

their receivers are therefore officially liable to punishment. Everybody, including the authorities themselves, who now, under certain conditions, tolerate the sale of objects obtained from digging, became more or less accomplices of diggers from whom no information was forthcoming till they were assured of not being in danger of punishment.

The stories which went round about the 1947 discovery were many,[1] but none of them satisfied the American journalist, Edmund Wilson. In an article of 111 columns,[2] and later in an interesting volume,[3] he made known the results of an intense investigation which he had carried out. He no longer believes the story about the strayed sheep. The Bedouin who found the cave were smugglers—which explains many things. According to him, the Bedouin did not part with their rolls between the spring of 1947 and the month of July, when the Syrian Metropolitan was sounded about buying the manuscripts. This is an important point, in view of certain revelations recently made (see below) which are supposed to explain the state of the manuscripts by the conditions under which they were kept between the time of their discovery and that of their sale. Edmund Wilson reports that the Bedouin themselves offered their rolls to a Jewish dealer in Jerusalem, who could not buy them through lack of ready money. It was only after this check that they entrusted their wares to a Bethlehemite go-between, who through the medium of Kiraz sold them to Mar Athanasius Samuel. Edmund Wilson thinks that this transaction was carried out with five rolls and a few fragments, the price paid being 50 Palestinian pounds. On the other hand, Mr. G. Lankester Harding is convinced that the Bedouin took only three manuscripts from the cave,[4] while Dr. Millar Burrows, on his part, states that in February 1948 five rolls and some fragments were shown to the American School of Oriental Research, but one of these rolls comprised merely a column and a half detached from one of the manuscripts.[5]

Edmund Wilson goes on to relate what he had learnt about the journeyings of the rolls. They were taken by Mar Athanasius Samuel in search of expert advice, first to the Syrian Metropolitan of Antioch, and then to the University of Beirut. So we arrive at the visits made to the

---

[1] A résumé of the stories is given by W. Baumgartner in *Theologische Rundschau*, XIX (1951), pp. 101–6.
[2] *The New Yorker*, 14th May 1955, pp. 45–131.
[3] *The Scrolls from the Dead Sea*, New York, 1955.
[4] *Qumrân Cave I*, p. 5.
[5] *The Dead Sea Scrolls*, pp. 6, 12, but see also pp. 13ff. Sukenik also stated that he saw at one time five rolls in the hands of his vendor.

Syrian monastery by T. Wechsler. He is absolutely categorical: his visit took place during the month of July 1947, and he maintains that he was shown two manuscripts—one the *Isaiah* roll and the other a roll of *Haphtarôth*. At St. Mark's Monastery they are just as categorical: the visit was made in September, and "perhaps" he was shown a roll from the monastery library. Later on, however, when most careful search was made, the only Hebrew manuscript found in the whole of the library was a modern Pentateuch which could not possibly be mistaken for a roll of *Haphtarôth*. There we have a mystery which perhaps will never be cleared up. All the same, a hypothesis may be put forward. Perhaps the Metropolitan bought four manuscripts from the Bethlehemite dealer— the *Isaiah* roll, the *Habakkuk Commentary*, the *Manual of Discipline*, which turned up later in two pieces, all easy to unroll and examine, along with a roll of *Haphtarôth*, coming from elsewhere, and which the dealer had slipped into the collection in order to make it look more attractive. Even in July 1947 this was recognised as modern, and there was a risk that this might lower the value of all the rest. It is easy to imagine all the protestations which followed, and how in the end the dealer was led to replace the roll of *Haphtarôth* by another which was really ancient and had come from some subsequent digging, perhaps the Aramaic roll of the *Genesis Apocryphon*.

It was in June 1954 that Mar Athanasius Samuel, in New York since January 1949, had the announcement made in the *Wall Street Journal* that "four" Dead Sea scrolls were for sale. General Yigael Yadin, son of Professor E. L. Sukenik, who had died on 28th February 1953, instructed a New York lawyer to enter into negotiations, and thus it was that finally the State of Israel was able to acquire these rolls for the sum of a quarter of a million dollars, thanks to the help of a wealthy patron, Mr. Samuel Gottesmann of New York. The rolls are now in Israel, and the then Israel Prime Minister, Mr. Moshe Sharett, was able to announce on 13th February 1955 that they would be exhibited in a special museum along with the other rolls acquired earlier by Professor Sukenik and certain ancient and medieval manuscripts.

Mr. John M. Allegro of the University of Manchester also made use of his stay in Palestine to try to solve the mystery surrounding the first discovery.[1] The story, rich in sudden turns and unexpected changes, might be compared with the plot of a good detective thriller. It is followed by an account of the facts which led to the centralisation of all subsequent

[1] *The Dead Sea Scrolls*, 1956 (Penguin Books Ltd.).

discoveries by the Department of Antiquities of Jordan and the Jerusalem Ecole Biblique.

According to Mr. Allegro's account, the Bedouin saw seven or eight complete jars lined up on the two sides of the cave. The first two which they opened were empty. In the third they found the manuscripts, looking like bundles of rags. As soon as they got to Bethlehem, they entrusted the rolls to a general dealer called Kando, whose name is here revealed for the first time. Accompanied by an accomplice named George, Kando at once went and explored the cave, and it was only after he had completely emptied it of its contents that he made contact with Kiraz and the Syrian Metropolitan. In his turn, the Syrian Metropolitan organised an expedition to the cave, and the only result of this was to destroy completely whatever earlier digging had spared.

It appears now that it was Kando himself who sold to Professor Sukenik the three manuscripts and two jars which the latter took back to Jerusalem on 29th November 1947, but we are still in the dark as to whether Kando sold or handed over to the Metropolitan, or to any collectors, some further manuscripts. A few fragments from Cave I were later bought from him by the Palestine Archaeological Museum. The fate of the remainder of the finds he made is still unknown. He maintains that most of the documents taken from the cave were buried by him in his garden, where they quickly deteriorated into a useless, sticky mass, but is this really true? Fragments which he sold later do not seem to have suffered much in his keeping.

It was not easy to enter into relations with Kando. When the Department of Antiquites of Jordan learned of the existence of the manuscripts, and especially when their age was no longer in question, it wanted to find the Bethlehemite dealer who had sold the rolls to the Syrian Metropolitan, and still more, to know the site of the cave from which they had come. As might be expected, it was not a simple matter to get tongues loosened. In the end, Harding gave Joseph Saad, the Secretary of the Palestine Archaeological Museum, the rôle of detective, allowing him a free hand in his efforts to recover, regardless of cost, the fragments which were still for sale. This piece of detection with its breath-taking adventures is related by Allegro. Nothing is missing—meetings in doubtful places, men watching every movement of the detective, etc. The rule of "No questions to be asked" was observed, and in the end Joseph Saad was able to buy a collection of fragments for 1,000 dinars.[1]

Allegro continues with the account of later discoveries, and of the

[1] About £1,000 sterling.

fruitless chase for clandestine diggers in the hilly, difficult neighbourhood. He tells the story of the haggling by the Ta'amireh Bedouin, which began again every time a fresh cave with manuscripts was discovered. These men, now under the protection of their sheikh, defended bitterly their monopoly of prospecting. They were determined not to reveal the position of the caves from which come the manuscript fragments which they offered for sale. Promoted to the position of accredited intermediary, Kando often carried through the negotiations with the Ta'amireh and, as far as funds allowed, paid the price of £1 per square centimetre.

As regards the greater part of these documents, their place of origin and condition when found is unknown, so it will be very difficult to draw any conclusion from them beyond what the texts themselves reveal.

Interest in the other objects discovered in the cave of the manuscripts seems to have ceased completely. The present writer expressed some slight doubts about the two jars bought by Sukenik in 1947. The Israeli professor had been told that the Bedouin did not wish to part with them, as they were used for carrying water. But what is to be made of this third jar, almost intact, which Allegro says he bought from Kando in 1953? It "had probably been used all this time by the Bedouin in their camp as a storage vessel".[1] Obviously, that tells us nothing as to when it was discovered nor in which cave.

*          *          *

The above is a very brief résumé of the results of investigations made by Edmund Wilson and John M. Allegro. Light is being thrown on what took place behind the scenes, but many problems remain. Following Edmund Wilson's reports, an Israeli journalist, Irene Lurie,[2] raised a few questions. Others appear as the history of the affair is studied, but no conclusive answer can be given.[3] It should be remembered that in order to talk about a library which had been stored away in a safe place, it is indispensable to know the exact state in which the manuscripts were found. There is a desire now to blame Kando for the dilapidation of certain manuscripts, but the condition of fragments found in the same cave, and which had become separated from these rolls, leaves no room for this late incrimination of the Bethlehemite dealer.

In a word, it is absolutely necessary to know:

[1] Allegro, *ibid.*, p. 77.

[2] The *Jerusalem Post*, 17th June 1955.

[3] Solomon Zeitlin, *The Dead Sea Scrolls and Modern Scholarship*, Philadelphia, 1956, asks a number of questions to which up till now no answer has been given.

(1) Which are in fact the rolls carried away by the Bedouin on the occasion of their first visit to the cave? Where were they found? In a single jar? Or partly on the floor of the cave?

(2) Which are the rolls actually bought by Mar Athanasius Samuel in July 1947? Had not the Bethlehemite dealer slipped into the collection a roll of *Haphtarôth* which had come from the plunder of some synagogue? On being recognised as modern, was not this roll then replaced by the fourth roll, the *Genesis Apocryphon,* which seems to have come from the digging done by Kando, and not from that done by St. Mark's Monastery? There is one point which should be noted. This fourth roll was stuck together, whilst the others in this collection were not. At the present time, Kando asserts that manuscripts which came from his explorations deteriorated in his garden where he had buried them. What had been the fortunes of this roll between the time of its discovery and that of its sale?

(3) Where are the fragments of the Book of Daniel which were in the possession of the Syrian Metropolitan? They do not seem to have formed part of the collection sold in New York. Their contents, but not their photographs, have been published in the Appendix to *Qumrân Cave I* (pp. 150-2). Mention has been made of a fifth roll in the hands of Mar Athanasius. Is it certain that this roll does not exist?[1]

(4) How did the Bethlehemite dealer come by the rolls which he sold to Sukenik? Did he get them from the Bedouin? From the personnel of St. Mark's Monastery? Or from his own excavations? Is it true that all these manuscripts spent some time underground in his garden?[2]

It is not only concerning the state of the manuscripts coming from Cave I that one has the right to ask questions. We have been told that the cave could only be entered by a small opening high up the rocks, and "hardly larger than a man's head",[3] and that the present opening was cut through

---

[1] Millar Burrows, *The Dead Sea Scrolls,* pp. 1-23, suggests that the mention of a fifth roll may have been due to the fact that the *Manual of Discipline* had been shown him in two pieces. This roll had been frequently handled, and he could not say if the break was ancient or not. Photographs show that one of these pieces consisted of only a column and a half, which would hardly allow it to be called "a roll". As to the three fragments of the Book of Daniel, they seem to come from two different manuscripts. According to Millar Burrows, the Metropolitan must have acquired them at a later date.

[2] It is important to know if the manuscripts have really suffered through this alleged burial in Kando's garden. In any case, the fragments which he sold later to the Department of Antiquities of Jordan do not appear to have become sticky during the long months that they were in his possession. Of all the rolls sold to Sukenik, only Isaiah "B" was stuck together, but Kando can hardly be held responsible for this, as detached fragments from the same roll found in the cave were in practically the same condition as the manuscript.

[3] Allegro, op. cit., p. 16.

the rock by the clandestine diggers. It is obvious, then, that the Bedouin could not have brought out through this opening the jars bought by Professor Sukenik. At the beginning of his negotiations with the Bethlehemite dealer, the professor had asked to see "the" jar from which, he was told, the manuscripts offered to him had been taken. The reply was given that this was impossible, as the Bedouin had put it to domestic uses and were not willing to sell it. Finally, he bought "two" jars which it is certain did not come from the first visit of the Bedouin to the cave. We are told that agents of the Syrian Metropolitan saw "a" complete jar, but could not carry it away because of its weight. One wonders if the dealer from Bethlehem did not sell to Professor Sukenik two jars *similar* to those from the cave, but which had come from some older excavation and which he knew could be found in the hands of the Bedouin.

Where did the almost complete jar come from which Allegro was able to buy from Kando in 1953? How long had the Bedouin had it and put it to ordinary use? How many other objects found in diggings still exist in Bedouin camps? How many come from caves at Qumrân discovered since 1947?

We are told that two groups of clandestine diggers visited Cave I. If they went back there after the sale of the jars to Professor Sukenik, they must have known that these objects had a certain commercial value. Did they not take from the cave some other objects to which no reference has ever been made, and about which nobody seems to trouble? Certain details should be recalled which may be important:

(1) The archaeological mission which visited the cave in February 1949 found pieces of wood lying on the floor of the cave, some small, some large. Where did they come from? Might they not have formed part of chests or other objects which have now disappeared?

(2) This mission noticed on the floor of the cave a quantity of olive kernels and date-stones, "much gnawed by rats". The present writer has first-hand acquaintance with the rocky desert near to the Dead Sea, and knows that there are no rats there. Had there been any, in the course of 2,000 years they would have finished off a few kernels and not left untouched the leather rolls and the linen coverings. Here is a problem which should have attracted the attention of scholars. Approximate dating of an olive kernel is now quite feasible by the carbon 14 method. Why has the test not been tried?

(3) Several "*great* blocks of conglomerate dung" were found in the

cave,[1] and the conclusion was drawn that the cave must have served as a shelter for some "*small* wild animals" during a long period. There we have a somewhat surprising contradiction! But would it not have been possible to analyse what was called "conglomerate dung"? What was for a long time thought to be asphalt or pitch turned out to be only a paste produced by the decomposition of leather.

★      ★      ★

Such accounts as have been published up till now can hardly be said to confirm the theory of the Essene library put away for safety. It is now insisted that there is a distinction to be drawn between Cave I and all the other caves with manuscripts which were discovered later. Because of certain later revelations, there is a desire to attribute to the Bedouin and to Kando the dilapidation of some of the rolls. Even if these points could be granted, it would remain none the less true that the excavation of this cave has brought to light some disturbing facts. A library is not the place for fragments of manuscripts rolled up into a ball, or folded concertina-wise, for bits of pure linen patched and useless, nor for so many other objects found in the cave. On the other hand, these things may be found in a cemetery for books, in a *geniza*.

What explanation can be given for the presence of olive kernels and date-stones in an uninhabitable cave, difficult to reach, and which certainly cannot have served as a store for foodstuffs? These kernels were found to have been gnawed. As there are no rats in the caves of Qumrân, it is right to assume that these kernels were probably in much the same condition when they were taken there as when they were found. That is understandable if the cave was a *geniza,* but it is illogical if one wants to look upon it as a hiding-place for a library.

On this matter, we may recall that Leviticus laid down that the sons of Aaron should take as their due a part of all the sacrifices offered in the Temple. "They shall eat it in a holy place", it was said. The suppression of the Temple sacrifices led the rabbis to constitute for themselves a slaughtering-tax, and to demand a part of the tithes and first-fruits as "worship-dues". But as the Temple no longer existed, what "holy place" could be thought of other than the synagogue in which to keep these products? The "pure things of the rabbis", the *terumah,* to which frequent reference will be made, attracted mice even into the Ark, where the rolls

---

[1] Which must not be confused with the "guano of bats" with which one chamber of Cave II was filled, *Revue Biblique*, LXIII (1956), p. 573.

of the Law were kept, this "very holy" place serving also as a food-safe. The rabbinic authorities issued many decrees to put an end to this unwarranted interpretation of texts. What was to be done with any foodstuffs which had been in contact with the Sacred Books? They could not decently be thrown away on to refuse heaps. They had to end up in a *geniza*. Appropriately, an old tradition on this subject was recalled: when the Ark of the Covenant was buried, the pot which had contained the manna was also carried away to the *geniza* because it had been in contact with the Tables of the Law. Moreover, when a synagogue was declared unorthodox, all the "pure things" of the rabbis had to suffer the same treatment as their books. When Rabbi Eliezer ben Hyrcanus was excommunicated, his "pure things" were burnt at the same time as all the books of his school.

Obviously, the many jars of which the debris has been found in Cave I must have been carried there for some good reason. Some were broken into the smallest fragments, and these breakages were ancient. Others were found empty, we are told, and no analysis could possibly be made to show what they had contained. But there were also found in the cave those "great blocks of conglomerate dung". "Small" animals cannot be held responsible for these "great" blocks, nor can it be supposed that the dung massed together spontaneously. Nobody seems to have tried to find out if these blocks did not result from the natural decomposition of some kind of organic matter, such as foodstuffs.

This is an important point when there is a wish to prove the existence of a buried library. In order to be able to talk about rats, it would have been wise first of all to be sure that rats could exist in the desert region of Qumrân, 1,000 feet or more below sea-level. At the present time, we are asked to believe in these hypothetical rodents; we are asked to believe that they had a marked predilection for the lower parts of certain rolls, but that they never attacked the upper margins; we are asked to believe that they had such a preference for certain books of Scripture as to leave remaining only a few insignificant fragments, and that they had an absolute aversion for the Isaiah roll; that they had a liking for some psalms, but respected certain other ones; that they could finish off all of an apocryphal roll except for two or three columns which were hardly touched in the space of 2,000 years, etc.

The caves of Wadi Murabba'at, which are above sea-level, have been inhabited. Birds have built their nests there, and there is much evidence of typical destruction by rodents. Nothing of the kind has been found in the caves of Qumrân. Not a single rodent's nest has been found, whilst in the

Wadi Murabba'at caves, most of the manuscript fragments were found in such nests. That is an important point.

*      *      *

To a large extent, the problem of the Dead Sea manuscripts is what one wishes to make it. Because of reasons of finance for some, and of legal immunity for others, essential facts have been hidden or distorted. We have not been told the whole truth and nothing but the truth. On many points where it should have been possible to have certainty, we are reduced to conjecture, and even here the enquirer is often more hampered by affirmations which are open to question than by the absence of precise facts.[1]

In brief, it is in this way that the problem of the Dead Sea manuscripts has become obscure. We are asked to believe, and frequently the evidence with which we are supplied demonstrates the opposite to what is put forward. Theories are erected, and after a little while their premises are found to be false. There are times when one can say to oneself, "What do they want to prove?" By talking about a buried library, by ante-dating certain manuscripts in which some Christian ideas are expressed, are they wanting to establish a belief in a "pre-Christianity" as there has been a talk of "pre-Qaraitism" by means of a comparison with the medieval fragments from Cairo? By insisting on the Essene monastery of Qumrân, do they wish to instil a belief that there was in Judea a Jewish "pre-monasticism"?

There has been the desire to identify the sect which is said to have hidden its precious books in this way with that of the Essenes, whose "monastery" is said to have been found in the ruins of Khirbet Qumrân, a few hundred yards away from the cave where the first manuscripts were found. It therefore becomes necessary to make clear what we know about the Essenes, and to show precisely what those could have known who wrote about them.[2]

---

[1] For a long time it was stated that Cave I had contained 200 to 250 manuscripts, a number arrived at from the number of jars which must have been deposited there. Today seventy-five rolls are spoken about, the number being based on the classification of the fragments which have been collected (Harding, *Qumrân Cave I*, p. 3.) As we do not know how many rolls were really taken from the cave by clandestine diggers and are now in the hands of dealers or collectors, and as we cannot be certain that all the recovered fragments come from complete rolls, would it not be better to admit our ignorance on this point? It should also be remembered that for a long time there was talk of rolls covered with pitch or bitumen when in reality it was simply a matter of decomposed leather.

[2] *Les Esséniens dans l'œuvre de Flavius Josèphe*, a study which appeared in *Byzantinoslavica*, XIII (1952), pp. 1-45, 189-226. This subject will be further developed in a forthcoming book.

# II

# Possible and Probable Authors

I. The most ancient reference to the Essenes is found in the works of Philo of Alexandria.[1] The *Essaioi*, as he called them, were said to be living in Palestine, "in villages, avoiding the cities, because of the iniquities which have become inveterate among city-dwellers". A question that at once arises is: "What did he know about them?" He was born in Alexandria about 30 B.C., and although he could not speak and write Hebrew, he was chosen as ethnarch by his Greek-speaking fellow Jews in Egypt. He was a Neo-Platonist, and wrote in Greek. He was about seventy years of age when he left Egypt for the first time, to go to Rome to plead before Caligula the interests of his community. He seems never to have been in Palestine; the short stay which he is said to have made in Jerusalem on his way back from Rome is very doubtful. These virtuous *Essaioi*, inhabitants of an idealised Palestine, seem to have been invented by him using any material that came to hand.

Why did this Alexandrian philosopher want to have *Essaioi* in Palestine among the Jews? Probably because he hoped to demonstrate to the pagans that monachism, a typical and exclusively Egyptian phenomenon in the first century A.D., was not incompatible with Judaism. He would have liked to prove that Jews also could practise the Egyptian ideal of virtue. In another writing,[2] he boasted about the *Therapeutai*, who lived in monasteries on a hill near to Lake Meriotis and even in the outskirts of Alexandria. Even if there was a sort of Jewish monasticism in Egypt, it is certain that there was nothing of the kind in Palestine. Palestinian Judaism was completely opposed to any idea of monastic chastity, celibacy being considered a grave sin. It has been rightly emphasised that "there is nothing to hinder

[1] *Quod omnis probus libersit*, ch. XII–XIII in *Philonis Iudaei Opera* . . . edited by Thomas Magney, London, 1742, pp. 457–9. Also in Loeb Classics (London), with English translation.
[2] *De vita contemplativa, idem.*, pp. 471ff.

64

us from believing that Philo somewhat stretched his material, finding in it an opportunity to develop the ideal of the perfect and happy life as he conceived it at the time of writing. It is a picture by a man who at times saw things in a dream."[1]

There is nothing that supports the statement that there really were some Jewish monks in Egypt, such as the *Therapeutai* described by Philo. And certainly there was no Jewish monasticism in Palestine in the first century A.D. In spite of his ignorance of the country, Philo did not dare to go so far as to state that his *Essaioi* (probably a translation into Aramaic of the Greek *Therapeutai*), were cenobites. According to him, the *Essaioi* were sturdy villagers who avoided all abstract philosophy and all logical discussion. They lived in the world while observing the same principles of virtue as the *Therapeutai* in Egypt. In short, it is very clear that there is nothing absolutely certain about these *Essaioi* of Philo's, and it is impossible to say that we have here a piece of unimpeachable evidence.

II. The second piece of evidence upon the Essenes comes from Pliny the Elder. As he had never been in Judea, it is not difficult to find the source of his quite fantastic information. He just embroidered what Philo had written. For reasons of euphony, he inserted an *n* into the name *Essaioi*, so that they became *Esseni*, or Essenes. Perhaps he was also thinking of the Essenes, "kings of the hive", who formed a body of priests at the temple of Artemis in Ephesus, and where it was said that priestesses were called *melissai*, or bees. Pausanias mentions this, but nothing really definite is known on the subject.

Pliny had little cause to fear contradiction when he invented a brotherhood of Essenes living together in one of the most inhospitable parts of the world, the desert of Engedi, to the west of the Dead Sea.[2] It was there that men "tired of life" came to "end their days" with only palm trees for company, in a community with no women, as the members "had renounced everything that had to do with Venus".

All attempts to show that this barren region could have been fertile in the first century A.D. have come to naught. Nothing that Pliny says about the Essenes can be called the truth. Moreover, his writings swarm with

---

[1] H. Leclercq, in the *Dictionnaire d'Archéologie Chrétienne et de Liturgie*, article "Cénobitisme", col. 3,057. J. L. Teicher, in *Studia Patristica*, I, Berlin, 1957, p. 541, goes so far as to suggest that if Philo was the author of these writings on the Essenes, he must have composed them under the effect of a touch of schizophrenia.

[2] *Natural History*, V, 15. To get an idea of the region, see photographs published in A. Dupont-Sommer, *Aperçus préliminaires* . . . p. 13; English translation by M. Rowley, *The Dead Sea Scrolls*, Fig. 1. Allegro, *op cit.* Figs. 9, 25, etc.

C

similar ramblings. And yet it is Pliny who is frequently being called upon to give evidence. Even so, contrary to all the rules of scientific honesty, the only words quoted are those which support the theory being maintained, and these are removed from their context. The calm Essene retreat for disillusioned old men placed in the neighbourhood of Engedi is, however, no more credible than the luxuriant vegetation which the myth-loving Pliny made to spring forth in that barren desert.

III. The third "witness" to the Essenes would have been, we are told, Dio Chrysostom, a Greek teacher of rhetoric in the first century A.D. This writer's complete works have not come down to us, but from what Synesius of Cyrene (A.D. 370-413) wrote we learn that Dio had made a eulogy upon a "city" of the Essenes, "situated on the shore of the Dead Sea, near to Sodom, in the heart of Palestine". In the same work, Dio is said to have given a description of the Valley of Tempe, and of the statue of Memnon. As we read Synesius, we gather that he blamed the Greek orator for having made use of sources which were not always reliable, and to have consulted books which had been too much "touched up". Had Dio Chrysostom really believed that in the Valley of Tempe the Peneus refused to mingle its waters with those of the Styx? Had he believed that the statue of Memnon in the temple of Serapis sent forth a sound when the rays of the sun touched it? Had he believed in the city of the Essenes near to Sodom? One thing seems clear enough. These items of information, all three of them fantastic, had been drawn by him from the same source, Pliny.[1] In short, we cannot speak of the "evidence" of Dio Chrysostom, and it is impossible to take seriously what Philo and Pliny say. Neither Philo, nor Pliny, nor Dio Chrysostom had ever been on the shores of the Dead Sea, and not one of them had ever met an Essene.

IV. It remains to be seen what we are to think of the evidence of Flavius Josephus, the most important of all, and also the most frequently invoked.

When one speaks of the works of Josephus, the reference is to Greek texts supposed to be translations from Aramaic (!). The Greek versions of the *Life, Jewish Antiquities,* and the *Jewish War* cannot in any case be considered original writings. They are translations, and have been subjected to various additions. There are several versions of a Jewish compilation known as the *Yossipon,*[2] of which a number of chapters seem to go back to

---

[1] *Natural History,* IV, 15 (8), 3; XXXVI, 11, 4; V, 17.

[2] Mantuan edition of about 1476, compiled by Abraham Conath: first edition of Sebastian Münster (Worms, 1529); second edition with different text (Bâle, 1541); Venetian edition, a different version (1544). See also the Hebrew manuscript No. 1280 in the Bibliothèque Nationale at Paris, which has important variations.

the Hasmonaean period, although the collections as a whole only crystallised after the invention of printing. There is a Christianised version of Josephus in Latin, and known as *Hegesippus*.[1] There is also the Slavonic version of Josephus.[2] Comparison with these works allows certain observations to be made concerning the references to the Essenes in the Greek text of Josephus.[3]

(a) In the Hebrew text, the *Yossipon*, the Essenes are *never* mentioned. All the episodes in which the Essenes figure in the Greek version also occur in this text, but the persons involved are never called Essenes.

(b) In *Hegesippus* there is *never* any mention of the Essenes, except in a passage which occurs in a few manuscripts, and is probably corrupt, where a person is sometimes called Johannes Esseus, Esseus, or Etseufa.

(c) The Slavonic version reproduces partly the well-known passage on the Essenes which is found in the *Jewish Wars* (II, viii, 2-14), but omits all the other references to the Essenes which are found in the Greek text (II, vii, 2-3; xx, 3-4; V, iv, 2).

Questions of style and other reasons have caused it to be recognised that in the Greek text of what is usually called "the works of Josephus" there have been many interpolations, and that these vary a great deal. As regards the Essenes, the famous passage, Chapter II, viii, 2-14, was introduced into the *Jewish War* by a Greek who probably lived in Italy at the beginning of the third century A.D. To the same interpolator we owe certain satirical phrases introduced into the *Life*. Enriched by only this one addition, the Greek version of the *Jewish War* was translated into Old Russian, whilst the Greek text received a fresh series of interpolations about the beginning of the fourth century. These can be easily recognised by their vocabulary and the ideas which they set forth, and are the work of a Christian. The same person introduced references to the Essenes in the *Jewish Antiquities*, (XIII, v, 9, x, 5-7, xi, 2; XV, x, 4; XVII, xiii, 3; XVIII, i, 2-6), and added to the interpolation of his predecessor the phrases which are not found in the Slavonic version.

It remained to discover the source from which the first interpolator drew his documentation, and the purpose of his interpolation. It has been possible to establish both.[4]

[1] Edited by V. Ussani, *Corpus Scriptorum Ecclesiasticorum Latinorum*, LXVI, Leipzig, 1932.
[2] Critical edition and translation into French, A.Vaillant and P. Pascal Paris, 1934-38.
[3] Critical edition in seven volumes by E. B. Niese, Berlin 1887-95; Loeb Classics (London); text with English translation, in nine volumes, in progress.
[4] *Les Esséniens dans l'œuvre de Flavius Josèphe* in *Byzantinoslavica*, XIII (1952), pp. 1-45, 189-226.

About A.D. 200 St. Hippolytus had written a treatise on religions which he entitled *Heresies*. This treatise is known under the name of *Philosophumena*.[1] In it the author deals with the "heresy" of the Jews (IX, iv, 18-20). He had doubtless heard of the Essenes, but he sought in vain for any confirmation of what was related about them. He must have said to himself that the name Essene had probably been badly transcribed, and finally he identified these virtuous men with the *hazanim*, the overseers of synagogues who were also responsible for the education of children. Though he devoted a few sentences to them at the beginning of his account, all the rest concerns the Jews in general. He describes very objectively the customs of the Jews, their doctrines, their way of living in the towns of the Diaspora, where they formed themselves into colonies, poor, but remarkable for the solidarity existing between fellow members of their religion. At the close of his account, Hippolytus seems to have changed his mind: the Essenes might well be the Elkazaites, who practised a kind of religious syncretism. The members of this religion dwelt mostly to the east of the Dead Sea in Transjordania. Epiphanius (*Adv. haer.*, XIX, 1) later called them *Ossaioi*. The author of the *Philosophumena* devotes a few sentences to them (iv, 28a), calling them "another order of Essenes". After that he goes back to the main currents of Judaism, and from this to the close of his account he speaks only about the Pharisees and the Sadducces.

In brief, if one takes out the name of Essene which is wrongly used, once for the *hazanim* of the synagogues and once for the Elkazaites, then everything that Hippolytus says about the Jews is correct and can be confirmed by what one finds in Jewish literature. Naturally, in his eyes, Judaism was a "heresy", but he refrained from making any offensive or prejudiced remarks about the Jews or their religion.

It is this chapter that was borrowed and deprived of its real meaning by the first interpolator of the *Jewish War*. He cleverly changed a few words, sometimes merely a simple prefix, so as to impart to the words the air of a stinging satire upon the Jews. Naturally, he attributed everything to "those called Essenes", who, "though of the Jewish race, are more altruistic than the others". It is surprising that the prejudiced nature of his sentences was not noticed earlier, and that no one realised that a Jew like Josephus could never have written such absurdities. The satire is clearly seen as soon as one sets oneself to translate the Greek text word for word,

---

[1] The only known manuscript is in the Bibiothèque Nationale. The text was edited by E. Miller, Oxford, 1851, and later in 1860 with a Latin translation by Patricius Cruice (Paris). See also Hippolytus of Rome, *Philosophumena*, edited and translated into English by F. Legge, London, 1921.

and still more when it is compared sentence by sentence with the *Philosophumena*.[1] If modern readers have not noticed the offensive nature of this well-known chapter of the *Jewish War*, it was certainly felt by readers in antiquity. Thus it was that the second interpolator introduced into this chapter a few sentences with a view to toning down the impression given by certain passages which he may have thought belonged to the original. As already said, these sentences did not figure in the exemplar which was used for the Slavonic translation.[2]

What is to be said about the insinuations which the first interpolator slipped into the *Life* of Josephus? Ancient readers cannot but have smiled at this unblushing declaration of Socratic manners which, supposedly, the author set out with such effrontery, yet modern readers do not seem to have had even a suspicion of the baseness of this passage. Moreover, no one noticed that it is impossible to discuss simultaneously three sects which mutually excommunicate each other.

The *Life* does not seem to have been revised by the second interpolator of the *Jewish War*. He simply revised the *Jewish Antiquities*, and naturally must have been astonished not to find even the least mention of the Essenes in the pages corresponding to those where his predecessor had introduced his chapter upon the Essenes. He therefore set himself to fill up this gap by reference to the *Jewish War*. It is to him that we owe the brief mention of them in XIII, v, 9. This passage is so much out of place that T. Reinach thought it worthwhile to remark; "One does not know what to do with this titbit which Josephus has made up on his own. Here as elsewhere, he makes the Jewish religious sects which had a totally different character into schools of philosophy on the Greek model." The other uses of the name Essene (XIII, x, 5-7, xi, 2; XV, x, 4; XVII, xiii, 3), where it is given to sages and soothsayers, and the paragraph on the Essenes in the passage (XVIII, i, 2-6), where the doctrines of the Jews are set out, are also from his hand. In reading the sentences which he devotes to them, one realises that he too must have sought to obtain evidence about the Essenes, but that he had not been able to find anything which would have confirmed the statements of his predecessor. He probably knew the works of Philo, but may have been ignorant of Pliny and Dio Chrysostom. One fact, however, stands out in his lines: he had not come across the Essenes and perhaps assuming, like Hippolytus, that the name had been deformed, in the end he thought he could identify these

[1] See *Byzantinoslavica*, XIII/1 (1952), pp. 16-26.
[2] *Ibid.*, XIII/2, pp. 193-200.

men with the country peasants whose manners he faithfully describes. Everything that he says about the Essenes fits in perfectly with Jewish peasants of the first, second and third centuries A.D., those who called themselves "the poor", and is confirmed by Jewish literature. If the name of Essene is left aside, and the interpolator, moreover, sees that it is a kind of nickname, then what this second interpolator said in this chapter about Jewish doctrines is perfectly correct. Here again it is astonishing that no one should have seen that his Essenes were peasants "entirely given over to working on the land".[1]

The additions of the first interpolator can be dated with sufficient precision from the fact that the approximate date of Hippolytus writing his *Philosophumena* is known. The second interpolator's additions are marked by a distinctive vocabulary and by sentences damaging to the Greeks, whereas the first interpolator always praised them. They may be dated by his allusion to the habits which were attributed to the Dacians in the fourth century.

Far from recognising that the references to the Essenes in the Greek version of Josephus are due to two interpolators, all the easier to distinguish because they frequently contradict one another, some people now are trying to bend the text to fit in with the theories which they wish to maintain, at times proposing quite daring emendations. Believing that the Essenes of whom he had heard were the *hazanim* of the synagogues, Hippolytus had written:

> These practise the more holy life, serving one another and observing continence. And they turn away from every deed of concupiscence, holding it even hateful to listen to such things. They renounce fornication, and when they agree to accept others' children, they bring them up in their customs, educating them and causing them to progress in their studies.
>
> They forbid them to commit fornications, even as they themselves abstain from it. As to women, although it is necessary to listen to their benevolent advice, they do not confide in them, for they distrust women altogether.

The first interpolator of the *Jewish War* has paraphrased this passage, sometimes by merely changing a prefix, so as to attribute unusual habits to the Essenes:

Although of Jewish race, they are more altruistic than the others.

[1] See *Byzantinoslavica*, XIII/2 (1952), pp. 215-20.

Whilst they shun pleasures as a vice, they regard abstinence and the control of the passions as a special virtue. As to marriage, they disdain it, but they carry off the children of others at a tender and pliable age, and, as if they were their parents, they mould them in accordance with their own principles.

They do not condemn marriage in itself, nor the offspring which results from it, but they themselves avoid the wantonness of women, and are of the opinion that no woman remains faithful to one and the same man.

This violent satire was certainly not to the taste of the second interpolator, who thought he could identify the Essenes with the country people. In the *Jewish Antiquities* (XVIII, i, 5) he wrote:

They do not bring in concubines, neither are they desirous to acquire slaves, the one tending towards injustice, and the other to domestic quarrels. They live the one with another and in a spirit of friendliness, rendering mutual service.

They appoint upright men as stewards of the tithes of all that the ground produces, and these are the priests who watch over the preparation of bread and other food. They therefore do not live in any unusual fashion, and certainly not in that about which taunts are made to some of the Dacians, who are styled "the superfluous".

This last word may be a corruption, but the reference is none the less clear. Strabo (VII, iii, 3) in fact mentions certain Thracians who live without wives and are nicknamed creators.

Hippolytus had given the idea that the *ḥazanim* whom he called Essenes, were virtuous, and that when children were entrusted to them they educated them and inculcated moral principles. The first interpolator of the *Jewish War* turned the Essenes into men with peculiar habits who carried off other people's children and moulded them to their own way of life. Naturally, they did not condemn the marriage of others, since it was the only way for them to procure the young. The second interpolator clearly recognised the vileness of this passage, and in the *Jewish Antiquities* he attempted a correction. The country people (according to him, the Essenes) abstained from bringing in concubines or having slaves, and they helped each other in their agricultural labours. That was all, for, besides, they did not live in any extraordinary fashion, and had nothing to do with such customs as those attributed to some Dacians and Thracians.

That is about all that the second interpolator had to say about those whom he called Essenes. Why did he not take up also the other passages of his predecessor? It may be that he knew the *Philosophumena* and had understood that everything that one read further on in the *Jewish War* referred to the Jewish communities in the Diaspora. One fact is worth noticing, however. Further on he made another correction when speaking of the Zealots, the sect which had branched off from that founded by Judas of Galilee.

When quoting the evidence of Josephus upon the Essenes, it is a good thing to refer to the Greek text and not rely upon old translations, which often are only approximate. And, more important still, the honest thing is not to extract only those phrases which seem to support some theory. The contradictions between the different passages in which the name of Essenes figures are sufficiently eloquent, and at least ought to be mentioned.

There has been much talk about the "sacred meal" of the Essenes. As a matter of fact, Hippolytus had given an account of a custom of the Jews living in the Diaspora, "travelling around their native land, in order to settle down in any foreign country".

(21) They always pray at dawn, not speaking before they have praised God. After that they go forth, and each one does the work which he wishes to do. After working till the fifth hour, they leave off. . . . And after having purified themselves, they gather together in one dwelling . . . and take their place around the refectory. They sit down in order, and in silence they are given bread, and then some one kind of food from which each has a sufficient portion. But no one tastes anything before the priest has blessed it. At the end of the meal, a benediction is again pronounced as at the beginning, and then they finish by again offering praise to God. After that . . . they toil again at their usual work until the evening.

The first interpolator of the *Jewish War* did not fail to be ironical over this custom as over the others. Under his pen, the sentences are deformed into (II, viii, 5):

128. In fact, their piety towards the Deity takes a peculiar form. Before the sun is up, they utter no word on mundane matters, but offer

to Him certain prayers which have been handed down from their forefathers, as though entreating Him to rise.

129. They are then dismissed by their superiors to the various crafts in which they are severally proficient, and are strenuously employed until the fifth hour, when they again assemble in one place. . . . Pure now themselves, they repair to the refectory, as to some solemn shrine.

130. When they have taken their seats in silence, the baker serves out the loaves to them in order, and the cook sets before each, one plate with a single course.

131. Before meat, the priest says a benediction, and none may partake till after the prayer. When breakfast is ended, a further benediction is pronounced. Thus at the beginning and at the close, they give thanks to God as the bestower of life. Then . . . they return anew to their labours until evening.

The irony of this passage has not been noticed, nor its anachronisms and inexactitudes (for example, Jews never served individual loaves, a loaf being broken by the person presiding at the meal). Nor has it been seen that the morning prayers and these meals in common were Jewish customs (correctly reported in Hippolytus), and had in them nothing Essene or monastic. The early Christians adopted these customs, and an echo of them is found in the younger Pliny's famous letter to Trajan, a letter which Tertullian analysed in his *Apologeticum,* Chapter II:

They affirmed the whole of their guilt, or their error, was that they met on a stated day before it was light, and addressed a form of prayer to Christ, as to a divinity, binding themselves by a solemn oath, not for the purposes of any wicked design, but never to commit any fraud, theft, adultery, never to falsify their word, nor deny a trust when they should be called upon to deliver it up; after which it was their custom to separate, and then reassemble, to eat in common a harmless meal. From this custom, however, they desisted after the publication of my edict, by which, according to your commands, I forbade the meeting of any assemblies.[1]

The letter of the younger Pliny to Trajan speaks of Christians of Bithynia who had adopted or continued Jewish practices. They also

[1] Translation by W. Milmoth ,*Pliny's Letters,* Bohn's Classics, London 1909, p. 395.

C*

offered morning prayer and it was quite well known that it was not to beseech the sun to rise. They too had their meal in common, quite an innocent custom against which nothing had been said before the prohibition of assemblies. So as to make the morning prayer and the common meal a uniquely Essene practice, this letter of Pliny's is usually passed over in silence.

It is, moreover, rather significant that the passages in Josephus which speak of the Essenes are the subject of skilful discrimination. Certain facts which do not fit in with the desired picture of these virtuous monks are never quoted, nor are certain passages which are too improper. If the evidence of Josephus is to be invoked, it would be right to report *all* that is found in these writings which concerns the Essenes, and not merely a few sentences carefully chosen and arranged. It is clear, for instance, that in the author's eyes the sanitary practices of the Essenes (*Jewish War*, II, viii, 9) had an importance at least equal to that given to the famous sacred meal.

Neither the interpolators of Josephus nor Pliny the Elder have ever suggested that the Essenes were said to be monks copying out manuscripts. No one has said that each man "had a writer's inkhorn at his side" (Ezek. 9.2, 3, 11), so that today any place may be called Essene where a Roman inkwell is found. According to the first interpolator, the instrument from which the Essene was never separated was a mattock, used to dig latrines, and by which an Essene could be recognised.

But that is not the question. What matters here is to emphasise a particularly important point, which is that originally the works attributed to Josephus *never* mentioned the Essenes, *who have never existed*. All which is found today in the Greek version is due to two interpolators. What they wrote is neither found in the Jewish version, the *Yossipon*, nor in the Christian version, *Hegesippus*. The phrases of the first interpolator, a violent satire against the Jews made by distorting the chapter upon them in the *Philosophumena*, are only found in the Slavonic version, and somewhat watered down there. The references made by the second interpolator of the *Jewish War*, and the sentences which he added to the interpolation by his predecessor, certainly did not figure in the copy used by the Russian translator.

★      ★      ★

This brief summing up of the "evidence" upon the Essenes ends therefore in a negative result. It was to be expected. *There never were any Essenes.*

The name was invented by Philo. Their town near to the Dead Sea with its luxuriant vegetation sprang from the imagination of Pliny the Elder. Certain persons believed that there were Essenes. Dio Chrysostom may have been one of them, and Synesius seems to have blamed him for doing so. Others wanted to make sure about their existence. Hippolytus found nothing to confirm what Philo and Pliny had said. He may have believed that the name was a corruption of the Hebrew *hazanim,* the superintendents of the synagogues. Later he believed that the name had been given to the Elkazaites of Transjordania and Samaria. The second interpolator of Josephus, in the *Jewish Antiquities,* identified the Essenes with the people of the countryside. Neither of these conscientious authors found the least trace of a Jewish cenobitism, of a monastic tendency nurtured in the bosom of Judaism.

There would therefore have been no need to come back to this satire of the first interpolator of the *Jewish War* if only he was not continually quoted as unimpeachable evidence—Josephus, the only Palestinian Jew who is said to have known the Essenes and "made trial" of their sect—and if only there was not an attempt to confirm what is found in the Greek text by two infallible proofs, the excavations at Khirbet Qumrân and the so-called *Damascus Document.*

## ii

## THE RUINS OF QUMRÂN

Between the mouth of the Jordan and the promontory called Ras Feshkha, the western shore of the Dead Sea forms a kind of beach which becomes more and more narrow. Near to the first cave where manuscripts were discovered, the distance from the cliffs to the water's edge is roughly a mile. On this strip of land is a small hill whose summit forms a plateau which is almost oval. Its dimensions are 360 yards from north-north-west to south-south-east, and 260 yards from east-north-east to west-south-west. The plateau is divided into two unequal parts by a straight line. The eastern and larger part contains a cemetery with nearly 1,100 graves perfectly arranged in lines. The western part was separated from it by a wall, parts of which remain, and this part has the form of a segment of an oval, almost a triangle. The longest side follows the wall and is about 320 yards in length. The greatest breadth is 72 yards. To the north-north-east, for a length of 120 feet, the wall also acts as the western wall of a rectangular building 96 feet wide; 130 feet further on, this wall forms the eastern side of a cistern along a further 130 feet. After that, the wall continues to the south-south-eastern edge of the plateau.[1]

In the cemetery, all the graves are aligned parallel to the wall. The bodies were buried on their backs with their heads towards the south-south-east. Not one of the graves so far excavated contained the smallest object, a coin or a jewel, nor any trace of any fabric. The age of the dead at time of burial varies from twenty to fifty years. A number of the skeletons found were those of women. Later some skeletons of children were found.

It is at a distance of 300 yards from the Dead Sea, and on a plateau more than half of which is a cemetery, that some people have wanted to place the flourishing Thebaid of Pliny's dreams. First of all it was in the main building 100 feet by 96, and later in the adjoining buildings, that the "monastery" was placed. The results of the excavations have not all been published as yet, but reading or listening to the explanations offered to visitors, one would imagine oneself back in the Middle Ages. They are reminiscent of the stories told to the Russian pilgrims, Ignatius of Smolensk, Anton of Novgorod and others, who visited the Holy Land, and whose credulity was systematically exploited. The story of one of these visits to the "monastery" of the Essenes has been related by an American journalist,[2] and it is not lacking in liveliness, especially since it is concerned with a scientific excavation.

The first comment to be made is this. The arrangement of the site alone shows that the buildings which still exist were constructed for purposes connected with the cemetery, and not that the cemetery is a consequence of the occupation of the site. No one would divide a small plateau by a straight line of wall, leaving the greater part for graves, if the building was the essential part and the cemetery only the accessory. This argument does not seem to have struck the excavators. Their primary idea was to find the date of the ruins, and as a criterion they used the coins found in them. When coins are found in the course of excavations, unless they were deliberately placed in the foundations, they are coins which someone has lost there. The conclusions that anyone is entitled to draw from them are subject to the same caution as those deduced from pottery and other finds of accessories. First of all, it is not certain that all the lost coins had only just been minted. Secondly, one cannot say that all those who inhabited the site did of necessity strew coins there to mark their passage.

---

[1] Approximate figures only whilst awaiting a detailed report.
[2] Edmund Wilson in the *New Yorker*, 14th May 1955, pp. 76–82.

At Qumrân, coins have been found which were struck between 136 and 37 B.C., and others from between 4 B.C. and A.D. 68. From this fact, the deduction has been drawn that the site was abandoned by the Essenes for thirty years, following an earthquake which had damaged the buildings. Later, two coins were found dating from this period, that of the reign of Herod the Great, but the theories have remained unchanged: these two coins, and just these, could have been in circulation at a later period. Moreover, it is not very clear why an earthquake must have led to the abandonment of the site for thirty years.

Other and later coins were also found in the course of the first excavations at Qumrân. Three date from the reign of Bar Kochba, three others are marked JUDAEA CAPTA, and a few carry the sign of the Tenth Legion. That has been looked upon as the proof that the site was occupied by the Roman legionaries after A.D. 70, and by the Jews of the Second Revolt about A.D. 132. But three Byzantine coins were also found, and two different Arab ones. These, we are told, can only have come from travellers who accidentally lost them.[1]

In this way, the story of the "monastery" is related year after year before proceeding to make the round of the ruins and the Essene remains which have been found there. One is shown at the extreme north what was the "kitchen", and at the extreme south, only to be reached after an impossible distance of over 60 yards, what was the "refectory", near to which there have been found over "1,000 pots and cups carefully arranged" Admittedly, this quantity of broken vessels strangely stacked is rather surprising. It sets a serious problem.[2] A few fragments of brick and plaster found in a long chamber, and which are held to have fallen from a supposed upper story when this gave way, have been assembled to form long benches. They come, so we are told, from the *scriptorium*, where diligent monks drew up, or re-copied, the rolls which were going to form their precious library, now partly recovered. Three inkwells have been found, one in bronze and two in baked clay. One of them still contained a little dried ink, the ink with which the rolls were written. All that is authentically Essene. Naturally, there is talk about the reeds which formerly grew on the shores of the Dead Sea in spite of its high salt content, and from which the monks cut their reed pens. There has even been talk of the rearing of sheep whose hides, tanned on the spot, served for making the

---

[1] In the course of the 1954-6 excavations, 415 further coins were found: 233 could be dated, 4 were from the reign of Herod the Great, and 6 were "late".

[2] See Question 2 in the next section, p. 90.

leather rolls of the manuscripts. There have been found, in two different parts of the building, it is true, the millstones which the monks used to grind their corn. Even their potter's shop has been found, with the place for the potter's wheel.[1]

One understands how such methods were used in the Middle Ages to exploit the credulity of pilgrims, and one smiles about them. It is difficult to allow that they may be used again by scholars in the middle of the twentieth century. The number of possible interpretations of these objects is considerable. Is it indispensable to make Essene relics of them? A Roman guard-post, a refuge for members of the Jewish resistance movement, would sufficiently explain the presence of inkwells, since reports were dispatched and received. But what can we say about the desks of the anachronistic *scriptorium*? Or of the Essenes' potter's shop? Where did this get its clay from, and its material for firing? Generally, potters' kilns are built far away from all dwellings. At Qumrân, where there is parching heat, the Essenes are said to have manufactured their pottery close to their living quarters. It is true that an enormous amount of domestic pottery has been found at Qumrân.[2] A jar in all respects similar to those discovered in the caves with manuscripts has been found intact, "sunk into the ground of one of the rooms". Pains have been taken to prove that it had not been imported from Egypt. Was that to insinuate that it had been made at Qumrân? Is it suggested that the Essenes had the monopoly of making these jars? That they had clay and firing material brought from afar so as to make them on the spot, and have them ready in case they should have to put their library into safe keeping in the caves?

The skill with which the romance of the Essenes has been built up has probably never had its equal. The region is dry, barren, and uninhabitable, but that counts for little, as a number of large and small open cisterns have been found. They served, we are told, to conserve the rains which rarely fall in this region. Knowing what to do with this water after months of stagnation and in the event of it not having evaporated is quite another question. The buildings are too restricted to shelter a large community.

---

[1] See Question 5 in the next section, p. 93.

[2] For the description of the potsherds found in Cave I, see *Qumrân Cave I*, pp. 8ff. As regards the jars, it may be noticed that "the mixture is invariably fine as a rule, combined with a slight and varying amount of chalk. The baking is always good, and frequently has been very thorough. On the outside, the surface has usually received a white, pink or cream wash". The bowls are distinguished by "a more refined mixture, an excellent baking". A lamp "which appears to have been imported from some other country can be distinguished by its grey earth". These facts alone are sufficient to eliminate the theory that the jars and other utensils found in Cave I had been manufactured in the "pottery" of Khirbet Qumrân.

That is explained by saying that these were reserved for certain chosen persons. The rest of the community lived in uninhabitable caves or in tents in the surrounding desert. Naturally, these "novices" depended upon the monastery cisterns for their water, but they kept their utensils in inaccessible clefts of the rock. Thus for some centuries Jews are supposed to have been camping at the side of a cemetery in a parched desert infested with vipers, scorpions, and centipedes, and as the very crown of asceticism they lived there with their wives and children whilst the monks went on calmly copying manuscripts in their *scriptorium* on locally produced leather, papyrus, or copper, with pens which they had cut from the reeds of the Dead Sea! They must have lived on air, whilst their seniors, protected by their walls and watch tower, baked their bread and ground the corn of their never-failing provisions! By an inexplicable marvel, clay and firing material kept arriving at the monastery for the manufacture of jars and household utensils. Regularly at fixed dates coins were strewn on the ground and never picked up, so that later on it would be possible to give precise dates to this curious community, remarkable for its thousands of dead!

A new chapter of this romance is now being elaborated. Three miles south of the ruins of Qumrân, where, we are told, the general services of the monastery, the reserves of food, and the workshops were all centralised, the ruins of a building have been found which one hastened to identify with the "community's farm". We are told that "a number of small, brackish springs made possible a certain amount of cultivation, and probably a palm-grove. Flocks could be watered at the spring of 'Ain Feshkha, which is also brackish".[1]

The idea of a "farm" is curious in itself, especially when one thinks of this strange community whose members are supposed to have lived "for the most part in caves or in huts all along the rocky cliff on a strip of five miles". Why was not the whole community settled around this one and only farm? Why were the "general services" set up two or three miles away? Why should they construct buildings for cattle whilst men and women were living in caves which we are told were "uninhabitable"?

It is clear that excavations will be carried out in the ruins close to 'Ain Feshkha, and it must be expected that the results will be interpreted in accordance with the theory that it is wished to maintain, without taking into account the climate, the potentialities of the soil, and the distance.

[1] R. de Vaux, "Les Manuscrits de la Mer Morte", in *La Table Ronde*, 107 (November 1956), p. 76. See also *Revue Biblique*, LXIII (1956), pp. 576f.

This time it is no longer a matter of a text drawn from Josephus. It is from the "evidence" of Pliny that support will be sought. There will be a desire to prove the existence of palm-groves on the shore of the Dead Sea to the north of the town of Engedi, by giving the Latin text a slight twist.[1] Few ancient geographers have described this inhospitable region, yet in the same *Jewish War* of Josephus, so often invoked when the Essenes are spoken about, this curious description of Lake Asphaltitis is found:

(IV, viii, 4.) Adjacent to it is the land of Sodom, in days of old a country blest in its produce and in the wealth of its cities, but now all burnt up. It is said that, owing to the impiety of its inhabitants, it was consumed by thunderbolts—in fact, vestiges of the divine fire and faint traces of the five cities are still visible. Still, too, one may see ashes reproduced in the fruits which from outward appearance would be thought edible, but on being plucked by the hand dissolve into smoke and ashes. So far are the legends about the land of Sodom borne out by ocular evidence.[2]

Why this belief in the palm-groves boasted about by Pliny, and not in the barren region described in Josephus? If the so-called "ocular evidence" of the latter is to be rejected, is it not necessary to reject at the same time all that he is supposed to say elsewhere about the customs of the Essenes? In any case, no text, however corrupt or interpolated it may be, has ever said that the Essenes passed their time in copying out manuscripts. No ancient historian or geographer has ever supposed that this mania should drive men to continue the practice, even when they had to be engaged in the work of a farm. For the announcement is made that "the Essene origin" of the ruins near to 'Ain Feshkha "is confirmed by the discovery *of an inkwell* and of some potsherds similar to those coming from the monastery".[3] Is it necessary to believe that the Essenes were the only people in Judea to use inkwells?

There is still another point to which it would be well to draw attention. We have been told about the monastery of the Essenes, we have

[1] The text says "above". It is only on modern maps that the north is placed at the top.
[2] This passage raised doubts in the mind of T. Reinach when he made his translation, and he remarked that "Josephus and Tacitus (*Hist.*, V, 6f.) appeared to follow a common source, perhaps Posidonius, known by Tacitus through Pliny". As a matter of fact, we have here one of the many interpolations in the Greek version of the work of Flavius Josephus, to whom the Biblical text would not have been a matter of "It is said".
[3] Fathers J. Starcky and J. T. Malik, "L'Enigme de la Mer Morte", in *Plaisir de France*, 218 (December 1956), p. 23.

been shown the desks from their anachronistic *scriptorium*,[1] and the inkwells which they used to write the manuscripts found in the caves of Qumrân. But *all* the results of the excavations have not yet been published. Perhaps there is an important part of the file which does not fit in so perfectly with the Essene hypothesis! Now, it happens that besides the coins found scattered about the area of the excavations in various rooms and in different layers, three jars were found at Khirbet Qumrân containing a treasure of 563 silver coins. Visitors have seen them and spoken about them, but a long time has passed without any publication mentioning them. In the same way, not much has been said about a number of jars which were found in the course of the excavations, and which contained bones often broken, roasted, or boiled, and coming from joints of animals.[2] Not much has been said about the two bases of columns (? Byzantine) solidly fixed into the ground, nor about a number of fragments which seem to have come from a portico or colonnade.

Only recently, Father R. de Vaux has published an important *Preliminary Report on the Third, Fourth and Fifth Campaigns of the Excavations at Khirbet Qumrân*.[3] An area of about 400 feet by 250 feet has been conscientiously excavated. This has allowed some very interesting hypotheses to be formulated about the successive constructions erected on the site, their re-use, and their abandonment at different periods. It would seem that originally there was a fortified enclosure there in the eighth or seventh century B.C. A series of constructions, including a round cistern, were adjoining. Two or three periods of later constructions have been identified following the abandonment of the site from the fifth to the second centuries B.C. First of all there is a vast system of rectangular cisterns, provided with wide, descending steps. These cisterns, curiously enough, are arranged round three sides of the original complex system of buildings as if they were moats designed to protect a fortified enclosure. But the arrangement of the place which seems to go back to this period is most strange. Two groups of buildings were erected outside this aquatic belt, one in the north-west corner and the other in the south and south-east. These have no connection with each other, nor do they seem linked in any way with the ruins of the ancient Israelite quadrilateral. The north-west group consisted in the main of two large rectangular halls, which,

---

[1] The name *scriptorium* appeared for the first time in the Middle Ages, when Christian monks at St. Gall devoted themselves to copying ancient manuscripts. Before then, the *scriptorium* was unknown even to the monks of Egypt and Asia Minor.

[2] See Question 3 in the next section, p. 91.

[3] *Revue Biblique*, LXIII (1956), pp. 522-77, with plan and 10 plates.

curiously, were divided by brick partitions. More than 50 yards away is a bath at the bottom of a large basin in the extreme north-west corner.

The construction to the south-east includes the famous great hall, 75 feet long and only about 15 feet wide. This, we are repeatedly told, was used by the Essenes for meetings, prayers, and banquets. It was in an adjoining chamber to the south-west that 1,080 pieces of pottery were found, of which 210 were dishes and 708 bowls. "The greater part of this pottery was manufactured on the spot", we are told. And in fact it was there at the south-west corner of this refectory that the potter's workshop was found, with its kilns, the place for the wheel, its basins where the clay was washed, the ditches where it was stored, etc. The destruction of all this pottery is put down to the earthquake of 31 B.C.

The reoccupation of the site, which is always supposed to have taken place thirty years or so later, brought about modifications in the plan of the existing buildings. Some were transformed and some abandoned. It is interesting to read all the hypotheses put forward upon the occupation of the site during the first century A.D., the only period which can have an interest for the connections which it is desired to make with the manuscripts from the caves.

The places where bones of animals were deposited are now known. With the exception of a single jar found in the courtyard of the ancient Israelite quadrilateral, all the deposits are situated definitely in the neighbourhood of the buildings in the north-west or of those in the south-east. The greater part of the jars, thirty or so, were found between the small bath, and the buildings to the west—a few even in the reservoir itself. The other jars were found to the east or the west of the great hall of the south. Six were found near to the potter's kiln, and others were buried along the length of the wall which limits to the east the whole complex layout of Khirbet Qumrân.

Whilst awaiting precise knowledge of *all* the excavations carried out at Khirbet Qumrân, certain remarks can be already formulated, and they are in direct opposition to the theory of an Essene monastery.

(1) As already stated, there never were any Essenes.

(2) There never was a Jewish monasticism in Palestine, neither in the first centuries of the present era nor before. Not a mention of this kind of life is to be found in the vast Jewish literature, and it is well known that the Jewish religion considers celibacy a grave sin. We should remember that Christian monasticism is of Egyptian origin. It was on the 16th April 339 that Rome saw for the first time two Christian monks. They were

named Ammon and Isidore, they came from Egypt, and they accompanied Bishop Athanasius of Alexandria. It is also known what difficulties Christianity had to contend with in introducing monasticism into Palestine. In Syria the most ancient monastic buildings date from A.D. 420.

(3) The site of Qumrân could never have been continuously lived in, for the region is uninhabitable. There may have been a lodge for the cemetery-keepers, for the grave-diggers, etc., as there were in the early centuries in the open-to-the-sky burial places used by Christians. Later on, semi-nomad Arabs may have set up temporary camps there, but they too would not have made a permanent resting-place of it. Even in the neighbourhood of Christian cemeteries, there is no evidence of monasteries till the fifth century, when Sixtus III (A.D. 432-40) founded a monastery *in catacumbas* near to the Basilica of St. Sebastian, and when St. Paulinus set up a monastery to serve the basilica of the cemetery of St. Felix.

(4) Except temporarily during a war, or at least through having voluntarily sacrificed his purity by becoming a grave-digger or cemetery-keeper, no Jew could have had his dwelling at Qumrân. The necrophobia of the Jews and their horror of tombs is well-known. It cannot therefore be supposed for a single moment that Jews could have deliberately chosen to live in the proximity of a vast cemetery.[1] When a Jew became a grave-digger, he made a real sacrifice. In the Middle Ages it was considered a very meritorious deed. One document found in a cave at Qumrân proves that in the early centuries of our era there already existed an equivalent of those associations of men, the *Ḥebra Qadiša,* who devoted themselves to the burial of the dead, and whose merit was held up to praise.

(5) Never has it been possible for any inhabitants of Qumrân to devote themselves in any continuous fashion to any industry whatsoever, whether that of copying manuscripts or that of making pottery. The region does not lend itself to the rearing of sheep and cattle, and therefore to the tanning of leather. Papyrus does not grow there. It is short of all clay and of burning material. If a potter had exploited the layer

---

[1] Of all the taboos imposed by the Jewish religion, that of the dead is the most severe. No sect of Judaism, no unorthodox school, however schismatic it might be, has ever set itself free from this taboo. He who touches a corpse "defiles his hands", and in consequence everything he touches becomes unclean. A corpse was unclean to the highest degree ('by 'bwt htwm'h). Anyone who had stayed, even accidentally, in a room where there was a dead body or who had passed the night near to a tomb became unclean. It may be recalled, in this connection, that in the Parable of the Good Samaritan (Luke 10.30-6) a priest and a Levite, on seeing at the side of the road a man who seemed to be dead, would have had to make a detour so as to avoid the risk of defilement through contact with a corpse.

of clay which had been deposited at the bottom of the disused cisterns during the course of the years (*Revue Biblique,* LXIII (1956), p. 543), this industry could only have continued a short while, till all the sediment was used up, and at a period when the site was abandoned (see below, p. 94).

(6) It is possible that guard-posts had been set up at Qumrân at different periods. The tower which flanks the main building seems to show that the site had been able to play a strategic rôle under the Hasmonaeans, under the Romans, and also in the second century A.D. It may be supposed that the post was abandoned under the Idumaeans, when the frontier no longer ran along the Dead Sea. Its reconstruction as a funerary building may also be admitted. It may be understood how a Roman guard was installed in the cemetery for a time, and how later members of Bar Kochba's movement temporarily occupied the site. In all this, however, there is no place for the romance of the Essenes.

At the commencement of our era, Jews had themselves interred in caves (cf. John 11.38, etc.). The bodies were placed in sarcophagi, after having been wrapped round in shrouds.[1] Moreover, at first sight it is possible to doubt if the graves at Qumrân were Jewish. It has been said "they could very well have belonged to some pagan Arab tribe of the period which Moslems call Jâhiliyâh—that is to say, before the time of Mohammed".[2] It remains none the less true that the actual site of Khirbet Qumrân is first and foremost a cemetery, belonging to which are some buildings, separated from the graves by a wall. Even if the cemetery was set up near to the ruins of some ancient military constructions, it is certain that the present buildings were part of the installation of the necropolis. This arrangement of the area is nothing new. It is found in the cemeteries of the early Christians in Italy and in Africa. It is found in Rome in the cemetery of Callistus, and is shown in outline on the famous marble plaque from Urbino. These Christian cemeteries, called *areae,* probably go back to a prototype such as we see in the layout at Khirbet Qumrân. The Christian *areae* of the early centuries included lodges for the keepers, the grave-diggers, etc. Before the time of Constantine and the cessation of persecution of the Church, Christians sometimes had their meetings in these

[1] The Romans unearthed the sarcophagi and used them as mangers for their horses, so that it came to be said that there was not a Roman horse which had not eaten its oats in the coffin of a Jew. In the period of persecutions, some Jews at times sought refuge in caves. Rabbi Baana was then charged to indicate the caves into which they could not go for fear of being defiled by contact with the dead already interred there.

[2] A. Dupont-Sommer, *Nouveaux Aperçus* . . . p. 16.

cemeteries, profiting from a certain measure of protection and liberty allowed under Roman laws concerning burials. Funerary *agapes* took place in the *cellae*. Food was served on *mensae,* which sometimes were the sarcophagi, and it was not till the fourth century that this practice was forbidden.[1]

The only explanation for the jars containing bones of boiled or roasted animals, sheep, goats, and an "abnormal" ox, is that funerary *agapes* took place at Qumrân as in the *cellae* of early Christians cemeteries. The limited number of deposits which have been found, in any case, rules out the hypothesis that the custom had been in use during many centuries. Orthodox Jews were forbidden to eat or drink in cemeteries, and could only do so at a distance of at least 50 *ells* from the graves. The fact should not be lost sight of that the site of Qumrân is far away from any large centre of population. Even if there is no evidence of funerary *agapes* with Jews, it may be assumed that the annual visits to the tombs at Qumrân must at times have been accompanied by some meal in the vicinity.[2]

In the light of information now supplied upon the excavations at Khirbet Qumrân, a hypothesis can be formulated upon the existing ruins and upon the adjacent necropolis. It is put forward tentatively, as all results of the excavations are not yet known.

At a time which we believe can be put within the reign of Alexander Jannaeus (103-76 B.C.), the ancient Israelite strong-point was reconstructed as a military post. Ditches serving also as cisterns were made, partly as a means of defence, and partly to supply the needs of the small garrison. Under Herod the Great (37-4 B.C.) the post was abandoned, the frontier no longer passing by the Dead Sea. As Father de Vaux has pointed out, in the course of the centuries a certain amount of clay could have collected at the bottom of the cisterns. This could have tempted a potter to set up a workshop in this desert spot, especially if the ruined buildings for a time supplied him with wood for the heating of his kiln. Some years later, when the Romans emptied sarcophagi to make mangers of them for their horses, some Jews may have had the idea of buying the potter's field so that they might bury there the bodies of their dead. In the cemetery of

---

[1] See Question 1 in the next section, p. 89.

[2] In the Middle Ages, the advice was given to choose a day of fasting for visiting tombs so as not to be tempted to eat or drink in a cemetery. It should be noted that at Qumrân bones have been found of joints of animals, not of entire lambs, bones too of animals of the ox family, and bones which appear to have been boiled, not roasted. These facts rule out the suggestion that they were connected with the Paschal feast.

Qumrân the bodies have been found which had been brought there in wooden coffins, apparently after having been unearthed from their first place of burial.

A tradition is reported in the Gospel according to St. Matthew (27.3-8):

Then Judas, who had betrayed him, when he saw that he was condemned, repented himself, and brought back the thirty pieces of silver to the chief priests and elders, saying, I have sinned in that I betrayed innocent blood. But they said, What is that to us? See thou to it. And he cast down the pieces of silver into the sanctuary, and departed; and he went away and hanged himself. And the chief priests took the pieces of silver, and said, It is not lawful to put them into the treasury, since it is the price of blood. And they took counsel, and bought with them the potter's field, to bury strangers in. Wherefore that field is called the field of blood, unto this day.[1]

Were there a number of "potter's fields" which had been transformed into cemeteries in the first century A.D.? That of Qumrân corresponds to this description, and all the more because it seems to have sheltered "strangers", at least at the beginning. Judging from the arrangements within the buildings erected around the ancient ruins at Khirbet Qumrân, one would get the impression that two distinct Jewish communities had shared this cemetery, where the needs of the moment made neighbours of the orthodox and the schismatic. One fixed its quarters in the north-west corner of the ruins, the other to the south-east, near to the former potter's workshop. It is not possible to determine up to what date the cemetery was in use, nor if later it belonged only to the orthodox, or to the unorthodox. At the time of the Second Jewish Revolt, followers of Bar Kochba seemed to have entrenched themselves there. It is possible that later on Christians held funerary *agapes* in this place.

During the time that the cemetery was in use—till the second century at least—the two communities which had their dead there each had a group of funerary buildings. One large hall in the north-east and another in the south could have served for the recital of prayers. Other rooms could have been reserved for the ritual cleansing of the dead. Such cisterns and baths as were still in a serviceable condition could have provided water for the washing of the dead, and for the purification of persons who had formed part of funeral processions or who had been visiting the graves, etc. Other

1 See Question 5 in next section, p. 93.

reservoirs could have supplied water for the personnel of the cemetery.[1]

In short, the information so far published on the excavation of the ruins at Khirbet Qumrân rules out the possibility of seeing in them a monastery with its dependencies on the medieval model. It may be necessary to change one's mind on certain points of detail, but in any case the arrangement of the site and the results of the excavations do not give grounds for supposing that men lived there who for centuries gave themselves to the making of pottery, and who copied out manuscripts solely for the purpose of creating a rich library for the use of those of their order who had chosen to live in the desert.

In talking about this Essene library, which is supposed to have contained over 1,000 rolls, not much attention has been paid to the arrangement of the site and its remoteness. Yet a library is created essentially for readers. It is true that the library as described to us differs considerably from anything that we have been accustomed to call by this name. The libraries of antiquity, of which names have come down to us—Athens, Pergamum, Alexandria, Rome—were all composed of very diverse works. They were collections formed at great cost, but they by no means represented the beliefs of the owners. Thus we know that the library at Alexandria was said to have contained a translation of the Pentateuch, yet this was not Holy Scripture to the Ptolemies. The picture given us of the Essene library is of something totally different: a collection of works which were all Essene, written by Essenes and for Essenes. Is it necessary to follow this train of reasoning to its logical conclusion? The monks of St. Gall copied out more than one profane work, and a fragment of the *Andromache* of Euripides has been found among the traces of the library of the monks of Khirbet Mird, but we have to suppose that at Qumrân books were produced one after another in the *scriptorium*, but only such as were written by Essenes or adapted to Essene beliefs. As to Biblical texts, we are told that the Essenes had a "mixed tradition", and that they took such liberties with the sacred text as "would have horrified a later copyist".[2] But if there is not a stable Essene tradition, by what may it be possible to recognise that a book is Essene?

[1] In the first century A.D. Jewish cemeteries were situated well outside the towns (cf. Luke 7.12). Women were forbidden to enter them, and even the cemetery-keepers had to live 50 *ells* from the tombs. From the Middle Ages onward it was not always possible to observe all these rules to the very letter, but a Jewish cemetery always contained a place where prayers could be recited, a chamber for the ablution of the dead, and a well or cistern which supplied the water for this rite.

[2] J. M. Allegro, op cit., pp. 65, 69.

Naturally, all idea of a book having been imported or bought in trade must be put aside; in such a case it could just as well have fallen into other hands, and then it would not have been Essene. This implies that there must have been Greek calligraphers among the monks of Qumrân, and a good many other things still less easy to maintain.

In conclusion, we have to suppose that these rolls were classified, arranged, and kept in good condition by librarians in rooms specially arranged for this purpose. We have also to suppose that at times the Essenes left their rocky dwellings to consult these books in the reading-rooms. And it is further necessary to believe that all that could be done in the neighbourhood of the Dead Sea, and in proximity to tombs.

To sum up, the very idea of a purely Essene library as some persons have conceived it is unimaginable, while to suppose that this "museum" could have been set up at Qumrân, at the side of a pottery factory, is a thought that surely would have occurred to no one. It is just a vicious circle. Starting out from the premise that two works from Cave I could very well have been Essene, a search was started for the ruins of the monastery. Then on the basis of the monastery and its *scriptorium* people talk about an Essene library. And it is put down as an axiom that this library was preserved in the Essene monastery of Qumrân, but that "it is unsafe at present to draw historical conclusions from the texts".[1]

iii

# SEVEN QUESTIONS RELATING TO THE RUINS AT QUMRAN[2]

The preliminary reports published on the excavations at Khirbet Qumrân and the reconstruction of the history of the site by Father de Vaux[3] and Father J. T. Milik[4] cannot satisfy anyone who has even only a slight acquaintance with Christian archaeology. The lack of precise details has not allowed me to formulate more clearly my theory concerning the final period of the site at Qumrân—a period lasting perhaps to the fourth century A.D. Moreover, the period fell outside the scope of my study. All the same, I am led to ask several questions, some of which might be

[1] T. H. Gaster, *The Dead Sea Scriptures*, New York, 1956, pp. v-vi.
[2] Substance of an article in *Sanctuaires et Pélerinages*, No. 9, October 1957.
[3] *Revue Biblique*, LX (1953), pp. 83-106; LXI (1954), pp. 206-36; LXIII (1956), pp. 532-77.
[4] *Dix ans de découvertes dans le désert de Juda*, Paris, 1957.

answered by a re-examination of the site, whilst others will probably require long research.

1. *The Masonry Tables with Shallow Hollows.* As J. L. Teicher has already shown,[1] the two tables with shallow hollows, found at Khirbet Qumrân, but not *in situ*, and now in the Palestine Archaeological Museum,[2] have nothing whatsoever to do with a hypothetical *scriptorium*. They belong to a well-known type of *mensa* used in funerary offerings.[3] They may have been used first by non-Christians, and have been taken over later by Christians, but it is absurd to imagine that the little, saucer-like hollows could have been used by Jewish scribes for their ablutions, which have never been "symbolical".

*Mensae* of another type, also in masonry, have been found in Algeria, and in other places as well. At Bonn in the Rhineland they seem to have been used by the pagans before the Christians took over those places towards the end of the third century.[4] In that town, their position is marked by cubes in masonry, roughly 32 inches in each direction, placed in the centre of a rectangular enclosure about 10½ feet long and 5 feet broad. In a number of places at Qumrân a similar arrangement is found, though here it appears that we are dealing with Christian *mensae*.

Three low pillars have been found on the axis of the long chamber 77, at the eastern end of which a column of the same height is built into the wall. The interpretation offered is that "these supports made the covering-in easy, but this expedient was not made use of in the western part so as to leave the place of the president free, and visible by the majority of the persons present".[5] No information is given as to the dimensions of these pillars, and they are not indicated on the plans of the building. We are informed, however, that they were "built on the underlying soil". In that case, they could hardly have functioned as supports for the roof. The weight of the pillars alone, if carried up to the height of the roof, would have made solid foundations necessary. Further, one cannot understand why this "expedient", if it was of any use, was not employed in the western part of this chamber.

Two more pillars of the same kind can be seen in the photograph of the small room, 86/89. These are marked on the plan. One is in the centre

[1] *Journal of Jewish Studies*, V/4, (1955) p. 147.

[2] J. M. Allegro, *The Dead Sea Scrolls*, Plate 34.

[3] *Dictionnaire d'Archéologie Chrétienne et de Liturgie*, articles "*Agape*" (I, 823-30) " *Martyr*" (X, 2,458-62), "*Mensa*" (XI, 440-53) *et passim*.

[4] André Grabar, *Martyrium*, Paris, 1946, I, p. 51.

[5] *Revue Biblique*, LXIII (1956), p. 546.

of the room, the other is built into the middle of the southern wall. No information is given either as to their dimensions or the nature of their foundations. No theory is put forward as to their purpose.

From the photographs, all of these pillars look like cubes the height of a table.[1] Their resemblance to *mensae* in masonry cannot be denied. Their surface appears smooth, but a closer examination might reveal some interesting details. Would it not be possible to see if those two plaques with shallow hollows found broken at Khirbet Qumrân did not fit one or another of these pillars? Is not the "block, the cutting of which had not been completed", found at the end of enclosure 102,[2] also a *mensa* like the other blocks and pillars?

We would recall the great table in stone and stucco, the fragments of which were found in the chamber 30, though not *in situ*. J. L. Teicher[3] considers that it also was used in *agapes*. In our opinion, it must have belonged to a *triclinium*—certainly not to a rather anachronistic *scriptorium*.

2. *The Broken Earthenware.* A large quantity of broken earthenware of the kind used at meals has been discovered in the southern group of buildings. In the corner of room 89 adjacent to the long chamber 77, 1,057 objects have been counted heaped on the ground, and the greater part broken. Their destruction has been attributed to an earthquake, but the nature of the breakages hardly warrants this. For one thing, not a single article has been found crushed, as by the collapse of the roof. Then, again, these vessels were piled together on the ground, not scattered about as they normally would be as a result of a seismic shock. A parallel deposit was found in room 114, a dependency of the north-western group of buildings. Though of much less importance, consisting only of 167 pieces, yet it forms a substantial collection. No information is given about the condition of this find *in situ* in a tiny room. The pottery of room 114 is said to be later than that of room 89. As a matter of fact, all that can be made out are shades of difference in the "finish", edge thicker or not so thick, and so on, and these differences can be perfectly accounted for by different places of origin without it being necessary to bring in the question of date. Moreover, there could only have been a space of a few years, not time enough to bring in radical changes in technique and style.

There is a similarity between the arrangements of the north-western

[1] *Revue Biblique*, LXIII (1956), Plates VII, IX.
[2] *Ibid.*, p. 563.
[3] *Op. cit.*

buildings (long room 111 with deposit of broken utensils in the adjacent room 114) and those of the southern buildings (long room 77 with deposit of utensils in the adjoining room 89). This resemblance suggests that the two groups of constructions, at one time, had analogous uses, perhaps with certain differences not yet noted. A comparison might be attempted with certain places where funerary *agapes* were celebrated. In the ruins of the basilica of Morsott in Algeria, to the north of Tebessa, over 4 kilogrammes of broken glass cups were found in a part of the building adjoining the apse.[1] Similar finds have been made at Rouis,[2] etc. One will also think of the bases of glass cups found at Rome in the catacombs and elsewhere. The faithful who took part in funerary feasts there brought their own provisions and their cups and plates, which were often broken after the feast.

We are thus led to suppose that *agapes* were celebrated in two places in Qumrân: in the southern group of buildings, where the masonry *mensae* were found, and in the northern group, from which perhaps comes the table of the *triclinium*. In both cases we seem to be dealing with buildings which were successively put to a number of different uses. For some time they appear to have belonged to two distinct Jewish communities. They may afterwards have been taken over again by pagans, and then by two different sects of Christians. Comparison with other finds of pottery—in Palestine, in Transjordania, and in Syria—should make it possible to establish the origin of the two types of utensils, and in consequence the areas from which came the two groups of pilgrims who used to visit the sanctuaries of Qumrân.

(3) *The Deposits of Animal Bones.* Several deposits of bones from quarters of meat, boiled or roasted, have been found buried at Qumrân. From the information so far available, with the exception of one jar found in the courtyard 135 of the ancient Israelite fort, all the deposits of the remains from meals are situated either in the area around the north-western buildings or around the southern ones. The facts so far given do not amount to much. There are:

26 deposits, each containing the bones of 1 animal
9 deposits, each containing the bones of 2 animals
3 deposits, each containing the bones of 3 animals
1 deposit, containing the bones of 4 different animals

[1] *D.A.C.L.*, I, 830; XII, 12–13.
[2] *Ibid.*, XV, 139–140.

It is established that these bones belong to:

5 fully grown sheep
5 fully grown goats
21 sheep or goats, no precision being possible
15 lambs or kids, no precision being possible
6 calves
4 cows or oxen
1 large animal not specified (perhaps an unusually large ox)

It would have been a good thing to have made an inventory of these remains, jar by jar, indicating where they had been found. Given that these bones must have come from joints of meat brought from afar, and probably already cooked, one may assume that no bones belonging to the skull, neck, or tail have been found. If one really wants to find out what these discoveries can teach us, then it is necessary to know if certain food taboos have been observed by one or the other of the groups of people who buried these remains from their feasts. Have broken bones been found, or hip-bones, or bones from the feet? (We call to remembrance that Jews and Judeo-Christians did not eat of the hip—Gen. 32.32—and that among the Syrians the feet of cows or sheep were taboo.) What of the bones of the "large, unspecified animal"—where were they found? Were they by themselves, or along with other bones? Could they have belonged to a buffalo or a camel? What of the bones from roasted meat, and those from boiled meat—how were they distributed? Jar by jar? All these questions are important when dealing with religious customs.

The presence at Qumrân of masonry *mensae,* some with saucer-like hollows, and of a *triclinium* table, of two groups of broken earthenware, and of deposits of bones from quarters of animals in two clearly marked-off areas leads one to imagine that two distinct communities have celebrated *agapes* around a single holy centre. As the custom of funerary feasts near to a cemetery cannot be attributed to Jews, one wonders if these repasts had not been organised in the first case by pagans, and afterwards by Christians at a time when the Jewish cemetery had ceased to be used as such. That brings us to the end of the second century, a turning-point in Jewish history. But to be able to formulate a likely theory on the subject it is necessary first of all to establish that the site of Qumrân could have been considered a place of pilgrimage for pagans, and that it could have harboured later two Christian sanctuaries commemorating one and the same event.

(4) *The Circular Pavement and the Apse of the Long Chamber* 77. At first, Christian *martyria* were not of necessity built around the tomb of a martyr. In Palestine especially, one finds *martyria* "which protected a holy place— that is, a place or object which had been *witness* of a sacred event".[1] But that does not imply that Christians did not later place the remains of holy personages near to ancient *martyria*. In the East, burial *ad sanctos* was a common practice.

The western end of the long chamber 77 presents a rather peculiar arrangement, shown in the photograph, but not on the plan.[2] No details are given about the two masonry pillars which mark off a kind of recess at the western end. Nothing is said concerning the curious construction which seems to back on to the eastern wall and extend into the enclosure 81. In this same chamber 77, at a short distance from this eastern wall, there is "a paved circular space distinct from the surrounding plastered floor". The interpretation given is that it "marks the place where the president of the assembly stood".[3] It would be interesting to know if anything lies concealed under this circular pavement. It might be useful to make a "sondage" against both sides of this eastern wall, if only to obtain the negative certainty that nothing was there.

(5) *The Potter's Workshop.* It seems that before the time of the cemetery the site of Qumrân had been used temporarily by a potter. This deserted workshop was covered over later by the steps of cistern 49.[4] Another potter's workshop, perfectly preserved, has been found in the enclosures 64-65 and the neighbouring courtyards. It backs up to the wall of the cemetery, and its arrangements are decidedly strange.

An ancient tradition recounted in the Gospel according to St. Matthew (27.2-10) makes much of a potter's field bought for thirty pieces of silver and made into a burial-place for strangers. The version in the Gospel relates that the purchase was made with the money that Judas had received as the price of his treachery. It may be supposed that for a certain time pagans came on pilgrimage to this "strangers' cemetery", but that afterwards the potter's field must have become a Christian "witness", a *martyrium,* for there was fulfilled the prophecy of Zech. 11.13 (which in Matt. 27.9 was attributed to Jeremiah). The present writer had seen a possible connection with the Qumrân potteries, but of which workshop could the Apostle have been speaking? Was it the former one, the kilns

[1] André Grabar, *op. cit.,* I, p. 49.
[2] *Revue Biblique,* LXIII (1956), Plate VIII.
[3] *Ibid.,* p. 542.
[4] *Ibid.,* p. 538.

of which have been covered over by the steps of the cistern, or was it the second, which certainly seems to have been built *after* the erection of the wall which runs all the length of the cemetery?

If, as already suggested, a potter set himself up at Qumrân to exploit the layer of clay that in the course of the years had been deposited at the bottom of the disused cisterns, that could only have happened when the site was deserted. It is easy to understand that in such a case, when the sediment had all been worked out, the potter's field would not be worth more than "thirty pieces of silver". But it is difficult to admit the working of a pottery at Qumrân at a time when there was a cemetery there with its cluster of funerary buildings, and when the water of the cisterns was being used for ablutions. If the apostolic tradition really refers to the first workshop, then that was destroyed at the time when the buildings serving the cemetery were built. Is it not possible to suppose that at a time when pilgrims wished to *see* the "witness", a new potter's workshop was constructed on the same site, but never put into use? In fact, is it not surprising that the potter's wheel was set up so near to the kiln, which would hardly be workable and is found nowhere else? It is true that attention has been drawn to a layer of clean clay of unknown origin found at the bottom of the basin 75, a basin which is "not deep and has a carefully applied coating of plaster". This, however, is the only sign that the workshop was ever in use, and, on the other hand, the perfect state of its preservation arouses suspicions. Generally potteries can be recognised by a heap of débris, pots broken in baking, or thrown away as misshapen, but nothing of this sort has been noticed here.

An objective and careful study should make it possible to say when the second workshop was built, and for how long it could have served as a "witness" for some Christian sect. But before anything else, it should be possible to determine whether it was a real potter's workshop or only a sham one, a mere piece of stage scenery.

The tradition related by St. Matthew does not seem to have been favoured by all Christians. In the West, the other version given in the Acts of the Apostles (1.18-19) was apparently preferred. Not a single pilgrim whose recital has been preserved seems to have been interested in "the potter's field". On the other hand, they are many who visited Aceldama, the "field of blood", bought by Judas and where "all his bowels gushed out". In A.D. 333 the Bordeaux Pilgrim makes reference to the Rock of Judas Iscariot. The Pseudo-Antoninus of Piacenza saw it about A.D. 570. At that time there was an orchard and a vineyard there. When, about a century later, Arculf visited "the field of blood" to the south of Mount Zion, the tradition had already been growing: it was a charnel ground where the bodies of *strangers* were thrown without taking the trouble to bury them. We can therefore suppose that from the fourth century the apostolic tradition of the "potter's field" was progressively abandoned in favour of that of the "field of blood", nearer to Jerusalem and easier to visit. In the sixth century we are in the presence of a fusion of the two traditions. The orchard bought by Judas has become the place of burial for strangers—what the Apostle had related about the potter's field bought by the priests.

The problems which arise in connection with the potter's workshop found at Qumrân are very delicate. The solution of them will depend to a large extent on the relative dating of the constructions, wall by wall, care being taken not to overlook the renovations that were carried out.

(6) *The Smelting Furnace.* In the early centuries of Christianity there must have been a rather mixed tradition concerning the potter's field purchased with the thirty pieces of silver. For one thing, the version in the Gospel did not agree with that of the Acts. Moreover, the quotation attributed to Jeremiah reproduced imperfectly the Old Testament text. Even as regards the prophecy by Zechariah, the faithful cannot have been in agreement. If one turns to the Syriac version, one reads that the thirty pieces of silver were to be given over to the Treasury. In all likelihood, the Hebrew text is corrupt. In the present version, the thirty pieces spoken of by the prophet were to be cast "to the potter". Doubtless the text of Matt. 27.7 goes back to this reading, for it was clearly "the potter's field" (*tou kerameôs*) which was bought with the money received from Judas. But there is also the Greek version, and in the Septuagint the prophecy is quite different: the destination of the thirty pieces of silver was the "smelting furnace" (*chôneuterion*).

Now, among the north-west group of buildings at Qumrân there has been brought to light in the enclosure 101 "a large furnace constructed in small bricks, which have sustained an intense heat".[1] Most visitors speak of a metal furnace, a forge, or a foundry, and the arrangement of the place as described to us seems to fit in with such a purpose.

At first sight it would appear difficult to imagine that any metal-working installation could ever have existed at Qumrân. It is also quite difficult to see how an intense fire sufficient to melt metals could have been maintained in the enclosure 101, so close to other buildings. Father de Vaux

[1] *Revue Biblique,* LXIII (1956), pp. 546–47, Plate VII.

announces "that no significant object has been recovered . . . samples have been taken, and when analysed may give the purpose of this installation".

After the considerations to which the potter's workshop led us, and in the absence of any trace of the furnace having been used, should we not ask ourselves if we have not here another fictitious reconstruction? The tradition which made of the "potter's field" a *martyrium* where the prophecy of Zechariah was fulfilled could not have altogether satisfied the faithful who knew the Greek version and were ignorant of Hebrew. Whilst admitting the facts, they could be in doubt as to the correctness of the quotation in Matthew. Can we not suppose that a smelting furnace was added to the ruins so as to give satisfaction to Greek-speaking Christians, for whom the "potter's workshop" alone was not a sufficient "witness"? Can we not allow that there were thus two distinct sanctuaries within one and the same place of pilgrimage, as the two deposits of broken earthenware and the two groups of remains from *agapes* seem to indicate?

A meticulous study of any remains in the enclosure 101 should make it possible to see if the smelting furnace really was only a symbolic reconstruction. Search into the writings of the Fathers of the Church perhaps will make it possible to identify among the Christian sects those in Palestine who would be more attached to the Greek version of Zechariah than to the text of the Gospel according to St. Matthew.

(7) *The Buried Treasure.* The smelting furnace was probably not the only "witness" to which came the pilgrims who celebrated their *agapes* in the north-west group of buildings. It is well to recall that, buried in enclosure 120, three jars were found containing respectively 223, 185, and "over 150" coins, almost all tetradrachma from Tyre and dating from before 9 B.C. It is reported that two of the jars are of a type otherwise unknown at Qumrân, and these were found to the right of the doorway leading into the enclosure 111. They were closed by means of a stopper made of palm fibre. The third jar was found on the opposite side of the same enclosure, against its northern wall. This jar is of a type quite common at Qumrân. The neck was too narrow to allow the coins to go through, so a hole was pierced in the body of the jar, making it into a kind of money-box.[1]

The theories put forward hitherto concerning the origin of the treasure and the date when it was deposited do not seem satisfactory. Is it not possible to suppose that it formed part of the "witnesses" around which the *martyrium* of Qumrân was set up? We may recall that the thirty pieces of

[1] *Revue Biblique,* LXIII, p. 567.

silver had a certain vogue, and that a number of legends were recounted about them. In the sixteenth century one of these pieces was preserved in the Treasury of St. Sabina at Rome. (As a matter of fact, it was a Carian coin from Rhodes of the third century B.C.) Another was in St. Peter's at Rome. In the Capuchin convent at Enghien an octogramme of Syracuse was called "denarius of Judas".[1]

By analogy, it may be supposed that legends grew up around the "large money" (Matt. 28.12-15) which the chief priests gave to the Roman guards to induce them to say that the disciples had stolen away the body of Jesus. In accordance with a well-known pattern, these soldiers, like the legionaire Longinus, became converts, and probably took steps to rid themselves of the money which they had accepted, burying it in a fore-ordained spot which eventually became a Christian *martyrium*. St. Cyril of Jerusalem (c. A.D. 315-86) reports a tradition on this subject: "A witness was given by the soldiers, and by the money with which they were bribed." That allows one to suppose that in the fourth century this money was "witness" of the Resurrection, in the same way as the Church of the Resurrection, "the place that you can still see".[2]

It is unlikely that any useful information can be deduced from the coins found in these vessels. Like the thirty pieces of Judas, long before the "invention" of these relics, they had probably ceased to be legal tender. On the other hand, it should be possible to draw useful conclusions from the jars and the places where they were discovered.

In the Western tradition, of which the Munich Ivory has preserved for us an echo from the fourth century, the sepulchre guards were two. On the other hand, the apocryphal *Gospel of Peter,* written in Syria in the middle of the second century, carries the number to three, two soldiers and a centurion named Petronius. This tradition seems to have influenced the miniaturist of the *Gospels of Rabbula* in the sixth century.[3] One can thus see two stages in the "invention" of the treasure of the Roman soldiers. At first two jars with their ancient coins were considered as "witnesses" of the Resurrection by those following the Western tradition. Then a third jar was discovered in the same enclosure, but at a different spot, not far from the others, to satisfy the Syrian tradition.

The conditions in which were found the jars containing the tetradrachma of Tyre seem to give support to this hypothesis. Obviously it will be

[1] *D.A.C.L.*, VIII, 278-9.
[2] A. Grabar, *op. cit.*, II, p. 157.
[3] *D.A.C.L.*, III, 2929, Fig. 988.

D

difficult to give precise dates to these jars, but that is only of relative importance. It should be possible to discover the origin of the two stoppered receptacles, which are said to be of a type foreign to Qumrân. Could it not be that they were a kind of jar which at the time would pass as "ancient"? An analysis of the radioactivity of carbon 14 contained in the palm-fibre stoppers might give an approximate date for the deposits within a century or two. Research into the legends which came to birth around the treasure of the Roman guards at the Sepulchre, especially in Syria, Mesopotamia, and Armenia, might give us valuable information.

★          ★          ★

The foregoing are the seven questions which the writer believes he should ask before being able to formulate with precision his theory on the cemetery and ruins at Qumrân during one of the last periods of its history. It is not necessary to underline the fact that this history is quite apart from that of the Dead Sea manuscripts, even if the site knew a Jewish occupation until the second century A.D. In the writer's opinion, this history extends from the end of the second century as far as the middle of the fourth century. It is, however, possible that the site has a longer history than has been thought. It will certainly be useful to reconsider what may be known from those remains labelled "Byzantine" or "late" which were cleared away in the course of the excavation, and to undertake afresh the interpreting of those "lower mill-stones" and of a number of pieces of worked stone.

Up till now there has been no announcement of any Christian inscription or symbol being found at Qumrân, but should not account be taken of Mohammedan iconoclasm and what it could have done during the many centuries that the site was abandoned? Let it be kept in mind that the tables with saucer-like hollows, perhaps of pagan origin, were found broken, and that several pieces are missing. A more thorough examination of all the recovered fragments might make it possible to arrive at some interesting conclusions.

iv

## THE DAMASCUS DOCUMENT

The second main argument invoked to prove the existence of the Essenes and their buried library is represented by what has been called the *Damascus Document*. In 1910 S. Schechter edited a few pages of manuscript found in one of the buildings of the ancient Qaraite synagogue in

Cairo,[1] but it is only quite recently that these fragments have been published in facsimile by S. Zeitlin.[2] Schechter thought that the texts had been composed between 196 and 176 B.C., and that the fragments discovered in Cairo had come originally from a "Zadokite book". According to R. H. Charles,[3] the Zadokites were neither Samaritans nor Essenes, but were a sect related to the Sadducees of the second century B.C. He too had no doubts about the high antiquity of the text. To S. Zeitlin belongs the credit of having taken up his predecessors' arguments, and of having proved in an irrefutable manner that we have here medieval Qaraite texts.[4]

The *Damascus Document* was presented by Schechter as a single text preserved in two versions. The version "A" represented by sixteen pages of writing, eight sheets written on both sides. The version "B" is written on both sides of a much larger single sheet. As a matter of fact, what has been called the version "A" comes from a number of texts, as the photographic reproduction clearly shows. Pages I-VIII, each of twenty-one lines, reproduce part of a text the end of which, pages VII-VIII, is found with several variants at the beginning of the fragment "B". Pages IX-XII are of twenty-three lines each, are in a different handwriting, and come from another text. The lower lines of page XIII-XVI are missing, and it is possible that these pages formed part of the same second manuscript, but there is nothing which permits a positive statement to that effect, neither the number of lines, which is unknown, nor the writing, nor the ink. It may be that these last pages come from another copy of the writing which is called "A2", to distinguished it from pages I-VII ("A1").

There is general agreement that all these pages may be dated between the tenth and the twelfth centuries A.D. That is possible, but not certain, for Hebrew palæography is a somewhat uncertain science. It can distinguish between pages which are properly written and those which are badly written, it can tell the difference between one handwriting and another, but it is ill at ease if called upon to give a precise date for a single piece of writing. Thus it is practically impossible to say at first sight if the two pages of sheet "B" are more ancient or less ancient than the manuscript

---

[1] *Documents of Jewish Sectaries*, Vol. I, Cambridge, 1910.

[2] *The Zadokite Fragments*, Philadelphia, 1952.

[3] *Apocrypha and Pseudepigrapha of the Old Testament*, Vol. II, Oxford, 1913, pp. 785-834.

[4] *Op. cit.*, referring to the different opinion put forward upon these texts. See also S. Zeitlin, *Jewish Quarterly Review*, N.S. XVI (1925-6), pp. 385 f. Dr. P. R. Weis, *ibid.*, XLI (1950-51), pp. 137-42. J. L. Teicher, *Journal of Jewish Studies*, II/3 (1951), pp. 115-43, considers these texts to be of Jewish-Christian origin.

"A". On the other hand, it can state definitely that these pages are from the hand of a scribe familiar with Syriac writing and the Babylonian vowel system, and that his handwriting is more "cursive" than that of the scribes who wrote the sheets "A". However that may be, it was not by palæographic criteria that the high antiquity of the *Damascus Document* was established. Nobody has any doubts about the pages of manuscript being medieval. They are written on paper, a detail not often mentioned by authors who connect these texts with the Dead Sea Scrolls and the Essenes.

To suppose that a text said to date from the second century B.C. was recopied in the Middle Ages amounts to admitting that a group existed at that time to whom it was of particular interest. In a word, that is to say that the Essenes survived to the time of the Crusades! There has been talk therefore of Essenism being a "pre-Qaraitism", and it has been considered a perfectly natural phenomenon that the rule of this Palestinian Jewish sect of the pre-Christian era should be faithfully copied out at Cairo in the Middle Ages.[1] As to the high antiquity of the text itself, there has been a wish to prove it by its contents, style and phraseology. The contents of these manuscripts are analysed below. The style, the vocabulary, and the ready-made phrases which recur in them leave room for no other view than that these writings are medieval.[2]

The pages of the *Damascus Document* were found in a part of the ancient Qaraite synagogue in Cairo. It is natural, therefore, to suppose that the text was written by Qaraites and for Qaraites. The existence of an old

[1] After his study published in *Vetus Testamentum*, II (1952), pp. 343-8, S. Szyszman returned to the question of pre-Qaraitism in his review of L. Nemoy's *Karaite Anthology, Vetus Testamentum*, V, (1955) pp. 328-55.

If we are going to talk about a pre-Qaraitism, we can just as well talk about a pre-Islam, a pre-Protestantism, a pre-Mormonism, etc. When the founder of a religion finds his followers, it is obvious that these share his views. So, as Qaraitism in its beginning made proselytes not only among Jews, but also among the heathen, it cannot be said that the Qaraites persevered in the views of the founder of the movement. The Qaraitism of the tenth century already bore little resemblance to Qaraitism in its beginnings. Founders of religion always draw support from existing beliefs, and even Joseph Smith felt he needed the support of the Bible which he interpolated. As the movement raised up by Anan was directed against rabbinic authority, it is only natural to find in the origin of Qaraitism some principles already found among the Sadducees at the beginning of the Christian era. An analogous phenomenon is seen in anti-Papist movements, all of which without exception demand a stricter observance of the Bible and the Gospels. But to claim that Qaraitism goes back to the Essenes and perpetuates their teaching is hardly more consistent than the Mormons' belief in the Lamanites and the Nephites.

[2] Medieval Hebrew was not a living language; all Hebrew writings of that time were packed with ready-made phrases. Quotations from the Bible were not treated as such, but formed part of the current speech.

Qaraite community in Cairo is perfectly attested,[1] and, as will be seen from the text itself, everything seems to confirm the medieval date and the Qaraite nature of these writings.

*The Qaraite Movement.* Medieval Judaism knew a number of movements opposed to the rabbinism, which, according to a current Biblical phrase (Ezek. 13.10), tended to "build walls of partition" around the Jews. These schisms were particularly noticeable among the Jews of Islamic countries. The movements begun about A.D. 720 by Serene in Syria and by Abu Issa in Persia were followed in 762 by the schism provoked by Anan, the founder of the Qaraite movement. Well versed in Biblical and and Talmudic knowledge, and also well acquainted with Islam and Christianity, Anan had hoped that on the death of his Uncle Solomon he would be appointed the Jewish Ethnarch. Upset by the fact that his brother was appointed in preference to himself, he separated from rabbinism. He denied the authority of the Talmud, and demanded that his followers restrict their study to the Scriptures, including the Books of the Prophets, whose authority, we remember, was not accepted by the Sadducees. His disciples called themselves "the masters of Scripture" (*Ba'ale Miqra*) or "Qaraites".

The essential points of difference between the Qaraites and the rabbinic Jews were:

(1) The strictness with which they observed the Sabbath. They would not allow any fire or light to be lighted on this day, even by a non-Jew working for them. They did not leave their homes unless that was unavoidable. They would not circumcise on the Sabbath, nor administer any remedy to the sick, and they forbade the taking of help to either men or animals in danger.

(2) They did not recognise the calendar established by the rabbis, and they fixed the beginning of the months by the actual appearing of the new moon.

(3) They had their own interpretations for Biblical rules concerning worship and feasts.

(4) They forbade the marriages between uncle and niece authorised in the Bible and in the Talmud, and they extended the list of prohibited degrees.

(5) They very strictly observed the laws regarding food. For instance,

[1] Apart from S. Zeitlin's publication already mentioned, see especially Jacob Mann, *The Jews in Egypt and in Palestine under the Fatimide's Caliphs*, Oxford, 1920-2, and the studies by S. Szyszman in *Vetus Testamentum*, III/4 (1953), pp. 411-13; IV/2 (1954), pp. 201-5; VI/3 (1956), pp. 309-15.

they did not eat chickens, as these birds were not named among the clean animals mentioned in the Bible. By what was probably a very correct translation of the word *ḥlb*, which means entrails as well as milk, they forbade the slaughter of pregnant cattle (Exod. 23.19.,34.26).

*The Qaraites in Egypt.* It is not easy to establish the date of the first Qaraite communities in Egypt.[1] Their presence at Fustât, Cairo, in the ninth century seems to be certain. It was the residence of their highest religious authority, the *Nasi*. As in Constantinople and Jerusalem, the Jews in Cairo dwelt in a separate quarter of the town, but we do not know if within this enclosure the Qaraites lived apart from the other Jews.[2] It is certain that there were many incidents between the rabbinic and the Qaraite Jews in Cairo, to which a temporary stop was made by the edict of toleration of 1024.[3] That did not prevent strife over prestige and friction between communities from continuing until recent times.

The echo of these dissensions is brought to us by these fragments from Cairo. The so-called *Damascus Document* ought not to be looked upon as something by itself, but should be integrated within the whole collection of documents which the Cairo *geniza* yielded up. It is only in this way that one can get the meaning of its pages and understand its terminology.

*The Damascus Document.* As in every religious sect, the Qaraites must have wanted to carry back their origin to the most remote periods of history. It was by arguments drawn from the Book of Judges that the Palestine rabbinate and that of Egypt discussed their respective rights as to the administration of the Jewish community in Ascalon.[4] Should it be surprising after that if the Cairo fragments "A1" and "B" present a rather fanciful history of the Qaraite movement? They are strewn with comments on Biblical texts intended as violent attacks against the rabbinists, on the one side and as a defence of the Qaraite rules on the other. A translation of these texts, accompanied by a commentary, is given in Part Three of this present work.

[1] J. Mann, *op. cit.,* I, p. 177. The colophon of a Pentateuch presented to the Qaraite synagogue at Fustât seems really to bear the date 1047 where there had been the wish to read 847 (*ibid.,* I, 80).

[2] In the twelfth century the Jews in Constantinople were not allowed to reside in the city itself. They had their quarter on the left bank of the Golden Horn, and within this Ghetto a wall of partition separated the dwellings of the Qaraites from those of the other Jews (Joshua Starr, *The Jew in the Byzantine Empire,* Athens, 1939, pp. 41, 231). At Jerusalem the Qaraites inhabited a quarter called that of the "Easterns", and there they adopted the mode of life of the "mourners for Zion". (J. Mann, *op. cit.,* I, p. 61).

[3] J. Mann, *op. cit.,* I, pp. 134-5.

[4] J. Mann, *op. cit.,* I, p. 191, II, pp. 225ff.

From the beginning, one is struck by the reference to a "Teacher of Righteousness", who, from the context, can only be Nehemiah. Naturally, this title has been connected with that of a personage referred to in the *Habakkuk Commentary* found in Cave I of Qumrân, without taking sufficient account of the fact that we have here a title which is not uncommon, and which the author of this fragment wished to apply to a personage of antiquity.[1]

Is it necessary to recall that in Hebrew there is a distinction between "master" in the sense of one who is in possession of a country, of riches, or of knowledge, where the word used is *ba'al*, and "master" in the sense of teacher, where the word used is *môreh* (*mwrh*). The Qaraites called themselves "masters of the Scripture" (*ba'ale miqra'*)—that is to say that they alone possessed the true interpretation of the Scriptures. On the other hand, a "master of Righteousness" (*môreh ṣedek*) is one who teaches that it is necessary to be righteous. In publications on the manuscripts from the Dead Sea, there is a tendency to confuse the two meanings of the word "master", and the "Master of Righteousness" of the Essenes is spoken of as if invested with almost supernatural knowledge and power. It is necessary, therefore, to point out that in the Qaraite writings, as in the manuscripts from Qumrân, the title is "Teacher of Righteousness", which approximates to the title of "Professor of Law" and by no means implies the far-reaching sense which some people would like to give to it.

When, later on, there is reference to Cohens and Levis, it must not be overlooked that in the nature of the case we are there dealing with patronymics to which in the Middle Ages the Jews attached more importance than they do today. Even in the eleventh century anyone who said his name was Cohen could administer justice in a strange town, and, collecting worship dues,[2] live on the fat of the land. Glaring abuse led eventually to the verification of the identity of those who said they were Cohens or Levis. Nor should they be identified with the priests (*Kohen*) and the Levites of the Temple at Jerusalem, and even less with the priests sometimes referred to in the Dead Sea manuscripts.

The continuation of the text, with its stereotyped phrases, brings us

---

[1] The Jews of Egypt made use of a long list of titles (see J. Mann, *op. cit.*, I, pp. 257-68). That of "Teacher of Righteousness" is found in the twelfth century (*ibid.*, I, pp. 244,267, II, pp. 315, 322). We find the title given to Maimonides, whose high authority was recognised throughout the Jewish world. Is it possible to draw the conclusion that the "Teacher of Righteousness" of the Habakkuk Commentary would be Rabbi Joseph ben Maimon, or that the theologian of Cordova lived in the Maccabaean time?

[2] See J. Mann, *op. cit.*, I, p. 172, II, p. 206.

the defence of Qaraite customs and the condemnation of the rabbinic laws. Every sect wishing to defend its point of view has to make use of similar exhortations. If the fragment of the so-called *Damascus Document* does not include the classical formulas of blessing and cursing which could be expected in a work of this kind, it must not be imagined that the *geniza* did not yield a text of this order. It can be found reproduced in the work by J. Mann (*op. cit.,* II, pp. 155-7). It would have been easy to add this page to the *Damascus Document,* and to push still further the analogy with the *Manual of Discipline* from Cave I. Probably no one has thought of it.

The reference to "camps" in the Cairo fragments has naturally given rise to comparisons with the military camps sometimes mentioned in Dead Sea manuscripts. Is it necessary to remind readers that all Jewish quarters in Egyptian towns were named *maḥanoth,* "camps", and the word should be simply translated "ghetto"? There is evidence of the title *negîd ha-maḥanoth,* commander-in-chief of the Ghettoes among the Qaraites of Egypt (J. Mann, *op. cit.,* I, p. 138).

Towards the end of the fragment "A1" the rabbinists are threatened with the wrath of God. This will show itself by ill-treatment at the very hands of those whose favours they had sought. The "kings of the peoples" (the Fatimides), whose wine they had accepted, and the "kings of Yawan" were about to inflict vengeance upon them. As a rule, commentators of our texts have passed rapidly over these embarrassing expressions. They have translated "the kings of Yawan" by "the Hellenistic world", overlooking a simple detail—one which is perhaps insignificant in their eyes—that "the Hellenistic world" is an artificial creation of the modern mind. For Jews living in the third century B.C. there was a Seleucid kingdom and there was an Egypt, but they certainly had no reason for combining them under the collective name of Ionia. In the whole of the Jewish apocryphal literature, Ionia (Yawan) only occurs in a single Sibylline Oracle (V, 288) and there it is unmistakably situated in Asia Minor. In our text, as in all medieval Jewish literature, Yawan denotes the Byzantine Empire. In all likelihood, the phrase in question made allusion to the victories gained in northern Syria by Nicephorus Phocas (968-9), to the exactions against the Jews to which they led, and to the still more terrible ones they had to fear if the Christian advance continued.

The right side of the fragment "B" reproduces fairly faithfully the text of the fragment "A1", starting from line VII, 1. The differences, however, are sufficiently noteworthy to discountenance all the attempts that have been made to join the two texts into a single one. The reverse gives us the continuation of this typically Qaraite writing.

In spite of the numerous expressions borrowed from Biblical Hebrew and from post-Biblical literature, the writing "A1"—"B" is unquestionably medieval. It is possible, and even probable, that the first author of this Qaraite history, transformed into a pamphlet against rabbinic Jews, was acquainted with the rules of certain Zadokite or other societies belonging to the early centuries of our era, or even later. Rabbinic "schools" kept up their activities in Mesopotamia and Persia till the twelfth century, and preserved many ancient traditions. It would be strange if they had not had their regulations, as did those in Palestine in the early centuries. In any case, nothing warrants the view that this writing is the copy of an ancient Zadokite document, as has been claimed. On the contrary, many passages allow a dating for this work which in any case could not be earlier than the Arab conquest. The text "A1" reflects the flourishing state of the community, whilst the text "B" presents the community as relatively poor. A certain time must therefore have elapsed between these two redactions. On the basis of facts in the texts themselves, for the palæographic criterion cannot be called in here, the present writer would put the date of the version "A1" before that of the version "B".

The original title of this work, often recopied and adjusted to the taste of the day, must have been the *Book of the Divisions of the Ages*. Almost all the Jewish communities of the Orient have their archives and preserve some oral traditions about their origins. Sephardic synagogues often carry even now the name of some town in Spain. There is therefore nothing surprising in the Qaraite community in Cairo preserving a tradition according to which it had its origin in Damascus, the town where Qaraitism came into being. Moreover, the Cairo Qaraites maintained commercial and cultural relations with their fellow members in Syria. It may also be noticed too how much the handwriting of the fragment "B" has been influenced by Syriac writing. All the same, the real reason for this book of history taking the form which it has in the fragments "A1" and "B" must be sought for in the hostility between the Qaraite and rabbinic communities. The book of history became a pamphlet against the rabbinists. Other Qaraite communities probably had their *Book of the Division of the Ages*. We have every reason to suppose that Byzantine versions of this work must have differed in more than one point from those found in the *geniza* at Cairo.

\*          \*          \*

The fragments "A2" and "A3" (pp. IX-XVI) form part of a different work altogether. The text even gives us its title: the *Sepher HHGW*, the *Book of Deductions*.[1] It may be that this work was afterwards replaced by another collection of laws to which was given the name of *Sepher Hamiṣwôth*, the *Book of the Commandments*.[2] From the very first sentence onwards, we find in these fragments a regulation of the Qaraites which appears in the form of an anathema in another document of the same sect:[3] legal proceedings between Jews were not to be taken before the tribunals of unbelievers! Another document brings us the confirmation that the Qaraites of Egypt punished with excommunication anyone who had brought a false accusation against a fellow member of his religion.[4] Further on there is the subject of the judicial organisation of the Qaraite community and of its "overseers" (*pqyd*). Judges had to be versed in the sect's *Book of Deductions*. The age limits imposed on them is in sharp contrast with the Zadokite rule by the elder members, and proves clearly that the document is dealing only with Qaraite tribunals, to the exclusion of all others. The title of *pqyd* (pronounced *paqîd*) given to the overseers or inspectors is equally a Qaraite one. Among other things, these inspectors had to see that whatever was sold in Qaraite shops conformed to the ritual requirements,[5] for the Qaraites had no trust in other Jewish butchers, and had their own.

Our text goes on to reproduce a list of regulations which were Qaraite, and uniquely Qaraite. It is surprising that some people have been able to

[1] There is nothing mysterious about this name. Its origin is clearly given in the Talmud: *nh hgh twrh mtwk twrh*—Noah "deduced" the Law in setting out from the Law. The laws "deduced" from the Bible were the cause of differences between the various schools of Judaism. There was not one single *Book of Deductions* going back to Noah, as some sects claimed. Each sect had its own. Thus the Zadokites had a *Book of Decisions* which was known in the tenth century (Poznanzki in the *Revue des Etudes Juives*, XLIV (1902), p. 176). Qirqisâni spoke of a *Book of Knowledge* (Yaddua'), which came from a cave near Jericho. *The Manual of Discipline* contains passages which could have come from a *Book of Deductions*. Perhaps the Qaraites got suggestions for the juridical style of their work from some ancient manuscript, and they may even have borrowed from it the title of *Sepher HHGW*. But there the similarity ends.

[2] J. Mann, *op. cit.*, I, p. 255, note 1, raises a doubt about the authenticity of the colophon reproduced by Firkowicz, according to which, in 1064-5, a Qaraite, author of this work, gives himself the title of *Nagid*. Throughout the eleventh century this high position was in the hands of rabbinists who had the right of jurisdiction over the Qaraites and the Samaritans. The title may have been false, but all the same a pretentious author may have attributed it to himself. Perhaps the *Book of Commandments* in the eleventh century was aimed at taking the place of the *Book of Deductions*.

[3] *Ibid.*, II, p. 156, line 8.

[4] *Ibid.*, I, p. 141, II, p. 158.

[5] J. Mann, I, p. 261, II, p. 137. The right accorded to Jews to have their own markets and organise their own police was confirmed by ‹*Theodosian Code* of A.D. 425 (XVI, v, 5).

connect these with the Dead Sea manuscripts and the pretended rule of a monastic sect. The gravity of the defilement contracted by contact with a dead body is considerably extended among the Qaraites (XII, 17-18). It goes as far as the nails in the wall of a house in which someone has died. That is in evident contradiction with the vicinity of a cemetery so curiously sought after by the monks of Qumrân.

The authority conferred by the Qaraites on persons with the names of Cohen or Levi has already been pointed out. It went much further than among other Jews, and it is not surprising that our text envisages the case of a "simple-minded" Cohen who has to be told what to do.

And so, right to the end, only typically medieval Qaraite arrangements can be found in this manuscript. Though the author made use of certain formulas better known to us since the discovery of the Dead Sea manuscripts, yet that does not justify at all the putting back the date of these fragments to a remote age. In all languages there exists a legal style. It always goes back to ancient prototypes, the tradition of which is handed on from generation to generation. But does that permit the making of such connections as have been made between the *Damascus Document* and the *Manual of Discipline*?[1]

If the fragments "A1" and "B" formed part of the *Book of the Division of the Ages*, the fragments "A2" and "A3" can have come from the famous *Sepher HHGW*, the *Book of Deductions*. They formed the code of the Qaraites of Cairo, the statutes of their communities. Naturally, they would resemble the statutes of other religious communities in form, whilst differing fundamentally from them in substance. All analogies that may be drawn allow of only one conclusion: that we are dealing with the regulations of a "religious community".[2]

*　　　*　　　*

There has been a desire to draw chronological data from the *Damascus Document* which would make it possible to determine the origin of the Qumrân sect. Much discussion has taken place over the statement that, 390 years after having delivered them into the hands of Nebuchadnezzar, God would cause a remnant of Israel and of Aaron to return. Whatever

---

[1] So far no one seems to have pointed out the resemblance in style and the other unquestionable parallels between the *Damascus Document* and the *Epistle of Barnabas*, especially Chapters XIV-XVI.

[2] Whilst admitting that the data should be taken *cum grano salis*, E. Wiesenberg, in *Vetus Testamentum*, V (1955), pp. 284-308, shares the opinion that the Cairo fragments and the Dead Sea Scrolls come from the self-same sect.

may have been the wish on the part of the author in Cairo to carry back Qaraitism to a remote age, he certainly had no intention of fixing so precise a date. The 390 years belong to Biblical phraseology. According to Ezekiel (4.5-6), the iniquity of Israel ought to last 390 years, or not quite 400, whilst that of Judah would last forty years. It is a case of the use of conventional figures, a practice already referred to. But the author of the Cairo fragment could not allow prophecies to be untrue, and so, according to him, a remnant of Israel did return from exile 390 years after having been delivered into the hands of Nebuchadnezzar, King of Babel.[1] Not only can no chronological data be drawn from this phrase, but the phrase itself only claims to be giving the story of Israel's straying, not the history of the sect.

Further on there is reference to the "Teacher of Righteousness" raised up by God twenty years after the return from exile. These twenty years are also part of Biblical phraseology, they mark (symbolically) the beginning of Nehemiah's mission (Neh. 1.1). There again the reference is to Israel and not to the "sect". Israel did not listen, and so fresh disasters occurred.

In what follows, it is always the history of Israel which is retraced. It is practically certain that the author had not understood that, in the text from which he drew his ideas, it was Agrippa II who was meant by the Man of Lying, who had "moved the frontiers".[2] In his mind there was one single story of the transgressions of Israel, a story which began with the creation of the world and went on to the birth of Qaraitism. This story, having once been told, is later taken up in detail for some periods of the Bible, and it is only then (IV, 2ff.) by the interpretation given to Ezekiel (44.15) that the Qaraites, those "who call upon the Name" are mentioned for the first time. He sees in them the true descendants of the priests, of the Levites, and of the Sons of Zadok referred to by the prophet. Apparently, in his mind, there were always the righteous whom God preserved from destruction. Their names had been lost and there only remained their teachings to which the Ananites wanted to be faithful, entering into a fresh engagement with God, "the New Covenant". The

---

[1] The Kingdom of Israel was destroyed in 722 by Shalmaneser, King of Assyria. The date of the Edict of Cyrus is 538, and the first of the returning exiles arrived in Palestine the following year. Thus for Israel the exile had lasted 185 years. It may be worthy of notice that in the LXX version of Ezekiel the period of Israel's iniquity is given as 190 "days".

[2] It was Agrippa II who, in exchange for Chalcis, obtained the tetrarchies of Philip and Lysanius, together with a small province belonging to Varro. Later Nero added to his kingdom further regions of Galilee and Perea, including Tiberias and Bethsaida.

foundation of the New Covenant had been laid before the creation of the world (II, 7), and doubtless the first Qaraites were the angels who did not let themselves be seduced by the beauty of the daughters of men (II, 18f.). This detail deserves as much credence as does the reference to the 390 years already referred to.[1]

The tendencious interpretations which have been given to the *Damascus Document* will never allow of the least connection between the very real Qaraite community of Cairo and the hypothetical monastic sect of Essenes at Qumrân. In the same way, any connecting of the *Damascus Document* with the manuscripts of the Dead Sea should be avoided. The only things which these writings have in common is the Hebrew language with its vocabulary and ready-made phrases. Just as "Messiah" had become a current term, so the expression "Teacher of Righteousness", which was derived from Hos.10.12, was a title which had been given to a number of persons. The same thing can be said about the "Orator of Untruth" and a good many other stereotyped phrases.

Of course, there is no need to give the least credence to the opinion of an eighteenth-century traveller quoted by S. Szyszman, according to which the Qaraites "are the ancient Essenes". The Qaraites have never claimed that, and even had they done so, in the same way as the Hassidim of Galicia claimed to belong to the ancient Assideans, they would not have merited belief thereby because of this claim. The opinion of a Maimonides that the Qaraites were descended from the Sadducees would have been more worthy of credence was it not that the Qaraites attached great authority to the books of the Prophets, and even to certain books of the Apocrypha. We may recall that in the buildings of the Qaraite synagogue at Cairo there were found fragments of four copies in Hebrew of the Book of *Ecclesiasticus*, all of them medieval. Fragments in Aramaic of a *Testament of Levi* also came from this Cairo *geniza*, and we know from the *Damascus Document* itself (IV, 15) that the Qaraites made reference to this apocryphal work.

It is very probable that the Qaraites had known the apocryphal writings discovered in a cave near Jericho in the ninth century. It is likely that they drew ideas from an ancient Zadokite or other kind of "Rule", or even from a collection similar to the *Manual of Discipline*, when they were

[1] The Mormons do not claim to go back to the angels. They are content to descend spiritually from the Jaredites, who emigrated to America at the time of the building of the Tower of Babel. Their history was written by Ether, the last of their prophets. Their true ancestors are the descendants of Laman and of Nephi, sons of the Prophet Lehi, who left Jerusalem about 600 B.C. and settled in the state of New York.

drawing up writings for their own sect. It may even be admitted that at a time when Hebrew was no longer a living language for the Qaraites, as several passages in their *Ecclesiasticus* show, they were fond of expressions taken from apocryphal works of the early centuries of our era, and had neglected somewhat purely Biblical ones. But it is at least risky to state that there have been found in the Qumrân caves fragments of the Cairo Qaraite document, which would prove the antiquity of that text and its Essene or Qumrânian origin.

In the *Revue Biblique*,[1] Father J. T. Milik has announced that Cave 4 has supplied seven manuscripts of the *Damascus Document*, "two of them comprising a number of fairly large fragments". But "nearly all the manuscripts contain regulations which are not found in the Cairo manuscript". And everything else beside that we have been told suggests that these fragments can only have had a very distant connection with the Qaraite writing.

The fragments from Cave 4Q have not yet been published, but Father M. Baillet has announced that he has also found fragments from the *Damascus Document* among those which came from Cave 6. These have recently been published[2] and are already referred to as certainties.

Fragment 1 has in line the letters *pšym* with, underneath, the letters *h zkr*. That is all that can be "read" on it. Fragment 2 is hardly more eloquent. One line has the three letters *'šw*, and the line below allows the reading *h . . b 'ly*. The first fragment has been inserted in IV, 19-21, of the Cairo document, and the second in V, 13-14. Without taking account of the fact that such ordinary passages could be found in any writing whatsoever, it is clear how arbitrary is the attributing of them to the Qaraite document.

The third fragment is the only one which gives complete words, and it has been attributed to the passage V, 18-VI, 2. The words which can be read are by no means significant: "Aaron" in line 1; "when Israel was saved" in line 2; "they made Israel to wander" in line 3; "by the holy anointed ones" in line 4, "And God remembered the covenant with the forefathers" in line 5. Surely one does not have to talk about the *Damascus Document* at the sight of such everyday phrases. And further, to incorporate this fragment into the passage in question, it is necessary to suppose that line 1 contained forty letters, line 2, fifty-one, line 3, forty-three and so on.

The same remark applies to the fragment 4, which, it is held, belongs

---

[1] *Revue Biblique*, LXIII (1956), p. 61.
[2] *Ibid.*, p. 55, pp. 513-23, and Plate II.

to the passage VI, 20–VII, 1. Here the first line would have thirty-six letters, the next, twenty-two, and the third thirty. The words which have been preserved do not yield a satisfactory meaning. As to the fragment 5, the insertion of it into the *Damascus Document* has not been renounced even though the only words which can be read fit into no known passage of the Cairo manuscript.

We have still to be informed about the fragments which came from Cave 4. Even if the passages discovered bear a great likeness to the Cairo document, all that can be said is that texts similar to those found in Caves 4 and 6 may have given ideas to the Qaraites for the drawing up of their rule or of their history. They may have served as models. That is absolutely all that one can conclude from these points of agreement, which at the moment are limited to ready-made expressions which one would be bound to come across in all works of the same nature. In any case it seems most improbable that there will ever be found among the fragments from Qumrân certain rules of purity which are definitely Qaraite, such as those regarding the cooking of fish and of grasshoppers.

The Cairo documents have their importance for the history of medieval Judaism, but the study of them should be free from all improper association with the manuscripts, caves, ruins, and cemetery of Qumrân.

v

# THE EBIONITES

It would be well to give here a variant of the theory of a buried library. It is that which attributes to the Ebionites the whole of the writings and other objects found in Cave I at Qumrân. Dr. J. L. Teicher,[1] propounder and chief defender of this thesis, quite rightly recognised that a number of manuscripts which came from this cave could not have been pre-Christian. From the reference to the "poor" (*'ebyônîm*) in the *Habakkuk Commentary*, and as a result of some other comparisons, he came to the conclusion that we must be dealing with Ebionite writings buried about A.D. 303 at the time of the Diocletian persecution. His views have been discussed and refuted.[2]

The information which we have concerning the Ebionites is little, and frequently contradictory. The name seems to have been used for

---

[1] See especially "The Dead Sea Scrolls, Documents of the Jewish-Christian Sect of the Ebionites", in the *Journal of Jewish Studies*, II (1951), pp. 67–99.

[2] H. H. Rowley, *The Zadokite Fragments and the Dead Sea Scrolls*, Oxford, 1952, pp. 54–6.

the first time by St. Irenaeus. Epiphanius (*Adv. Haer.*, XXIX, 7) says that the Ebionites were established at Pella in Transjordania, where, according to one tradition, the first Christians took refuge before the fall of Jerusalem.[1] Dr. Teicher admits the establishment of the Ebionites at Pella, but the distance—about sixty miles—between that town and the cave at Qumrân does not seem to have struck him, yet it is difficult to imagine that persecuted people, burdened with a whole library, would have made a journey of several days, solely with the intention of hiding it in a cave.

However, in the light of recently published texts, Dr. Teicher's theory may find confirmation, to a certain degree at any rate. The Qumrân caves did not shelter a library: they were *genizoth*. It may very well be that some writings found in the hands of Ebionites and seized by the rabbinic authorities may have been interred there. The Ebionites were Jewish-Christians, not completely heretical, for they considered themselves still to be Jews. They saw in Jesus a reformer of Judaism, and because of this they believed themselves authorised to criticise the Old Testament, and to make distinction between what was true and what was false in the Scriptures. But above all it would seem that they wished to make theirs a world religion through syncretism and propaganda.

The details that one can find in passages of the *Gospel of the Ebionites* preserved in Epiphanius and in the pseudo-Clementine *Homilies,* are very fragmentary. Nothing of what can be read there is clearly expressed in any writing whatsoever found in Cave I of Qumrân. But that is not a sufficient proof for saying that no manuscript found there was not at some time in the hands of Ebionites. When further on in this work we deal with Jewish-Christian and Gentile-Christian fragments, thought will be given to the Ebionites, who were by no means hypothetical. Unlike the Essenes, the Ebionites certainly existed, though their history is surrounded by mystery. We will merely recall that Eusebius[2] did not know that '*ebyônîm* meant "the poor" and that, following Tertullian, Hippolytus, and Epiphanius, it was thought that this sect took its name from its founder, someone named Ebyon.

[1] Eusebius, *Hist. Eccl.*, 3, 5.
[2] *Ibid.*, 3, 27.

# III

# The Translating of Hebrew Manuscripts

The attempt to translate a Hebrew text often results in a kind of vicious circle.[1] Hebrew vocabulary has not changed much. It is very little enriched by borrowings, and neologisms are rare. Biblical forms of speech have been slavishly followed throughout thousands of years, and phrases conform to earlier models. But, on the other hand, meanings of words and phrases have been constantly changing, and so it sometimes happens that it is impossible to translate a word or a phrase without knowing the period and region from which the document comes. And as, on the other hand, it is impossible to date a text unless one knows its contents, there is a danger of making serious anachronisms. To cite only one example, there is a Hebrew work called *Yossipon,* which is a medieval compilation of several historical books. According to the age of the different fragments, one and the same term, *zqn,* should be translated by "old man", "bearded", "venerable rabbi", or even at times by "patrician". The *ṣdwqym* are sometimes the Sadducees and sometimes the Zadokites. We may recall also that in the course of the centuries *ywn,* "Ionian", has been used to denote successively the peoples of Asia Minor, the inhabitants of Greece, the Macedonians, the Byzantine Empire, and even at times Christians in general.

What has been said about vocabulary applies equally to ready-made expressions. In turn, the descriptive term *rš‘,* "wicked" or "impious", was given to the Romans, the Arabs, the Turks, etc. Even at the beginning of this century, when Eastern Jews used the word *rmy* ("false") they meant

[1] A difficulty of this kind has been pointed out in connection with the translation of the *Damascus Document.* Although the text reads *'yš khn,* "a man Cohen", this expression has usually been translated by "a priest". It is true that at the time when there was a temple the *Kohanim* were sacrificing priests. After its destruction, Cohen was no more than a simple proper name, all the more frequent because so many Jews liked to claim descent from the ancient priests.

"an Armenian". Many of these expressions are known through the Bible, but even there their meaning varies from text to text. One knows well enough that it is impossible to give the same meaning to "Messiah" in Leviticus and in Isaiah. Other and similar terms may have been found in apocryphal books which have not come down to us. A few have survived in Jewish jargon, but it is not known with what meaning they were originally employed. We have an example of this in the expression "Teacher of Righteousness" met with in the Dead Sea manuscripts. Till now it was only known by the use the Qaraites made of it, sometimes to denote Anan and his alleged forerunners, sometimes to pay respects to a Maimonides. In every place, and at all times, different people have been called "Sons of Light" and "Sons of Darkness"; others have deserved the title "Teacher of Righteousness" or been called "Orators of Falsehood". It is of first importance, therefore, to know approximately from which period and which region a text comes, for otherwise there is danger of making serious mistakes.

ii

## THE MAIN STREAMS OF JUDAISM

In the first centuries of the present era, the period to which we assign the Dead Sea manuscripts, there were three main streams in Judaism, both among the Jews of Palestine and those of the Diaspora. They need to be clearly distinguished both as regards doctrines and as regards the manner of life of their adherents. We have also to bear in mind a fourth stream, Christianity. Among the Jews of Palestine, this appears more as something new grafted in than as a result of an evolution.

(a) *The Pharisees.* Two very different words, but with the same sound, are confused in the name of "Pharisees" (*prwšym*). Successors to the Chassidim or Hassidaeans, the Pharisees of the second century B.C. lived "separated" from the ordinary people, so as not to be contaminated by all the Greek customs which had been introduced into Judea. Their struggle against Hellenism came to an end in 37 B.C., when Judea became tributary to Rome, and they vanished from the political scene.

By another interpretation of the same word, the name of Pharisees was given later to followers of Hillel, who had made it their mission to reduce oral tradition to writing. The world had evolved, and it was impossible to observe the laws of the Bible to the very letter, and yet it was necessary to avoid certain pagan customs which had been implanted in Palestine.

So the Pharisees became the "interpreters" of the Law, and it was to them that Rome entrusted the religious administration of the Jews in Palestine. Whilst "erecting a wall of partition" around Judaism by the many prohibitions ('*issûrin*) or taboos which they enacted, the rabbis of the Pharisees collaborated willingly with the Romans, and because of this were accused of hypocrisy.

The Pharisees believed in the survival of the soul after death. Until the Last Judgement, the souls of the righteous would dwell in the presence of God, whilst the wicked were given over to the torments of Gehenna. The Pharisees practised charity and had a highly developed sense of solidarity, but they were greedy for honours, and styled themselves "the Great" (*rbym*). Looking upon themselves as the successors of the former priests, they levied worship dues upon their flocks, both in money and in kind.[1]

The rabbinic schools from which the rabbis were drawn were often in conflict with one another on grounds of prestige, though their differences were given out as doctrinal. A number of schools were excommunicated by the *Nasi*, the religious head recognised by the Romans. The most outstanding excommunication was that of the school of Lydda, presided over by Rabbi Eliezer ben Hyrcanus.

The Pharisees had to struggle against the conversion of orthodox Jews to the Zadokite movement and to Christianity on the one hand, and to paganism on the other. They were also strongly opposed to the conversion of Romans to Judaism. A relation of the Emperor Domitian, Flavius Clemens, having been converted to Judaism along with his wife, Domitilla, Rabbi Gamaliel II went to Rome in order to prevent Jews from making proselytes there.

(*b*) *The Zadokites.* Under the reign of John Hyrcanus (134–104 B.C.) the aristocrats—important officials of the Temple, the administration, and the army—had formed a party of "The Righteous" (*saddîqîm* or Sadducees), so-called because their intention was to observe Biblical righteousness in all its rigour. Wishing to recognise only the Law of Moses, they demanded, for example, the strict applications of the law of retaliation. In this they were in opposition both to the Helleniers and to the Pharisees, who spoke about unquestionable oral traditions. For a time they were the dominant party. Then Salome Alexandra (76–67 B.C.) put the more gentle laws of

---

[1] The right granted to rabbis to levy a worship tax, a right for which the evidence goes back as far as the second century, was confirmed by the *Theodosian Code* (XVI, viii, 29). Julian the Apostate asked the patriarch to lighten this burden, which had become too heavy.

the Pharisees into force, and influential Sadducees were exiled. Hyrcanus II looked to the Sadducees for support in his efforts to seize the power from his brother Aristobulus. Pompey's entrance into Jerusalem put an end to the fratricidal war, and the Sadducees disappeared from the political scene.

When the Procurator Coponius in A.D. 6 ordered a census of all persons and all property so as to draw up a taxation register, a pupil of Rabbi Shammai named Zadok or Zaduk urged the people to revolt. Subsequently, he formed a party from among the rich proprietors who had been dispossessed by the Romans. It had as its leaders the Aaronite priests whom the ethnarchs had removed from office and deprived of their privileges.

The Zadokites took over the strict rules of the former Sadducees. They did not go so far as to deny all authority to the books of the Prophets, but they refused all elucidation of the Mosaic law. It was within the Zadokite environment that the idea of revenge took form which was to culminate in the disaster of A.D. 70. Even after the fall of Jerusalem, the Zadokites did not renounce the privileges due to birth, and for a long time they cherished the hope of setting up once more the theocratic State.

The Zadokites denied the survival of the soul. It was in this life that the good would be rewarded and the wicked punished. For them, death was the end of everything. In very crude language, they expressed their thoughts upon the mystery of birth, and from it they deduced that the human being was destined to rot in the grave. They believed in a divine judgement upon earth, and the early coming of the Day of Yahweh. In consequence they attached great importance to the purity of the individual, the only way to be sure of survival in the cataclysm which would engulf the godless.

Keeping to the letter of the Mosaic law, the Zadokites would not recognise the "easements" or accommodations allowed by the Pharisees. They even went further, and were ready to add fresh "prohibitions" to those already existing. In the Diaspora, where they were in a minority, the Zadokites sometimes formed themselves into distinct communities. Thanks to Rabbi Simon ben Gamaliel I, the Zadokites were never excluded from Judaism, as the Pharisees demanded. Ultimately, the word "zadokite" became the synonym for heretic (*myn*). In the Babylonian Talmud, all heretics are called "zadokites", and Rabbi Samuel the Younger introduced into the prayer of thanksgiving, the praise of God for not having been born a Zadokite.

It is difficult now to know if all the personages said to have been converted and become "zadokites" had not joined some other sect or religion. The real Zadokites did not hold greatly to the making of proselytes, but there were many sects derived from them, and some of these sought to make converts.

(c) *The Baptists*. The sect to which John belonged presented numerous analogies with the Zadokite movement:

(a)   John offered expiation by fasting (Matt. 9.14, 11.18, etc.).
(b)   He administered the baptism of purification and repentance (Matt. 3, 11, etc.).
(c)   He was opposed to the Pharisees (Luke 7.30, etc.).
(d)   He belonged to the priestly class (Luke 1.5, etc.).
(e)   He did not believe in the Kingdom of Heaven (Matt. 11.11, etc.).
(f)   He believed that the Judgement Day was at hand (Matt. 3.7, etc.).
(g)   He was expecting the coming of the Messiah (Matt. 3.11, 11.3, etc.).
(h)   He was called "born of woman" (Matt. 11.11; Luke 7.28, etc.).

When we also find in the Qumrân manuscripts the expression "the being born of woman" we do not realise that it is not a chance phrase, but a characteristic expression used by a branch of the Zadokites.

The Baptist sect was not Christian. There was even a marked opposition between the Baptists, attached to this world, like all the Zadokites, and the Christians. An echo of this is found in the Pseudo–Clementines (*Homilies*, III, 22): "Since the same spirit rules in this present world, which is feminine, she [Eve] passed for the first prophetess, prophesying among all those *born of woman*; but the other, inasmuch that he is *son of man*, of masculine sex, announces what is important for the world to come, which world is male." See also *Homiles*, II, 17.

One is also aware that the Qaraites claimed to descend from the Zadokites who emigrated to Damascus. This opinion was shared by Maimonides, who saw ancient Zadokites in the twelfth-century Egyptian Qaraites.

(d) *The Zealots*. This movement arose among the people of the countryside at the beginning of the first century. It was a reaction against the double imposition to which the rural populations were subject under Roman rule. Hostile both to the Romans and to the Temple priests, the followers of Judas of Galilee showed their zeal for God by appointing their own priests and in refusing to pay the Temple dues demanded by the

Jerusalem priesthood. As one would expect, all kinds of belief, however strange, came to be accepted in the country. Gnosticism claimed quite a number. An unrestrained belief in angels and demons found a favourable soil.

Sometimes the Pharisees tried to lead the country people to renounce certain beliefs, especially under Rabbi Gamaliel II. At other times, they tried to adapt the orthodox religion to Gnostic doctrines. At the beginning of the second century, Rabbi Aqiba introduced the teaching of Gnosticism in the school of which he was head, but a short time later his two assistants, Ben Asai and Ben Soma, died, and this attempt to take into account the aspirations of the people had no sequel.

The pride of the rabbis was the chief hindrance preventing the country people from adhering to Pharisaism. The rabbis looked upon the "poor" as mere cattle, and treated the peasant as stupid. The term for peasant, *'am ha'ares,* came to have the sense of "simpleton". Whilst the peasants boasted of their material and intellectual poverty, the rabbis laid down a number of rules aimed at maintaining their purity through the avoidance of contact with this class of the population. Zealot writings, especially commentaries on the books of the Prophets, were often seized and consigned to the *geniza.* It was principally among the "poor" (*'ebyônîm*) that Christianity spread.

Among the beliefs of the country people were many that were foreign to Judaism. The Zealots believed in the other world, but they pictured it in some very strange ways. Among other things, they believed that this present world would be destroyed and that the elect would work together with God to build up a new universe.

It was in Zealot circles that there arose about A.D. 60 the political movement of the Sicarii. These, armed with daggers, committed acts of terrorism. Their victims were not only the Romans, but also Zadokites and certain Pharisees whom they supposed to be traitors. If taken prisoner, the Zealots endured all sorts of torture without betraying their comrades. Some even seem to have sought martyrdom so as to instil courage into their fellows.

Though kept at a distance by the Pharisees, the men of the people were never in so many words considered as heretics so long as they did not belong to some branch of the Zadokite movement or to Christianity.

(e) *The Christians.* Information from Jewish sources upon the beginnings of Christianity is rare. All the same, we can gather from the New Testament certain indications as to what the Pharisees found fault with in Christianity.

In their hostility to the Pharisees and the Zadokites, the Christians were not different from the rest of the "poor". The humility which they displayed was in line with the conduct of the Zealots. On several points, their beliefs could be confused with those of the people. The essential point by which the Christian movement differed from the others lay elsewhere. It lay in the idea that the pagans could be brought to embrace Judaism by giving them an example of toleration, and that once the Romans were converted there would be an end to the sufferings of Israel. The commandment, "Love your enemies" (Matt. 5.44), is characteristically Christian, as is also fraternisation with the publicans (Mark 2.15-17) and the reproach made to the Pharisees of treating proselytes badly (Matt. 23.15).

To Judaism, the teaching of Christ and His disciples had the inevitable result among Christians of relaxing certain taboos. The Sabbath rest (Matt. 12.1, etc.), ritual washings (Matt. 15.1ff.), taboos as to food (Matt. 15.10ff.) and the avoidance of contact with the dead (Luke 10.30), etc., were less strictly observed. The use of foreign languages (Acts, 2.1ff.) and the complete assimilation of converts which resulted from it, in the end made Christianity a different religion from Judaism.

For nearly two centuries, the Pharisees considered Jewish-Christians to be heretics, and persecuted them. But from the end of the first century there were Christian communities of foreign speech, and it would seem that the rabbis had no authority over these. As among the Pharisees, the Zadokites, and the Zealots, so among the first Christians of Palestine there were many sects. Certain characteristics, however, are common to them all, and in a Hebrew text these are easily recognised.

iii

## THE STUDY OF SOURCES

Before being able to give an accurate translation of a Dead Sea manuscript or of a passage from a composite work, it is clearly necessary first of all to determine if it comes from a Pharisaic, a Zadokite, or a Zealot source, as words will differ in meaning in each case. From the fact that the roll was placed in a *geniza* and not completely burnt, it is also clear that it was not held to be entirely heretical. There must at least have been a doubt about its author, for to save a book from being burnt, even one found in the hands of an unbeliever, it was enough that it had been written by a Jew who had not been excommunicated. Yet a Jewish scribe could have copied the texts of a sect to which rabbinism was opposed: he could have hired out his services to heretics. Thus, even if the circumstances of the find and the condition of the manuscript when found do supply some indication as to its source, yet the problem is not solved. That can only be done by a study of the contents.

Naturally, it is difficult to determine with precision to what school within the larger movements of Judaism a particular work or passage should be attributed, but all the same the identification of sources, even if it is only approximate, is an indispensable stage in all translation.

A Christian point of view in a number of Dead Sea manuscripts has often been pointed out. Quite recently, J. M. Allegro[1] and Otto Eissfeldt[2] have tried to make out that Christianity borrowed a great deal from "the Qumrân sect". There is talk of a "pre-Christianity". Parallels and differences have been sought between the teaching of Christ and what is persistently regarded as a completely homogeneous presentation of the doctrine of a sect. The problem is seen in a very different light as soon as one gives up the theory of a buried Essene library, and as soon as one puts back the date of most of the non-Biblical material to the first centuries of the Christian era. The passages with a Christian outlook which have been detected in a number of writings are not pre-Christian, but really Christian. Very often that was the reason why the rolls were taken to the *geniza*. Admittedly it is surprising not to find the name of Christ mentioned nor that of any of His Apostles. We may be surprised not to read what would clearly recall all that the Gospels tell us, and which is the foundation of present-day Christianity, but we should not overlook the fact that it is the same with a quantity of apocryphal writings the Christian origin of which has never been in question. And the fact should not be lost sight of that the *genizoth* have not given back to us the whole of the literature of the early centuries. The writings carried away to these cemeteries by orthodox Jews, from the very nature of the case, were Jewish writings, not the works of Gentile-Christians. If there had been writings which were clearly too Christian in the sense that we today give to that word, they would certainly have been burnt when seized by the rabbinic authorities. In the present case, it cannot be argued that some fragment is not Christian because no other fragment more typically Christian has been found in the same cave.

Further on in this book consideration will be given to the relations

---

[1] *The Dead Sea Scrolls*, 1956 (Pelican Book), p. 376.
[2] *Conference of 26th October 1956, Academy of Maintz*, 15 pp. and 47 figures.

between the Jews of Palestine and those of the Diaspora, and of the stream of ideas which flowed from Italy to Palestine and Palestine to Italy during the early centuries. "Jewish fables" which came into being in the Diaspora of Syria and Mesopotamia and found a ready hearing among the country people of Palestine will also be considered. But these are secondary matters, and the important thing is, first of all, to distinguish the main sources of our texts.

So far, the outlook of Palestinian Pharisees is only represented by a few passages in the composite manuscript which has been called the *Manual of Discipline*. They are easily recognised because of their references to rabbis, and to a number of distinctively rabbinic institutions known to us through Jewish literature. It should not be surprising that no complete orthodox work of the Pharisees has been found in the caves of the Judean Desert. The place for a roll of the *Mishna,* for instance, would not be in a *geniza*. On the other hand, certain dissenting Pharisaic schools seem to be represented by passages here and there in the midst of other writings. There are indications that the authors of these passages belonged to the Diaspora, probably to Syria.

Zadokite works and Zadokite fragments incorporated into composite works have two characteristics which can be easily recognised. First of all there is the importance given to the Sons of Zadok, the legitimate successors of the Aaronite priesthood, to Cohens and Levis, to the Temple and to the Law of Moses. Secondly, there is the lack of references to the prophetical and didactic books of the Bible, the absence of belief in the other world, and the disparagement of the human being, made from the dust and destined to return to it. Within the Zadokite movement itself there are some tendencies which reveal themselves immediately: the Zadokites of the Diaspora showing themselves less strict and even seeking converts, the Baptists calling themselves those "born of woman", and making frequent use of a commentary on the Book of Isaiah.

The popular writing of the Zealots is marked by their beliefs in angels and demons, by their views of the other world, and by certain Gnostic features. Occasionally, but rarely, peculiarities of vocabulary show that authors came from the Syrian Diaspora, or from Italy.

By the use of these preliminary criteria, the first steps can be taken in sorting out what the Dead Sea manuscripts have brought us. Passages embroidering eternal life in the next world in company with saints and angels can be marked off from others which deny any life after death. Fragments dealing with the Sons of Zadok, Aaronite priests and their rights and privileges, can be separated from those which avoid all mention of priests, and which sing the praises of poverty, as well as from those dealing with precedence among rabbis, etc. It is only in this way that an approach can be made towards the understanding of these texts which seem so contradictory at first glance.

iv

## THE *MANUAL OF DISCIPLINE*

All the arguments invoked to prove the existence of the Essenes, the evidence from Pliny, Philo, Josephus, and Dio Chrysostom, the ruins and cemetery at Qumrân, with numerous relics which have come to light, the *Damascus Document*—they all pale before one massive argument: Cave I has provided undeniable proof of the existence of this Jewish monastic sect, for the "rule" of the sect has been discovered! The document referred to is that which has been called *The Manual of Discipline*, though today preference is given to the title, *The Rule of the Sect*. Since its publication,[1] it has been frequently and very differently translated.[2] Although the present writer has already published his opinion on this manuscript,[3] he thinks it necessary to repeat certain facts which seem to have been deliberately ignored.

When one speaks about the "rule" of a community, whether monastic or lay, obviously one is talking about a coherent, homogeneous document. The Qaraite "rule" found at Cairo is unquestionably such a document. None of its phrases contradict each other. But this is not so with the *Manual of Discipline*, which is a composite work—one, moreover, which is marked out as such by the many lines and signs in the margin indicating the beginning of the different fragments copied out one after another, without any connection between them. The writer has been accused of having separated the different fragments, and of then regrouping them according to certain criteria, "a process which seems premature at least".[4] As we shall have to break up in the same way two other manuscripts which are translated and commented on below, we may see first of all if the

---

[1] Millar Burrows, *The Dead Sea Scrolls of St. Mark's Monastery*, Vol. II, fasc. 2, New Haven, 1951.

[2] See Bibliography in G. Vermès, *op. cit.*; English translation, *Discovery in the Judean Desert*, New York, 1956.

[3] *Deux Manuscrit Hébreux de la Mer Morte*, Paris, 1951.

[4] J. van der Ploeg, "Quelques traductions du Manuel de Discipline", in *Bi. Or.*, IX (1952), p. 131.

*present state of our knowledge* allows us to act in this way with a Hebrew text belonging to the beginning of our era.

Formerly there was not the same respect for ancient writings as we have today. When we happen to possess a number of manuscripts of the same text, the variants are often so considerable that in critical editions we have taken account of several traditions. But, quite apart from glosses and interpolations by different scribes, the "original" redaction appears to a modern scholar as a composite work.[1] It is impossible to understand these books unless the elements composing them are studied separately, placed in their proper settings, and dated as far as that is possible. Most of the books which make up the Old Testament are composite works, "compilations of earlier works which the editors combined whilst reproducing them almost textually. . . . This was the method often followed by Arab historians and the chroniclers of the Middle Ages. It is the way Israelite and Jewish scribes worked . . . they copied from end to end, and with a pious respect, fragments of earlier collections which they had under their eyes, even when these fragments did not agree with each other, or were repetitions."[2] Obviously it is necessary "to be convinced by the evidence of several typical cases" of the composite nature of a book. In the case of the *Manual of Discipline*, this certainly presents less difficulty than when dealing with the Pentateuch or other books of the Old Testament which can still spring many surprises upon us.

What do we find in the *Manual of Discipline*? First of all a series of fragments[3] referring to "The Sons of Zadok", a society or "union" which they had formed, and to the admission of new members into that society.

The Union of the Sons of Zadok was a secret society (V, 11). Initiation was in the presence of members and, following a ritual described in detail (I, 16-11, 18), after certain prayers, Cohens who belonged to the society gave the history of the movement and read the statutes; then they pronounced a blessing upon the other members, and the Levis pronounced curses on the enemies of the society, while, finally, both Cohens and Levis together laid curses on members who had betrayed the secrets of the union. Every year, in the course of a solemn session, members were examined, and according to their conduct were promoted in rank or otherwise (V, 22-5). The society was divided into "lodges" distributed

[1] See introductions and commentaries to separate books in R. H. Charles, *The Apocrypha and Pseudepigrapha of the Old Testament*, Oxford, 1913.

[2] A. Lods, *Histoire de la Littérature hébraïque et juive*, Paris (1950), pp. 11, 15-16.

[3] These fragments, in the order in which they should be read, are: V, 1-13; IX, 2-5, 5-11; VIII, 4-7, 1-4; I, 1-11, 10; II, 11-18; V, 13-25; II, 19; III, 12.

throughout the country, some more important than others. For valid discussions in any lodge, there had to be present fifteen members, including three Cohens (VIII, 1). Cohens always had precedence. Then came the Levis, with ordinary Israelites in the last place.

The aims of the society are clearly set out: to strive by all possible means for the re-establishment of the Temple services and the privileges of the Cohens as priests. Naturally, the Sons of Zadok held themselves to be the true followers of the Law of Moses, the only persons pure and able to confer purity on members of their union. As Zadokites did not believe in another world, in these fragments there is never any mention of angels or of a resurrection. It is in this world that the wicked will be punished and the good rewarded. Members were not sought for, new members having to offer themselves spontaneously on their own initiative. They took an oath to love all the "Sons of Light", and to hate all the "Sons of Darkness". They promised to put at the service of the society all their knowledge, ability, and possessions. They had to swear to be regular in their attendance at sessions of the society, and to carry out the orders which should be given them. They were forbidden to seek for proselytes, lest they should be corrupted by the wealth of "men of falsity". In spite of its religious colouring, this society was obviously a militant political organisation.

However little inclined to *dissect* the *Manual of Discipline,* one cannot help noticing that the other passages in this writing have nothing to do with the above Society of the Sons of Zadok. A number of passages reveal a mutual affinity. They emanate from a rabbinic school sometimes called "the Union", and its *yeshivah,* "session of the rabbis" (*mwšb hrbym*).[1]

Before speaking, permission had to be asked for from the rabbis (VI, 10-13). It was the rabbis who examined a new candidate. After the first inscription of his name, he had no right to any part of the *terumah,* "the pure things of the rabbis" (VI, 16-17). Instead, anything he could gain from his work was his own. After having followed a year's course of study, he was again examined, and if successful he could exercise certain rabbinic functions, and whatever he received for these services were put into the common fund, but not shared out. After a second year's examination, a successful candidate had a right to the "wine of the rabbis", and it was only now that he received a fixed stipend, as his colleagues did. This

---

[1] Re-grouped, these passages should be read in the following order: V, 8-23; V, 25-VI, 1; VI, 1-8; VIII, 16-19; VIII, 20-IX, 2; VI, 24-VII, 25.

was taken from the common funds of the rabbis, and the amount varied according to seniority.

New rabbis who were in excess of the number required had to set themselves up in other towns and villages. Wherever ten rabbis met together (a *minyân*) they formed a new *yeshivah*, elected a head (who had to be named Cohen), and took their meals in common. The study of the Law had to be carried on, day and night, by rota (VI, 1-18). As a consequence of certain delinquencies, a rabbi could be excluded temporarily from the Union. If he had acted through lack of understanding, he received advice from the other rabbis, and when he had amended his ways he was restored to his position (IX, 2).

The order of precedence with the rabbis was not the same as that with the Zadokites. Those named Cohen always had the first place, but they were immediately followed by the "venerable" rabbis (*zqn*), and those named Levi enjoyed no special prerogative (VI, 8). The aim of the Union was to promote the study and interpretation of the Bible.

Either the same or a second society also ran a *midrash* (elementary and secondary school), and the rules of this school (VI, 24-VII, 25) show that punishments most frequently took the form of fines. These were inflicted upon both pupil and teacher for all sorts of breaches of good conduct, ranging from the pupil who laughed stupidly in class to the teacher who let down the reputation of the school.

The term *rbym*[1] has been translated in a variety of ways. Even though there may be uncertainty in some other texts, there is none here. The references to typically rabbinic institutions, the *yeshivah* of the rabbis, the "pure things" of the rabbis, the *midrash*, etc., are too many to leave the least doubt as to how this term should be translated.

With the exception of the four psalms copied out at the end of this roll, and of the very curious passage found in VIII, 7-16, all the other passages in the *Manual of Discipline* seem to emanate from a Zealot society, *hostile* to the Sons of Zadok (IX, 14). These fragments seem to be extracts from three different pieces of writing, a "rule", a "doctrine", and a "history".[2] In these fragments there is frequent mention of the "zeal" of

[1] This term can be rendered by "the many" or by "the great". The first translation, "the many", is unwarranted. As to the second, it should not be forgotten that for Jews a "great" one was, above anything else, a rabbi. It is almost like translating the title "Excellency" by "goodness" and the title "Eminence" by "altitude" or "hill".

[2] These fragments may be considered as belonging to the "rule"; IX, 12-16, 21-6, 16-21; III, 13-17. The following, perhaps originally inserted in the same writing: IV, 6-8, 2-6; III, 17-IV, 1, belong to the "doctrine". The historical fragments, which may also come from the same initial work, are: IV, 15-26; X, 1-9; IV, 9-14.

the members of this Union constituted so as to form a clandestine army for the liberation of the country. The young, in whom a spirit of vengeance was to be inculcated (IX, 23), were to feign humility, hide themselves from the men of perdition and not dispute with them, and not reveal plans except to fellow members (IX, 16-19). They were to receive their military and their civil training in hidden places in the desert (IX, 19-21; III, 13-16). Thus, furnished by God with everything necessary for them, they would be able to defeat the enemy on the appointed day.

As one can see, we are far from the Zadokites preoccupied with their privileges, taken up with their ritual purity, very far from their lodges, where initiations were carried out with a ceremonial calculated to strike the imagination. We are also far from the rabbis with their petty rules of precedence, far from their schools and academies with their rules of decent behaviour, and also far from their financial arrangements. These differences stand out still more clearly as soon as we read the passages where the Zealot "Sons of Truth" set forth their doctrine. It is essentially the teaching of "The Two Ways" that is found in these much-erased pages, where phrases borrowed from most schools of Judaism stand side by side. The historic fragments, one of which (X, 1-9) is the paraphrase of a prayer found in the *Book of Thanksgiving Hymns,* are as a rule very obscure, and filled with things hinted at, like all other such works. There is also an apocalyptic vision with references to angels, to whom the rabbis attached little importance, whilst the Zadokites ignored them on principle.

The most difficult fragment to understand is VIII, 7-16. It appears to be an extract from a *Commentary on Isaiah* written to explain the coming and mission of John the Baptist. As to the four psalms copied out at the end of the roll, the first (X, 9-17) may well have come from a Pharisaic environment. On several counts, the second (X, 17-XI, 2) seems to have originated in some Jewish-Christian circle. The third, filled with visions of the life beyond the grave and pictures of a new world, can only be the work of a man of the people. It was among such that the Zealots gained recruits. As to the fourth (XI, 15-22) it denies all survival after death. It is therefore a Zadokite work, whilst the use of the expression "he who is born of woman" seems to indicate that its author belonged to the Baptist sect.

     ★    ★    ★

That is what the *Manual of Discipline* consists of: a mixture of the most incongruous fragments which even the copyists did not attempt to arrange in a logical fashion. It is incomprehensible how anyone could see in this manuscript the "rule" of the supposed Essenes, or of "the monks of Qumrân", as some scholars will call the 1,100 dead, men and women, who lie in a cemetery close to the Dead Sea. The doctrinal views set out in this manuscript are frequently so contradictory that one cannot help wondering who can have had a reason for joining these fragments together. Merely looking at its good state of preservation, one would be inclined to imagine that this roll was written in some dissident rabbinic school, but closer observation, and especially comparison with other manuscripts recently published, makes it very apparent that this roll also has been passed through the flames. Therefore it can only have belonged to some unorthodox Jewish sect.

The roll consists of four sheets of leather. The first sheet has three columns, the second, four, the third, three, and the fourth only one. Three scribes have taken part in the copying of this roll, and they were all as little calligraphers as the many others who made corrections to the manuscript by additions between the lines, by erasures, washing out, and by writing over other words. Columns I-V are very unequal in width and have each twenty-six lines. Columns VI-IX have twenty-seven lines, less equally spaced, and with some left blank. Column X has twenty-six lines, and column XI is two-thirds written on, with twenty-two lines very close together. The columns were not ruled for writing—just the margins being marked off by a line. A number of signs can be seen, including some "signatures of the rabbis", these naturally illegible. The roll must have been carefully examined by the rabbinic authorities, the same as those who inspected the roll *Isaiah "A"* before its fate was determined. Perhaps there was an attempt to save it from burial by making a number of corrections to the text. Nevertheless, it was passed through the fire: and yet to such a small extent! The flames only injured the lower margin and the last two lines.

On the publication of the photographic reproduction of this roll, the present writer saw in the *Manual of Discipline* a kind of memorandum-notebook. For the date of its compilation, he suggested between A.D. 90 and 110, with about A.D. 115 as the latest date for its consignment to the *geniza*. Whilst some other opinions have had to be revised, he still considers these dates as the most probable, in spite of all that has been published.

The date of compilation cannot be earlier than that of the latest fragment copied into the roll. Signs of date are rare, yet the following points may be noticed:

(a)   A Zealot fragment (VI, 13-14) includes an allusion to the eruption of Vesuvius in A.D. 79.

(b)   The title of *Nasi* which occurs in a fragment (VIII, 13) only appeared in connection with a rabbinic academy about the year A.D. 90.

The latest pieces of evidence concerning date therefore come from about A.D. 90, a time when more or less secret societies with initiatory rites were flourishing in Palestine. Some group or other may have wished to draw up its statutes after getting ideas from those of already existing societies.

Contrary to current opinion,[1] rabbinic *haburoth* can only have taken definite form after the destruction of the Temple. In fact, they are based on the recognition of privileges to which the rabbis could only have laid claim after the suppression of the regular clergy of Jerusalem. Many details concerning these societies can be found in rabbinic literature. They are often contradictory, for the rabbinic societies were never in perfect accord with each other, and even went so far as to mutually excommunicate each other.

Before the fall of Jerusalem there were already priests in the countryside. They were appointed by Zealot peasants who refused to pay tithes and other dues to the Temple, and who showed their "zeal" by fulfilling their religious duties towards upright men (see above, p. 71, the interpolation in Josephus, *Jewish Antiquities*, XVIII, i, 5). This institution was the foundation on which rabbinism established its cultural primacy in Palestine.

Rabbi Yohanan ben Zakkai, who had managed to escape during the Siege of Jerusalem (legends say he was carried out of the city in a coffin), founded in A.D. 72 a rabbinic school at Jabneh (Jamnia) halfway between Jaffa and Ashdod. The Jews, who had need of a religious authority if only for the fixing of the calendar, unanimously recognised that of Rabbi Yohanan, but after his death this harmony came to an end.

Rabbi Gamaliel II wished to succeed to Rabbi Yohanan. He took to himself the title of *Nasi* (prince), and about A.D. 90 he obtained from the Roman procurator in Antioch official recognition of this title, which till then had only been carried by two chiefs of the Sanhedrin, Rabbi Gamaliel I and his son Simon, in the early years of the first century A.D.

---

[1] See *Jewish Encyclopedia*, article, "Ḥaber".

This title was taken over by the successors of Gamaliel II, and till A.D. 135 it was the acknowledged right of the head of Palestinian rabbinism.

At first, however, a number of the disciples of Rabbi Yohanan refused to acknowledge the authority of Gamaliel II. He was deprived of his rank, excommunicated, and then later restored to his office. It was then that he began to take vigorous action against his former fellow disciples who had founded rival academies. The most important of these schools was that of Lydda, with Rabbi Eliezer ben Hyrcanus as its head. This academy had been conceived on the lines of Greek schools. It was even said to have included a stadium. The excommunication of Rabbi Eliezer caused a great sensation. Some books from his school and all the provisions ("pure things") accumulated there were burnt. Some other writings, however, were consigned to the *geniza*. Another disciple of Rabbi Yohanan ben Zakkai, the Rabbi Eleazar ben Arakh, had also founded a school at the instigation of his wife, who was very ambitious. He had only a few disciples, and although he was not excommunicated, his school did not survive his death.

Other rabbinic schools were founded later, and all of them had their statutes, and some of the provisions in these have been preserved in rabbinic literature. The schools around which communities gathered had strict rules of rank and precedence, and whatever may have been the later developments, this movement, and above all the drawing up of "statutes" for the schools, began round about A.D. 80.

Zadokite societies came into being about A.D. 60. They were not named after David's high priest, but after Zadok, an ally of Judas of Galilee, who founded the Zealot movement. Until A.D. 66 Zadokites and Zealots marched hand in hand, but after the war with the Romans had broken out frictions occurred and they became bitter enemies. After the defeat of A.D. 70 the Zadokites and the different sects which had developed out of this movement had to struggle against the hostility of the Pharisaic rabbis. They were often excommunicated, and it would have needed little for them to have been put out of Judaism completely.

As the Zadokites always entertained ideas of vengeance, it must be supposed that soon after Rome had recognised the *Nasi* as the official Jewish authority, they formed themselves into a secret society, with ranks and rites of initiation. Thus it must also be round about A.D. 90, that we must place the drawing up of the statutes for the Zadokite lodges, and fragments of these have been preserved in our manuscript.

It is impossible to give even an approximate number of the Jewish and Jewish-Christian sects which arose in Palestine in the first two centuries

E

A.D. The Qumrân manuscripts have made known a number of these with their pompous names, but the list is far from complete. But it can hardly be imagined that a series of memoranda notes, such as the *Manual of Discipline*, could have been of interest to them all. Many of the fragments recopied into our manuscript could only have interested some rabbinic school. From that we can therefore suppose that the collection was compiled during the period that dissident rabbinic schools were being set up—that is to say, *after* A.D. 80.

It is very likely that the *Manual of Discipline* was compiled during the first years in authority of the *Nasi* Rabbi Gamaliel II, the time when that authority was challenged. Although containing fragments from the statutes of Zadokite and Zealot societies, the roll could only have been drawn up in a rabbinic school. No other group would have been interested in rules for seemly behaviour in class. Naturally, there are many other things in this roll. That goes without saying. A rabbinic school could only exist on condition that it gathered a community around it. It had to rely on the financial help of its faithful supporters, and we know that Jewish beliefs in the first century were very divided. The school at Jabneh, strictly Pharisaic, did not succeed in imposing its point of view every-where. Would it be surprising if one or another of the dissident schools which arose at this time attempted some degree of syncretism so as to draw from a wider community? One of the accusations against Rabbi Eliezer ben Hyrcan of Lydda was that he had perhaps admitted certain Zadokite and Christian points of view.

The present writer at one time suggested associating the *Manual of Discipline* with the school of Emmaus, founded towards the end of the first century by Rabbi Eleazar ben Arakh. He still holds that it is in such an environment that the compilers of this roll should be sought. It is known that Rabbi Eleazar did not have many disciples. A more important school would have entrusted the compilation to better calligraphers. The corrections made in the manuscripts and, still more, the signatures of rabbis in the margins show that the roll was examined, if not to say censored. That would have been admissible only if the possessors had not been excommunicated, and the school of Emmaus was not excom-municated. If the gentle treatment given to the *Manual of Discipline* is compared with that inflicted on some other manuscripts found in Cave I, it must be admitted that its owner had benefited from considerable indulgence. This can be understood when it is remembered that the wife of Rabbi Eleazar ben Arakh was said to be descended from Hillel.

Of course, the roll could have emanated from the school of some other disciple of Rabbi Yohanan. We do not know them all, but information about the activity of some of them has come down to us. None of these could have had any interest in putting together the fragments which we find in the *Manual of Discipline*.

Rabbi Haninah was an enthusiastic supporter of collaboration with the Romans. His motto was that it was necessary to pray for the good of the government because, were it not for fear of the Romans, the Jews were capable of devouring each other.

Abba Saul of Botnith gave up teaching and became a wine merchant.

Rabbi Nahum of Gimzô, whose life is surrounded with legends, was the founder of a school of optimism, very far from anything we find in the *Manual of Discipline*.

Rabbi Nehoniah ben Haqanah, a renowned stylist and a learned exegete, was a stern Pharisee who took an active part in the suppression of subversive writings. By a play of words upon his name, he came to be called "digger of pools and caves"—that is to say, of *genizoth*.

Rabbi Elazar ben Azariah, who was appointed head of the school at Jabneh when Rabbi Gamaliel was removed from office, and who was sixteen years of age at the time, continued to be attached to this school when Gamaliel was reinstated.

Thus, by a process of elimination, one comes back to Rabbi Eleazar ben Arakh and the school of Emmaus. At the present time, it is the only school known to the writer where the *Manual of Discipline* could have been compiled at the end of the first century or during the very early years of the second. By A.D. 115 at the latest, the roll must have been seized by the orders of the *Nasi* Rabbi Gamaliel II, and taken to the *geniza*.

Several fragments of other copies of the *Manual of Discipline* are said to have been found in other caves. As the roll found in Cave I was in reality a collection of fragments, the question arises as to whether other similar collections existed, as was the case with the *War,* or whether these more recently found fragments are not parts of coherent rules of societies—Zadokite, Zealot, etc.—and not sets of diverse extracts copied out one after the other. To be clear on this point, it is necessary to await the publication of these texts.

★      ★      ★

It remains to say a few words about the attribution to the Essenes of the *Manual of Discipline*. The customs and doctrines which are given to this supposed sect are very contradictory. We have seen that the information concerning them which is found in the Greek version of Josephus comes from two interpolators. The first put to the account of the Essenes all that Hippolytus had said about Jews in general, at times changing certain words so as to produce a stinging satire against the Jews. The second interpolator tried to tone down some of his predecessor's phrases, and in the *Jewish Antiquities* he painted a very different picture of those whom he thought had been falsely "called by us" the Essenes. These two groups of data contradict one another on more than one point. They are also in contradiction with what one reads in Philo and Pliny. But if one will connect them with the *Manual of Discipline*, then one cannot help noticing that there are countless divergencies.

As the *Manual of Discipline* itself shows, it cannot be attributed to any one sect. The collection was formed with the view to extracting from it elements which could be used by a rabbinic school in drawing up its own set of statutes and regulations, for making the same kind of thing as that from which come the Cairo Qaraite fragments. But in its present state it could never have served as a set of rules to which reference had to be made. As to attributing it to the Essenes, that is something which could only be imagined by those who give this name "a meaningless indefiniteness".[1]

v

THE DETACHED SHEETS

Mention has often been made of sheets which had become separated from the *Manual of Discipline,* and which were said to have been bought by a collector. These sheets were found in the hands of the Bethlehemite dealer and, along with a part of the fly-leaf bearing several letters of the title of the roll, were acquired by the Palestine Museum in 1950. These sheets have been published, translated, and provided with commentaries, but the problems which they set are far from being all settled.

(a) *The Fragment of the Title.* This quite insignificant fragment is of great importance, for it proves that no sheet is missing from the *Manual of Discipline.* The holes made by stitching which it bears correspond exactly with those on the right-hand edge of the first inscribed sheet of the roll. The title was written on the back of the fly-leaf, and from bottom to top, but as the sheet is incomplete, it is impossible to determine of how many

[1] M. H. Gottstein, "Anti-Essene Traits in the Dead Sea Scrolls", in *Vetus Testamentum,* IV (1954), p. 142.

words it consisted. There has been a desire to read on the part which remains the words "[*sr*]*k hyḥd wmn* [. . . . . . . .]"—"Rule of the Union and (extracts) from . . . . . . . . .", but this is by no means certain. The first letter is not complete, only the lower part remaining, and it does not have the form of final *k*, which is usual in this manuscript. It could just as well be a *q*. As to the last letters, it is very difficult to justify the reading, *wmn*. The word for "union" and the conjunction are all that are certain, and this is insufficient ground for stating that the roll contained anything more than memorandum notes and the four apocryphal psalms which have been preserved.[1]

(*b*) *The Sheet of Two Columns*. This sheet has marks of stitching both on the right and the left edges, so it must have formed part of a roll, though certainly not that of the *Manual of Discipline*. The holes at the beginning of that document correspond with those of the fly-leaf, whilst the last column of it is only inscribed for two-thirds of its length, and the final, the left, edge has no signs of stitching. It is difficult to understand why that last sheet was not wider, and why the last column was only partly written, if the document was to continue. The observations about "rat-bites" at the bottom of the columns is no proof whatsoever, even if it could be admitted that this separated sheet had been rolled round the *Manual of Discipline*.

This sheet of two columns, therefore, may be considered as having formed part of another roll, not the same as the *Manual of Discipline*, though similar. The arrangement of the columns and the number of lines to the column, twenty-nine instead of twenty-six to twenty-seven, confirm this impression.

The text is that of a composite work having as a basis a Zadokite Constitution which was to be put into force for the nation of Israel *after* its liberation. The nation was to be organised on the Biblical model, in tribes and families. The State was to be responsible for the education of the children from the age of ten, and at twenty-five the young man was to put himself at the service of the State. Unless affected by some vice or physical defect, he was to be incorporated into the army or the civil administration, according to his degree of instruction. Sexual impotence, vouched for by the wife, on principle disqualified him from any office or function. There was a provision for an age limit to active service, but the text does not indicate what it was.

The Constitution made provision for convocations of the nation in

[1] D. Barthélemy and J. T. Milik in *Qumrân Cave I*.

certain circumstances. Those with the right to vote are mentioned. There was also a specific regulation that the godless should not take part in these meetings. It may be noted that only those Levites who performed active service in the Temple could be present in these convocations. The others were to fulfil police duties.

These passages are followed by some other arrangements which have nothing to do with Zadokite Constitution. They come from the rules of a popular Zealot society, but all the same are very strict about everything which had to do with ceremonial purity. These Zealots looked forward to a visit of the Messiah of Israel. The Warrior Messiah, realised in Bar Kochba, would naturally be accompanied by the *Nasi,* the religious head of the Jews. In anticipation of this eventuality, the Zealots laid down the rule regarding precedence. The first members of the group to present themselves were to be those whose name was Cohen. They were to be followed by chief military officers, and in third place would come the heads of the civil administration of the camp (or colony?). All were to be in order of rank. If the reception was followed by a banquet, naturally it fell to a Cohen to pronounce the blessing over the food and drink, and then to break the bread and pour the wine. The Warrior Messiah was to help himself next, and after that the other guests could help themselves, each in order and according to rank. A final sentence states that this was to be the procedure whenever ten persons were united at table, even when they were not honoured by a visit from the *Nasi.*

★　　　　★　　　　★

To all appearance, the "sheet of two columns" was written by one of the scribes who together produced the *Manual of Discipline.* It is therefore in the same circle that we must place the compiler of this second roll, of which only two columns have so far come to light. The date of the elements composing this fragment can be established by the mention of the *Nasi,* the title borne by Gamaliel II and by his successor. The messianic hope and the idea of preparing a constitution to come into use after the coming victory suggest that the elements of which this manuscript was composed must have been written towards the end of the first century A.D. There is nothing which is against the theory that they could have been recopied during the same period by a syncretistic school—that of Emmaus, for example—and that the manuscript was also seized about A.D. 115 and taken to the *geniza.*

It is also possible that the manuscript itself was burnt, and that this single sheet was detached and taken to the cave, whilst it is also possible that the rest of the manuscript was regarded as less pernicious and left in the hands of those with whom it was found. On this matter, all theories are permissible.

## vi

## THE BENEDICTIONS

A mass of manuscript fragments was purchased by the Palestine Museum from the dealer in Bethlehem. We are told that they belonged to the same manuscript as I.QS (=the *Manual of Discipline*) and I.QSa (="the sheet of two columns"). Nothing, however, could be less certain. It has already been pointed out that "the sheet of two columns" could not have been sewn to the beginning of the *Manual of Discipline*, nor to the end. The same remark applies also to the other fragments.

With a perseverance which cannot be too much admired, Fathers Barthélémy and Milik[1] have been able to distribute these fragments into five very incomplete pages of a manuscript. Naturally, some of the groupings are quite theoretical, but, on the other hand, some are quite certain. One fragment had, stuck to the back, two little heaps of three sheets of leather one upon the other, and also a layer of a single sheet. Some of these pieces could be detached, and for these fragments at least the succession of the columns was certain. They came from a manuscript rolled *inside out*. Some approximate calculations show that the roll must have been more than 2 inches in diameter. The roll of the *War of the Sons of Light* was less than that. One fact is certain. These fragments come from a single roll and from the latter part of the manuscript. Two fragments bear signs of sewing. We have to suppose that all these fragments come from a rather voluminous manuscript, rolled back to front, and that some parts near the edge stuck together and broke off. What did this roll contain? Does it still exist or is it lost? It can be hoped that one day it will be found in the hands of a dealer or a collector. All that can be said at present is that this roll terminated in a series of benedictions, like the *Manual of Discipline* did with four psalms.

The benedictions seem to have been rather numerous. They were composed in one and the same environment. The order in which they are set forth and the persons to whom they are addressed are most significant.

To these benedictions the author also gives the title of *maskîl*, a term

---

[1] *Qumrân Cave I*, p. 119.

borrowed from the Psalms, and probably taken in the sense of a mascot or charm to bring good luck. The first group is addressed to the members of the sect or school in which the manuscript was drawn up. If really this group of benedictions comes first, we have a fact of great importance when it comes to determining the environment from which the roll comes. Unfortunately, apart from the echoes of some popular beliefs, there is nothing to show precisely what were the aims of the school or sect from which the manuscript emanated.

The benedictions of the second group seem to be addressed to the Warrior Messiah, the future ruler of the liberated people. Those of the third group are addressed to the Zadokites, destined to form the future government. The fourth group are addressed to the Nasi, the religious head of the Jews. In all probability the list of these good wishes went on and on. All the future dignitaries of the State and of the army must have had a right to these benedictions proportioned out so learnedly, whilst the "poor", the ordinary folk, were probably not overlooked. The passages which have been preserved or reconstructed from this curious work allow of certain possible conclusions.

We are not dealing here with copies of fragments from various sources, but with benedictions composed within one single environment. It was syncretistic, desiring to take account of the aspirations of all movements within Judaism. The Zadokites and their ex-priests were blessed before the Nasi of all Israel. That suggests that these benedictions were written before the breach between the Pharisees and the Zadokites had become complete. More important still, the members of the sect or school from which the manuscript comes were the first to be blessed. That could only be conceived where rabbis, steeped in their privileges, considered themselves the equals if not the superiors of princes. This rabbinic school had come to be greatly influenced by beliefs which were current among the peasants, especially that of the power of the word, capable of destroying the enemy "by the magic of the lips". We do not know the exact sense which was given to the word maskíl. Maybe these benedictions were intended to be carried as amulets by the persons for whom they were written.

It is hardly possible to give a date when these pieces were composed and written out at the end of the lost roll. It must be after A.D. 70 and before the revolt of A.D. 132. Perhaps it was during the Patriarchate of Rabbi Aqiba, the Nasi who was going to anoint Simon Bar Kochba and proclaim him the Messiah of Israel. It is unlikely that these maskíl were composed after the defeat of 135, as was the case with the roll of the *War*. The lost roll could have been placed in the *geniza* at a time when the Jews wished to remove from sight anything which recalled the ephemeral reign of him whom they now called Bar Kosibah, "the son of the lie".

vii

## THE *HABAKKUK COMMENTARY*

This roll is one of the St. Mark's Monastery collection of rolls, and consists of two sheets of leather sewn together. The first sheet contains seven columns of writing. The second sheet was ruled and had margins set out for seven columns also, but only six were used, and of these the last column has only four lines of writing. Following a kind of spiral line, the lower edge of all the columns has been destroyed, with signs of scorching, especially of columns II and III. This indicates that the roll has been passed through flames. The first column must have been wider than the others, but only some odd words at the end, the left-hand side, of the lines have survived. The second column has a considerable gap right down the middle. The other columns are relatively well preserved, especially in the upper part, where the edge is almost intact.

The writing on the whole is good, but without showing signs of exceptional care. Corrections have been made to the text, sometimes by another hand, and written between the lines. The concluding lines, the bottom of column XII and the four lines of column XIII, are an addition. In the quotations from the Book of Habakkuk, the name Yahweh is written in ancient "Phoenician" letters. In one place (II, 5) there is a letter *aleph* at the end of a line, and in eleven other places a cross shows that the space at the end of the line is not to be taken as an *alinea*.

The author has taken many liberties with the text of the Prophet's book. Moreover, the comments which he gives show that he frequently makes a play upon words, giving them a meaning that does not properly belong to them. The commentary is not one following the rules of the *pirûsh* or the *midrâsh*, but something quite different.

The author's method is to make a more or less free quotation of a verse from the prophet, and to follow it with a *pšr*—pronounced *pêsher*— saying, "its *pšr* concerns . . ." or, "its *pšr* is that . . .", etc. At times, the same verse, or some part from the verse, is given two different *pšrym*. There has been much discussion as to the precise meaning to be given to this word, but everybody agrees that the general sense is that of "explanation".

E*

"Interpretation", as the word is used in connection with dreams, oracles, etc., would appear to be the best term to use, yet in spite of this our roll is still called the *Habakkuk Commentary*.

It is characteristic of prophetic books that they lend themselves to a number of interpretations. The Book of Habakkuk in its present form in the Bible is a composite work, and, moreover, is always considered to be somewhat of a mystery. Never since it has been studied has there been agreement as to the events to which it refers. As a rule, prophetical books are written after the events to which they refer, and are dated back so as to prove that "it was written". That does not prevent the appearance of new interpretations of the Book of Habakkuk whenever there is another war, in the same way as there are published the predictions of Isaiah, Daniel, St. Odile, or the quatrains of Nostradamus, always with the purpose of showing that these works clearly refer to current events. This sort of thing must have been going on a long time. The roll we are considering is proof of that. Actually, the studies[1] made on this roll have not been concerned with the situation or the situations dealt with by the original authors of the Book of Habakkuk, but on what was the position of affairs when the interpreter wrote his *pêsher*.

Research on this point has produced very different results. Some discussions have arisen on points which are open to different interpretation; others where there is no possibility of uncertainty. Thus there have been long discussions as to whether or not the *Kittîm*, to whom there seemed to be reference in this text, were indeed the Romans. As a matter of fact, there is no mention *whatsoever* of the *Kittîm* (*ktim*). On the contrary, what is found is the word *kty'im* to be read *katya'îm*, "the legions", and clearly the reference is to the Roman legions. Where the text is supposed to report that "the *Kittîm* sacrificed to their standards", it has been asked if that could not apply to the Seleucids, etc.

It is, however, quite natural that the question should be raised as to what were the events to which the author of the *Commentary* made reference. What personage is hidden under the description "Teacher of Righteousness" (a title frequently given to very different persons)? Who were "the man of treachery", "the house of Absalom", "the wicked priest", the last-mentioned bearing "a theophorous name"? How should definite dates and facts presented in the *Commentary* be identified? What identifications are to be made of "the wicked priest who ground down the people",

---

[1] For a summary of the different theories, see H. H. Rowley, "The Internal Dating of the Dead Sea Scrolls", in *Ephemerides Theologicae Lovanienses*, XXVIII (1952), pp. 257-72.

and "the last priests" of Jerusalem who had had to give over to the legions all their gathered riches? Who was the speaker of untruth who had built a town of nothingness destined to destruction? Which massacres took place on a Sabbath, a day of fasting?

There can be no question but that the *Habakkuk Commentary* was a political pamphlet, intended to be widely circulated. Its aim was not to replace the Prophet's predictions by some new ones, but to show that what he had foretold had actually come to pass. Of whom was he speaking? To what was he alluding?

So long as the archaeological criterion supplied by the "Hellenistic" jars seemed assured, there was a desire to place in the second century B.C. the facts alluded to in this document. Some writers thought it possible to come down as far as the middle of the first century B.C., but that was regarded as almost the utmost limit. Since then the dating of this pottery has been recognised as an error, even by those who proposed it, yet the logical consequences which follow from it do not seem to have been acknowledged by an attempt to find a later date for the events referred to in the *Commentary*.

Moreover, all the efforts to identify persons and events in the end run up against contradictions which one tries to elude. The advocates of the theory that in the disaster which occurred on a Sabbath, a Day of Atonement (10th Tishri), there is an allusion to the taking of Jerusalem by Pompey on a day of fasting in the 179th Olympiad[1] overlook the fact that the Day of Atonement (*Yôm Kippûr*) is not the only Jewish day of fasting. It is the only one that coincides with a Sabbath day, but it is known that after a long resistance the Temple was taken by Pompey on "the seventeenth day of the fourth month [Tammuz], a day of fasting",[2] therefore not the 10th Tishri, the day of *Kippûr*, and consequently not on a Sabbath day.

The Wicked Priest may have many traits in common with Hyrcanus II, but it so happens that Hyrcanus II did not have a theophorous name, nor did he amass great wealth. We are told that he was "poor", and, "poor-spirited", forced to surrender to Antipater the greatest part of his income. Some people have liked to think that Absalom was maternal uncle to Aristobulus II and therefore brother to Alexandra, but as a matter of fact the Absalom in question was the fourth son of Hyrcanus I. At the time when many people wished to place the disposing of the manuscripts in

[1] Josephus, *Antiquities*, XIX, ii, 3.
[2] The date is given in *Yossipon*, Edition Bâle, IV, p. 23; Edition Venice, 39, p. 58a. The fast of 17th Tammuz (cf. Zech. 8.19) had been established in remembrance of the first Tables of the Law, broken by Moses (Exod. 32.19).

the cave at the end of the second century B.C. it was the fashion to identify the wicked priest with Alexander Jannaeus, but this also comes up against insurmountable contradictions. In spite of the play on words in Joel 11.23, where *mwrh* could mean either "teacher" or "rain", it is hardly possible to see a "Teacher of Righteousness" in Onias "the rain-maker". As a matter of fact, this personage has never been called "the rain-maker", but *ha-maghîl*, "the drawer of circles".

Others have wanted to carry the events even further back and identify the Wicked Priest with Menelaus, who had been nominated High Priest by Antiochus Epiphanes (187-163 B.C.), and who had assassinated a predecessor, one of the many bearing the name Onias who had become High Priest. Apart from other impossibilites, this would compel the identification of the Legions (*kty'îm*) with the Seleucids, which by no means would be in keeping with other facts in the text.

Among those who doubted if the archaeological criterion was sound and who sought to place the events in the first century A.D. were some who would have identified Jesus with the Teacher of Righteousness and St. Paul with either the Orator of Falsehood or the Wicked Priest. It is not easy to see how such a conclusion could be arrived at without giving a purely symbolic value to the whole of the "interpretation" of Habakkuk. The attempt has even been made to identify the Teacher of Righteousness with John the Baptist.

In the opinion of the present writer, there is only one interpretation which agrees with *all* the facts of the *Habakkuk Commentary*—the Teacher of Righteousness was named Menahem, and Absalom was his minister; the Wicked Priest with the theophorous name was Ananias; and the Orator of Falsehood should be identified with Agrippa II. The City of Nothingness which the last-named founded is Caesarea-Philippi, which Agrippa greatly beautified and to which he gave the name of Neronias. It is well known that it was one of the last of the Temple priests who did in fact himself hand over the treasury of the Sanctuary to the legionaries of Titus. The following is a brief summary of the facts:

Agrippa II, who had the habit of removing High Priests from office and putting in their place even Gentiles newly converted to Judaism, in A.D. 62 had bestowed the High Priesthood on a Zadokite, Anan, the son of Anan. Already subjected to all the Roman taxation, the country people were bowed down under the weight of a further burden, for the Zadokites would in no wise give up the ancient rights belonging to Anan's priesthood, and they showed themselves hard and haughty. There were protests. In consequence, Agrippa removed Anan and nominated as High Priest a person *"with a theophorous name"*—Ananias, "who was a priest of great merit, and who won the heart of everybody". At his accession, Ananias enjoyed therefore a degree of popularity, but that was not to last. Later on, Ananias was going to deserve the epithet, "The Wicked Priest".

As the inhabitants of the country districts, "the poor in Judah", still refused to contribute to the costs of the Temple administration in Jerusalem by the payment of tithes and first-fruits, Ananias had to resort to the employment of energetic collectors: "He had agents so evil that with others as bad as themselves they went into the barns to take by force the tithes due to the priests, and they beat up those who refused to surrender them." That was to lead to a state of civil war between the Temple and the rural population, from which the Zealots recruited their "men of the *maquis*", the Sicarii. One of Ananias's sons was taken prisoner by the Sicarii, who only released him after ten of their own number, prisoners in the hands of the Romans, had been given back. The liberation of these had been obtained by Ananias from the Procurator Albinus, and in everybody's eyes it proved that the High Priest was in league with the Romans. Moreover, it was known that he had officially introduced the worship of the Emperor into the Temple, and that he made no difficulty over gifts and sacrifices offered by pagans and apostates because he was short of money and the country people still refused to pay the Temple dues.

It was from his own family that arose the revolt against his proceedings. A grandson of Ananias, Eleazar ben Simon, and not a son, as Josephus has it, put himself at the head of a group of determined men, and took upon himself to forbid the priests to receive gifts from pagans. The priests were at pains to show that the greater part of the decorations of the Temple came from gifts made by foreigners, and that they could not refuse to sacrifice animals to the honour of the Emperor without incurring the hostility of the Romans, but it made no difference. Eleazar came with his men, occupied the Temple, and entrenched himself there. His grandfather Ananias had to ask for Roman troops to restore order.

Florus had succeeded Albinus as Procurator of Judea, and it was he who received the delegation headed by Simon—perhaps the Simon who had been held prisoner by the Sicarii—the son of Ananias and the father of Eleazar. The legionaries tried to drive out the insurgents from the Temple, but failed. Repulsed, they fell back on their barracks, where they were besieged by the followers of Eleazar.

We have no precise knowledge of the origins of Menahem nor of where he was at the time all this happened. In the light of events, it may be supposed that he was related to the former High Priest Anan, and that he had followed him into exile when he was deprived of his office in A.D. 62 or 63. In any case, it is certain that Menahem was not a son of Judas of Galilee, founder of the Zealot movement, as it says in Josephus.[1] All the information that we have about him confirms that he was a Zadokite, even if, a few days later, numerous Zealots joined him. Was it because he wished to re-establish Anan in his former office of High Priest that Menahem joined in with Eleazar's sedition? We cannot tell. All that Josephus[1] tells us is "that, having won over some men of note"—that is to say, some Zadokites—Menahem marched on Jerusalem, which he entered on a Saturday, the 8th Ab (July-August) A.D. 66. The following day, 9th Ab, a day of fasting in remembrance of the destruction of the Temple of Solomon in 586 B.C., the anniversary of so many misfortunes, Menahem won his first victory over the Romans.

The understanding between Eleazar and Menahem, if ever it existed, was of short duration. The Feast of Xylophoria, when they consecrated the wood brought to the Temple for the everlasting fire, was observed on the 15th Ab. This year it fell on a Saturday, the Sabbath. Trouble broke out between the supporters of Eleazar and those of Menahem. The latter set fire to several public buildings. The Public Records Office and the High Priest's Palace were given to the flames. That same day, the Saturday following the 9th Ab, Menahem's troops attacked the fortress of Antonia and cut to pieces the Roman garrison. The High Priest Ananias and his supporters tried to save themselves and hid in the sewers, and stayed there three weeks.

That Saturday, Menahem became master of the place. A short time afterwards, he left Jerusalem with a small company to capture the Roman armoury at Masada. "After having armed a number of his own people who had nothing to lose, and some robbers who had joined him, he returned to Jerusalem in royal state, made himself head of the revolt, and gave orders for the siege of the upper palace to be continued."[2] These events should be placed towards the end of the month Ab. Having in vain asked Menahem that he would assure their voluntary retirement, the Romans had to abandon the Stratopedon and defend themselves in the royal towers. On the 6th Elûl (August-September), Menahem's troops gave

[1] Josephus, *Wars of the Jews,* II, xvii, 8.
[2] *Ibid.*

themselves to pillage and massacre. Ananias and his followers were discovered in the sewers and the next day, also a Saturday, put to death.

This act could only aggravate the division between Eleazar, grandson of the High Priest and still master of the Temple, and Menahem, master of the town. This state of affairs continued till the month of Tishri (September-October) which marks the beginning of the Jewish religious year. On 1st Tishri, the Feast of Trumpets, Menahem in royal robes and accompanied by many armed men, went to the Temple to worship God. "Then Eleazar and several others assembed there said that, having revolted against the Romans for the purpose of recovering their freedom, it would be disgraceful if they accepted as master a man inferior to themselves, even if he had not been as violent as Menahem. . . . They threw themselves upon him, and the people took up stones to stone him."[1] Abandoned by his followers, Menahem fled, but, having been found in a place called *Ophlah,* where he was in hiding, he was dragged out and publicly executed, after having endured countless tortures. The principal ministers of his tyranny, and especially *Absalom,* were treated in the same way. Eleazar had betrayed his ally.

The date when Menahem and his ministers were put to death is not given by Josephus, but can easily be reckoned. It could only have been the 1st Tishri, the Jewish New Year.

Eleazar now found himself at the head of a revolt which was greater than he had foreseen. It was to him that the Roman besieged in Jerusalem turned to arrange a capitulation. The pourparlers lasted a whole week. In the end, Eleazar promised under oath that their lives would be spared if they laid down their arms. Menahem's followers had no such intention. As soon as the Romans were unarmed, they fell upon them and massacred them. "Mutitius, the Roman commander, was the only one not slain, for he not only implored that his life should be spared, but went so far as to promise to be circumcised."[2]

The massacre of the Romans plunged all the town into grief and sorrow, for the "carnage was so much more horrible because it took place on a Sabbath day, a day on which our religion required us to abstain from all work even if it is sacred".[3] This particularly sacred Sabbath was the 10th Tishri, the *Yôm Kippûr,* the Day of Atonement, which this year fell on a Saturday. The date is easily arrived at. The Roman repression followed

[1] Josephus, *Wars of the Jews,* II, xvii, 9.
[2] *Ibid.*
[3] Josephus, *Wars, passim.*

almost immediately. Cestius Gallus, the Governor of Syria, marched on Jerusalem, and must have reached Gibeon, half a dozen miles from Jerusalem, on the 17th Tishri, at the time of the Feast of Tabernacles, which lasted a week from the 15th to the 21st Tishri. "The Jews . . . abandoned the ceremonies of this great feast and, without even observing the Sabbath, which hitherto they had kept so religiously, they ran to arms."

The day of *Kippûr,* A.D. 66 was to be a date particularly inauspicious for the Jews: "It happened as if by the act of Providence that on that same day and at the same hour the people of Caesarea cut the throats of the Jews, so that of 30,000 living in that town, not one escaped." At Scythopolis, the Zadokites joined with foreigners and massacred 13,000 Jews and pillaged their belongings. Such a deed can only be accounted for if Menahem was a Zadokite, and the Zadokites there were avenging his death. Other massacres took place in Ascalon, Ptolemais, Tyre, and even in Alexandria. Josephus saw in this divine retribution for the crimes committed by the followers of Menahem. On the other hand, the Zadokites interpreted these disasters as the vengeance of God for the treacherous assassination of his "Elect", the "Teacher of Righteousness".

To the very day, four years after the first arrival of Menahem at Jerusalem, the 9th Ab, A.D. 70, the Temple became a prey to flames, and the armies of Titus pillaged Jerusalem. One of the last of the priests, a man "named Jesus the son of Thebuth, whose life Titus had promised to preserve on condition that he handed over a part of the Temple treasury, took out and passed over the wall of this holy place two candlesticks, some tables, cups and vases, of heavy massive gold, and also some veils, precious stones, and a number of vessels appertaining to the sacrifices".

As to Caesarea-Philippi, formerly an object of strife between Jews and Syrians, and on a number of occasions the scene of bloodshed, it was abandoned by the Jews, who left carrying away their sacred books. The town was later rebuilt by Agrippa II and given the name of Neronias in honour of the Emperor. "So as to embellish this town, he had brought there the greatest part of all the rarest things in his kingdom, and also a number of excellent statues of the greatest men of antiquity. This display made him odious to his subjects, who could not bear the fact that he robbed their towns of their greatest ornaments in order to embellish a foreign town." Caesarea, however, was indeed a *Town of Nothingness.* The Jews who went back to live there were massacred two years after its new foundation on the 10th Tishri, A.D. 66. The Zadokites could see in all that a punishment from God.

The death of Menahem, and the valiant conduct of his brother at Masada, must have greatly encouraged the birth of legends around him whom many Jews still considered to have been the Messiah. "Is not his name clearly stated in the Bible (Lam. 1.10)?" they said. Shortly after the fall of Jerusalem, it would appear that there was a belief that he was going to come to life again. Perhaps it was even believed that he had appeared to his disciples some days after his execution: "We have the firm conviction that even if the Temple was destroyed because of him [Menahem], it is still because of him that it will be re-built." It was recalled that Aaron died on 1st Tishri (Num. 33.38), the Jewish New Year's Day, "date on which die all the just (*saddiqîm*)". The anniversary of his death is put on, however, to the 10th Tishri, for on that day of *Kippûr* seven disasters at once fell on the people of Israel: following the death of priest, prophet, and judge, innocent blood had been spilt. It was the Sabbath day and also the day of *Kippûr*. It was further said that it was sufficient for the name of Menahem to be invoked, and Jerusalem would be reborn.

Even in our days, the name of Menahem is often given to children born round about the 9th Ab. Is the thought there that perhaps one of them may be the reincarnation of the Messiah? The name Menahem is given to all the month of Ab,[1] and in some parts, the Saturday following the 9th Ab is called "Shabbat Menahem".

R. Eisler seems to have placed the events in the same period, whilst identifying the Prophet of Lying with Menahem, and the Teacher of Righteousness with John the Baptist.[2] For Menahem to have been regarded as the Prophet of Lying, the writer of the *Habakkuk Commentary* would have had to have been pro-Roman, opposed to the liberation, and that was not the case.

★      ★      ★

There would have been no point in bringing the *Habakkuk Commentary* into the discussion about the Essenes if certain people did not still persist in seeing in the Teacher of Righteousness mentioned in the text the founder of this hypothetical sect in the second century or the middle of

[1] It may be pointed out that the Preface to *Meghilloth Genuzoth I* is signed by E. L. Sukenik and dated from Jerusalem, Menahem, Ab 5708 (August 1948).

[2] In a letter to *The Times*, 8th September 1949, referred to by H. H. Rowley, *The Internal Dating*, pp. 268-9. When somebody is regarded by one person as a Teacher of Righteousness and by another as a Prophet of Lying, it does not necessarily mean that they are both mistaken. R. Eisler speaks from a non-Jewish point of view, and in his opinion Menahem was a "false messiah". As a matter of fact, the present-day point of view is that any messiah who did not succeed was "false". People reasoned at times in a different fashion in the first century A.D.

the first century B.C. It is a very curious thing that this identification and this dating of events is still maintained, although the *Habakkuk Commentary* is *dated* by an expression, or, rather, a grammatical form, which only appeared in Hebrew towards the end of the 1st century A.D.[1] It is also found in a text from Murabba'at which can be dated A.D. 132.

Were we not dealing with a pamphlet on current affairs, it might be admitted that a copyist of the first century could reproduce an older text, but as the facts present themselves this hypothesis cannot be sustained. Who is interested today in the interpretations of the Book of Daniel which were current in 1916 and 1917? Can we imagine a Jew after the events of A.D. 70 lamenting the entry into Jerusalem of Pompey 139 years before?

The *Habakkuk Commentary* found in a cave near to the Dead Sea was a political pamphlet. It cannot have any connection with some sort of confraternity of hypothetical Essenes or of "monks of Qumrân".

★       ★       ★

At the end of the eighth century A.D., the newly formed sect of the Qaraites must have known about certain manuscripts coming from *genizoth* in the neighbourhood of Jericho or Qumrân. Among all that Qirqisâni styled useless verbiage, were there any writings that told of the dismissal from office of the High Priest Anan, his departure into exile (Damascus) and the coming to Jerusalem of his son (?), Menahem? It was said that one of the names of the Messiah foretold in the Bible was Anan, the "cloud", by whom God was going to manifest Himself. Now, it happened that the founder of the Qaraite movement was also called Anan. Certain Qaraites of the ninth and tenth centuries may have come to believe that the ancient manuscripts discovered in the caves included the prediction of what had happened a century or so before their own time.[2] They may have come to confuse the High Priest Anan of the first century with the Qaraite Anan of the eighth century, and they may have applied to the latter the title of Teacher of Righteousness. Obviously that

---

[1] See p. 147.

[2] Simply as a curiosity, it may be recalled that a Constantinople rabbi, Abraham Yakhini, agent of the Dutch collector, Varner, in 1651 produced an old manuscript, probably faked, in which was written: "A son will be born to Mordechai Zvi, and this child will receive the name of Shabetai [the name of the planet Saturn, predestined to be the name of the liberator of Israel]. He will save Israel and put the dragon to death." Shabetai Zvi, born at Smyrna in 1629, had worked out from the Zohar that the Messianic Age would begin in 1666. He was one of the last "messiahs" of Judaism, and the sect founded by him even now has numerous adherents, officially Moslems.

is no reason for us to make confusion in the opposite direction. To claim that whenever in a text one comes across the expression "Teacher of Righteousness" it must refer to just one and the same person is the same as saying that whenever there is mention of an "Anointed" this word should be translated by "Cyrus" (Isa. 45.1).

Even if the Qaraites did more or less deliberately mix up Anan and Anan, even if they did use a form of speech copied from ancient manuscripts which came from caves in Judea, there is no need for similar confusions to be made in our time. There is no reason for directly connecting the medieval fragments from Cairo with the *Habakkuk Commentary* or with the *Manual of Discipline*, which has already been dealt with.

At the time that the Book of the Prophet Habakkuk was written, it was a "tract for the times". When it was "interpreted", whether after the war of A.D. 70 or during that other war of 1914-18, it served the same purpose for the events of those later days. Once those events had passed, all these interpretations would lose their interest—unless they themselves were also given a sibylline character and considered as capable of providing fresh interpretations. In principle, therefore, the *Habakkuk Commentary* was neither a library volume nor a book to be carefully preserved for the ages to come. It was a "present-day pamphlet", intended to be broadcast among the people. Two points, therefore, remain to be established: (a) When and by whom can it have been written? And (b) when and by whom can it have been seized and consigned to the *geniza*?

In dealing with writing which, like Hebrew, is considered as almost sacred, the palæographic criterion is far from sure. The shape of letters is preserved unchanged for a long time. One can distinguish greater or less skill of the scribes, and also certain regional forms, but, for the present at any rate, precise dating is out of the question. From the use of the form *'bît,* one can conclude that a text was written towards the end of the first century A.D., or it may be necessary to date it as late as the early years of the second century. In any case, the pamphlet was written after the fall of Jerusalem in A.D. 70. The present writer had put the date of composition between 74 and 78, most probably about A.D. 75, though he had not ruled out the possibility that in column X, lines 3-5, there might be an allusion to the eruption of Vesuvius in A.D. 79. A better acquaintance of the Jewish world in the first centuries of our era, obtained from further manuscripts from the Dead Sea published more recently, has compelled him to put the date a little later.

The pamphlet seems to have been written with the intention of creating a fresh understanding between the Zadokites and the Zealots, in view of a new rising against the Roman rule. In the new army, the Zadokites would take command, and the "simple" of Judah should follow their orders (XII, 3-4). The (or, a) Teacher of Righteousness was going to reappear and lead the people to victory. It is therefore undeniably a writing that cannot be styled purely Zadokite. The very fact that a Book of the Prophet was taken as the starting-point puts it outside Zadokite circles, where no importance was attached to such writings. We therefore need to seek its author in a popular environment which was unorthodox from the rabbinic point of view, yet not hostile to the Zadokites. Because of this, the author can hardly be looked for in Palestinian surroundings, nor in any which were strictly Zealot.

The *Habakkuk Commentary* was written in popular Jewish circles, where the belief in Menahem had been kept up. It may have been composed in a town of the Diaspora during the years between the destruction of the Temple and the first ideas of revenge and the rising of A.D. 115 which followed the earthquake at Antioch. We think we shall not be far out if we suppose that the pamphlet was published towards the end of the first century A.D., perhaps first of all in a town in Syria, and from there introduced into Palestine. Two arguments strengthen this hypothesis:

(1) Corrections have been made to the text by an unskilled hand. This leads one to suppose that the roll, written by an expert scribe, afterwards passed through the hands of someone less used to writing.

(2) The second writer was not satisfied with making corrections. He also completed in his own way the interpretation of 2.18, and added the two verses, 19 and 20, with a short commentary from the same point of view which was not that of the author.

This last remark suggests that in the version of the Book of Habakkuk known to the writer of the *pêsher* the Book went only as far as 2.18. When and by whom were added the last two verses of that chapter and the prayer which forms Chapter 3 in the present-day version? It is difficult to say, but most probably the addition was made in Palestine in the first century A.D. We can therefore suppose that the writer of the roll, who had at his disposal only the ancient version of the Book of the Prophet, was living in the Diaspora. The handwriting places him in a cultured class.

On the other hand, the person who corrected and continued the *Commentary* knew a version of the Book of Habakkuk which was longer by two verses. His handwriting and spelling show that he did not belong to a very cultured class. It will be noticed that he did not use the final *m* and displays some hesitation in writing $t$ and certain other letters. It will also be noticed that although the author at times uses the long form of the pronoun *hmh*, he always writes the short form, *-hm*, when the pronoun is preceded by a preposition, as in *'lhm; 'lhm*. The continuator, however, writes *lhmh* in XII, 14, using the long form with a preposition. As to his interpretation of verses 19 and 20, it cannot be said to be very brilliant. We think, therefore, that he should be placed in a peasant community of Palestine at the end of the first century A.D.

It was the time when in Palestine Rabbi Gamaliel II was given the title of *Nasi* by the Roman Procurator of Antioch. Rabbi Gamaliel strove vigorously against dissident rabbinic schools and everywhere made them take their books to the *geniza*. By this order, a number of other writings were burnt. It is not therefore ruled out that the *Habakkuk Commentary* may have been seized in his time and placed in the cave after having been "half" burnt, this being the reason for the loss of the lower part of all the columns.

The drawing up of the *Commentary* can hardly be dated in the second decade of the second century A.D., preceding the rising of Bar Kochba in A.D. 132. An allusion to "the Star", though slight, must have been seen in it. Shortly after the death of Rabbi Gamaliel II, the centre of Jewish authority was moved from Jamnia to Usha, and Rabbi Aqiba, the head of this school, was a supporter of the new war. It would not, therefore, have been he who would have seized a work encouraging a war of revenge, as the *Habakkuk Commentary* does. It is not possible to place the work at any later date. Books written after A.D. 135 bear unmistakably the mark of that period.

There are thus two possibilities: either the *Habakkuk Commentary* was seized by the rabbinic authorities of Jamnia and taken to the *geniza* about A.D. 110—which does not exclude the possibility that other rolls may have been placed there later—or the roll may have been a chance discovery during one of the searches made under the Patriarchate of Rabbi Simon III, and consigned to the *geniza* at the beginning of the reign of Marcus Aurelius, round about A.D. 163. In that case, it would have to be admitted that the roll had been preserved by its owners for more than half a century, which would hardly be probable when one thinks of the war that had taken place during that time.

Obviously, had the *Habakkuk Commentary* been found *in situ*, and not after it had been passed from hand to hand, it would have been much easier to settle the question, manuscripts having been deposited in the *geniza* at several successive dates. If only it was absolutely *sure* that the roll was found in the same jar as the *Manual of Discipline*, there would be serious grounds for supposing that it had been part of a collection—according to the present writer's hypothesis—the collection seized from the school of Emmaus. But it is certain that the manuscript was not drawn up there, and the handwriting of the continuator bears little resemblance to that of the scribes of the *Manual of Discipline*.

viii

## THE *BOOK OF THE WAR OF THE SONS OF LIGHT AGAINST THE SONS OF DARKNESS*

This manuscript is the best preserved of those bought in 1947 by the Hebrew University of Jerusalem. It was found rolled inside out, and so the beginning of the text is fairly well preserved, but the end has suffered from the ravages of time. It is impossible to say how long the original roll was. We possess the upper part of eighteen columns written on four sheets of leather sewn end to end, with a fragment of the nineteenth column, the remainder of which is lost. As already indicated, all the lower part of the sheets, almost half, has been destroyed below an almost regular spiral line. In places, this line shows clear signs of scorching, and from this fact we can conclude that the roll was passed through flames. The upper part of the sheets shows little sign of deterioration, and the margin is preserved throughout its whole length. Some fragments, separated from the rest of the roll by the action of time, have been restored to their respective positions. Inside the roll was found a leather strap 14 inches long, which originally served to keep the roll closed.

The text is in beautiful writing, and has only a few corrections. The greater part of these are by the hand of the same scribe, and have been inserted between the lines. One alteration by erasure or washing out has, however, been found (XI, 6). It refers to a Biblical quotation.

The leather of the roll is exceptionally fine. Its light-grey or bluish tint distinguishes it from all other rolls published up till now. One can assume that the holes visible on the right of the first page indicate where the strap was attached. This would be at about half the height of the roll. If the lower margin was of the same width as the upper, each column must have had about twenty-three lines. Actually, no more than fourteen have been preserved.

One notices immediately that the roll does not contain a continuous text. A number of dissimilar fragments, separated from each other by *alineas,* and even frequently by blank lines, have been copied out, one after another and in no definite order. One is surprised at the number of repetitions and parallel versions of the same text that one meets. These different sections often reflect contradictory ideas, and it is quite evident that they emanate from different tendencies in Judaism, very much opposed one to another. In some places it is easy to recognise a gloss by the compiler, or some phrases which can only have come from his pen, yet on the whole it may be said that the copyist has faithfully reproduced the passage that he had before him. Frequently even he gives the impression that he had not got hold of their real meaning. At times he makes a mistake and copies texts which have nothing to do with the *Battle Manual* which he wanted to compile.

As with the *Manual of Discipline*, the present writer has endeavoured, as far as possible, to assign authorship to each of these fragments, and to establish its date. That does not mean that a number of these pieces may not go back to some older prototypes, nor that different authors may not have elaborated themes already known, and each one in his own way. These older elements can be reconstituted by bringing parallel passages together and noting their points of agreement. As the base for quite a number of regulations, old Biblical injunctions will be found.[1] Research for the original texts, which are not found in their pure state in this manuscript, would lead us too far. It has seemed more useful to tabulate first of all the fragments which make up this roll:

| | | |
|---|---|---|
| I, 1-7 . . . | | Introduction in the form of an historic survey. Extract from a popular work composed in the Diaspora, probably on the left bank of the Euphrates, a little before A.D. 130. |
| I, 8-10 . . | | Interpolation by the compiler. |
| I, 10-15 . . | | Continuation of the historic survey. |
| I, 16-17 . . | | Interpolation by the compiler. |
| II, 1-6 . . | | Regulations about service in an idealised Temple. Extract from a Zadokite work of the Diaspora, composed after A.D. 70. |
| II, 6-9 . . | | Gloss by the compiler. |
| II, 9-14 . . | | Preparation for the coming war. The work of the compiler or emanating from his circle. |
| II, 15ff. . . | | Incomplete fragment. |
| III, 1-11 . . | | Regulations for the *seven trumpets with long inscriptions*. Extract from a popular writing, composed before A.D. 66. |
| III, 13-IV, 5 . | | Regulations for the *numerous ensigns with long inscriptions*. Extract from the same work. |

[1] For the quotations from the Old Testament, see J. Carmignac, *Revue Biblique*, LXIII, (1956), pp. 234-60, 375-90.

IV, 6-8 . . Regulations for the *four ensigns with short inscriptions*. Extract from another popular work, dating from before A.D. 66.

IV, 9-14 . . Regulations for the *eight ensigns with short inscriptions*. Extract from a third popular work, dating from before A.D. 66.

IV, 15ff. . . Regulations concerning the length of the staffs for the ensigns. Extract from the same work.

IV(?)-V, 2 . . Inscription on the *Nasi's* shield. Extract from a popular work.

V, 3-14 . . Regulations for the formation of front-line troops and description of weapons. Extract from a work probably written in the Diaspora after A.D. 135.

V, 16-VI, 6 . First version of the battle. Extract from a popular work by the author of the long inscription.

VI, 8-11 . . Description of the cavalry. Extract from a writing composed in the Diaspora.

VI, 11ff. . . Regulations for the chariots and the cavalry. Extract from a Zadokite writing from before A.D. 66.

VII, 1-2 . . Conclusion of an extract from Zadokite regulations.

VII, 2-7 . . Regulations for troops and the "purity" of camps. Extract from a Zealot work of before A.D. 66.

VII, 9-VIII, 12 . Second version of the battle. Extract from a Zadokite work written before A.D. 66, with an interpolation at the beginning describing the costume of the High Priest.

VIII, 12ff. . . Third version of the battle. Same date and place of origin.

IX, 1-9 . . Fourth version of the battle. Extract from a Zadokite work written after A.D. 70 and perhaps after A.D. 132.

IX, 10-16(?) . Regulations for certain military formations called "towers". Extract from a popular writing, composed before A.D. 66.

IX(?)-XII, 5 . Commentaries on Biblical passages, and praise of "the poor". Extracts from a writing probably drawn up before A.D. 130, but recast with interpolations by the compiler.

XII, 7-16 . . Popular version of an ancient hymn.

XII, 17ff. . . Fragment of a popular work.

XIII, 1-6 . . Extract from the initiation regulations of a Zadokite lodge in the Diaspora, written between A.D. 70 and A.D. 130.

XIII, 7-16 . Popular prayers, probably re-edited about A.D. 130.

XIII, 18-XIV, 1 . Fragments of popular prayers.

XIV, 2-4 . . Regulations for after the battle. Extract from a Zealot writing from before A.D. 66.

XIV, 4ff. . . Collection of popular prayers.

XV, 1-3 . . Fragment from a *Commentary on Ezekiel*. Extract from a popular writing composed after A.D. 70 and before A.D. 132.

XV, 4-XVI, 1 . Ritual for entering into war. Extract of a Zadokite writing from the Diaspora.

XVI, 3-9 . . Fifth version of the battle. Extract from a Zadokite writing.

XVI, 11-14 . Fragment of a version of the battle, in which a reverse is anticipated. Extract from a Zadokite work written in the Diaspora.

| | | |
|---|---|---|
| XVI, 15-XVII, 3 . | | Commentary on those dying in the war. Comes probably from a popular writing of before A.D. 130. |
| XVII, 4-9 . | . | Another version of the call to battle. Probably an extract from the same work. |
| XVII, 10ff. . | . | Sixth version of the battle. Extract from a later Zadokite writing (about A.D. 130?). |
| XVIII, 1-8 | . | Fragment of a compilation drawn up in the Diaspora, with an historic preamble (1-3) and a call to war. Probably written about A.D. 160. |
| XVIII, 10ff. | . | Prayer for liberation. Extract from the same compilation. |
| XIX, 1-7 . | . | Second and less popular version of an ancient hymn already reproduced in XII, 7-16. Taken from the same compilation. |
| XIX, 9ff. . | . | Regulation for after the battle. Comes from a Zadokite writing drawn up in the Diaspora about A.D. 130. Extract from the same compilation. |

The first remark that will be made on going through this long and varied list of documents is that none of them agrees with the Pharisaic tendencies of before A.D. 66, nor with those of the school of Jamnia (A.D. 80-130), nor with the teaching of the rabbis after A.D. 135. All are unorthodox, some to a greater, others to a less degree, and at the same time are often in opposition one to another. What explanation can be given for the compilation of such a roll as that of the *War of the Sons of Light against the Sons of Darkness?* By whom can it have been written, and for what purpose? All these questions find their answers if one studies carefully the last two columns of the roll. What do we find there if not extracts from another compilation in all points similar to the one we have here? We read there an abridgment of the same historical introduction, and even the same hymn which had been copied out earlier in the roll. All this shows that the editor of this roll was not the first person who had wanted to draw up a *manual of tactics,* utilising Hebrew fragments more or less ancient. He had had a predecessor, and even believed that he should add to his own work material copied from that predecessor's book.

There was therefore a moment in Jewish history, subsequent to the defeat of A.D. 135 when in certain circles it was thought that the hour for a war of revenge had again struck, and that preparations for the war should be made by studying the instructions written either on the eve of the war of A.D. 66 or before Bar Kochba's rising. The former writings, which had circulated among the Zadokites and Zealots, certainly had not all been destroyed. Some fragments of them had been preserved, especially in the Diaspora, where rabbinic censorship was not so strict. Whatever tendency they represented, all these writings had a naïve side to them. Excessive importance was attached to the external signs of Roman power—to ensigns, to the decoration of weapons, to trumpet-calls. Yet at the same time there was an anxiety to conform with the Biblical commandments for the War of Jahweh. The Zadokites would not so much as dream that anyone other than a priest could take military command. The ordinary people interpreted the texts from the Bible in the sense that "the poor"—"the cattle", as they called them—would be called to free the country from the Roman yoke.

What had been collected as fragments of this kind had then been recopied, in no fixed order, but somewhat haphazardly, by Jews who belonged to no definite school of thought. They looked upon themselves as Jews, even if their beliefs had been somewhat affected by contact with Greek and Persian civilisations. We should probably look for these Jews on the banks of the Euphrates, at Dura, or even further north at Carchemish and Edessa. They too had hopes of a liberation, and must often have dreamed of the land of their fathers being reconquered. The fact that the writer of our roll had copied out so many fragments which could not have been written in Palestine is in itself a sufficient indication that he lived in the Diaspora. Certain geographical indications allow the placing of him on the left bank of the Euphrates.

It remains to discover the time when these Jews of the Diaspora could have believed that the moment for world-wide freedom had come. Several passages in the manuscript say clearly that *all* the inhabited world was to be freed from the Roman domination. Israel, in its turn, would be called to colonise vast territories where the legionaries were provisionally living as masters. That moments had indeed seemed to have come at the beginning of the reign of Marcus Aurelius, when, in A.D. 161-3, the Parthians began to harass the eastern frontier of the Roman Empire. Threatened on several fronts, the Emperor entrusted the conduct of the war in the East to his half-brother, Verus, who had only weak forces at his disposal. It was thought, therefore, that this time the Parthians would really liberate Judea, and not merely for a few months, as it had been two centuries before when, in 40 B.C., with their aid, Antigonus had succeeded in driving out the ethnarch, Herod. The Jews in Palestine were to take an active part in this new war for freedom, but, as is well known, the rabbinic authority was opposed to any new rising.

The accession of Antoninus Pius (A.D. 138-61) had brought to an end in Judea the persecutions which had stained the reign of Hadrian and led to the revolt of Bar Kochba. There had in fact been a few sporadic risings, but the repression of them had not been the occasion of great massacres. That was partly due to the wise diplomacy of Rabbi Simon III, who had even succeeded in having the authority of the Palestine Sanhedrin re-established and himself given the title of *Nasi*. Rabbi Simon III fixed his residence at Usha, and from there maintained an energetic oversight of the Jews placed under his control. Even if he could not prevent all uprisings, he at least used his influence to see that there was no great bloodshed when they were put down. When the Parthian attacks raised new hopes among the Jews, Rabbi Simon took energetic measures to prevent a fresh war in Judea, which could only have led to further disasters.

Rabbi Simon III possessed sufficient authority and power to seize subversive writings introduced into Palestine by Jews from the Diaspora. It can also be admitted that it was under his patriarchate that such a roll as the *War* could have been taken to the *geniza*. It is also about this time that it would have been possible to write the roll, while the nature of the leather clearly indicates a foreign origin.

One more question may be asked: Why was not the roll put into the fire and destroyed? It was subversive enough to merit such a fate, but, on the other hand, it contains quotations from the Bible. God's name was written there, and twice it was written in a form regarded as particularly sacred. In such cases the law of *meḥeṣeh* comes into play: thus it is that half this roll was burnt, and the other half placed in the *geniza*.

The roll of the *War* is a composite work, like the *Manual of Discipline* and the *Book of the Hymns of Thanksgiving*. The date of the different component parts stretches out probably from Maccabean times (XII, 7-16, XIX, 1-3) to the end of the reign of Antoninus Pius, or the beginning of the reign of Marcus Aurelius. Our roll must have been taken into Palestine shortly after it was written, and was probably seized immediately. After having been passed through the flames and half-burnt, the remaining part was taken to a *geniza* near to the Dead Sea. That is the only explanation that the present writer can see for this curious find.[1]

\*　　　\*　　　\*

[1] Several writers have tried to interpet the *War of the Sons of Light against the Sons of Darkness* from the point of view of an association with Essenian monks of Qumrân. Theodor H. Gaster, in his *The Dead Sea Scriptures*, London, 1957, pp. 257-60, sees in it a call to a mimic combat to hasten the triumph of spring over winter. This drama, echoes of which can be found in the folklore of most peoples, would here be carried from the sphere of the seasons to that of eschatology, and we would have a sort of sham fight in preparation for the day when the forces of Good would do battle with those of Evil. This roll would be a "kind of G.H.Q. manual" for the guidance of the Brotherhood at Armageddon (Rev. 16.16).

The problem arises once more as to the date when the manuscripts in Cave I at Qumrân were placed there.

Pottery fragments of different periods have been found in this and several other caves. These finds have been interpreted on the supposition that the caves had been "visited" on various occasions and that the diggers took away certain manuscripts and left the others. Is it still necessary to emphasise how unlikely that is? When an order was given to carry away one or more manuscripts to a *geniza,* the instructions would be rather vague from the very nature of the case, a *geniza* being a place secret or hidden. Probably the place where it would be found was only indicated very approximately. If those bringing the manuscripts happened to find the exact place, they would put the manuscripts at the side of those already there. This is just what seems to have happened on several occasion in Cave I. If those whose duty it was to inter the books did not find the *geniza,* they carried out their duty by putting them in some neighbouring cave—which thus became a new *geniza.*

When one or other of these *genizoth* was dug into during the Middle Ages, it would be emptied of all its contents. It would be an astonishing thing if these excavators sorted out their finds on the spot, taking some and leaving others. As a matter of fact, the discoveries in the region of Qumrân seem to give good proof that a number of caves were emptied of their contents long ago, there being found there now only some débris of pottery and some minute scraps of manuscripts. On the other hand, those caves which the excavators had not discovered contained whole rolls and complete sheets of manuscripts in more or less good condition.

The roll of the *War of the Sons of Light against the Sons of Darkness* was certainly not a unique specimen. As stated above, this copy from Cave I reproduces at the end several columns of a similar compilation. The works themselves, from which the fragments joined together here were subsequently borrowed, must have had a wide circulation. In other caves of Qumrân, a number of similar writings have been found. As yet it is impossible to say whether they are pages from a homogeneous work, more or less ancient, or if, with these also, we are dealing with pages separated from compilations of the same kind as the roll of the *War of the Sons of Light against the Sons of Darkness* found in Cave I.

ix

## THE *THANKSGIVING HYMNS*

A description has already been given of the state of this manuscript at the time it was bought—just a couple of shapeless bundles. The first contained three sheets of leather, not sewn one to another, and each having on it four columns of writing. Two sheets were filled with regular and well-shaped writing. This has been put down as the work of Scribe "A". It is also to be noted that in two places (I, 26 and II, 34) the word "God" is written as it were in italics, an imitation of ancient Hebrew writing being used. There are very few corrections, and these have been inserted between the lines or in the margin, and as a rule they are by some other hand. The third sheet contains two and a half columns in the writing of Scribe "A", and the following one and a half columns are in the writing of Scribe "B". This writing may be described as crude and careless. It would look as if the second scribe had not often had occasion to use a pen for writing Hebrew. There are many more corrections in his work than in that of his predecessor. That is about all that one can say about the hand-writing of this scroll. The palæographic criterion, so often appealed to in the dating of Dead Sea manuscripts, in this case gives no clue. In fact, would not the kind of arguments put forward up till now prove that the second scribe wrote some centuries before the one who wrote the preceding lines on the same page!

The second bundle yielded one sheet from Scribe "A". It contains three columns, but neither the first nor the third has the characteristic holes made by a needle at the beginning or end of a sheet forming part of a roll. There was also a fairly large piece of leather with signs of sewing on the right, and another fragment revealed holes made by a needle on the left. Can it be that there was a single sheet of five columns? That is hardly probable, yet the text has been edited as if it was so. A dozen fairly large fragments covered with the handwriting of "B" have made possible the partial reconstruction of two more columns, two fragments of the first, three of the second. But traces of sewing to the right or left of certain other smaller pieces suggest that there must have been at least four columns from the hand of this scribe. It may be agreed that they were a continuation of the third sheet of the first bundle. There are sixty-six other pieces found in the second bundle, some in the handwriting of "A", and others in that of "B". As a rule, they are very small and only bear a few words, sometimes even only a few letters.

Naturally, it is impossible to re-establish the order in which these reconstructed columns followed each other. The most that can be said is that the columns in handwriting "B" should be placed in the latter part of what was originally a single roll. Though it may be well to establish the sequence of the fragments, yet the question is not so important as one might suppose, for the manuscript is not of a continuous text, but of a collection of hymns, very different one from another, and having no connection with each other. The different hymns are quite distinct, and easily separated from each other, thanks to a formula at the beginning of each which runs as a rule, "I give Thee thanks, my Lord . . ." It is because of this formula that the roll has been named *The Book of the Hymns of Thanksgiving*. In addition, these hymns come from different environments, and at times give expression to definitely contradictory religious ideas. Frequently it is found that a hymn is in reality a composite work made up of different fragments.

It is difficult to make out the rôle of the scribes in the editing of these hymns. Did they limit themselves to copying faithfully, and without troubling about their order, certain texts which they wished to collect, as was the case with the scribes of the *Manual of Discipline*? Did they add to it anything of their own, as the scribe of the *War* did? Provisionally we may suppose that their personal contribution to the texts is negligible, and we may take the different hymns as relatively faithful copies of the original pieces.

Following the order of the texts as published we find:

| | | |
|---|---|---|
| I, 1–20 | . . | A popular fragment which could have been written after A.D. 6 and before the war of A.D. 66. |
| I, 21–31 | . . | A Zadokite fragment of uncertain date. |
| I, 32ff. | . . | A popular fragment in which there is reference to the "poor", probably written before A.D. 70. |
| | | These three fragments are joined together in one hymn. |
| II, 1–19 | . . | A Gentile-Christian hymn from the end of the first century A.D. |
| II, 20–30 | . . | Popular hymn written in Judea after A.D. 70. |
| II, 31–9 | . . | A work by a Jewish-Christian "poor" (Ebionite?), composed in Palestine after A.D. 79. |
| III, 1–18 | . . | A popular apocalypse written in Syria between A.D. 115 and 132. |
| III, 19–36 | . . | An apocalypse written in Italy a little after A.D. 79. |
| III, 37–IV, 4 | . . | Two fragments of one or two texts of unknown date and origin. |

| | | |
|---|---|---|
| IV, 5-29 | . . | A pamphlet by a false prophet (a dissident Pharisee), native of Palestine, but living in the Diaspora (Syria), between A.D. 135 and 150. |
| IV, 29-41 | . . | Confession of a renegade who comes back from his apostasy, probably dating from the beginning of the second century A.D. |
| V, 1-4 | . . | A passage which may have been a continuation of the preceding text. |
| V, 5-19 | . . | Prayer of a Jew condemned to meet wild beasts in the arena, written in Italy after A.D. 70. |
| V, 20-39 | . . | Prayer of a heretic imprisoned by the Zadokites (at Damascus?). |
| VI, 1-36 | . . | A Jewish-Christian Gnostic hymn, probably written in Italy by an emigrant from Palestine who must have left his country a little before A.D. 66. |
| VII, 1-5 | . . | A fragment by a pacifist who lived in Italy during the war of A.D. 66-70. |
| VII, 6-25 | . . | Hymn by a Zadokite of Palestine who hoped to rule over that country. Written after A.D. 70, and perhaps even after A.D. 135. |
| VII, 26-33 | . . | Hymn by a convert to the Christian sect of the Sons of the Truth, probably written in the Diaspora in the second half of the first century A.D. |
| VII, 34-VIII, 3 | . | Two fragments of an anti-Zadokite writing. |
| VIII, 4-40 | . . | A composite work comprising the legend of the trees of Eden, the parable of tongues like to overflowing rivers, and a description of the final cataclysm, written in Italy by a prisoner after A.D. 79. |
| IX, 2-36 | . . | Hymn by a Zadokite recently converted to Christianity. |
| IX, 38-X, 10 | . | Two fragments of a Zadokite writing. |
| X, 14-XI, 2 | . | Prayer of a Jewish-Christian of Palestine, written after A.D. 79. |
| XI, 3-14 | . . | A Jewish-Christian Gnostic hymn, written in Palestine after A.D. 70 by a member of the sect of the Sons of the Truth. |
| XI, 15-22 | . . | An anti-Zadokite fragment. |
| XI, 21-7 | . . | A fragment of unknown date and origin. |
| XI, 29-35 | . . | A series of current Jewish benedictions, first century A.D. |
| XII, 1-3 | . . | A fragment of which only a few disconnected phrases remain. |
| XII, 3-11 | . . | A current Jewish prayer (first century A.D.). |
| XII, 11-24 | . | A Christian fragment. |
| XII, 25-37 | . | A Zadokite fragment. |
| | | These three fragments are joined together in one hymn. |
| XIII, 1-21 | . | A hymn from the Zadokite sect of Baptists; from the beginning of the Christian era. |
| XIV, 1-8 | . | A fragment which is probably Christian. |

| XIV, 8-22 . | . | Apologia by a Zealot who had been playing a double game, written about A.D. 130. |
| XIV, 23-8 . | . | A fragment of unknown date and origin. |
| XV, 9-26 . | . | The writing by a Zadokite priest of Palestine before A.D. 66. |
| XVI, 2-7 . | . | An anti-rabbinic Zadokite fragment of uncertain date. |
| XVI, 8-20 . | . | A prayer by a man from the ordinary people admitted into a Zadokite society, written after A.D. 70. |
| XVII, 1-15 . | . | A Zadokite work, written after A.D. 70, but of unknown place of origin. |
| XVII, 17-28 | . | A Zadokite fragment, written in Palestine towards the end of the first century A.D. |
| XVIII, 1-32 . | . | A hymn by a Gentile propagandist who had joined the Baptist sect. Date and place of origin unknown. |
| Fragment 1 . | . | Of Zadokite inspiration. |
| Fragment 2 . | . | Of Christian inspiration. |
| Fragment 3 . | . | Too fragmentary for any definite judgement to be formed upon it. This is also true of Fragment 4, and sixty-one other and smaller fragments. |

It is naturally impossible to affirm that originally this manuscript did not include any text corresponding to the orthodox Jewish outlook. All the same, from this long list hardly a couple of prayers can be found which could equally well have been in use in the rabbinic synagogues (XI, 29-35, XII, 1-11). All the others are unorthodox, and even heretical from the rabbinic point of view.

As in the other manuscripts, the popular pieces can be recognised by their angelology and their descriptions of the Beyond. Those of Zadokite origin disparage the human race and deny any survival after death. Prayers from false prophets rub shoulders with apocalypses and "Jewish fables" circulating in the Diaspora. As to the date of these fragments, they stretch out from the beginning of our era or even before, to the middle of the second century A.D. Not only peculiarities of vocabulary, but also subject matter allows a distinction to be drawn between what was written in Palestine and what saw the light of day in Syria, Italy, or elsewhere.

It has already been pointed out that it is necessary to look within the Zadokite circle for the members of the Baptist sect, "Born of the woman". Some groups of this movement may have been converted to Christianity, but many others seem to have preserved the Jewish character of their sect. The Zadokite converted to Christianity from whom comes the prayer (IX, 2-36) of our manuscript does not seem to have belonged to the Baptist sect.

As regards Christian texts, our manuscript contains few elements which could be attributed to the outlook of the church of Jerusalem. If speaking with tongues, so important an element in Pauline Christianity, was unknown in Palestinian Christianity,[1] then II, 1-9 must be attributed to a Greek-speaking author. The texts emanating from the Christian sect of "The Sons of Truth" (or "of the Truthful") reflect a definitely Gnostic outlook (VI, 1-36, VII, 26-33, X, 14-XI, 2, XI, 3-14). The Christian nature of two other fragments is not certain (II, 31-39, XII, 11-24). On the other hand, the prayer of the converted Zadokite (IX, 2-36) contains a clear echo of Matt. 7.1-2 and 6.14-15. It is also in this text that we have a prayer asking God to assure His worshipper of his food, even to old age (Matt. 6.11). We also find God called "Father" (Matt. 6.9; Rom. 8.14) in not quite the same sense as in the Old Testament.

The only reference to Jesus which we believe we find in the Christian fragments is one met with in the hymn attributed above to a Greek-speaking author (II, 1-19): "If all the men of treachery roar against me . . . and if they turn back to bring to naught the life of the man whom Thou hast appointed by the word of Thy mouth, and also that of his disciple. . . ." One is tempted to see in this passage a reference to Christ whose disciple the author says he is. Even if he has to suffer abuse and perhaps even be put to death, yet others will come after him who will translate the teaching "into uncircumcised tongues, and into the speech of strangers, for the [foreign] nations who do not understand Hebrew, so that they may let fall their errors". It is quite the Pauline programme for Christianity that we have put forward here.

Yet in other fragments we find an attitude which is completely anti-Pauline. In three Jewish-Christian hymns, the belief in the resurrection from the dead is clearly set forth. In one (VI, 34) the author says that "those who are lying in the dust shall lift themselves up like a flagstaff, and those risen from the dead shall raise a signal". Another author (X, 33-4) proclaims that he will be saved from the abyss, and even in the halls of Sheôl God would set free his soul. A third (XI, 12) knows that after his death, and being purified from sin, he will arise from the dust of the worms which consume the dead, and shall present himself before God. In all these poems, it is not a question of the immortality of the soul, but of the resurrection of the body, as in Dan. 12.2 and Acts, 24.15. It should be noted that these three authors are anti-Pauline: the third clearly affirms that he is of the Hebrew tongue, while the second, propagandist that he is, recalls the prohibition to mingle with the uncircumcised (VI, 20).

[1] M. Goguel, *La Naissance du Christianisme*, Paris, 1955, p. 113 and note 1.

F

As already stated, a number of texts recopied into this manuscript must have come from the Diaspora. The Syrian origin of some is easy to detect. Further, it is well-known that in the first, and early part of the second, century A.D. there was a very live intellectual exchange between the rabbinic schools of Syria and Mesopotamia on the one hand and those of Palestine on the other, but what appears here for the first time, but quite clearly, is that the Jews of Italy were also in continuous communication with their fellow Jews of Judea, and that each circulated the writings of the other. The flow of ideas from Palestine to Italy is easily understood. The flow in the opposite direction has never been suspected till now. It was known, however, that even in Crete there were authors of "Jewish fables" (Titus 1.14). "Profane and old wives' fables" (1 Tim. 4.7) saw the light among the Jews almost everywhere in the Diaspora, and were afterwards introduced into Palestine. There was also a Jewish community at Rome, and probably also at Pompeii, where a Christian *graffito* has been found.[1] We must now suppose that the Jews who witnessed the eruption at once set about to find a meaning for this cataclysm, and passed it on to their fellow Jews in Judea. The eruption of Vesuvius, in fact, seems to have left a deeper mark on Jewish and Christian apocalyptic literature than did the fire of Rome in A.D. 64. What the prophets had foretold was about to happen: the godless were about to meet their doom. Had there not perished in Pompeii along with his bride, the son of Agrippa's adulterous and apostate sister, Drusilla, by the Procurator Felix? (Josephus, *Antiquities,* XX, vii, 2). For those living at that time, it was a certain sign that the Day of Yahweh was at hand.

Those passages of our manuscript which could be described as "Christian" frequently emanate from a sect calling itself "The Sons of Truth" (or "of the Truthful"). Now a sect bearing a similar name has already been met with in the *Manual of Discipline,* and it is named in two passages there (IV, 2-6 and 6-8), where its doctrine is partly set out. But reference is also made there to the "zeal" which its members should show in carrying out the purpose of God—that is to say, in fighting the Romans. It is also said there that the Sons of Truth should keep aloof from those who made a pretence of submission, meaning by that the Pharisees. If they followed the leading of the Spirit, they were to be rewarded by rich harvests. All this shows that the Sons of Truth were recruited among the peasant class. Putting these facts together, one can regard the members of the sect as forming part of the Zealots who took an active part in the

[1] *Dictionnaire d'Archéologie Chrétienne et de Liturgie,* XIV, 1,403-8.

guerrilla warfare against the Romans before the war of A.D. 66-70. We may recall that the *Manual of Discipline* includes also a Christian passage (X, 17-XI, 2) which is definitely anti-Zealot. There one reads, "To no man will I return evil for evil. . . . I will not be full of zeal to carry out wickedness." That can only mean that at the time when the *Manual of Discipline* was drawn up, the Sons of Truth were not Christians. On the other hand, in the *Thanksgiving Hymns,* in spite of opinions frequently of a heretical nature, the Sons of Truth appear as a Christian sect. Unless one imagines that there were existing at the same time two sects of the same name, but of definitely different principles, one must feel that a certain lapse of time has to be allowed between the time when the Zealot Sons of Truth insisted that its members not only kept aloof from those collaborating with the Romans, but showed their zeal in acts of terrorism, and the time when they accepted pagans into their ranks and spread abroad Christian ideas.

As a matter of fact, it would seem that this lapse of time was relatively short. The Zealot fragment of the *Manual of Discipline* (IV, 9-14) can hardly have been much older than Hymn VI, 1-36, of the *Thanksgiving Hymns.* But while the first was written in Palestine, it can be accepted that the second was composed in Italy, perhaps in Rome itself. From this it may be inferred that it was in Italy that certain Sons of Truth were won over to Christianity. They may have been converted in prison by fellow prisoners, or in some other circumstances where they were thrown into contact with Gentile Christians under sentence, like themselves. A stream of Christian propaganda must have taken its rise among the rank and file of the people and gone from Italy into Palestine: Roman Christianity set out for the conquest of Judea. It is thus that an explanation can be given as to how a Palestinian Zealot group could have been won over by Christian ideas coming from Rome.

It has been frequently pointed out that in the fragments written by the second scribe of this roll, and above all in XVIII, 1-41, great importance is assigned to "light" in contexts which recall the Gospel of St. John (1.4-10, 3.20-1, etc.) and still more the First Epistle of St. John (1.5-7, 2.8-11, etc.). It is also in St. John's Gospel (14.17, 15.26, 16.13) that there is mention of "The Spirit of Truth", but "The Truth" in the sense that this expression has in our roll seems to have particularly influenced the author of *The Shepherd of Hermas* (Mandate III), a Christian apocryphal work written in Italy about the middle of the second century A.D. In the same work (Mandate X) we come across the invitation "to seek the Truth", meaning to seek God, the Truthful ('*mt*).

A question now arises which is difficult to answer. Did the Italian Christian sect, whose existence we have been led to suppose, call itself "The Sons of Thy Truth" or "The Sons of Thy handmaid"? Both expressions are written alike in Hebrew, *bny 'mtk*. Whilst mention of "Thy Truth" is frequently found in the Bible, the other expression "Thy handmaid" is also found as in Ps. 116.16, where one reads: "I am Thy servant, the son of Thy handmaid." As far as the present writer is aware, there is no case of the expression "Son of *Thy* Truth" ever being used. This invites comparison with Luke 1.38, and suggests that certain Christians may have called themselves "Sons of Thy handmaid". In any case, one fact is certain: the expression *"Ancilla Dei"* is very common among the Christian inscriptions of Italy during the first centuries A.D. It is simply a sign of humility, and in no ways implies a monastic vocation, for quite a number of handmaidens of God were buried with their husbands and children. There is nothing to hinder the supposition that by association with Ps. 116.16, some worshippers called themselves not just "Thy servant" as in several of our hymns, but also "Son of Thy handmaid". If, as we may suppose, the expression came into use in Italy, it is very possible that it was not properly understood in Palestine, above all at a time when writings of the type of *The Shepherd of Hermas* were being introduced, and when further, as we have seen, a Zealot sect of "The Sons of the Truth" already existed there. In two of our hymns we have a definite impression that the copyist must have confused "Thy truth" and "Thy handmaid". To what degree was this confusion accidental? To what extent was it deliberate by the Christian propagandists in Judea? Both questions remain unanswered at present.

A new chapter in the history of Christianity seems to be opening before us, and it may be that the necessary details will be supplied by these Dead Sea manuscripts. There have been doubts, and justifiably so, as to the accuracy of the information given by Eusebius (*c.* 265-340) in his *Demonstratio evangelica*, III, v, 10, that a very large Christian church existed in Jerusalem until the destruction of the city by Hadrian in A.D. 131. According to Epiphanius (A.D. 315-402) in his *De mensuris et ponderibus,* XIV, 1, there was in his time only a little church on Mount Zion, and that was in ruins. On the other hand, Eusebius affirms in his *Historia Ecclesiastica,* IV, iv, 3-4, that the church which was set up in Jerusalem when Hadrian rebuilt and repeopled the town was composed of Gentiles. Must it be understood that at the beginning of the second century the number of Jewish Christians in Palestine was almost nil?

During the first generation, Christianity certainly had Jewish members in Palestine. After A.D. 66 all trace of them disappears. We are led to suppose that in the first century A.D. it was above all in Italy, Asia Minor, and Egypt that Christians made proselytes, both among the Jews and the Gentiles. We are brought to the conclusion that by the end of the first century or the beginning of the second the Christian tradition in Palestine had been lost, and it was the Christianity of the West that was then infiltrating into Judea and attempting to win over the Jews. We may recall that it was in Italy in a Jewish-Christian but Greek-speaking circle that the Epistle to the Hebrews was written about the year A.D. 90.[1] It is also in Italy that we should look for the author of several hymns of Christian inspiration that are found in the roll of the *Thanksgiving Hymns* coming from Cave I at Qumrân.

$$\star \qquad \star \qquad \star$$

The manuscript of the *Thanksgiving Hymns* presents this peculiarity: that the handwriting of the Scribe "A" was beautiful and regular, with even touches of refinement, especially in the letter *l*, whilst that of the Scribe "B" was almost shapeless.[2] "B" presents a number of different forms of the letter *š*, was obviously at pains to write correctly the *y*'s and the *w*'s, and his ignorance of the final form of *ṣ* attracts attention, as do a number of other points. As it cannot be supposed that this scribe was a young scholar practising his first lessons, it has to be admitted that this manuscript was begun by a Jew well accustomed to write in a running hand, but was continued by a converted Gentile, a novice to Hebrew writing. This hypothesis is supported by a further fact.

As far as we are able to judge, the Scribe "A" had only copied out unorthodox texts. The collection on which he was working must have had a well-defined purpose, and for that end there was no need to copy out ordinary everyday prayers and blessings. But a clear impression is given that when the Scribe "B" took in hand the incomplete roll of his predecessor, he began to copy out quite ordinary texts. He restarted, and

[1] The author sends the greeting of those "of Italy" (13.24). The Epistle, quoted for the first time by Clement of Rome in A.D. 96, could not have been earlier than the reign of Domitian (A.D. 81-96).

[2] Of all the manuscripts published up till now, there is no question but that the roll of *The War of the Sons of Light* is the most carefully written. The writing of the *Habakkuk Commentary* is also very good, and *Isaiah "B"* was written by an expert hand. On the other hand, the *Manual of Discipline,* in which several copyists have collaborated, shows much less care, while no one would suggest that *Isaiah "A"* is a piece of good penmanship. All the same, these last two were clearly the work of persons well used to writing Hebrew.

now only copied out unorthodox texts, as his predecessor had done. That leads us to the supposition that "B" was a recent convert. Not only was he unaccustomed to write Hebrew, but he could not even as yet distinguish prayers in ordinary use from those used by heretics.

The fact that a manuscript of this kind should be compiled and the work of copying entrusted to a newly converted pagan seems to imply that the very idea of getting together all these unorthodox texts arose within a sect that was itself heretical, and which gathered its recruits from among the pagans. The date of the compilation of this manuscript must have been later than that of the latest fragments in it (IV, 5-29, VII, 6-25, XIV, 1-22)— that is to say, later than A.D. 135. We are not very well informed concerning Jewish and Christian heresies in Palestine in the second century. Epiphanius (*Adv. haer.*, 9ff.) mentions five Christian heresies, seven Jewish, and, further on, three Jewish-Christian ones, the Nazaraeans, the Ebionites, and the Sampsaeans. The Elkazaites, at times confused with the Ossaeans, are also mentioned in some other passages without it being possible to say whether they have been brought in twice (*ibid.* 19, 30, 53). It would appear at once that none of these sects or heretics would have been interested in such a heterogeneous collection of texts. The explanation of our manuscript must be looked for in another direction.

The second century A.D. must certainly have brought about in Palestine an important change in the relations between Jews and Christians. After the fall of Jerusalem, and still more after the defeat of Bar Kochba, it was no longer the Jewish-Christians who sought to bring Gentiles into a religion which they considered the true Judaism. More and more, it was the Gentile-Christians who sought proselytes among the Jews. For example, they introduced into Palestine Hebrew writings of a Christian nature, such as the Epistle to the Hebrews and certain of our hymns which had seen the light of day in the Diaspora. They must also have used in propaganda material which was already there.

It has long been known that the different schools of thought in Judaism supported their doctrines by quotations from the Bible—quotations often altered and interpreted in a tendentious manner. The books of the prophets were often exploited in that fashion—witness the *Habakkuk Commentary*. Even current prayers were at times paraphrased, as the pamphlet incorporated into the *Manual of Discipline* shows (X, 1-9). In a similar manner, Jewish apocryphal and pseudepigraphical writings were composed in Biblical style and attributed to Jacob, Baruch, Moses, Enoch, etc. Christian propaganda did the same thing. Christian points of view were interpolated into passages quoted from the Old Testament, and apocrypha and pseudepigrapha were presented as the works of ancient writers—the *Assumption of Moses,* etc. For the composition of these books, their authors must have drawn up some sort of note-books from which they could draw their stock phrases and their ready-made expressions, which would awake in the reader or the hearer a feeling that they were familiar—and therefore authentic.

The existence of these "aids to memory" had already been assumed by a number of scholars who had studied this problem. One document of this kind has in fact been found—the *Manual of Discipline,* which, for a different purpose, had been compiled by Jews with the intention of uniting items from it in the drawing up of the rules for a society. The roll of the *Thanksgiving Hymns* is another "aid to memory", this time compiled by Christians so as to facilitate the employment of expressions in common use by certain Jewish sects when composing apocryphal books. These would thus have the air of being genuine. If the anthology found in this roll is essentially unorthodox, that is explained by the fact that Christian propaganda could be carried out more easily in circles already opposed to rabbinic authority. Once the apocryphal book was written, in Palestine and in Hebrew, it could go back into the outside world. Translated into Greek, Syriac, or Latin, it could serve as propaganda in the dissident Jewish circles of the Diaspora.

Now, there are actually a number of Christian apocryphal writings which do systematically make use of the forms of speech met with in the *Thanksgiving Hymns.* One of the most typical is known as the *Sixth Book of Ezra.* In all known manuscripts, it is joined on to the Jewish apocryphal *4 Ezra,* of which it forms Chapters 15 and 16.[1]

*6 Ezra* present several problems which have not yet been solved. It is not known in which language it was originally written but it is supposed that it was Greek. The date of composition is put down approximately

---

[1] There is much irregularity in the numbering of the books which bear the name of Ezra, or Esdras. Following Labourt in the *Revue Biblique,* 1909, pp. 412-34, and H. Weinel in Ed. Henecke, *Neutestamentliche Apokryphen,* 1924, pp. 394-99, the following system is used in this book:

*1 Ezra*=Canonical Ezra.
*2 Ezra*=Canonical Nehemiah.
*3 Ezra*="The Greek Esdras" called *1 Esdras* in A.V. and R.V. and *3 Esdras* in the Vulgate.
*4 Ezra*=The main part, Chapters 3-14, of what is called *2 Esdras* in the A.V. and R.V., and *4 Esdras* in the Vulgate, and often referred to as *2 (4) Esdras.*
*5 Ezra*=Chapters 1 and 2 of *2 (4) Esdras.*
*6 Ezra*=Chapters 15 and 16 of *2 (4) Esdras.*

between A.D. 120 and 300. An indication of date may be seen in the mention of "wild boars", the wild boar being the badge of the Tenth Legion Fretensis, which was in barracks at Jerusalem up till A.D. 132. In the Latin translation, *mṣrym*, "the land of anguish", has been rendered by "Egypt", though there can be no question but that it is Italy that is referred to where "My people have been led like a flock to the slaughter" (15.10). "All the country will be destroyed" we read further on (15.11) and "its trees will be devasted by fire and hail" (15.13). "Thus saith the Lord God, My right hand shall not spare the sinner, nor my sword draw back from those who spill on the earth the blood of the innocent. A fire shall come forth from His wrath, and shall consume the foundations of the earth with all sinners, like to lighted straw" (15.22).

All these expressions are found in the *Thanksgiving Hymns,* and this leads one to suppose that the original language of *6 Ezra* was Hebrew, hardly classical Hebrew, but Hebrew all the same.

The mention of Karmonians in this apocalypse places in the early part of the reign of Marcus Aurelius the events referred to in *6 Ezra*, *qrmn'y* being the name given to the Parthians in rabbinic literature. The composition of *6 Ezra* therefore should be placed a short time after A.D. 166.

Though the Christian sect in which this apocryphal work was produced had members speaking Hebrew, Greek, or even Latin, it was Palestinian none the less, and it may be accepted that it possessed an "aid to memory" on the lines of the roll of the *Thanksgiving Hymns* until the time that *6 Ezra* was written. Naturally, it is impossible to say if other such rolls did not exist, nor if there were not a number of copies of the *Thanksgiving Hymns.* For the present, we should treat this "note-book" as a manuscript separate from anything else, as we have done with the *Manual of Discipline.*

The date of the compiling of this roll can only be given as later than the latest fragments included in it, and that would appear to be about the middle of the second century A.D. The copyists of the manuscript should be sought for in a Christian sect in Palestine to whom this collection was to serve as an "aid to memory" in the composition of a work of the type of *6 Ezra.* It should be remembered that this work could not have been composed before A.D. 166, and it should be further remembered that the sect comprised not only Jews, but also Gentiles who were not in the habit of writing Hebrew.

To understand how this roll could have been confiscated by the rabbinic authorities in the second half of the second century, partly destroyed in accordance with rules of which we have only imperfect knowledge, and then consigned to the *geniza* near the Dead Sea, it is necessary to take account of the reconstitution of the Palestinian Sanhedrin under Rabbi Simon ben Gamaliel II (140–63), and the recovery of authority enjoyed by his son and successor, Rabbi Yehuda ha-Nasi, the friend of the co-Emperor Lucius Verus, who lived at Antioch till A.D. 166. It was under the Patriarchate of Rabbi Yehuda that the collection known as the *Mishna* was formed, and that led to a fresh seizure of aprocryphal writings similar to that which took place when the canon of the Old Testament was fixed. Rabbi Yehuda's successors were not able to maintain their authority over Judaism, and shortly after A.D. 230 the centre of spiritual authority made another move towards Mesopotamia. From the middle of the third century, Palestine, moreover, came under the growing influence of the Palmyrene syncretism championed by Queen Zenobia.

It may therefore be supposed that the roll of the *Thanksgiving Hymns* was seized by order of Rabbi Yehuda ha-Nasi some time during the later decades of the second century. Only Rabbi Yehuda could have had sufficient authority to act in this way with regard to certain writings accounted pernicious or unorthodox, and in the possession of Christians in Palestine or of people influenced by Christianity.

Thus one comes back to the conclusion that Cave I of Qumrân, like many other *genizoth,* received consignments of manuscripts at dates considerably distant from one another, in the same way as sometimes the dead are interred in old cemeteries which had passed out of use. Besides, no one has ever imagined that all the writings recovered from the Cairo *geniza* had been placed there the same day!

x

## THE ROLL OF *ISAIAH* "*A*"

Among the rolls purchased by the Syrian Metropolitan of Jerusalem, the first to be identified, and the one which seemed the most important, was a roll of the Book of Isaiah. Although not dating from before the Exile, as one liked to think at first, it was still unquestionably the oldest copy of the book of this Prophet known up to date, and, what was remarkable, it was practically complete. Seventeen sheets of leather sewn end to end gave to the roll a length of 7 metres 34 centimetres. A further sheet, the fly-leaf, had been cut off with a knife. The manuscript was found correctly rolled, and wrapped up in a linen cover.

It is evident that the roll must have been a long time in use in some synagogue before being carried to the *geniza* in the jar in which it would seem it was discovered. The effects of its long interment are less than those produced through use. Two torn sheets had been patched and re-sewn. Other tears of less importance had been darned. In the margin of its fifty-four columns of writing, eighteen signatures of rabbis may be noticed, and eleven X's. There has been much discussion over this sign. Some scholars wish to see in it a Greek *chi*, the initial of Christ. Others regard it as the Hebrew *taw* in ancient script.[1] It seems certain that the passages marked by this sign are those which have often been interpreted in a messianic sense. It may be supposed that the roll belonged to a community whose members drew support from the Book of Isaiah to prove that "it was written". But that does not necessarily imply that they were Christians or that the passages in question were applied by them to Jesus. These signs by themselves are not sufficient proof for stating that the roll had been taken to the *geniza* as it had been found in unorthodox hands. From a rabbinic point of view, there were many reasons for withdrawing a canonical book from use and for consigning it to a *geniza*.

Although the writing of the scribe is good, yet the roll *Isaiah "A"* is far from being the work of a calligrapher. There are occasional corrections where the roll differed from the orthodox text. Omissions have been made good in the margins or by writing between the lines. A number of words have been erased, crossed out, or written over.[2] According to rabbinic rules, a canonical book with more than five corrections to the page became *pasûl* and, for that reason, unfit for use. On that ground alone, the withdrawal from use of this book and its burial in a *geniza* would have been justified.

It might also have been that the owners put this roll away simply because it was too worn out and old. Many an ancient roll has finished up in a *geniza* in this way without there being anything unorthodox or irregular in its contents, and it is for such a reason that Jews of today take their sacred books to a *geniza*. The ancient sewings and darnings are clearly seen in the roll of *Isaiah "A"*, and if the community to which it belonged had decided to procure a new copy it could itself have decided to inter the old one.

The manuscript may be the work of more than one scribe, but all the same it contains the complete Book of Isaiah ,that is to say, Proto-Isaiah

[1] See the articles by J. L. Teicher in the *Journal of Jewish Studies*, III (1952), pp. 128f., I. Sonne in *Vetus Testamentum*, IV (1954), pp. 90ff., and J. L. Teicher, *ibid.*, V (1955), pp. 189ff.

[2] A list of the variants presented by the text in its present state is to be found in the new edition of R. Kittel, *Biblia Hebraica*, 1951-2. See also S. Loewinger, "New Corrections . . .", in *Vetus Testamentum*, IV (1954), pp. 80-7.

(1-39), Deutero-Isaiah (40-55), and the various writings gathered together under the title of Trito-Isaiah (56-66). The tradition which attributed to Isaiah the chapters 40-55 was only formed towards the end of the third century B.C., and it was probably in the second century B.C. that the book began to take its present form. It has been pointed out that many passages in this manuscript are closer to the Greek version, the Septuagint, than to Hebrew Massoretic text. Some scholars have wanted to draw the conclusion that Isaiah "A" was written before the canonical Hebrew text was definitely fixed, but this does not necessarily follow. It has already been pointed out that for a long time there was circulating in Syria a version of the Book of Habakkuk which was shorter than the ordinary version by two verses. For the Book of Isaiah, as for other canonical books, the Alexandrian tradition was kept up in the communities of the Diaspora during a rather long period.

From the corrections made to the text, and from the signatures of rabbis in the margins, it may be assumed that the manuscript was summarily corrected after the establishing of an official text in the first century A.D., and that about the same time it was censored by the same authority which examined the *Manual of Discipline*. But by this time the roll must have already seen much use. It could have been 150 years old at least, judging from its state of preservation. Whatever our ways of thinking, we are forced to the conclusion that the roll was written before the birth of Christianity. Even if it belonged to a community which eventually became Christian, even if the marks X were added at a later stage to mark Christological passages, the text itself was written before the beginning of the Christian era, and in consequence cannot bring back to us a Christian version of Isaiah.

The most important additions to the text are:

(1)  The last stich of verse 34.17, and the verses 35.1-3.
(2)  The verse 36.21.
(3)  Two words added to verse 37.4.
(4)  The verses 35.5-7.
(5)  Three words completing verse 37.31.
(6)  The verses 38.21-2.
(7)  Two stichs completing verse 40.7.
(8)  The verse 40.8.
(9)  The two last stichs of verse 40.14 and the verses 40.15-16.
(10) The last stich of verse 53.8.

The greater part of these passages add a note of confidence to the book. Verses 38.21-2 do not seem to have formed part of the original version of the book. Ought the conclusion to be drawn that originally the roll of Isaiah "A" contained a more faithful copy of the Book of the Prophet Isaiah than that transmitted not only by the Massoretes, but also by the Septuagint?

In the opinion of the present writer, Isaiah "A" could have been written in the second or first century B.C. It is hard to say when it was corrected. It may have been taken to Cave I at Qumrân towards the end of the first or the beginning of the second century A.D. It has now been acquired by the Israelite Government, and will doubtless be the subject of further study. It may be possible by the aid of infra-red rays to re-establish the text as it was before the additions and overwritings of the correctors, and it is in that text that its true value lies.

## xi

## THE ROLL OF ISAIAH "B"

A description has already been given (see above, pp. 50-51) of the state of this manuscript which was acquired by the Hebrew University of Jerusalem. On being unrolled, "only the upper part of the last third and a few fragments from the middle of the book have been preserved".[1] Other fragments which had disintegrated from it have since been bought from the dealer in Bethlehem.

At the time of the accident which caused the roll to be taken to the geniza, it was doubtless almost new, and it may be supposed that it contained the complete text of the Book of Isaiah from the first verse to the last, and of the same version as that in use today. In the parts that have been preserved, it is this version that is represented, and not a touched-up older and less orthodox version, as is the case with the roll "A".

From some points of view, it is possible to regard this roll as perfect. Not only was it beautifully written, but its text is very close to the current Massoretic version. The list of variants noted by S. Loewinger[2] is astonishingly short, and is mostly of slight differences in spelling. It was neither old nor worn, and no sign of repair has been discovered. Corrections made to the text are rare.

The roll Isaiah "B" could have been written at any time between the

[1] The Dead Sea Scrolls of the Hebrew University, ed. E. L. Sukenik (1955), p. 30.
[2] "The Variants of DSI, II", in Vetus Testamentum, IV (1954), pp. 155-63.

end of the first and the beginning of the third century A.D. Without any difficulty, it can be said that it must have been written after the fall of Jerusalem, but the present state of our knowledge does not allow us to state precisely where this copy was made. In spite of resemblances between the handwriting and that of the *Habakkuk Commentary*, it is by no means certain that the two manuscripts had the same origin. All that can be said is the roll *Isaiah "B"* may well have been written in some town in Palestine.

xii

## THE GENESIS APOCRYPHON

Of the four rolls exhibited in the United States by the Metropolitan, Mar Athanasius Samuel, one appeared to be a solid mass, all stuck together. The possibility of saving pieces large enough to reveal its contents seemed hopeless. Moreover, whilst it was in the United States, the Syrian Metropolitan refused to allow experts to attempt its unrolling. When once its contents were known, the manuscript was in danger of losing a great deal of its monetary value. It was therefore an unknown roll that was purchased by General Yigael Yadin, and it was in the University of Jerusalem that Professor Bieberkraut began the difficult task of separating the sheets of leather adhering one to another or covered by a white layer, the nature of which is not yet known. The work is on its way to being completed, and in the meantime a preliminary report has been published.[1] This publication only presents columns II and XIX-XXII. They are given in photographic reproduction along with transcription, and translation into modern Hebrew and English. A summary of other columns is given as far as it has been possible to open them out and form an opinion of their contents. The many notes on points of detail show how very interesting this manuscript is, but it is too early as yet to form a judgement on it as a whole. What is written here cannot be taken as final.

Judging from the few fragments which it was possible to read in 1948, it was supposed that this roll contained an Aramaic version of the *Book of Lamech*. As a matter of fact, the manuscript gives a kind of paraphrase of a part of the Book of Genesis, and in it each patriarch relates his own history, adorning it with curious legends. The work presents many analogies with the *Book of Jubilees* and the *Book of Enoch*, Jewish apocryphal writings which have only come down to us in translation. One wonders therefore

[1] N. Avigad and Y. Yadin, *A Genesis Apocryphon*, Jerusalem, 1956.

as to what degree those writings influenced the author of this manuscript. The *Genesis Apocryphon* is certainly not the basis of those two works, as some people have already wished to suppose.

Y. Kutscher is to publish a study of the language of this manuscript,[1] but one remark may be made here. It is not written in ordinary Aramaic, but in a most curious sort of Aramaic jargon.

Seeing that the first part of the roll has perished, it is obviously impossible to know how the book opened, but by analogy with the *Book of Jubilees* it may be supposed that the story of Genesis was going to be told to some personage, perhaps Moses, though not this time by an Angel of the Presence, but by the patriarchs themselves, who were to appear in turn, one after another.

Column II is the first that is moderately well preserved. In it Lamech relates how he had doubts as to the faithfulness of his wife, Bath-Enosh, and tells of all the oaths she made to persuade him that Noah was indeed his son, and not the fruit of an alliance with angels, those "Sons of God" who saw that the daughters of men were fair (Gen. 6.2.). The name Bath-Enosh means "daughter of man". Lamech wanted to be quite sure. As in the *Book of Enoch* (16.1-2), he prayed his father, Methuselah, to ask Enoch to let him know the truth. The succeeding columns must have covered Gen. 6-11, doubtless supplying a mass of geographical details and putting names to persons left unnamed in the Bible. Many analogies with the *Book of Jubilees* have been found in the few passages which it has been possible so far to decipher.

In column XIX Abram tells of the dream which he had when he arrived in Egypt, and of the interpretation of it that he gave to Sarai, his wife. Sarai was going to be taken by a Pharaoh named Zoan, and she would save her husband's life by declaring that he was her brother. The Bible frequently mentions the town of Zoan (Tanis), and in the corresponding passage of the *Book of Jubilees* (13.10) a phrase has been added referring to the building of the town of Zoan. There is no question but that our author here took Zoan for a man.

After having lived for five years in Egypt with his wife and his nephew, Lot, Abram received a visit from three Egyptian princes, who saw how beautiful Sarai was. Then follows a description of her beauty which one of the princes, Hyrcanus, gave to the Pharaoh Zoan. Here again a name is given to someone left unnamed in the Bible, and this name deserves special attention.

[1] *Israel Exploration Journal.*

Why was this princely pander called Hyrcanus, and who lies hidden behind the name? It can only refer to Hyrcanus of the family of Tobias, who was already the subject of legends when Josephus wrote his *Jewish Antiquities*. Stories of Egyptian marriages were told about his father, and Hyrcanus himself was noted for his cunning at the Court of Ptolemy V Epiphanes (203-181 B.C.). A brief reminder of some of the characteristics of these legends will make it easier to understand the strange anachronism by which in the *Genesis Apocryphon* he becomes the contemporary of Abram.

As it should do, the epic of the sons of Tobias begins with Tobias himself, the founder of the family which for a long time had the privilege of collecting the taxes in Judea on behalf of the Egyptian administration. While quite young, Joseph, the son of Tobias, went down into Egypt, where he won the heart of the Pharaoh. Like his Biblical namesake, he lived in the palace and ate at the King's table. Joseph was already the father of seven sons when, going to Alexandria in company with his brother Solomon, he fell violently in love with a dancer who had exhibited her talents at a royal banquet where he had been a guest. Joseph asked his brother to arrange a meeting between himself and this dancer, but Solomon, rather than see his brother dishonour himself, put in her place his own daughter, whom he had brought to Egypt in the hope of finding for her a husband suitable to her rank. (Theme of the substituted bride: analogy with Jacob's first marriage.) From this union was born the Hyrcanus whose story was to present so many parallels with that of Joseph. There was even a plot on the part of his seven brothers to put him to death. When the author of the *Genesis Apocryphon* wished to give a name to a Jew who was an Egyptian prince, it is easy to see why he would choose Hyrcanus rather than Joseph, especially as the use of the latter name might cause misunderstanding over the Biblical personage with whom he was going to deal later.

Such anachronisms and exaggerated precision are common in the formation of legends. In the Middle Ages they are found in the legends of the Holy Grail, of King Arthur and his Knights of the Round Table, of the Nibelungs, etc. As to taking the name of a town for that of a person, it is equally common. It may be recalled that in a Coptic version of the Gospel according to St. Luke, the name Nineveh is given to the rich man in the parable of Lazarus (Luke 16.19-31), and this same name is found in a number of Greek manuscripts. Confusions in the opposite direction are also frequent. Rameses becomes the name of a town (Exod. 1.11, etc.).

That can easily be understood, for among Oriental place-names a town often bears the name of its founder. It is harder to understand how it came about that an author whose aim was to relate Biblical history took the name of Zoan, a town frequently mentioned in the Bible, as the name of a Pharaoh.

When all the doctors and wizards of Egypt were found incapable of curing the Pharaoh and of putting an end to the pestilence that had been ravaging the country since "Zoan" had robbed Abram of his wife, Hyrcanus learned from Lot that the unique cause of all these disasters was to prevent the Pharaoh from having intimacy with Sarai. The beautiful Sarai was restored to Abram, to whom the Pharaoh gave much wealth on condition that he left the country. Thus, laden with presents, Abram and Lot set out, accompanied by Sarai, by Hagar, the Egyptian handmaid, and by the wife Lot had married in Egypt.

In column XXI we find Abram installed at Beth-El after having separated from Lot, and the account is given of how he made the circuit of all the lands that God had promised to his descendants. Much valuable information may certainly be drawn from the geographical names which occur in this passage, but it is difficult to follow on the map the highly fantastic course which is the result of the author's characteristic liking for exaggerated precision. It may be noted, too, that frequently the author has altered proper names, and this is specially noticeable in the continuation, in column XXI, 23ff. Here it is no longer Abram who is speaking in the first person. The events recorded in Gen. 14 are given as retrospective history: it was "before these days" that the battle had taken place in which four kings defeated the Kings of Sodom, Gomorrah, Admah, Zeboiim, and Bela. In this account, Arioch, King of Ellasar, becomes King of Cappadocia, while Shinab, King of Admah, is called "Lost-my-name", *šmy'bd*, literally "my name is lost". When Abram had defeated the four kings and retaken all their booty, the King of Sodom went out to meet him, and came to Salem, "which is Jerusalem". This identification, which is also given in Josephus, was not afterwards maintained. The pilgrim Etheria looked for Salem on the road to Samaria, close to the place where John the Baptist baptised (John 3.23).

As is often the case in late writers, "Melchizedek, King of Salem", has been made into a person,[1] and Abram gave to him the tithe of all that he had taken from the four kings in exchange for a blessing of God Most High. This personalisation (which may be due to the author of the Epistle

[1] See article, "Melchizedek", by the present writer in *Z.A.T.W.*, 1957, pp. 160-70.

to the Hebrews) comes from an erroneous interpretation of the Hebrew text: it is the King of Sodom, "a just king" (*mlk sdyq* and not *mlkysdq*), and "a peaceful king" (*mlk šlwm* and not *mlk šlm*), who offered his benediction to Abram and declined the tithe which the latter wished to give him, while demanding on the other hand that his providential ally should give up to him the men who had fought with him. In this manuscript, the King of Sodom came up at this moment (*b'dyn*) and offered to leave Abram the booty which the latter held, and on which he had paid the tithe. He only reclaimed the prisoners who had been set free. Abram gave to the King of Sodom all the goods and all the prisoners, and in addition he freed all the captives of "this country".

Although the Book of Genesis endeavours to draw a moral from this adventure (Gen. 15.1; *vide Jubilees*, 14.1), our text does not speak of a recompense promised by God to Abram to compensate him for his renunciation. On the promise of a rightful heir, our roll stops in the middle of a sentence. The following sheet has been cut off by a knife, as indicated earlier.

★      ★      ★

N. Avigad and Y. Yadin think that this roll was written at the end of the first century B.C. or during the first century A.D. They also think that the text is older still, has a close connection with the *Book of Enoch* and the *Book of Jubilees*, and "may have served as a source for a number of stories told more concisely in those two books". At the moment, it is impossible to give a definite date for this manuscript, but there is a clearly marked tendency in all writings of this kind which should not be overlooked: whilst an author leaves out a story he does not know, the general rule stands that "no author abbreviates; all amplify". It is at the end of the first century A.D. and the beginning of the second that Christian authors are seen giving names to persons unnamed in the New Testament, a tendency already noticeable in the Fourth Gospel. The *Acts of Peter*, the *Acts of Pilate*, and other such Christian apocrypha abound in examples of this kind. By analogy, we may conclude that the author of our roll did not escape this tendency. He also has filled out texts—often fragmentary—of which he had rather imperfect knowledge.

Moreover, it hardly seems probable that our roll could have been earlier to, or contemporary with, the *Book of Jubilees*, *Enoch*, etc., which are given dates from the fourth to the second centuries B.C. In the columns already published, we have noted the name Hyrcanus given to one of the princes of Egypt. But Hyrcanus of the family of Tobias lived about 200 B.C. For the legend to have formed about him as it is found in Josephus, nearly three centuries had had to elapse. How much longer is necessary for a popular author to be able to make Hyrcanus a contemporary of Abram, especially as this name borne by sovereigns and princes of the Hasmonaean house is here given to a doubtful character? What ignorance of the Scriptures could have led the author of our text to make Zoan a Pharaoh? Whence comes it that Salem is identified with Jerusalem and that Melchizedek is personified? In any case, the *Book of Jubilees* seems to be unacquainted with Melchizedek and the King of Salem, and the author of the Epistle to the Hebrews clearly indicates that he is giving a *new* interpretation to an expression which one rendered then as "the just king" and "the peace-loving king".

At the moment, the roll of the *Genesis Apocryphon* appears to us to date from the middle of the second century A.D. at the earliest. The manuscript itself may be of the same period, perhaps even later. It is impossible as yet to say when it could have been consigned to the *geniza*. In any case, that is only the place where such a writing would get landed, for a number of passages, even in Aramaic, are highly improper.

xiii

## FRAGMENTS FROM QUMRÂN CAVE I

As a result of long and painstaking work, the manuscript fragments collected in Cave I of Qumrân, along with others acquired by purchase, have been classified into different groups. Frequently when the letters which had been preserved did not allow of the identification of a text, the nature of the leather made it possible to differentiate the manuscripts. Any pieces of manuscript which presented more than a few parts of letters have been published.[1] They have been divided out into Biblical fragments and non-Biblical fragments.

### I. BIBLICAL FRAGMENTS

The Biblical fragments which have been identified come from eleven rolls written in what is called "square" Hebrew script. They are : Genesis, Exodus, Deuteronomy (two copies) Judges, Samuel, Isaiah (fragments of roll "*B*") Ezekiel, Psalms (three copies). Fragments have also been

---

[1] D. Barthélemy and J. T. Milik, *Qumrân Cave I*, Oxford, 1955. References to this work are given in the text between parentheses.

found of Leviticus and Numbers, coming from four rolls. These are all in the ancient "Phoenician" script. To this list may be added a phylactery reproducing the Decalogue in the version of Chapter 5 of Deuteronomy.

(*a*) *The Fragments in "Square" Script.* Looking at the reproduction of these fragments and in view of the information published about them, one can have serious doubts about their coming from complete rolls taken to the cave in their linen covers, as was the practice. It would have to be supposed that the effects of time had been greater on some writings than on others, which would be difficult to admit seeing that the conditions of preservation were identical. It has been remarked that the Genesis fragments seem to be "broken bits of a very limited number of larger pieces" (p. 49). The fragments of Exodus give the impression of having come "from the scattered remains of a little heap which itself came from a roll which had been gnawed to pieces" (p. 50). Six fragments from the Book of Samuel were found "in the form of a strip rolled together, crushed, bent back and nibbled at" (p. 64). Of the nine fragments from the third Psalter, eight "easily fitted into the framework of the same Forty-fourth Psalm" (p. 71). All the fragments from the second Psalter belonged to Ps. 126–8 —that is to say, to one and the same sheet (p. 71). Of the nine fragments of the Book of Judges, seven belonged to Chapter 9 (p. 62).

These facts ought to be sufficient to show that most of these fragments did not come from complete rolls, but from separate sheets which had been thrown into the *geniza* as torn and unusable. Some fragments had been rolled into a ball, and others were crumpled up like papers thrown into a waste-paper basket.

It is very difficult to get an idea of the manuscripts from which the fragments came, and many of these are extremely small. None the less, it is possible to remark that the two copies of Deuteronomy must have presented a text which was "hardly classical". Can it be inferred from that that they came from an ancient version or from an unorthodox one? We should like to suppose that all these small pieces came from detached sheets of manuscripts, as did the fragments which formed the book of *Thanksgiving Hymns,* but in this case it is impossible to pronounce upon the age of the manuscripts, as was done in the case of the two Isaiah rolls.

(*b*) *The Fragments in "Phoenician" Script.* Although in several non-canonical writings found in Cave I the name of God, whether Yahweh or simply El, was written in ancient "Phoenician" characters, no one thought to attach to this detail an importance which, as a matter of fact, it does not have. In the *Manual of Discipline* the name Yahweh is replaced by a series of four dots, symbol of the unpronounceable Tetragrammaton. The transcription of the NAME into ancient characters must have served the same purpose. It is in this script, too, that the Tetragrammaton is written in the fragments which come from the second Psalter of Qumrân.

On the other hand, the discovery in the cave of numerous fragments of Leviticus and Numbers, entirely in ancient characters, raises the problem as to whether these particular books, of which not a single fragment has been found written in "square" script, did not have to be written in this manner, and if so, till what period.[1] Ancient script is no evidence that a manuscript is ancient. The Samaritans still use the so-called "Phoenician" script. One cannot on that account say that these fragments come from books which had belonged to some Samaritan sect or other, particularly devoted to the ancient form of writing. Attention has been drawn to the fact that there are resemblances to the Samaritan Pentateuch, that certain spaces left blank do not correspond with the Massoretic divisions, but obviously these considerations do not carry much weight, for the Samaritan tradition which has come down to us today does not appear to go back to a very early period.

For the moment, nothing very definite can be said about these fragments, and no theory likely to win acceptance can be put forward concerning them. Judging from what we know about the pieces as they were found, the only possible inference is that they do not come from complete rolls, but from odd sheets—and that has not been suggested.

(c) *The Phylactery.* It is well known that the interpretation of the words found in Deut. 11.18 led, at a very early date, to the Jewish custom of wearing phylacteries. Little leather containers were made to hold the *Shema* and some other passages from Deuteronomy and Exodus, and these were worn attached to the hand or the forehead, "between the eyes", by means of straps. Sheaths called *mezuzoth* were nailed to door-posts. Naturally, there were many rabbinic rules as to how these pieces of parchment bearing verses from the Bible were to be drawn up, written, folded, and placed inside the little cases. For manual phylacteries, four passages from the Pentateuch (Exod. 13.1-10, 13.11-16; Deut. 6.4-19, 11.13-21) were to be copied on a single sheet of parchment and placed in a single compartment. For phylacteries to be worn on the forehead, these passages were to be copied on separate sheets and placed in four separate compartments. At a

[1] See article by J. L. Teicher on the Shapira manuscripts in *The Times Literary Supplement*, 22nd March 1957.

time when Gnosticism was infiltrating into Judaism, and the wearing of Gnostic amulets tended to become general, the rabbis had to watch very carefully that no confusion was possible between phylactery and amulet. Nor is it surprising that certain phylacteries declared irregular were seized and consigned to the *geniza,* though ordinarily a phylactery did not "defile the hands".

As the document found in Cave I consists of a single piece, it cannot have been a frontal phylactery, one for the forehead. We are told that it was found in the form of a "little flattened-out roll the ends of which had afterwards been bent over towards each other so as to form a sort of small ring" (p. 72). That certainly was not the usual way to roll the parchment of a phylactery, which also had to be fastened by a band of leather.

Unfortunately, the unrolling of this document practically destroyed it. The published information about it is somewhat contradictory. First we are told about the text of the Decalogue and it is said that "the sheet on which the copy had been made was rolled with this on the inside, and so it was better preserved", but from the attempted reconstruction of this passage (Fig. 10) the impression is given that the document was rolled inside out. Further on it is said that "the phylactery must have contained a number of passages which were not according to Jewish tradition" (p. 75). Apart from the Decalogue, these passages have not been indentified. Elsewhere we are informed that at first the lines increased in length as they went on, the first line with twelve letters and the fourteenth with nearly 100, and that then they decreased to eighty, a couple of score, and finally to ten. Does that mean that the text was written in the classic form of an abracadabra?

Other doubts crop up. Mention is made of eight fragments from Chapters 10 and 11 of Deuteronomy, the supposed ending of this document, and it is said that "it is hardly likely that the passage 11.13-21 was copied on the same sheet". In any case, neither the fragments from Exod. 13 which have been identified, nor the other passages which have not been identified, fit into a lozenge pattern. In a word, the learned labour bestowed on this document does not let us know if a number of sheets of leather were rolled together one over the other, or if a number of passages and other texts were found on a single sheet, arranged more or less fantastically in squares, lozenges, and other geometric figures. But already one thing is quite certain: this document from Qumrân Cave I *is not a phylactery.*

(1) As far back as Jewish traditions go, a frontal phylactery has always

consisted of four separate sheets inserted in the four compartments of a small case. A case of this kind, and fragments of a similar second one, have been found in Cave I, and that proves without any question, if proof was necessary, that this form of phylactery was current at the time, and that the discovered document did not come from a frontal phylactery (Plate 1, Fig. 5).

(2) A manual phylactery consisted of only a single sheet of parchment, inscribed with the four passages given above, and with nothing else. It was rolled with the writing inside and fastened with a band of leather. Although frequently written in microscopic characters, no fantasy was allowed either in the way of arranging the text or of folding the sheet of leather. In Cave I the complete case belonging to a manual phylactery has been found, though empty of its contents, and the remains of at least four others (Plate 1, Fig. 7). "Not one of them seems large enough to hold the phylactery which has been discovered" (p. 7).

To all appearances, the document was a Gnostic amulet. It contained the passages used in phylacteries, but they were arranged in a way which can almost be called cabbalistic. It also contained something else, but what we shall never know. Moreover, it was rolled up in a very strange way so as to form a ring, the extremities having been brought near to each other. For a long time what was rolled in this manner was an abomination to the Jews, and, among other places, an echo of this interdiction is found in the *Damascus Document*.

This Jewish amulet was certainly considered to be heretical, and taken to the *geniza* like any other unorthodox parchment written by a Jew and bearing the name of God. It is therefore impossible to compare it with phylacteries from any other age or region.[1] The publishing of the phylacteries found at Murabba'at and in Cave IV at Qumrân, if they really are *tephilin*, cannot supply any basis for comparison, in spite of certain resemblances which may exist between phylacteries and amulets.

## II. NON-BIBLICAL TEXTS

The non-Biblical fragments have been divided out into commentaries, apocryphal books, legal texts and liturgies, collections of hymns, and miscellaneous.

(a) *Commentaries*. The Book of Habakkuk was not the only one to serve as the theme for interpretations of current events. Those of Micah

---

[1] S. Zeitlin, *The Dead Sea Scrolls* . . ., pp. 35-9, thinks that what was found in Cave I was a Babylonian phylactery of the Middle Ages.

and Zephaniah were interpreted in the same way, and also connected with the fall of Jerusalem. The Orator of Falsehood and the Teacher of Righteousness are mentioned in the *Commentary on Micah*, and, as in that on Habakkuk, these names probably hid those of Agrippa II and of Menahem. Unfortunately, the texts are too fragmentary to give certainty on this point.

A *Commentary on the Psalms* seems to apply the verses of Ps. 68.30–1 to the "legions" (*kty'ym*). Unfortunately again, not much remains of this fragment, and probably it will never be known if the author rightly interpreted or not the words *hyt qnh 'dt 'byrym*, words which should be rendered by "the being who buys by the right of the strongest" and not, as is usually done, by "the beast of the reeds", etc. Other texts from Qumrân suggest that the correct meaning of this psalm had not yet been lost at the time, and frequently the plundering of the country was called "profitable buying".

(b) *Apocryphal Books*. Two fragments may have belonged to the *Book of Jubilees*, known only to us by translations which may be more or less close to the original. Some other fragments are thought to come from the *Book of Noah*, one of the supposed sources of the *Book of Enoch*, only known through Greek and Ethiopian versions. Some fragments broken off the *Genesis Apocryphon* have been found, and it may be possible to insert these into breaks in that manuscript when it is published. Other fragments, some exceedingly small, have been attributed to the *Testament of Levi* in Aramaic, the only one of these texts hitherto known in a Hebrew version through finds in the Cairo *geniza*.

The name of the *Sayings of Moses* has been given to another unknown apocryphal work. A few fragments of this have been found, but not a single complete sentence. About forty minute pieces have come from two books in Aramaic to which names have not been given. There are fifteen fragments which probably belonged to some book of prophecies, and five others have been attributed to some book of "Wisdom".

Of all these apocryphal or pseudepigraphic writings, only one fairly large fragment has been recovered. It comprises a few lines from one column and the beginnings of the lines in the next column. The book from which this part of a sheet comes has been given the name of the *Book of Mysteries*. The few complete sentences suggest that the text promised the coming of an age of peace and righteousness. It seems to be a Jewish-Christian work, but no precise dating of it is possible.

(c) *Legal Texts and Liturgies*. Fourteen small fragments seem to come from regulations for the service of the Chief Priest in the Temple when that should be rebuilt. In a context unfortunately lost, there appears to be mention of "tongues of fire". Twelve other fragments almost certainly belong to a similar work. A score or so of other small fragments cannot be placed.

(*d*) *Collections of Hymns*. Twenty-five fragments of apocryphal hymns or psalms have been collected in the cave. Judging by the nature of the leather and the characteristics of the writing, these must have come from four similar rolls.

(*e*) *Miscellaneous*. Among the fragments, often very small, which have been recovered in Cave I, some are on papyrus. Among these, some have writing both on back and front, with calligraphic script on one side and cursive on the other. As these pieces are so small, it is impossible to know what they contained, and conjecture alone remains. Merely as a theory, a comparison has been made with the Midrashîm, the Talmudîm, and other works which even in present-day printed editions use several kinds of script to distinguish texts from one another. It is quite possible that in these volumes the Biblical text or its translation was in one kind of writing and the commentary in another, etc.

★          ★          ★

Apart from the fragments collected in the cave, several pages bought from the dealer in Bethlehem by the Palestine Museum almost certainly originate from there. The Syrian Metropolitan had in his possession three fragments of the Book of Daniel. They were in two different handwritings and seemed to come from two rolls, which perhaps will one day be offered for sale. Some fragments from a collection of prayers, only one with a few complete sentences, and a few other pieces of papyrus 2 or 3 centimetres square complete the list of all that, up to the present, we can suppose to have come from the cave discovered by the Bedouin in the spring of 1947.

# IV

# Conclusion

The story which is told us by the manuscripts from Cave I of Qumrân is far from coherent. Apart from a few rare exceptions, there is nothing in one manuscript or group of fragments to relate it to another roll coming from the same cave. It is said that three of the four rolls formerly named after St. Mark's Monastery had been found in the same jar, but the statement to that effect was only made after a considerable lapse of time, and is very doubtful. Even if it is true, the only deduction that can be made from that fact is that the rolls were perhaps taken to the cave at the same time. But they are not equally old, nor are they from the same place of origin. The same is also true about the other manuscripts and fragments found in the same cave. In a similar way, within a cemetery may be found dead of all ages and of different countries.

The Biblical texts are not as ancient as was hoped, but is a document of the time of Julius Caesar necessarily more important than a piece of evidence from the reign of Marcus Aurelius? One can hardly agree that the Dead Sea Scrolls were "unquestionably the greatest manuscript find of modern times".[1] Other discoveries certainly more sensational have been made in other spheres of Orientalism. But for those who have a real, unprejudiced interest in the history of the small Jewish nation in the early years of our era, the Dead Sea manuscripts are of priceless value, and the study of them will be the work of decades to come.

Cave I of Qumrân can no longer be considered as unique. Not only have caves with manuscripts been discovered in the Wadi Murabba'at, but five others are known in the cliffs at Qumrân and five near to the ruins. Essential information is lost because many of the manuscripts from these caves are in Bedouin hands, and have to be purchased before their

[1] W. F. Albright in the *Bulletin of the American Schools of Oriental Research,* 110 (1948), p. 2.

contents can be known. Who would blame a scholar for having doubts about the exact origin of a roll which he knows has passed through the hands of a number of traffickers only more or less trustworthy? Who can stop a manuscript from being called a forgery, or "of uncertain origin", when it does not fit in with theories which are being maintained? Who can prevent the destruction or loss of a manuscript, or of a fragment from it, when a word, or even a letter, is going to reduce the market value of all that is being offered for sale? Bedouin have even been known to make up sheets of manuscripts out of very small fragments, and then to protest on oath that the sheets came to pieces in their hands. Our only guarantee is the alert attention of the scholars who are in contact with the diggers, but can the human factor be excluded? In every sphere of life the human mind works by selection in what it perceives. That is the price of attention. A scholar cannot be prevented from only seeing what he has in mind, even as a doctor will always see in his patients symptoms of the disease in which he has specialised, and may overlook others which are not familiar to him.

A typical case is that of rolls said to have come from Cave IV. Interest is centred round a sheet of a *Commentary on the Book of Nahum,* because it has been thought that there is a direct reference to Alexander Jannaeus and events which took place in 90 B.C.[1] Thanks to generous financial help, this fragment was purchased from illicit diggers in preference to a number of others, but there is no news of a roll said to contain the whole Pentateuch, which, according to rumours that cannot be verified, made part of the same collection. If this roll exists, like the incomplete roll of the Minor Prophets found in a cave of the Wadi Murabba'at, it cannot from the nature of the case be earlier than the second century A.D.

A dispatch from Chicago dated 30th November 1956, and reproduced in the Paris edition of the *New York Times* the next day, announced that the McCormick Theological Seminary had acquired nine rolls from the Dead Sea. The review published by this institute[2] gave more precise information. Thanks to the generosity of Mr. and Mrs. Rehnborg, the McCormick Theological Seminary had been able to put at Mr. Harding's disposition a sum of money enough to buy 2,100 square centimetres of manuscript. Mr. Harding received this news on 15th July, and at once

---

[1] See the articles by J. M. Allegro in the *Journal of Biblical Literature,* LXXV (1956), pp. 89ff., and H. H. Rowley, *ibid.,* pp. 188ff. The passage in question is very fragmentary, and can be translated in a number of ways. In any case, one fact seems certain: it is not an allusion to current events, but is a historical recalling of some past event.

[2] *McCormick Speaking,* X, 4 (December 1956), pp. 7-10.

informed Kando, the Bethlehemite semi-official intermediary between the Ta'amireh Bedouin and the Jordanian Department of Antiquities. At ten o'clock the following day, Kando arrived carrying a collection of large pieces, which apparently came from the bottom of the Bedouin barrel. After some sorting and the identification of fragments, some of which filled in gaps in other manuscripts, the McCormick Seminary was allotted the fragments of nine manuscripts described briefly as follows:

(1) An ancient copy of the Book of Jeremiah, probably dating from the end of the second century B.C.
(2) A very fragmentary manuscript of the Book of Daniel, dating from the second century B.C.
(3) A second copy of the Book of Daniel.
(4) A manuscript of Ecclesiastes, dating from about 150 B.C.
(5) A paraphrase of Genesis.
(6) An Essene liturgy (?).
(7) A collection of hymns.
(8) A "Wisdom" writing.
(9) A papyrus containing an unknown apocalyptic work.

Naturally, until these texts have been published, it will be impossible to know what arguments support their being dated to the second century B.C. It will be particularly interesting to learn why one of these copies of the Book of Daniel was made within fifty or sixty years of the original composition by the author.[1] Doubtless there were serious reasons for speaking of an "Essene" liturgy, and for having bought the fragments of it rather than the others which filled the bottom of the Bedouin barrel. The only precise information we have concerning this collection is that the Book of Jeremiah follows rather closely the Greek Septuagint version and departs a great deal from the classic Hebrew text. This is referred to below.

*The Temple Treasure.* Another case, equally typical, is that of the copper rolls found in Cave III at Qumrân. The discovery goes back to the month of March 1952. This cave is situated in the cliff not far from that called Qumrân I. In it were discovered "the débris of at least twenty-five jars and only a few fragments of writing". We are told that this hiding-place had never been violated. All details about the state of the cave at the

---

[1] It is generally agreed to place the composition of the Book of Daniel (apart from later additions) to the years 167-164 B.C. or, more precisely, between December 168 and June 164.

moment of discovery are therefore of the highest importance, and the publication of them cannot fail to give us valuable information.

The most important find made there consisted of two very curious rolls. These were neither in leather nor in papyrus! Three sheets of pure copper 1 millimetre thick (roughly $\frac{1}{16}$ inch), 30 centimetres (12 inches) in height and about 80 centimetres (32 inches) in length had originally been riveted end to end to form a strip of 2 metres 40 centimetres (8 feet). At some time—though when we do not yet know—one sheet was separated and rolled up with the inscription on the inside, and the remaining part was also rolled up in the same way, similar to the rolling up of manuscripts on leather. On the back of the rolls, the trace of some deeply indented letters could be seen in relief. The copper was much oxidised and brittle, and it was impossible to learn the contents of the roll.

Theories were afoot at once. There was talk of a religious text of the greatest importance, of the essence of the "rule" of the Essenes. This band of copper, we were told, must formerly have decorated the wall of the large chamber where the Essenes held their chapter; it must have borne very important admonitions to have been in such a prominent place, and in such a manner that every Essene had it before his eyes whenever he took part in the ceremonies of the order![1] It was imagined that about A.D. 66, when the community of the Essenes were about to disperse, these sheets of copper were unfixed from the wall and rolled up so that the monks could put them in safety, as they had done with the books from their library. And, as this copper band must have been exceptionally important, Cave III must have been the most secret hiding-place, the most inaccessible, etc.

In 1953 Professor K. G. Kuhn of Heidelberg was able to see these rolls preserved in a glass case in the Palestine Archaeological Museum.[2] He at once saw that there was no question of a religious text, and that these sheets had never been fixed to a wall. At the request of several specialists, notably Mr. Allegro, it was in the end decided to entrust this curious document to the University of Manchester, where in the course of the winter of 1955-6, Professor H. W. Baker succeeded in cutting the sheets into strips, which, placed end to end, revealed the most unexpected text. The first announcements made to the Press in June 1956 caused a sensation. It was a list of sixty places where enormous treasures, mostly in gold and silver, had been buried! In all it must have been about 200 tons of precious

---

[1] M. Delcor, *Contribution à l'étude de la législation des Sectaires de Damas et de Qumrân*, Paris, 1955, p. 8, had the idea of "some kind of calendar engraved on metal".

[2] K. G. Kuhn, in the *Theologische Literaturzeitung*, LXXXI/9 (1956), cols. 541-6.

metal, worth today about £30,000,000 sterling, without speaking of other objects of value. A short fragment of the text was given in translation:

> In the cistern which is below the rampart, on the east side, in a place hollowed out of the rock, 600 bars of silver.
>
> Close by, below the southern corner of the portico, at Zadok's tomb, underneath the pilaster in the *exedra,* a vessel of incense in pine wood, and a vessel of incense in cassia wood.
>
> In the pit nearby, towards the north, in a hole opening towards the north near the graves, there is a copy of this document with explanations, measurements and all details.

Obviously all that is in contradiction to the supposed monastic poverty of the Essenes. The fact that these rolls had been found in one of the Qumrân caves was left on one side, and the explanation was quickly given that these rolls had no historic value. It was the work of a crank, a romance of the imagination, and no credence was to be given to these supposed treasures. In any case, it was necessary to abstain from publishing this text, or at least to put off the publication as long as possible, lest illicit diggers should turn all the soil of Palestine upside down in their search for treasures which had never existed.

Until the whole text is published, it is, of course, very difficult to form any clear idea about it, but already Professor Kuhn has pointed out that the palæographic character of the inscription suggests that this roll could have been written about the middle of the first century A.D. He also made the observation that an imaginary list of hiding-places would never have been inscribed on material so rare and valuable as copper. No one would have had sheets prepared in this special manner and then had them riveted end to end unless there had been the idea to inscribe an important text on them.

Professor Kuhn considers that the copper roll gave the places where the Temple treasure had been put for safety, and quotes passages from Josephus where the plunder of this treasure is related in detail. He emphasises that only the Temple could have owned such riches, and only the priests would have thought of consigning to writing, and upon sheets of copper, the list of hiding-places. He believes that there were Essenes, and thinks that this copper roll was given into the care of these monks because of their contempt of riches and their undoubted honesty. It is difficult, however, to follow him on this point.

One fact is certain: The three sheets of copper originally formed one band. It can be assumed that one of these sheets was detached, not by those who had it in safe-keeping, but by those who "recovered" the roll and took it to the cave. The Temple treasure was discovered by the Romans, and many details about the plundering of it are well known. From what we can find out, it was far from reaching the fabulous sums mentioned on the copper roll. It did not consist of bars of gold and silver, but mostly of priestly ornaments, liturgical vestments, silver lamps and vases, etc.

Although the topographical indications given in the roll are very vague, there seems to be a real fear that to divulge the list of hiding-places would lead to a veritable treasure-hunt in which more than one tribe of Bedouin would like to join. Obviously, it is necessary to abandon the theory hastily put forward about the exceptional character of Cave III and its importance in the eyes of the Essene order. There are other facts calling for attention, and they deserve to be pointed out:

(1) From the beginning, the roll must have been unshapely and difficult to handle. It could not have been unrolled frequently, and yet it was a roll. It cannot have been manufactured so that a work of imagination might be written on it. And neither can it have been used for a list of real hiding-places. If the roll had been made with the idea of hiding it, a material would have been used that was not so heavy and so showy, and which was easy to conceal. A copper roll can only have been manufactured so that it might be exhibited, and naturally one's mind turns to the Zadokites, their lodges and their ceremonies of initiation. To get the new member to promise that he would put all his possessions at the service of the society, it must have been useful to unroll before him in all solemnity a shining copper roll setting forth the enormous Zadokite treasures. And as it did not give a list of real treasures, he must have been told that there was another more secret roll with exact information. That is what can be read in the passage from the roll given above.

(2) To take an oath "by the Law of Moses", one had to place one's hand on a roll of the Pentateuch. The Zadokites, however, did not administer the rabbinic oath. With them an oath was taken "by the Treasury of the Sanctuary" (cf. Matt. 23.16). This formula was still in use in the Middle Ages, especially among the Qaraites, as the *Damascus Document* shows. The mode of administering the oath is not known, but by analogy it may be supposed that he who took the oath had to place his hand on an inventory of this treasure. What was more natural than

to present this inventory in the form of a roll of semi-precious metal, the shining copper used for making mirrors?

(3) The Zadokites considered the Temple treasure to be their property, as they alone had the right to be priests. According to an old tradition, of which an echo is found in the Talmud, the origin of this treasure went back to Joseph and the riches brought back by him from Egypt on the death of his father. This treasure was buried, and was reserved for the "righteous" (ṣdyqym)—that is to say, for the Zadokites (ṣdwqym), the only true "righteous".

(4) The passage given in translation above refers to a tomb of Zadok. If the tomb of David's chief priest is meant, then the reference can only be to a mythical tomb. In David's day one did not build mausoleums with porticoes and *exedras*. Moreover, even if the memory of this tomb had been maintained, can it be supposed that the many conquerors who had occupied Jerusalem in the course of the centuries would not have violated it? It must not be overlooked that myths have a long life. Josephus relates (*Antiquities*, XIII, viii, 4), and many historians believe him, that John Hyrcanus violated the tomb of David, and took from it 3,000 talents of silver to pay his foreign mercenaries. It could also be that the tomb mentioned in the roll was that of Rabbi Zadok, the founder of the Zadokite sect, though this tomb would have been just as mythical as that of his namesake, David's chief priest. Yet if such a tomb existed, no Zadokite would have dared to dig there in order to make sure that the treasure was there.

According to the present writer's theory, therefore, this copper roll must have been an ostentatious, fictitious inventory of "the Temple treasure" used in Zadokite lodges of the second century A.D. It may be supposed that, after having been seized by the rabbinic authorities, it was placed in a *geniza* along with other unorthodox documents which could not be destroyed. Like the other Qumrân caves, Cave III can only have been a *geniza*. Had it been otherwise, and the copper roll had been put away for safety in a hiding-place, then it would have been found in one piece, for one can hardly see why three sheets riveted together should be separated into two by those who had taken charge of them. And on the other hand, if the inscription had been merely an imaginative romance with no taboo attached to it, those who separated the roll into two parts would have made use of the copper, and not have placed it in a cave.

★          ★          ★

Of the eleven caves at Qumrân which up to now have yielded manuscripts and manuscript fragments, the richest seems to be Cave IV, situated under the ruins and cemetery.

Numerous Biblical manuscripts have been found in this cave. Some are on leather and others on papyrus. As the papyrus certainly does not grow on the shores of the Dead Sea, for these latter rolls, at any rate, the theory of them having been written by monks in their *scriptorium* at Qumrân ought to be given up. As these discoveries in Cave IV have not yet been published, the present writer cannot do with them what he has tried to do with those which came from Cave I—separate writings imported from outside from those written in Palestine. Nor can he determine the reason why these writings should have been buried close to the cemetery. One fact, however, was made known: in the case of one manuscript at least, it was *certain* that it had been deliberately damaged before being placed in this hollow.

Thus, slowly and with some hesitation, truth begins to break through, in spite of a persistent desire to keep up the fiction of a library put away for safety by the Essene monks of Qumrân. The exact contents of everything enclosed in these eleven caves is not yet known, but two important facts are certain:

(1) No manuscript or fragment of the Book of Esther has ever been found in any of the caves of Qumrân or of Murabba'at.

Of all the canonical books, the roll of Esther is the only one that "does not defile the hands". It does not have to be wrapped up in a linen serviette like the other rolls, and may be kept in a Jewish home, whilst any other roll of a canonical book must be kept in a synagogue, and if it once leaves the synagogue it must be taken to a *geniza*. It is therefore quite a normal and natural thing not to find a Book of Esther in a *geniza*, but it is illogical to think that a library would have contained all the canonical books, and several copies of them as well as other non-canonical works, but not a single copy of the Book of Esther.

(2) There have been found, and especially in Cave IV, a number of canonical books in the Greek Septuagint versions.

*The Septuagint Version.* Rightly to appreciate this last point, it must not be lost to view that the Greek Septuagint version was not some sort of *Targum*. For the Jews of Egypt, who frequently knew no Hebrew, it had the value of canonical writings. At the beginning of the second century A.D., when Biblical texts were often adapted to fit in with the new beliefs

A view of the cliffs and the entrance to Qumrân Cave I

Two of the jars in which the
Dead Sea Scrolls were found

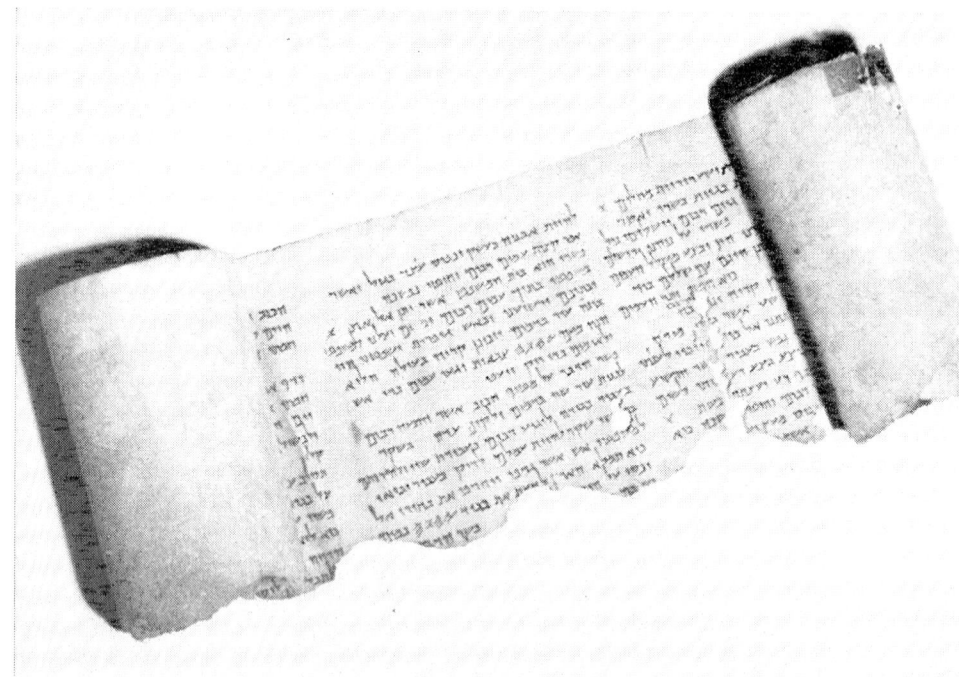

The *Habakkuk* Scroll showing the well-preserved upper part
and the wavy line which marks the line of destruction

A section of the *Manual of Discipline* showing insertions

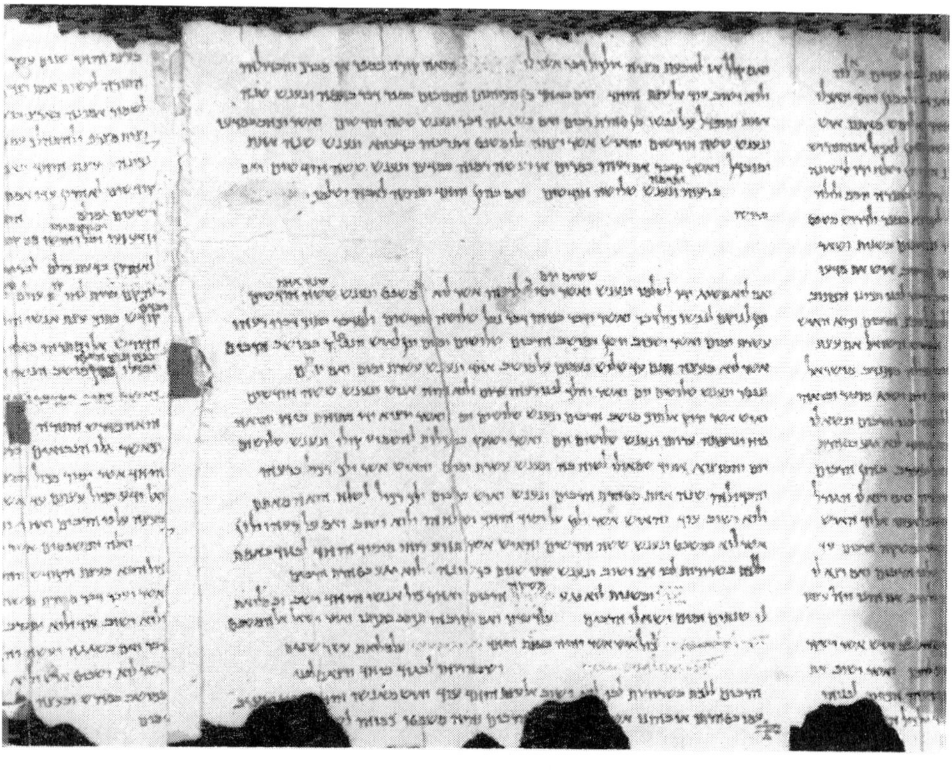

then coming into being in the heart of Judaism, a severe struggle began against translations in Aramaic, Greek, etc., which rendered imperfectly the meanings given to the Scriptures by the rabbis. It was then, under the direction of Rabbi Eliezer and Rabbi Joshua, contemporaries of Rabbi Aqiba, that Aquila, a Greek proselyte from Pontus, and said to be related to the Emperor Hadrian, was given the task of preparing a new Greek version of the Pentateuch. At the beginning of the second century, the older version, the Septuagint, was declared to be "apocryphal", and all copies in circulation in Judea were seized and taken to *genizoth,* and the Aquila version alone was permitted to be used by the Jews in Palestine.

If, as we are now told, most of the manuscripts found in Cave IV can be dated to the early part of the second century A.D., then it may also be assumed that the fragments of the Septuagint, some of which seem to be rather old, were placed there about the same time. That can only be explained by the fact that the Septuagint had just been declared "apocryphal", the official version, that of Aquila, having appeared. Until then no objection had been made to the Septuagint. In Palestine it was not looked on as canonical, and could circulate freely, like other *Targumim.* From the date of Rabbi Aqiba's edict, copies of it had to be taken to the *geniza.* Therefore it is in a *geniza* of the second century, and there only, that one can expect to find copies or fragments of the Septuagint.

*       *       *

Whilst on this subject, it might be useful to recall that other translations of the canonical books were not considered as sacred literature. Possession of these books was not forbidden. It was only forbidden to read from them in the synagogue, though they could be quoted from memory, which was not allowed for the books in Hebrew. Even worn and torn rolls containing the Aramaic versions of the Old Testament did not have to be taken to the *geniza.* Rabbinic literature mentions only a *Targum* of Job as having been seized and consigned to the *geniza.* Probably it had been judged seditious and unorthodox.[1] It may also be supposed that the Aramaic paraphrase of Genesis found in Cave I was likewise buried because of its unorthodox character. But it will be noted that, among the many Aramaic fragments found in the caves of the Judean Desert, not one comes from an ordinary *Targum* of a canonical book. There again the negative argument may be called in. It is impossible to think that a Palestinian

---

[1] The fragments of a *Targum* of Job have been found in Cave XI.

G

"library" did not contain the current Aramaic versions of the books of the Bible, which were far more widely distributed in Palestine than the Septuagint was, yet it is logical not to find the *Targumim* in a *geniza*.

The history of the Greek version of the Bible is even now not well known, in spite of many studies devoted to the subject. One fact is certain in any case. If it is necessary to believe the legend according to which, about 250 B.C., seventy-two learned Jews translated the Pentateuch into Greek, very little remains of their work. As to the other books which form the Bible of Alexandria, they were surely translated much later, and from texts which were not in all points in accordance with the Palestinian tradition. It has been maintained for a long time that certain deutero-canonical books were written directly in Greek. The Hebrew fragments of Ecclesiasticus or *Ben Sirach,* found in the Cairo *geniza,* have every appearance of being re-translations from the Syriac version of the book.

Now that the caves of the Judean Desert are yielding up to us pages of the Old Testament in Hebrew which are closer to the Septuagint than to the Hebrew text which eventually became the Massoretic version, there is one thing which is quite certain: these pages did not have the approval of the Palestinian rabbinic authorities, even if, according to the standards of modern textual criticism, they at times offer a better reading of some obviously corrupt passages in the Massoretic text. But that is about all that we can say. The study of each fragment ought to bring up a number of questions, and it would be very wise to ask oneself if the manuscript in question was written in Palestine or brought in from abroad. Frequently it will be necessary to see up to what point current Greek or Aramaic versions had been the basis for certain "emendations" of the Hebrew text. It may even be necessary at times to see if passages in the Alexandrine, Samaritan, and in the Judean Bible itself are not downright re-translations from the Greek. There again the easy solution which talks about an ancient Hebrew tradition always followed more closely by translators into Greek than by the rabbinic schools of Palestine and Mesopotamia, will sooner or later have to be abandoned.

In any case, it will not be easy to admit that the supposed Essene monks of Qumrân knew the Hebrew Bible in a variety of versions, but all of them unorthodox from the point of view of the Palestinian rabbis.

*          *          *

It is interesting to point out here that in the collection of manuscripts from Cave IV bought by the McCormick Theological Seminary a copy of the Book of Jeremiah was found which followed very closely the version transmitted by the Septuagint. It is well known that this version is shorter than that of the Hebrew Bible by about an eighth. Moreover, several passages are placed differently, Chapters 46-51 in the Greek version following 25.13 in the current Hebrew version. There are several indications which suggest that the Greek text was translated from a Hebrew manuscript which followed a different tradition from that which was to become official in Judea and Mesopotamia, but these same indications favour the attribution of this recension to an Alexandrine Jew of the third century B.C. They also imply that on being translated into Greek it was incorporated into the Septuagint.[1] Yet, if the Alexandrine version goes back to an ancient tradition (and the Book of Jeremiah dates from the sixth century), it has certainly undergone remodelling quite as apparent as that of the Judean version incorporated into the Hebrew Bible.

The fact that a copy of the Alexandrine version of the Book of Jeremiah has been found in Cave IV is a definite proof that this version was accounted "apocryphal" by the rabbinic authorities of Judea, and not that the Essenes of Qumrân had been the faithful guardians of a more authentic tradition going back to the fifth century B.C.

*     *     *

The problem of the manuscripts of the Dead Sea is a very involved one. One cannot try to solve it by a convenient solution which attributes all the finds to the same date and the same origin. Even if the theory of the Essene library is universally accepted, it must not be overlooked that scientific and historical truth is not established by a majority vote. An error, multiplied by no matter what factor, still remains an error. If an idea is obviously false, is it necessary to persist in it just because it has the approval of the crowds? In 1948, when only one cave with manuscripts was known in the Judean Desert, it was allowable to be mistaken by a few centuries, even though many of the mistakes could have been avoided. Today it ought to be possible to renounce untenable theories and take up the problem afresh, looking at it from another angle and in a different light.

As soon as it is possible to place it in its age and environment, each manuscript, and frequently every passage in a manuscript, has a story to tell us. It is this story which the present writer wishes to disentangle in the

---

[1] A. Lods, *Histoire de la Littérature hébraïque et juive*, p. 422.

short commentaries which follow his translation of the texts found in Cave I of Qumrân. When the contents of the other caves are better known, it will be possible to attempt a synthesis of all that has come to light, and perhaps it will be possible to take a comprehensive view of the political and religious movements in Palestine which were destined to be swept away by the triumph of Nicene Christianity.

# PART TWO

# Non-Biblical Texts from Cave I

Three non-Biblical works found in Cave I at Qumrân[1] are, in reality, compilations. No one has ever thought that the *Hymns of Thanksgivings* were other than a collection, and the composite nature of the *Manual of Discipline* and of *The War of the Sons of Light against the Sons of Darkness* has been recognised by the majority of the translators of these documents. These works, however, continue to be treated as forming a homogeneous whole, emanating from the same environment, and manifesting the same ideas. In the same way, for a long time, the whole of the Pentateuch was attributed to one sole author, Moses, the whole of the Old Testament Psalter to King David, and the whole Book of Isaiah to the prophet of the eighth century B.C. Thus there has been an inclination to seek the origin of all the writings found in Qumrân in one single sect, the Essenes.

To the present writer, it appeared useful before anything else to divide up these collections. Between the different passages there are sufficient contradictions, doctrinal divergencies, and other varying points of detail to justify the attributing of most of these passages to one or another of the main currents of thought and belief to be found within Judaism. Sometimes allusions to certain definite events make it possible to determine their approximate date. There are other divergencies, which though less clearly marked are yet quite noticeable, and these sometimes enable one to differentiate between schools of the same tendency: here a writer finds importance in the number "seven", while another writer is influenced by the number "four". On the other hand, peculiarities in the choice of words and phrases, and also the style, justify the attributing to one and the same writer of several fragments now found scattered here and there throughout a manuscript.

To get a clearer idea of the original documents which formed the basis of the collections and compilations coming from Qumrân Cave I, a re-grouping of the various fragments would be necessary. An attempt of this kind has been made in the present writer's first translation of the *Manual of Discipline.*[2] In this present work, the various fragments have been translated one after the other in the order in which they were copied out by the compilers of the manuscripts now discovered. Their attribution to different sources is indicated in the short commentary which follows each passage. The questions dealing with the compilation of these collections have been dealt with in Part One.

[1] See p. 11 of Preface for note on method of translating.
[2] *Deux Manuscripts hébreaux de la Mer Morte*, Paris, 1951.

# I

# The Manual of Discipline

Since the translation which the writer proposed in 1951, there have been numerous studies on this text. It has not been possible to accept all the suggested changes, but some, however, seemed feasible, and account has been taken of them.

The manuscript has been frequently corrected by scratching out the original word, by writing over it, and by phrases inserted between the lines. This makes it somewhat difficult to establish the text. The various alterations made by the scribes have been given in the earlier translation. In this present work, notes have been considerably shortened in view of publishing requirements.

## FRAGMENT 1

COLUMN I, LINES 1-11.

For . . . . . . . . . . . . on his life . . . . . . of the Community; to seek God . . . . . . . . . . . . . to do that which is good and right in His eyes, in accordance with what He has commanded by the hand of Moses and by the hand of all His servants, the prophets: to love all those whom He has chosen and to hate all those whom He has rejected: to keep away from all evil and to join in all good works: to practise truth, charity, and justice upon the earth: to walk no longer in the stubbornness of a guilty heart and of perverted eyes ready for every kind of evil: to bring into the Covenant of Grace all those who offer themselves for the observing of the commandments of God, so that they may be united in the counsel of God, conducting themselves before

Him correctly as regards all that which He reveals when they assemble to receive revelations: so that they love all the Sons of Light, each according to his lot in the counsel of God, and hate all the Sons of Darkness each according to his guiltiness which God shall requite.

This fragment is situated at the beginning of the roll of which a part of the fly-leaf has been recovered. It forms part of the initiation path of a Zadokite lodge, a community calling itself "The Covenant of Grace". The new member had to swear on his life to follow solely the precepts of the Law of Moses (and not the rules of the rabbis). The "prophets", servants of God, referred to here are Samuel, Elijah, etc., mentioned in the books of "The Former Prophets" (Joshua, Judges, Samuel, and Kings), the Zadokites recognising the authority of these books while denying that of the Prophetical Books, rightly so-called.

One will notice the engagement to bring in proselytes of whom it would be demanded that they conformed to all that was revealed in the sessions of the lodge. They were to love all their fellow members, the Sons of Light, and hate all the opponents of the sect, the Sons of Darkness. In other texts, these expressions have a more general meaning.

COLUMN I, LINES 11-15.

And all those who offer themselves to observe God's truth, shall contribute to the Community of God, all their knowledge, strength and wealth, in order to purify their knowledge by the truth of God's ordinances, to control their strength by following His perfect way, and use all their wealth agreeably to the counsels of His righteousness. Obedience to the words of God is to be without reservation, neither putting forward nor delaying any of the decreed times, and not departing from His truth by turning to the right hand or to the left.

The members of this Zadokite lodge should bring to it all their knowledge, strength and wealth, but that by no means implies that they should cede all their possessions to the society. The text says clearly that the engagement consisted solely in not making a bad use of their intellectual, physical or financial resources, not even by the subterfuge of any mental reservation which they might make. As the society followed political aims, common action was essential for success. The members therefore had to promise to undertake nothing before the fixed date should be revealed, but also not to delay when once the hour had struck.

G*

COLUMN I, LINES 16–26.

And all those who enter into the bond of the Community shall pass into the Covenant (*promising*) before God to act in accordance with all that He has commanded, and not to draw back in spite of any terror, or dread, or fiery trials in the realm of Belial. And as they are entering into the Covenant, the Cohens and the Levis shall be blessing God for His deliverances and for all the works of His truth. Those entering the Covenant shall repeat after them, "Amen, Amen".

The Cohens shall recount all the righteous acts of God done by mighty men, and what has been told concerning all the benefits bestowed on Israel by the Merciful One. The Levis shall recall the iniquities of the Sons of Israel, and all their sins, transgressions and crimes under the rule of Belial. [And all] those entering into the Covenant shall make confession, saying after them;

"We have been evil-doers, [we have sinned, we have been crimin]als, we have made ourselves guilty, we, and our fathers before us, walking [in a way which is not that of truth and justice. Therefore God has performed] His judgement on us and on our ancestors."

COLUMN II, LINES 1–18.

Yet it is by the mercies of His favours that He has repaid us, from the eternity past to the eternity to come."

Then the Cohens shall bless all the men of God's heritage, who walk rightly in all His ways, and they shall say:

"*May He bless you in granting you every good!*
*May He keep you from all evil!*
*May He enlighten your heart with a quick understanding!*
*May He give you knowledge of all things for an adorning!*
*And may He show you his favours for your everlasting well-being!*"

And, laying a curse on all who pertain to Belial, the Levis shall say:

"*May you be accursed in all the deeds of wickedness of which you have made yourselves guilty!*
*May God make you shake with fear because of all the seekers after vengeance!*
*May He set in pursuit of you the exterminating hand of all those who render retribution for crime!*
*May you be accursed without pity as the blackness of your doings is accursed!*

*May you be accursed by the darkness of the eternal fire!*
*May God show no kindness to you when you call upon Him!*
*May He not accept atonement for your deeds of wickedness!*
*May He turn towards you the face of His wrath, to bring vengeance upon you!*
*And may no one of your father's race give you his greeting!"*

Following those who bless and those who curse, all who are entering into the Covenant shall say, "Amen, Amen." And the Cohens and the Levis shall conclude by saying (*together*):

"Cursèd be he, who with guile in his heart, and with intent to transgress, enters into this Covenant, and who in the abomination of his wickedness purposes to return to his sin, and who, listening to the words of the Covenant in secret flatters himself saying, 'All will go well with me, and I shall go on doing what I wish, yet my thirsty soul shall join with those who are full.' With no possibility of pardon, the wrath of God and the fierceness of His judgements will burn in him for ever. The curses of the Covenant will fall on him, and God will sort him out for evil. He will be cut off from the midst of all the Sons of Light, because by his guile and by the abominations of his transgressions, he will have turned from following God. His lot will be in the midst of the accursed for all eternity."

And all those entering into the Covenant shall make response, saying after them, "Amen, Amen".

A stroke of the pen in the margin, and an *alinea,* mark clearly the end of this fragment, which gives us the initiation ritual of a Zadokite lodge. Like all Jews, the Zadokites attached certain prerogatives to the name Cohen, but in the whole of this passage it is necessary not to translate "Kohen" by "priest", nor "Levi" by "Levite". Here we are not dealing with a sacrifice, nor with a religious ceremony in the Temple. In the synagogue, even to our own days, only persons who inherit the status of Cohen have the right to pronounce a benediction. It seems that the right to pronounce an anathema was also accorded to them by the Zadokites, although certain anathemas might be pronounced by members of the society who had the status of Levi. The question will frequently arise as to the prerogatives attached to family names. Even if in some other texts, it is necessary to translate "Kohen" by "sacrificer" or "priest", that is not the case with the fragment dealt with here. It should be remembered, nevertheless, that many ancient priests and their descendants belonged to

Zadokite organisations which had as their aim the re-establishment of the Temple worship, and the restitution of their ancient privileges to the descendants of Aaron.

The Zadokite initiation ceremony began with an oath by the new members who promised, before God, not to betray the community whatever were the threats and sufferings which might be inflicted on them by the Romans—the dominion of Belial. Jewish history, accommodated to the tenets of the Zadokites, was then narrated to them. The Cohens read the pages which showed the glory of the men of valour, and the Levis read those pages dealing with the transgressions of Israel. All religious communities have had similar books of history. One has even been found with the Qaraites of the tenth century. It forms part of the fragments discovered in the Cairo *Geniza*, and was probably named "The Book of the Divisions of the Ages". In the Zadokite book of history, a very considerable place was given to Jewish betrayals under the Roman occupation. We may recall that the fall of Jerusalem in A.D. 70 was attributed to betrayals, first of Rabbi Zadok, and later of Menahem.

After the confession of sins, following a formula found with little variation in all Jewish prayers, the Cohens blessed the members of the community, and the Levis cursed all those who were in league with Belial, i.e. with the Romans. In conclusion, the Cohens and the Levis together laid a curse on all those who joined a Zadokite lodge with the idea of betraying it, or in a spirit of opportunism. To each blessing and curse, all the members present responded by the words, "Amen, Amen".

We should remember that, in order to prevent any mental reservation, the actual words of an oath were always pronounced by the person administering it, while he to whom it was administered had to respond by the word, "Amen".

A very curious expression is met with in the formula of the curse— "by the darkness of the fire eternal". It refers to Gehenna, the Valley of Hinnom, which is placed to the east of Jerusalem (the region of Qumrân?), Joshua 18.16. It was said that the entrance to the valley of Hinnom was marked by two palm-trees, and that a black smoke rose up from these trees. According to some who did not believe in survival after death, reprobates were condemned while still alive to spend twelve months there before experiencing eternal rest. According to others, they had to remain there throughout eternity.

## FRAGMENT 2

COLUMN II, LINE 19, TO COLUMN III, LINE 12.

The following is what shall be done year by year, so long as the domination of Belial endures:

The Cohens shall go in front according to custom, as they think fit, and in due order. Then the Levis shall follow after them, and in the third place, according to custom, all the people also in due order, by thousands, by hundreds and by fifties. Thus each and every man of Israel shall know "the house of his post" in the Community of God [* in the eternal counsel].[1] Let no one feel humiliated by "the house of his post", and let no one boast about his allotted position, for within the Community there should be nothing but truth, real humility, love of well-doing, and the consideration of what is right in respect of one's neighbour in the "Council of Holiness and of the Sons of the Universal Secret".

And whosoever is unwilling to enter . . . . . . . . . . so as to walk in the stubbornness of his heart [do] not [allow him to enter into the Comm]unity of His truth, for his soul is loathsome. The life of the apostate cannot be bolstered up by the penances which he inflicts upon himself through his knowledge of what is right. He cannot be reckoned among upright men. His knowledge, ability and wealth shall not be allowed within the Counsel of the Community. Shod with wickedness will he labour, a source of infection wherever he comes. He will not get right if one allows him licence in the hardening of his heart. It is darkness that he will see instead of the ways of light. In the eyes of the righteous, he will not be held in consideration. He will not be purified by ceremonies of expiation, nor cleansed by holy water. Neither in seas nor in rivers will he sanctify himself, and he will not purify himself in all the waters that cleanse. Impure he is, and impure he will remain, so long as he persists in the repudiation of what is according to the declarations of God, and until he finds in His counsel the way of amendment.

For it is by the spirit of the Council of the Truth of God, in respect to man's ways, that all a man's sins can be atoned and he can perceive the light of life. It is only by the breath of holiness, existing within the Community of His Truth, that one is purified from all one's iniquities, and it is by the spirit of uprightness and of humility that one's sins are atoned. It is the humbling of the soul before the commandments of God

[1] Inserted between the lines.

that purifies the flesh before ever it is sprinkled with holy water and sanctified by immersion in the waters of purification. Thus are the steps of a man made firm so that he walks perfectly in all the paths of God, even as He has commanded to the assemblies of His own. One must not depart from them, either to the right or to the left, nor transgress any of His words. Thus shall a man make himself acceptable to God by reconciling expiations, and find the Covenant of the Eternal Community.

This passage is marked off at the beginning and the end by strokes of the pen in the margin. It also is Zadokite, and seems to come from a society calling itself "The Sons of the Eternal Secret". We notice that the society has a number of lodges situated in different towns, and of greater or less importance. Some were grouped by thousands (?) of members, some by hundreds and others by hardly fifty. The members were exhorted not to feel any pride in belonging to an important lodge, nor inferiority if it should happen that they were inscribed in one of less importance, for in reality all these lodges formed part of one and the same Community, animated by the same spirit.

In all these lodges the order of precedence was the same. The members whose name was Cohen entered first without distinction of rank, then those whose name was Levi, and lastly all the other members. The Sons of Zadok are not specially mentioned; they formed "the people".

The remainder of this fragment reproduces a document which was probably read at every meeting. The reminder was given that collaborators with the Romans should not be admitted into the societies. For one thing, it would not be in them to recognise the light. As they laboured, shod with "sandals of iniquity" (an allusion to Isa. 9.4 and to the footwear of the Roman legions) they were capable of contaminating the others. It is well to note here the mention of penances (*ysuryn*) which the Zadokite added to the innumerable taboos with which the Jewish religion was already encumbered. Even in submitting to all these requirements, the apostate could not obtain his readmission into the community.

What follows lets us understand, though with difficulty, as the manuscript is very much crossed out and overwritten, that the purification of the soul had to precede the purifications by water and other baptisms, frequently daily ones, which certain Zadokites imposed on the members of their societies. Only those who shared in the holiness of the Community could obtain these purifications.

The importance given to baptisms and, above all, the allusion to a passage in Isaiah leads one to suppose that this fragment emanates from a Baptist sect.

## FRAGMENT 3

COLUMN III, LINES 13-17.

. . . to instruct, explain and teach to all the Sons of Light the genealogies of all human beings according to all their kinds of spirit, with their signs and how they make them, with their ages (*history*), and following what has been decreed as to their trials, the limits of their retribution.

From God is the knowledge of all that is and of all that is to be. Before things came to pass, He had determined all that was necessary in regard to them. When the Sons of Light are ready in their instruction, according to the designs of the Glorious One, they will accomplish what they have to do, and there will be nothing to repeat. In His hand are the judgements of all, and it is He who will provide for them all that will be necessary.

This extract from a Zealot rule is marked out at the beginning by an *alinea* with a stroke of the pen in the margin. The marginal stroke at the end is one line too low.

Here it is a question of instruction to be given to the young in view of the war against Rome. The fragment to which this seems to be the sequel (Fragment 21, column IX, lines 16-21) says that the young should receive their military training in the desert—which was actually done, if we are to believe Josephus. Here we are told that the young had to know foreign races, their beliefs, their military standards (or their manner of writing) their history, their justice, and the sufferings they were capable of inflicting. They were also told the date fixed for the revolt, when the Romans would receive retribution for all the evil they had done. A note of confidence is found at the end of the fragment. When the troops will have received their instruction, they will be ready with nothing to be repeated. God will supply all the arms necessary. Such seems to be the sense of this fragment, in which a number of words could be read in different ways.

## FRAGMENT 4

COLUMN III, LINE 17 TO COLUMN IV, LINE 1.

It is He who created man to have dominion over the world, and He has made for him two spirits, to be led by them until the date determined for him to render account. They are the Spirits of Truth and of Evil. In the Fountain of Light are the generations of the Truth, and from the Spring of Darkness come forth the generations of Evil.

In the hand of the Prince of Light is the power over all the Sons of Righteousness, and in the paths of light shall they walk. In the hand of the Angel of Darkness is the power over the Sons of Evil, and it is in the paths of darkness that they shall walk. The goings astray, and all the sins, iniquities, transgressions, offences, and guilty deeds of the Sons of Righteousness can be attributed to the Angel of Darkness. That will continue all the time that the Angel of Darkness reigns in accordance with the inscrutable purposes of God. It will be so until he comes to an end, which will also be the end of their sufferings and days of distress under the power of his enmity. And all the spirits allotted to him are there to make the Sons of Light to stumble, but the God of Israel and the Angel of His Truth are the help of all the Sons of Light. It is He who created all the Spirits of Light and the Spirits of Darkness, and it is on them that He has founded all His works. [On their] . . . [is based] all labour and on their ways every. . . . As to the one, God loves him through all the ages of eternity and is constantly delighting in all his works. As to the other, He has in abomination all his purposes and all his ways. He hates them for ever.

FRAGMENT 5

COLUMN IV, LINES 2–6.

The following are the ways of the Sons of Truth in this world. They are to enlighten the heart of man, and to make smooth before him all the ways of real righteousness; to make his heart fear the judgements of God, and to make his spirit humble. Long-suffering and abounding mercies, everlasting kindness and understanding, wisdom with true and mighty knowledge are in all the works of God when you put your trust in the multitude of His favours. The human creature has then a mind of wisdom in all his plans; a zeal for righteous judgements and the purposes of holiness, along with an immovable spirit. Thus will there be a multitude of mercies for all the Sons of Truth, and the purity of the divine Majesty will peal forth for him who detests all who wallow in impurity, and who, putting on a pretended humility, hide themselves from the truth of the mysteries of wisdom.

## FRAGMENT 6

COLUMN IV, LINES 6-8.

These are the secrets communicated by the Spirit to the "Sons of the Truth of the World". The proof of all who walk in conformity with them will be seen in healing and abounding health, in long life and fruitful seed, blessings without end and everlasting joys in the life eternal, fullness of glory with continual splendour in the Light Eternal.

These three fragments ought to be taken in reverse order—6, 5, 4. They form part of the statement of doctrine of a Zealot group calling itself "The Sons of Truth", (or of the "Truthful"). In frag. 5 there is a reference to "zeal" in its members. Judging by the *Hymns of Thanksgiving*, this society (or another of the same name, which is unlikely) had come to adopt some Christian ideas.

Quite ordinary people, very different from the Zadokites of the preceding passages, had been entrusted with certain secrets given to them by the Spirit. This knowledge (*gnôsis*) assured those who conformed to it of every good in this world (health, long life, and abundant harvests) and also in the world to come. What was necessary was to believe in the wisdom of God, to trust in Him, to make converts, and detest the Pharisees and their pretended humility.

The "secret" exposed in Fragment 4 is essentially the Doctrine of the Two Ways (*Testament of Judah*, 20.1-5). God has created the Angel of Light and the Angel of Darkness and, in order to test human beings, He has given the latter the right to reign for a certain time. Thus it is that at times the evil spirits have made the Sons of Righteousness (the Zadokites) to go astray, and have also tried to make the other Sons of Light to stumble. God, however, who has founded His creation on the struggle between the powers of Good and Evil, loves those who act according to the one, but hates those who follow the ways of the other.

Belief in the future life, and in angels and spirits, places these fragments clearly in a popular movement, that of the Zealots. One may even suppose that our text was written at a time when the Zealots and the Zadokites were in conflict, and the former were reproaching the latter of having been led astray by the Spirit of Evil. That would allow the redaction of this fragment to the years following the fall of Jerusalem in A.D. 70.

The *Epistle of Barnabas* (18.1-19.1, 20.1-21.1) repeats almost word for word several passages in this text, which appears to approach even nearer to the corresponding passages in the *Didache* (1.1-6.1). If it is accepted that the *Epistle of Barnabas* was drawn up about A.D. 120, then it follows that this version of The Two Ways may have been preserved in an environment which was Zealot, but at the same time influenced by Christianity. We should remember that this teaching was not unknown to the Pharisees, but these held that no one should go to extremes, that under many circumstances it was wise to follow the majority and discover a *via media* between the two paths.

## FRAGMENT 7

COLUMN IV, LINES 9-14.

And (*the following are the judgements of God*) for those who are of a spirit of wickedness, covetous and greedy in the exercise of justice, spiteful and untruthful, proud and haughty, untrustworthy and cunning, cruel and thoroughly unspeakable, quick-tempered and unrestrained, with an arrogant zeal for abominable deeds carried out in a spirit of lewdness. Their impure ways lead to a defiled worship, a mocking tongue, blindness of eyes, deafness of ears, stiffness of neck, and hardness of heart, so that they walk in all the ways of darkness and the wiles of wickedness. When all those who so walk shall be called to account, they will be given over to a multitude of torments at the hands of all the angels of destruction—to the everlasting Pit, by the fierce wrath of the God of Vengeance—to eternal horror and shame until their eyes are closed in final death ( '*d 'ms lmt klh* ) by the obscuring fire. Till their times are fulfilled, all their borders shall be in sorrowful mourning and bitter unhappiness. Theirs shall be a gloomy existence till they shall be utterly destroyed, not one remaining, nor one escaping.

This fragment between two *alineas* and also marked by strokes of the pen in the margin, appears to come from another Zealot work, a *Book of History* similar to that of which the Cairo fragments have given us a medieval Qaraite version. The detailed description of those who would be smitten by God leaves no room for doubt: this time it has reference to the Romans. The apocalyptic vision at the end, where the author makes use of a current phrase, seems to be influenced by the eruption of Vesuvius in A.D. 79. The author evokes the "obscuring fire" (the shower of ashes), and the unlimited number of bereavements which struck the legions on the frontiers. He foresees a further cataclysm in which no Roman will be able to save himself.

## FRAGMENT 8

COLUMN IV, LINES 15-26.

It came about that all the human race was enrolled, and in their (*conquered*) provinces, all their (*Roman*) armies were installed for the periods allowed them (*by God*). They marched along their roads, and the products of their labours (*idols or Roman ensigns*) were in their (*conquered*) provinces. From all the corners of the earth, according to each man's heritage, they carried off much or little. However, it was God who proportioned the part for each man, until the final end.

In the heart of their provinces He has put a continual hatred; injustice and wickedness which hates the truth and all its ways, and an eagerness to find fault with all the laws (*of conquered peoples*) because they did not conduct themselves in agreement with them.

But God in His inscrutable purposes and His glorious wisdom has decreed an end to wickedness and, at the destined time for the calling to account, He will destroy her (*Rome*) for ever, and thus the truth will shine forth again, and for ever. For it has been permitted that truth should be wrapped round by the ways of wickedness and under the sway of sin until the day of judgement should be determined. And then God by His truth shall purge all the works of the man of power. God has separated him from among other men in order to end the spirit of iniquity in his flesh, and by the spirit of holiness to purge him of all sin and wrong. He has therefore sprinkled him with a spirit of truth, as with water, washing away every abomination of lying. He was converted by the spirit of lustration so as to instruct upright men in the knowledge of the Most High, and in the wisdom of the Sons of Heaven, and to make known the way of perfection. For it is in them that God has chosen those destined for the Universal Covenant; all the glory of man shall be theirs; and then, sin shall be no more.

May shame overtake all deeds of falsehood, so long as the spirits of truth and of evil struggle in the heart of the man of power. They (*the men in power*) behave wisely or foolishly according to what a man's fatherland does. If it loves truth and justice, a man can hate iniquity. But if his fatherland belongs to the portion of iniquity, from that fact, he becomes wicked and detests the truth.

For to each one his portion—so God has decreed until the pre-destined end, and (*that of Rome*) the New Esau-dom. He knows the products of their (*the Jews'*) labours until all the limits (*of eternity*), and He has placed them in their heritage, while yet men, to know good (. . . . . . [And He has ca])st the lot for every living thing, according to his spirit (. . . . . . . . .) calling to account.

There has been much diversity in the translation and interpretation of this fragment. The language used gives the impression that the passage may itself be a translation. The author makes use of two forms of the plural, and we imagine that the plurals in -*hn* are used for conquered nations, and for the Jews, whilst those in -*hm* are used for the Romans.

The fragment begins with a reference to the census of A.D. 6, to which a Thanksgiving Hymn (1.17) and several other texts make allusion. Frequently there is the statement that God has fixed everyone's portion. The expression "the New Esau-dom" indicates the Roman rule which was exercised through the Idumaean Dynasty. Rome has similarly been called Edom or Esau elsewhere. The hostility of Rome towards the laws and customs of conquered countries will be finally punished by God, who will cleanse the countries under Roman rule of all that the conqueror had been able to accomplish.

A change of tense gives the impression that in what follows there is an allusion to something that had actually happened. We suppose it refers to the conversion of a Roman to Judaism—perhaps that of the procurator Vitellius, who, in A.D. 36, had relieved the Jews of certain taxes. The passage is most ambiguous and difficult to understand. It can be interpreted in the sense that even a converted Roman was not free to act rightly: that, his country being evil, he had to follow the instructions given him.

This passage also seems to be an extract from a Zealot *Book of History*. We should recall that it was the Jewish reaction to the census of A.D. 6 that gave birth to the Zealot and Zadokite parties.

## FRAGMENT 9

COLUMN V, LINES 1-13.

And this is the custom for the members of the Community who engage of their own will to turn back from all evil and to cling to all that which God has ordained as pleasing to Himself. They will promise to abstain from the company of evil men and to join in keeping the Law, in sharing of possessions, and in obeying the Sons of Zadok—that is, the Cohens, the (*recognised*) guardians of the Covenant—following the decisions of the majority of the members of the Community who cling to the Covenant. Their decisions will determine everything pertaining to the Law, or to possessions, or concerning things to be done in conformity with truth, humility, charity, justice and love of good. They (*the members of the Community*) shall practise humility in all their ways, in which no one shall walk in hardness of heart, as he did when he was going astray following his own desires, his own eyes, or the promptings of his own instincts. In order to lay the foundations of truth for Israel and for the Community of the Universal Covenant, a man must circumcise not only the foreskin of his instincts, but also the stiffness of his neck. His aim will be to make atonement for all those who have volunteered for the service of the Sanctuary of Aaron and the Temple of the True One of Israel, and for all who join with them to form a community for the judging and accusing of all those who transgress what is right. They (*the members of the Community*) will order their ways according to these precepts.

When joining the Community, all those who enter its council shall (*first of all*) join in the Covenant of God in the presence of all the volunteer members. Each one shall swear on his soul by a binding oath to return with all his heart and soul to the Law of Moses, and to all the Law enjoins as it has been revealed to the Sons of Zadok, the Cohens, guardians of the Covenant and seekers after His will, and to the majority of the members of the Covenant who have freely joined together on account of His truth, and to live as He desires.

Moreover, he who takes upon himself the oath of the Covenant shall promise on his soul to separate himself from all the men of evil who walk in the ways of wickedness, yet he shall do so in such a manner that they will not suspect that he belongs to the Covenant, to ask him questions about its laws and to know its secrets. Those who depart from their oaths by guilty deeds, and those who purposely stir up wrath by performing in a traitorous way what has been revealed, shall be handed over to the avengers of the oath of the Covenant. These avengers will carry out on them terrible judgements for their everlasting extermination, so that not one of them shall remain.

We have here the beginning of an initiation ritual of a Zadokite lodge, a ritual of which other fragments have been already met with (columns

I.i to II.17). Here the aims of the society are clearly set out: to re-establish the privileges of the priesthood, and to rebuild the Temple with its separation between the part reserved for the "clergy" and that accessible to the laity. (The word "Aaronic" does not occur in this passage.)

The Zadokite society was under the direction of the Cohens, former priests or their descendants. It was among these that the members could elect the leaders to whom they owed obedience. The Law of Moses was to be followed—that is to say, the Zadokites attached no value to what the rabbis laid down. But obedience also extended to what the Cohens and the majority of the members decided, or said had been revealed to them. Terrible threats were uttered against those who unveiled the plans of the society, and apparently it was the Levis who were charged with the execution of those verdicts. It was recommended that the members should hold themselves aloof from the non-initiated, so that no one should suspect that they belonged to the society and should question them about its rules and aims.

Like other Zadokite fragments, this passage appears to have been written after A.D. 70. In the manuscript there is the signature of a rabbi at the beginning, and the end is marked by an *alinea* and a stroke of the pen in the margin.

## FRAGMENT 10

COLUMN V, LINES 13-25.

Let no one lightly enter the water while holy men are purifying themselves in it, for those who are not initiated will not purify themselves that way, even if they are turning back from evil, for they are unclean, as are all who do not observe His word, and as he is who does not make common cause with His people, both by work and wealth. Lest he bring his guiltiness upon us, we must completely avoid him, for thus it is written, "*Keep thee far from a false matter*" (*Exod. 23.7*). Let no member of the Community fall in with what he may say concerning the Law or its implications. He should neither eat nor drink anything that belongs to him, and except by purchase, should accept absolutely nothing from him, for it is also written, "*Cease from man whose breath is in his nostrils (=who is violent) for wherein is he to be accounted of?*" (*Isa. 2.22*). Anyone who has not entered into God's Covenant must be avoided with all that belongs to him.

Let not the man of holiness put his trust in any vain work, for vain are they who know not His Covenant, and all who despise His word will perish from the earth. All their deeds are unclean in His sight, and impure all their possessions.

Moreover, all who join the Community to conform to the statutes in the hope of attaining to the Assembly of the Saints should examine each other within the Community concerning their spirit, their knowledge of the Law, and their deeds under it. This shall be carried out under the direction of the Sons of Aaron, who are volunteers within the Community for the purpose of maintaining God's Covenant, and of watching over all the statutes which He has laid down. It is the voice of the R:B in Israel that shall say how it will be possible for the volunteers, within the Community, to return to His Covenant. According to custom, they shall be enrolled one after another, each according to his knowledge and conduct, so that they shall all be in obedience to one another, the lesser to the greater. In proportion as they have watched over their thoughts and their actions, each year they shall be advanced or reduced in rank, these because of their knowledge and the correctness of their conduct, those because of their delinquencies. Each should reprove his neighbour . . . both in humility and love of the man's good.

The fragment which we find here comes from the rules of a Zadokite society, but a number of peculiarities in it lead us to think that this sect was already noticeably different from the warlike society of whose ritual of initiation several passages have already been given.

The importance given to baptism and the quotation from Isaiah allow us to imagine that we are here dealing with a Baptist sect, not the same, perhaps, from which comes Fragment 2. Less importance is given to the Law of Moses, though that does not lessen the responsibility of the ancient Aaronic priests within the society for the carrying out of the Mosaic requirements. In this fragment the expression "Sons·of Zadok" does not occur, nor the name "Cohen". A descendant of an Aaronic priest, who was a member of the society, examined the converts whose admission was subject to the approval of an R:B of Israel—that is to say, of a *Rab-Ba'al* or Grand Master. Ranks seem to have played a great part in this sect. A convert did not begin as a novice, but at the time of admission was given a rank after taking into account his knowledge and his past conduct. Then each year the members were promoted or reduced in rank according to their behaviour during the year.

In this society the members were also advised to keep apart from the non-initiated, but this passage deals more particularly with the heathen from whom nothing was to be accepted apart from what was bought in the market.

A stroke in the margin marks the end of this paragraph.

## FRAGMENT 11

COLUMN V, LINE 25 TO COLUMN VI, LINE 8.

Let not a fellow-member speak in anger, hatred, or stupid obstinacy . . . spirit of spite. Let him not bear a grudge . . . of his heart. He must bring his reproof the self-same day, so that he himself be not charged with fault. In the same way, no one should bring before the rabbis an accusation against a neighbour unless it can be supported by witnesses. These are the rules the rabbis should follow wherever they may be living. And whatever is good enough for one, is also good enough for his neighbour. The lesser shall obey the greater in affairs of work and of money, but they shall eat together, and take counsel together. Wherever there shall be ten men of the Council of the Community, let there not be missing one of the name of Cohen, and in his presence, they shall take their seats in order of rank. In this manner shall they make enquiry and consult together over any matter. On those occasions when the table is prepared for eating and drinking, it is the one named Cohen who shall first of all stretch out his hand to bless the bread and the new wine. Neither, in any place where there are ten members, shall one neglect the continual study, day and night, of the Law and of the beauties (*of the creation?*), each one studying along with his neighbour. The rabbis shall sit up together, a third of all the nights, to unite in reading the Book, and in studying the Law, and in praising God.

Marked off by a stroke in the margin, both at the beginning and the end, this fragment forms part of the Rule of a rabbinic society, very different from those of the Zadokites and the Zealots. It is possible the scribe, not a very expert one, for a long dittography occurs in lines 5 and 6, allowed himself to be influenced by the conclusion of the previous passage, where it was a question of reproofs between members of the Baptist sect.

The beginning of the fragment has reference to a rule of rabbinic tribunals. As in other texts, one finds the command not to hate anyone in one's heart (Lev. 19.17), a command which was interpreted in the sense that one should not maintain resentment but put an end to the quarrel the same day. The reminder is also given that no accusation could be received unless supported by witnesses.

Though the rabbis took upon themselves the authority to judge, yet they recognised certain prerogatives as belonging to the Cohens. It was to be desired that wherever ten rabbis were, one should have the name of Cohen. Precedence at table was to be accorded to him, the other rabbis taking their places in order of seniority. The same respect to rank held when rabbis spoke in their meetings, which had to have at least a *minyân* of ten persons.

The rule of this rabbinic society assumed, as a matter of fact, the presence of a number of rabbis in a town or village. They were recommended to share out equally among themselves their profits, and the money they received (for slaughtering, circumcisions, marriages, etc.). Further on, a more detailed rule about finance is given. If the rabbis instituted a *yeshivah,* or kind of academy, they were to arrange for the uninterrupted reading of the Bible, day and night. To make this easier, they were advised to limit their zeal, and only sit up one night in three.

## FRAGMENT 12

COLUMN VI, LINES 8-23.

This is the custom for a session (*môshab*) of the rabbis. Each man according to his rank! The Cohens shall take their seats first, venerable rabbis next, and the remaining persons each according to his rank. This is how they shall make enquiry about the laws or about any other matter under discussion. Each rabbi shall give his opinion to the Council of the Community. No one shall interrupt his neighbour by speaking before he has finished. Neither shall anyone speak out of his turn. If anyone wishes to raise a question, he shall do so when his turn to speak comes.

In the session of the rabbis, no one shall speak on any subject unless it has been sanctioned by the rabbis, even though it is a question concerning the rabbis. When someone is charged with a question from an absent person who seeks the advice of the Community, he shall rise and say, "I have a matter to bring before the rabbis." If they give him permission, he shall speak.

Every volunteer in Israel who wishes to join the Council of the Community shall be examined by the superintendent of the rabbis as to his knowledge and his conduct. If he has received sufficient instruction, he shall be admitted into the Covenant so that he may return to the truth and forsake all iniquity. He shall be instructed in all the laws of the Community, and later, when he enters to stand before the rabbis, they shall question him on all these subjects. Then, according to the vote in the council of the rabbis, he shall be admitted or rejected.

If he is admitted to the Council of the Community, he shall not partake of "the pure things of the rabbis", the *terumah*, until he shall have been further examined concerning his spirit and behaviour, and this not before a year shall have elapsed. Even then he shall not share financially with the rabbis. When he has fulfilled a year in the midst of the community, and the rabbis shall have held an enquiry into his case, about his knowledge and observance of the Law, if the voting shows he might be admitted into the secret of the community, then, on the proposition of the Cohens accepted by the majority of the members of their Covenant, his possessions and his income shall be received from him and handed over to the man in charge of the revenues of the rabbis, and he shall enter them on account. They shall not be distributed for the benefit of the rabbis. The new member shall not partake of the drink of the rabbis until he shall have completed a second year in the company of the members of the Community. When he shall have completed this second year, the rabbis shall examine him verbally. If the vote is in favour of his admission to the Community, according to custom, he shall be enrolled in his rank in the company of his brethren. From then onwards, he shall have the right to give his opinion on the Law and to share in "the pure things of the rabbis" his own possessions being incorporated with those of the other rabbis. Moreover, his advice will be valid in the Community and in the pronouncing of judgements.

As in other cases, this fragment is marked off by strokes in the margin. It is a further passage dealing with the rule of a rabbinic society. These societies called *habûrôth* were often the object of Roman sarcasm. The name given to their academies was *yeshivoth*, or "sittings", called here *mwšb hrbym*, and was due to the fact that the rabbis held their deliberations sitting down, whereas at the time of Rabbi Gamaliel I one stood up to discuss. A kind of open space was reserved at the back of the hall for an audience which had no right of speaking.

The first subject is that of precedence. Though the Cohens had the privilege of always being the first to take their seats, nothing is said concerning the Levis, to whom the rabbis accorded no special privilege. The second rank consisted of "venerable" rabbis, the *zeqenim*, or elders who had attained the highest position in the rabbinic hierarchy. In the *yeshivoth* one had to observe order in the discussions. In principle, the rabbis replied to questions put to them, but they had the right to refuse discussion on any subject that they thought unsuitable. All this is illustrated by numerous examples in Jewish literature.

Then comes the question of admission of new members into the *haburah*. A *mebaqqar*, an inspector appointed by the rabbis, first of all examined the candidate, and if he considered that he had had sufficient instruction, he informed him of the rules of the society which dealt mostly with finance. Afterwards the rabbis voted upon him, and if the vote was favourable, the candidate was admitted as *ne'eman*. For a year he had to live by his trade, and had no right to share in the *terumah*.

Having taken the place of the Temple clergy, the rabbis had established for themselves the privilege of slaughtering, of the preparation of un-leavened bread, etc. In addition to those parts of the sacrificial animals which had formerly pertained to the Temple clergy, they imposed the tithe of the threshing-floor and of the wine or olive press. These taxes in kind were called "the pure things of the rabbis". The Biblical laws relating to what was to be reserved for the priesthood in a "holy" place and eaten by only certain privileged persons had been the object of various interpretations. Often the unavowed motive of seeking the right to receive these dues was the cause of conflicts between different rabbinic schools. Moreover, when a rabbinic school was set up in a town, the first concern of the rabbis was to make sure of their influence over the community, and at times this involved making concessions in the realm of dogma.

The candidate when accepted received no stipend for a year and had no right to a part of the *terumah*. Most rabbis had a trade, and the *ne'eman* exercised whatever was his trade, and gave no return of what he gained. At the end of the year, if his conduct was satisfactory, he had a further examination. This time the lay members of the community had a voice. If the Cohens were agreed, and a majority of the community voted in favour, the candidate was advanced to the rank of *haber* or companion. This was not an exalted rank, and one did not have to rise if a *haber* passed. He could perform certain duties, could be a *šohet* and cut the throats of fowl, or be a *moel* and perform circumcisions, and so on. But all he received for fulfilling these functions he had to contribute to the common fund, administered by a rabbi who was an inspector.

Our text comes from a rabbinic community with its own particular rules. For a year the income of the *haber* was not put into the common fund, but held in reserve. Except for the tithe from the wine-press, he could share in the *terumah*. At the end of the second year, the *haber* was once more examined by the rabbis. If successful, he became *rab* (rabbi) and could wear the *taleth* (gown). He was said to carry on his shoulders all the burden of the community. This promotion had to be made in the presence of at least three rabbis. From now onwards he was a member of the *yeshivah*: had the right to express his opinion on all matters touching the community to which he belonged, or on questions of law submitted to the rabbis for judgement. All his income, whether personal or gained by his rabbinic functions, was passed into the common fund. In exchange, he was paid a fixed stipend, in cash or in kind, according to his position in the body of rabbis, and that depended on his seniority and his rank. Eventually he might become a "venerable", a *zaqen*, or elder.

It is not possible to state precisely the date of these rules, nor the community from which they come. From the mention of the "inspector of the rabbis", it is clear that this was an orthodox rabbinic school, recognising a central authority, probably that of the *Nasi* of Jamnia. This text cannot be earlier than A.D. 90, nor can it have come from a dissenting school, like that of Lydda or that of Emmaus.

## FRAGMENT 13

COLUMN VI, LINE 23 TO COLUMN VII, LINE 25.

The following are the rules for passing judgement in the *Midrash*[1] of the Community after a verbal accusation.

If a man is found among them (*the rabbis*) who cheated with regard to possessions, and this man is known, he shall be excluded from receiving "the pure things of the rabbis" for a year, and shall pay as fine a quarter of his income.

Anyone who stubbornly retorts and speaks violently to his neighbour with the intent to have cancelled the former inscription of his fellow in the "sayings", asserting that what he had said had been uttered by someone else—unless he was labouring under a misunderstanding—let him be fined during one year.

He who brings a report against the "venerable" who is above the . . . and if he has invoked a curse, either out of fear, or from some other

---

[1] Primary or secondary school.

personal motive quite different, even though he is a reader of the Book, or one who gives the blessing, he shall be put out of the Community, to return there no more.

If, carried away with passion, anyone speaks against the Cohens mentioned in the Book, he shall pay his fine during a year.

If anyone kept for himself a part of "the pure things of the rabbis", but says he did it unwittingly, he shall pay his fine during six months.

Whoever leads anyone into error shall pay his fine during six months.

The man who deliberately starts an unjust quarrel with his neighbour shall pay his fine during a year and be excluded (*from the Council*).

Whoever speaks words of deceit to a neighbour or puts false ideas in his mind shall be fined during six months.

But if he deceives himself at the same time he shall be fined during three months.

If it is concerning the goods of the Community that he makes mistakes, so that they suffer harm, he shall make good out of his poverty, and if he has not the means to make good he shall be fined sixty days.

Whoever is in anger unjustly with his neighbour shall be fined during six months [* a year],[1] and the same for anyone who takes vengeance for himself over anything.

He who allows his mouth to utter nonsense—three months.

He who interrupts a neighbour who is speaking—ten days.

He who lies down and sleeps while there is a session of the rabbis—thirty days.

Similarly, anyone who without compelling reasons goes out three times in the course of a session shall be fined during ten days. But if he had been posted as sentinel and leaves his post, he shall be fined during thirty days.

Anyone who exhibits himself naked before his neighbour, though there are no other witnesses, he shall be fined during six months.

Anyone who spits in the midst of a session of rabbis shall be fined during thirty days.

Anyone who uncovers his member, breaks wind, or exposes his nakedness shall be fined thirty days.

Anyone laughing inanely or loudly shall be fined thirty days.

Anyone who puts out his left hand to sign with shall be fined during ten days.

The man who goes about slandering his neighbour shall not partake

1 Inserted above the line.

of "the pure things of the rabbis" for a year, and shall be fined, but if he slanders rabbis, he is to be irrevocably expelled.

The man who murmurs against the whole basis of the Community shall be irrevocably expelled. But if it is against a neighbour that he unwarrantably complains, then he shall be fined during six months.

A man who becomes so afraid of the basic principles of the community that he is unfaithful to the truth and walks in the stubbornness of his heart, if he repents, shall be fined during two years. During the first year he shall not share in "the pure things of the rabbis", and during the second year he shall not partake of "the drink of the rabbis", and shall take his seat behind all other members. When the full period of two years has elapsed, the rabbis shall conduct an enquiry into his case, and if they are satisfied he shall be entered on the roll, but they shall proceed to discuss what they shall decide to do with him.

If any man who has been a member for ten years then falls away and is unfaithful to the Community, he shall be put forth from before the rabbis to go in the stubbornness of his heart. Let him never more return to the Council of the Community. And anyone from among the members of the Com(munity . . . . . . .) who shall have dealings with him, by his "pure things" or by his possessions . . . . . . . . . of the rabbis, let him be judged like the other, let him . . . . . . . . . .

The foot of these columns is incomplete, but a signature by a rabbi is clearly seen. Erasures are frequent.

The laws in this Rule do not all come from a rabbinic *Beth-ha-Midrash*. All the punishments are in the nature of fines. In some cases, a temporary or permanent exclusion from the community is pronounced—but not the great excommunication.

The fines are all monetary and give the length of time during which the delinquent had to give up a quarter of whatever income might be due to him. Naturally, a rabbi or *ḥaber* under sentence was automatically excluded from sharing in the *terumah*.

The first clauses deal with teachers guilty of negligence or inaccuracy. A sacred character was assigned to everything decided on in a *yeshivah* and put into writing.[1] A rabbi contesting or denouncing such a decision of a "venerable" of the society was to be expelled even though he was a reader (*ḥazan*) or one with the right to bless—that is to say, a Cohen. The same offence over the decision of a Cohen was punished merely by a fine

---

[1] The gathering together of such writings was later to form the *Talmudim*.

lasting a year. Inaccuracy over the distribution of the *terumah* was punished by a fine, etc.

There were rules as to what was right and proper in a session of a *yeshivah* or a class of a *midrash*. These add nothing to what is already known from rabbinic literature.

The last clauses anticipate the case of a rabbi who, overcome by fear, betrays the rules of the Community. If he repented of his apostasy, he was to be treated as a new candidate to the rabbinic order, but, in addition, for two years he was to pay as fine a quarter of his income. During the first year of his probation he would not share in the *terumah*. After two years, if he was readmitted there was another judgement on his case, fixing a punishment, probably less severe, or even holding that he had paid enough. (The text has been scratched out at the end of this *alinea*.)

Any rabbi of ten years' standing who betrayed the community was to be expelled for ever, and any rabbi who gave him a part of his own revenue in money or in kind was also to be expelled.

As with the preceding fragment, one cannot say precisely from which rabbinic community this rule came. The "venerable" mentioned here might be the head of the school. If it was necessary to assign this title to the head of the school at Jamnia, the rule would have to date before A.D. 90, when the title of *Nasi* was given to Rabbi Gamaliel II.

## FRAGMENT 14

COLUMN VIII, LINES 1-4.

In the Council of the Community, twelve laymen and three Cohens shall be the correct number to set forth what has been made known in all the Law. They are to set forth the practice of truth, the love of good, right conduct between man and man, to establish on earth an unshakable belief coupled with humility, the avoidance of the sin of those who worship molten images, and the ordering of one's life in all things by the standard of truth.

## FRAGMENT 15

COLUMN VIII, LINES 4-7.

And when the predestined time arrives that the Council of the Community alone shall be established as the planting (*of the Lord:* Isa. 60.21, 61.3), then the courtyard of the Holy Temple shall be for Israel, and the Holy of Holies for Aaron, witnesses of the Truthful

One, to pronounce judgement, and willingly to make atonement for the country, rendering to the wicked their reward.

These two fragments are marked by only a single stroke in the margin between lines 4 and 5, but two spaces are left vacant in the manuscript, and the following fragment, which has many erasures, seems to begin on line 7.

We have here two passages from a Zadokite text. Contrary to rules of rabbinic societies which insisted on the presence of a *minyân* of ten members, the Zadokite community could only have a valid session if fifteen members were present, of whom three had to have the name of Cohen.

The second fragment looks forward to the time when the Zadokites would be supreme, their society the only one in Israel. At that time the Temple would be rebuilt and the courtyard would be for the people, and the Holy of Holies for the priests, the sons of Aaron.

## FRAGMENT 16

COLUMN VIII, LINES 7-15.

For he is the approved wall, the precious corner-stone (*Isa. 28.16*) so that [* their foundations][1] shall not shake nor move out of their place. The dwelling of the Holy of Holies is for Aaron, who, as all know, is accepted for the Covenant of Righteousness, and for the offering of a well-pleasing sacrifice [* and odour].[1] And the Temple of the Perfect and Truthful One is for Israel, to confirm the Covenant according to the everlasting law [* and they will be accepted to make atonement for the land, and to wipe out the judgement of the wicked (. . .) and sin shall be no more].[1]

When these men are established in the fundamentals of the Community during two full years, in the path of perfection [* they are set apart][1] holy ones in the midst of the members of the Community. And all those things hidden from Israel, but found by the man who seeks God, they were hidden from them for fear of a rebellious spirit. But when there were only these [* in Community][1] in Israel, [* following these rules],[1] they withdrew themselves from the midst of the session (*moshab*) of the Nasi (*Prince*) of wickedness and went into the desert to make level His way before Him, as it is written, "*Prepare in the desert the way of. . . . (Yhwh), make level in the wilderness a highway for our God*" (*Isa. 40.3*).

[1] Additions written between the lines.

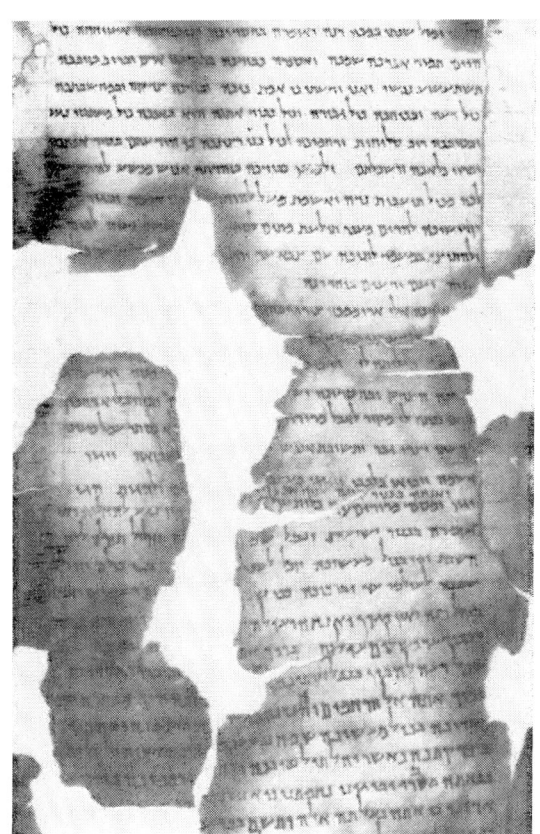

The *Thanksgiving* Scroll in which two different hands are evident

The destructive action of the ink used for the writing of the *Genesis*

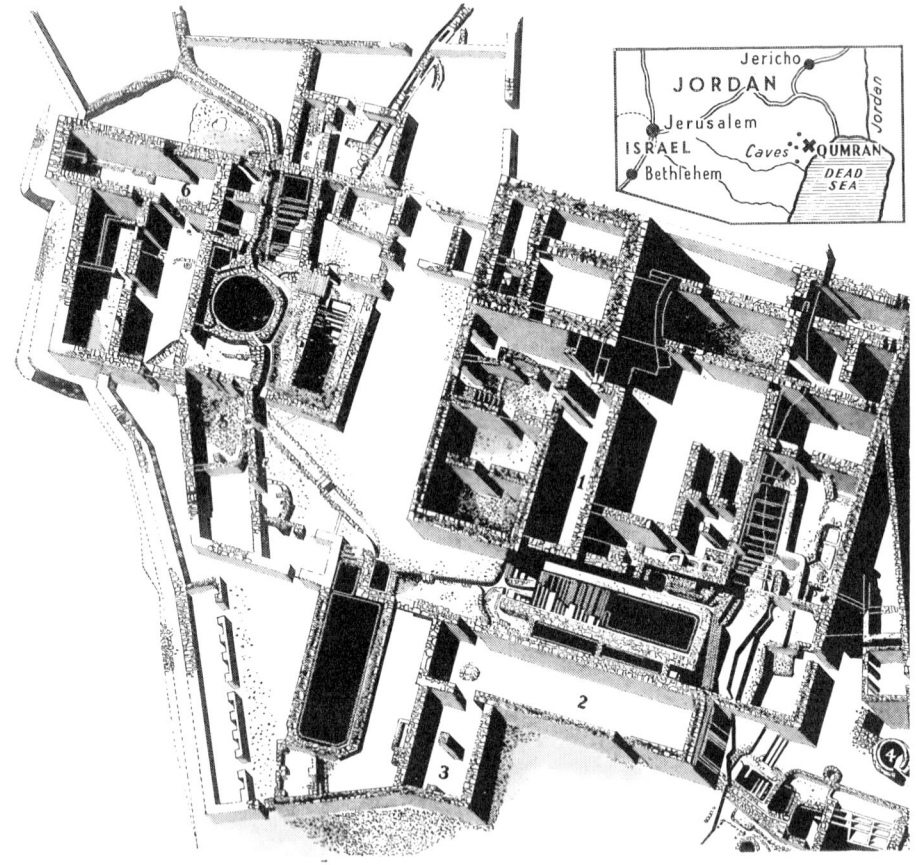

A GENERAL PLAN OF THE RUINS OF QUMRÂN

1. The so-called Scriptorium
2. Chamber 77 in which three low pillars have been found
3. The small room 86/89 in which two more pillars of the same kind were found
4. The perfectly preserved potter's workshop.
5. The smelting furnace
6. Room 120 in which a large number of ancient coins were found contained in three jars

He was therefore teaching the Law ordained by the hand of Moses, that it is necessary to perform all that has been revealed, age by age, in accordance with what the prophets have revealed through His Holy Spirit.

This fragment, which has more erasures and insertions than any other part of the manuscript, is marked off by two brackets in the margin. It is clearly made up of a number of pieces, and its translation presents great difficulties. It has been translated in widely different ways.

One of the fundamental elements in this composite fragment appears to be a *Commentary on Isaiah*, perhaps the same as was used in the New Testament in connection with John the Baptist, where the quotation from Isa. 28.16 is combined with Isa. 5.1-2 or Ps. 118.22. As in our text, the interpretation of the evangelists applies this verse to the "sanctuary" and to "the two houses of Israel".

The second quotation from Isaiah (40.3) is also found in the Gospels (Matt. 3.3, 11.10; Mark 1.3; Luke 3.4, 7.27; John 1.23). It is difficult to say if the author of our text wished to apply this verse to the study of the Law, or to him who studies it. In this quotation, the unpronounceable name of *YHWH* is replaced by four dots.

It may be supposed, therefore, that a *Commentary on Isaiah* existed, the words of which were applied to John the Baptist in the same way as the *Commentary on Habakkuk* was applied to Menahem. The sects of the Baptists, which came forth from the Zadokites, also aimed at the re-establishment of the privileges of the ancient priests. In this fragment the same idea is met with again, that within the Temple there will be a division between what is reserved for the priests and that which is accessible to the ordinary people of Israel.

This fragment contains an indication of date, but it is difficult to interpret it. It is the reference to the separation of the session from the Prince (*Nasi*) of Wickedness. At the time of John the Baptist the title *Nasi* was given to the Chief of the Sanhedrin, Rabbi Gamaliel I. However, there was no *yeshivah*, and the expression session (*mwsb*) brings us back to Rabbi Gamaliel II and the school at Jamnia (A.D. 90). Either one has to credit the compiler of this fragment with an anachronism—which is not impossible —or one must suppose that the Baptists applied the *Commentary on Isaiah* to a second personage. We are given to understand that there was a definite breach between the Baptists and the Pharisees after two years of

H

collaboration. It was then that the Man who sought God went into the wilderness. Our text styles him "Holy".

## FRAGMENT 17

COLUMN VIII, LINES 16-19.

Any man who is a member of the Community—the Covenant of the Community—and who departs from all commandment, will infect the others. Let him have no share in "the pure things" of the men of holiness and know nothing of their counsels, until he has cleansed his actions from all iniquity, walks in the perfect way, and has been readmitted to the Council by the votes of the rabbis. Then his name shall be entered according to his rank. This is the law that shall apply to all who join the Community.

This fragment is an extract from the rule of a different rabbinic society, and the provision laid down differs from that already met with (Fragment 13, column VII, lines 18-21). The rabbis call themselves "the men of holiness", a title which was only given to rabbis especially revered. The apostate who returned to the society was readmitted and restored to his rank after certain purifications, whereas the former society laid down two years' probation with loss of rank.

## FRAGMENT 18

COLUMN VIII, LINE 20, TO COLUMN IX, LINE 2.

These are the rules of conduct to be observed, each towards his neighbour, by "the men of holiness", all those who enter the Council of Holiness, walking in the perfect way which He has ordained.

Any member who violates a word of the Law of Moses, by hypocrisy or deceit, shall be irrevocably expelled from the Council of the Community. Let no man of holiness have anything to do with him, his possessions, his advice, or anything that is his. If he acted through a misunderstanding of the law, he shall be excluded from the "purification" and from the Council. For two years, when the Law—which is of no human origin—is being studied, he shall raise no question on any subject whatsoever. If he has amended his conduct in the *yeshivah,* the *midrash,* and the Council, the rabbis shall carry out an examination to see that during these two years, he has made no further mistake. Thus a mistake shall be punished by a fine during two years, but a deliberate deceit by irrevocable expulsion. It is only someone who acted through error that shall be on probation for two years, so as to amend his ways under the guidance of the rabbis. After that, he shall be enrolled according to his rank in the Community of Holiness.

This fragment is marked by a stroke in the margin at the beginning, and the signature of a rabbi at the end. It also seems to be an extract from the rule of a rabbinic society, that of the "Men of Holiness". Once again the question is raised as to the apostate who repents of his error. Here, however, he is not excluded from the society if he acted mistakenly. He was merely excluded from the purifications, but he had to attend all other meetings of the *yeshivah*, *midrash* or Council though with no right to speak during a period of two years. Naturally, anyone who broke the rules deliberately was excommunicated and one may suppose that this class of apostate would show no desire to re-enter the rabbinic society.

## FRAGMENT 19

COLUMN IX, LINES 3-11.

When the time comes in Israel that these rules will be observed and no others as a basis for a spirit of holiness and as eternal truth, then atonement will be made for the sins of guilt and the crimes of trespass, and the flesh and blood of sacrifices will be an acceptable offering for the earth. Till then, the offering of the lips will be the incense of righteousness, and the perfect way an agreeable oblation.

In that day, the members of the Community will make a separation. The Holy Temple will be for the Sons of Aaron, and they alone will go into the Holy of Holies. The Temple of the Community will be for Israel, for those who walk rightly. The Sons of Aaron alone shall pronounce sentence and decide law-suits. Everything that concerns the members of the Community shall be decided in accordance with their pronouncements. The wealth of those who behave righteously shall not be mingled with that of men of deceit who have not purified their ways by abstaining from sin and by walking in the perfect way. The Sons of Aaron, however, have not withdrawn from all the prescriptions of the Law to live according to the stubbornness of their hearts and souls, but they have judged themselves by the law of "the former prophets" which enable members of the Community to correct themselves while awaiting the arrival of "the prophet" and the Messiahs of Aaron and of Israel.

These two passages, separated by a stroke in the margin, are from a Zadokite society. Several phrases are parallel to those from other societies (Fragments 15 and 16). While awaiting the establishment of the Temple services with their sacrifices, prayer and righteousness should be considered as offerings to God. The Zadokites were not alone in holding prayer to be a temporary substitute for the sacrifices no longer taking place.

When, however, the services begin again, the Temple would be divided into two. One part, including the Holy of Holies, would be reserved exclusively for the Aaronite priesthood, and the other would be accessible to Israel. The rights of the true Aaronite priesthood could not be called in question, for they alone had conformed to the ancient laws, those of the Pentateuch and of the Former Prophets. They had not mixed their possessions with those of men of deceit—that is to say, unlike some priests (the word Kohen does not occur here), they have not accepted gifts from pagans and apostates. In addition, they alone have the right to judge people and settle questions about their possessions.

The last sentence of this fragment has aroused much discussion. The text is not clear. One cannot tell if the author was expecting the coming of a prophet who would also be the Messiah of Aaron and the Messiah of Israel, or the simultaneous appearance of a prophet, a warrior messiah and a law-giving messiah. The Law-giver had been expected long before the destruction of the Temple. In addition, every High Priest was a "messiah" in the sense of being an "anointed one". At his anointing, a cross was traced on his head by a line going from the middle of his brow to the first vertebra of the spine, crossed by another line going from ear to ear. The warrior messiah received the royal anointing, a circle being traced around the top of his head. It was only after A.D. 70 that one looked for his coming. So as to be acknowledged as leader, Bar Kochba had himself anointed by Rabbi Aqiba.

This fragment must have been written after A.D. 70 as it deals with the rebuilding of the Temple and the re-establishment of animal sacrifices.

## FRAGMENT 20

COLUMN IX, LINES 12-16.

These are the ordinances on which one must meditate and in accordance with which one's relations to other persons must be determined. The circumstances of each age, and the differing qualities of men must be taken into account. God's will must be done following what He has revealed from age to age. Knowledge from the past ages must be acquired, also the knowledge of what is right for the present age. Distinctions must be made between the Sons of Zadok and between the Elect of the Age, assessing them by the spirit which they manifest. One must keep to what God's Accepted One has said, even as He has commanded. To execute His judgements, one must take a man's mind into account. He should be approached as one deals with a bucket at a well: he should be held in consideration in proportion to the degree of knowledge that he holds. On this he should be loved or hated.

## FRAGMENT 21

COLUMN IX, LINES 16-21.

Since there is no need to scold or quarrel with men of perdition, the counsel of the Law must be kept to oneself when in the midst of wicked men. On the other hand, however, one must instil the knowledge of truth and the principles of righteousness into the minds of young people. As a man is moved, and in keeping with the conditions of the time, he should instruct the young, and by the mysteries which are marvellous yet true, should bring them up in the company of the members of the Community so that they behave rightly, each towards his neighbour, in all that has been made known to them.

It is the time for taking them into "the way of the desert", and for teaching them all that it has been found necessary to do in this age so as to to be separate from every man who has not departed from all iniquity.

## FRAGMENT 22

COLUMN IX, LINES 21-6.

Now these are the rules of conduct to be taught in this age so that the young will either love one or hate one with an everlasting hate. As regards the men of perdition, one must hide one's motives, and toil with one's hands as a slave toils for the person who governs him, and submits himself before the person who lords it over him. Yet one must be full of zeal for what is right, and when the day of vengeance dawns, must carry out the will of God on everything to which one can lay one's hand, everywhere in His realm, as He has commanded. All that one does for God, He will accept as an offering willingly made. But reluctance He loves not. The . . . . of the orders of His mouth He will accept, but let no one put forward as God's purposes what He has not

ordered. One must always be attentive . . . . . . . . . . He will bless
his deeds in all that which will be . . . . . . . . . by the lips we shall
bless Him.

All these three fragments, in which we find a number of doctrines
already met with in Fragments 3 and 5, have their origin in a Zealot
society which had borrowed several ideas from the Baptists, whilst making
slight changes in them.

Like all men of the people, these Zealots attached great importance to
learning. One should know the age in which one lived and understand
one's contemporaries. Above all, it was necessary to be on one's guard
against the Zadokites and the rabbis of the Pharisees called the "Chosen of
the Age". A sample of gnomic wisdom is seen in the allusion to the
proverb, "This world is like a well with a water-wheel: the full bucket
empties itself and the empty bucket fills itself."

The thing of importance was to instil into the young a hatred for the
oppressor. It was recommended to make a pretence of submission, and
renounce all enrichment, until the day of vengeance. Then one should
show one's zeal. Everything one could burn would be counted as a
sacrifice well-pleasing to God. There should be no going further than
what was laid down, and orders should be respected. It was enjoined that
one should continue in the teaching given by "The Accepted One of God"
(Judas of Galilee?).

These texts must have been written after the disaster of A.D. 70, when
the final breach between the Zealots and the Zadokites took place. A
paraphrase from the *Commentary on Isaiah* suggests that this Baptist work
was also known in Zealot circles.

## FRAGMENT 23

COLUMN X, LINES 1-8.

In accordance with the designs which He has allowed, the people of
His might must be in the government of the Realm of Light, whilst
his country shall be in the government of the Watchers of Darkness
under his "pick-up", the factotum. He has opened his cellar: he has given
him drink in full measure. Through his violence against the people,
they gather together because of the light when the lamps from the
people's Holy Dwelling shine out. He had them collected for the
glorious mansion, to place them in the entrance.

The feast days, he has put them together on days and months which are after their traditions and until they rebuild the terrace opposite the Holy of Holies. By his orders, the sign "N" replaces in every corner the key of God's everlasting mercies at the beginning of the festivals. At the new moons, following their way of fixing dates, at holy days as they establish them, and at days of remembrance as they count them, it is necessary by a lip-offering that we make, to give him a blessing, as if it was a right engraved in stone for all eternity. It is the same thing at New Year and following the cycle of their festivals. Putting an end to the privilege which he had conceded on the day when he gave judgement, he has fixed the feasts at wrong dates; thus the feast of harvests, which should be in the spring, now is in summer, and the feast of sowings is now at a time when the blades of corn are already green. He has established annual feasts according to their calendar, whilst at their New Year he has appointed a feast of licence. All the eternal rights of the Jews have been transformed into a fruit of praise and a tribute of the lips (*to the Emperor*).

This fragment, the last of what some would like us to consider as the *Rule of the Essenes,* was also part of a Zealot writing—a book of contemporary history. This passage has been given very different translations, and comparison has been made with the calendar in the Book of Enoch, a composite work in which many authors of several centuries have had a hand—at least in the versions that we possess. This fragment, a paraphrase of a current prayer, is not giving us some individual ideas concerning the calendar of festivals. It is a pamphlet directed against the government of Agrippa II. First of all, the author recalls that God has determined the lot of everyone. The Realm of Light must return to the "people of His Might"—that is, to Israel. Antonius Felix, someone "gathered" or "picked up", a freed slave, who had been steward and cup-bearer to the Emperor Claudius, and belonged to the Spirits of Darkness.

Following that, it is a question of the procurator who had the lamps of the Temple taken to the government palace. Rabbinic literature relates similar incidents. Then there is the question of the introduction into Judea of the Roman calendar, and at the time when a terrace was rebuilt opposite the Temple. That is an historic fact. It is well known how the Jews replied by setting up a palisade to mask the Temple, or at least to hide the faithful from Agrippa's excesses. He demanded the destruction of the palisade, and under the government of Porcius Festus (A.D. 61-2) the Jews sent a delegation to Nero, and obtained the right to preserve it. The event happened, therefore, under Felix.

The greatest complaint formulated in the text is the claim of the Romans to introduce their calendar into Judea. The feasts were in the wrong periods because of the difference of climate. In Judea, the feast of harvest fell in the spring. It was carried over into the height of summer so as to agree with the Roman Census, observed on 21st August. The feast of sowing now fell so late that the blades of corn were already green. Worse still, a licentious feast, the Saturnalia, had been introduced at the Roman New Year. The Jews considered this as particularly revolting.

Then there was the question of the sign "N", which had to be displayed everywhere at the beginning of each month and on Roman civic festivals. On these occasions it was obligatory to bless the emperor as if that was his right.

There has been much discussion over the meaning of the sign "N", which also carried the numerical value "50". But it is almost certain that we should see in it the initial of Nero Charles (*Apocrypha and Pseudepigrapha*, Vol. II, p. 397; *The Sibylline Oracles*, V, 28–34). Pontius Pilate had already decorated Jerusalem with shields bearing the initial of the Emperor Tiberius, and similar incidents are given in rabbinic literature.

These data allow us to place this fragment in the years A.D. 60-2, which would make it the oldest passage re-copied into *The Manual of Discipline*.


# FRAGMENT 24

COLUMN X, LINES 9–17.

*Psalm A*

*From a full understanding, would I make my song,*
*And all my music will be for the glory of God.*
*The strings of my harp shall chant His holy verdicts,*
*And the flute of my lips shall be a burnt-offering to the righteousness of His judgement.*
*At the coming of day and night, I will enter into the Covenant of God,*
*And when evening and dawn depart, I will recite His precept,*
*Even though fires surround me, and there is no way of escape,*
*And though the sentence of the oppressor strikes as if I had committed a crime,*
*Yet in my eyes my crimes are a right that cannot be denied.*
*It is God who can say if I am just,*
*And the Most High who can declare my innocence.*

*In Him is the well of knowledge, and the source of holiness,*
*The height of glory, and the almighty and eternal splendour.*
*I choose therefore what He has shown me,*
*And shall be content with the way He shall judge me.*
*Before I move my hand or foot,* *I will bless His* NAME.
*Before my going out and my coming in,*
*Before my sitting down or my rising up,*
*And when I lie upon my bed,* *I will magnify Him.*
*When I take my place in the ranks of men,*
*Before I raise my hand to profit from the the fruits of the earth,*
*I will bless Him with the offering of my lips.*
*In the realm of fear and terror,*
*In the land of woe and waste,*
*I will praise Him for his wonders,*
*I will bow before His might,*
*And will lean upon His kindness, all the hours of day.*
*For I know that in His hand judgement lies for all who live*
*And that all He does is truth.*
*When anguish comes upon me, I will glorify Him,*
*When He accords me His help, I will magnify Him.*

The four psalms which are found at the end of this roll are written out one after the other, and only the last one is marked off by a stroke in the margin. It is only by their contents, therefore, that they can be separated one from another.

The first psalm contains nothing unorthodox, and could easily have come from a Pharisaic environment. The hours of prayer conform to the rabbinic practice. Mention is made both of the prayers in the synagogue—"in the ranks of men"—and of the blessings to be pronounced before each meal.

*Psalm A* takes the form of a profession of faith by a believer who wishes to remain true to God even though the Roman oppressor persecutes him and treats his loyalty to his religion as a crime. He is sure that God, the only judge, will recognise his righteousness. He awaits a miracle that will save him, and even in his sufferings does not cease to bless God.

This psalm appears to have been written in Judea during one of the Roman persecutions which preceded and followed the war of A.D. 66-70. The phrases used by the author have so much in common with ordinary Biblical terminology that it is difficult to attribute this poem to any particular school.

H*

## FRAGMENT 25

Column X, Line 17 to Column XI, Line 2.

*Psalm B*

> To no one will I return evil for evil,
>   The man of might, I will pursue with goodness.
> It is for God to judge all who live,
>   And He it is who will render to man his reward.
> I will not be full of zeal to carry out wickedness,
>   My soul shall not long after goods got by violence.
> The quarrel with men of perdition, I will not make greater, before the day of
>       vengeance,
> Not a jot will I take back from wicked men,
> Not a tittle will I desire,
>   Till the sentence of God is determined concerning them.
> On that day, I will retain no rancour towards those who have turned from
>       their sin,
> But I will have no pity for all those who persist in the paths of rebellion.
> I will have no comfort for the defeated,
>   Until they have amended their ways.
> And I will not keep Belial in my heart.
> Folly and wicked guile shall not be heard from my mouth,
>   Nor treachery and lying be found on my lips.
> The fruits of holiness shall be heard from my tongue,
>   And things of horror shall not be found there.
> With thanksgiving will I open my mouth,
>   And my tongue shall ever relate the just dealings of God.
> My lips shall flee the blasphemies of men,
>   Who spit out oaths all the time of their sinning.
> My heart will do battle for knowledge,
>   And with counsels of prudence shall I proclaim understanding.
> Even surrounded by knowledge of treachery . . .
>   With a solid frontier for guarding the faith,
> In the verdicts of help and the righteous deeds of God, I . . .
> To Him belongs the right, with a plumb-line of the ages . . .  . . .  . . .
>       justice.
> Love of charity towards those who are bowed down,
> Strength of hand for . . .  . . .
> Understanding to those of a wayward mind,

*To make the humbled to understand instruction,*
*To reply with humility to those whose bearing is haughty,*
*And by a contrite spirit to men of the sceptre,*
*Who stretch out the finger, utter their insults, and are eager for wealth.*

A completely different spirit is found in this psalm, which had its origin in a Jewish-Christian environment of the first century, perhaps even of the first generation. Many passages are in harmony with phrases from the Gospels, the *Didache,* and the epistles of Barnabas, Polycarp, Clement of Rome, etc.

In a number of places, the text has been altered by erasures and additions, and some contradictions exist as a result. That does not prevent this psalm from echoing a spirit quite different from that in the corresponding Zealot passage, Fragment 22. The parts which can be recognised as the original version reveal a believer who desires to return good for evil, and not be a "zealot" in the sense of one who talks of war. It is God who judges men. The believer should not even reply to the haughty; in their presence he should show humility. Naturally, the phrases "men of the sceptre" and "those who stretch out the finger" refer to the Idumean government, and to the Romans. The latter phrase is frequently employed. It can be taken for granted that where the author is presented as expressing a desire to take part in the day of vengeance predestined by God, we have later additions to the text, as for instance in line 19, where the original wording has been erased and a sentence inserted between the lines.

In its original form, the psalm may have been composed about the middle of the first century, while its revision can be put to the years A.D. 80-90, and the reviser must be placed in a popular Gnostic circle.

## FRAGMENT 26

Column XI, Lines 2-15.

*Psalm C*

*As for me,*
  *God is my judge, and in His hand is the perfecting of my way, and the uprightness of my heart.*
  *In His acts of righteousness my sin will be lost.*
  *From the well-spring of His knowledge He has made light to spring forth.*
  *My eyes have seen His wonders, and my heart is enlightened by the mysteries of the future.*

*He is for ever, the support of my right hand on the rocks of help,*
*And the path of my feet, made wholly smooth so that I may not stumble,*
*For it is the truth of God that is the rock of my steps,*
*And His might, that is the support of my right hand.*
*From the well-spring of His justice go forth the verdicts of light.*
*In my heart are the wonders of His miracles in this present world.*
*My eyes have perceived the help which is hidden from the man of wickedness,*
*And from him, who among the Sons of Man makes with guile his plans.*
*I have seen a well-spring of righteousness, and a fountain of valour, hidden from human flesh.*
*To those whom He has chosen, God has given an everlasting possession, a share in the heritage which is the lot of the saints.*
*With the "Sons of Heaven" as companions, they work together for the Council of the Community,*
*For the foundation of the sanctuary, and for the planting of a universe which will endure to the end of all things.*

*As for me,*
*As a man of sin, and according to the nature of sinful flesh, I have fallen short.*
*I have sinned, I have been criminal, by following the sins of my heart,*
*Choosing the counsel of deceit, and the way of those who walk in darkness.*
*For according to his nature, so is the way of man,*
*And the human being, of himself, cannot control his steps.*
*Judgement is with God, and from His hand proceeds the perfecting of the way.*
*It is by His knowledge that everything will be, and all that now is has been controlled by His thought,*
*And without Him, naught is done.*

*As for me,*
*If I totter, the kindness of God will ever be my help.*
*If I stumble, by the sinfulness of my flesh, my verdict will be established for eternity in accordance with the justice of God.*
*If anguish makes itself known to me, He will save my soul from the Pit, and order my steps in the way.*
*He will grasp me with His mercy, and according to His kindness shall my verdict be pronounced.*
*According to the righteousness of His truth, will He judge me,*
*And in the multitude of His kindness He will wipe out all my iniquities.*

*By His justice, He will cleanse me from the pollution of the human flesh, and*
*from the sins of the Sons of Man.*
*So shall I give thanks to God for His justice, and to the Most High for His*
*splendour.*

In this third psalm, we once more come across the Zealot outlook. The doctrine of "The Two Ways" is the basis of the avowal of the helplessness of the human being. Unless God guides him, he stumbles because of the weakness of the flesh.

Further on, we find views which were current in the popular Zealot literature of the first and second centuries. The believer had contemplated God's miracles; he had perceived the source of justice and the fountain of valour. He also knew that God would give him in the other world a portion with all His elect. With angels as their companions, those whom God has chosen will have to prepare for the building of a future universe which would be eternal and governed by the Council of the Community.

The expression "Sons of Man" occurs twice in this poem in different contexts, not easy to reconcile. The use of the phrase may have importance. As a matter of fact, to use the terminology of the Pseudo-Clementines, first of all was he who was born of woman, and only later he appeared who belonged to the "Sons of Man". The expression "born of woman" has often struck the present writer as a characteristic mark of Zadokite-Baptist writings. It may be, therefore, that we have here a poem coming from a Zealot environment influenced by Christianity. In that case, it can only be that we are dealing with an anti-Pauline sect, in opposition to "him who from among the sons of man made plans of guile". The notion of the pollution inherent in the human being from the fact of his birth is a Zadokite idea. It appears to have been taken over in Zealot circles, and there it may have taken the form of "original sin".

## FRAGMENT 27

COLUMN XI, LINES 15-22.

*Psalm D*

*Blessed be Thou, my God, who dost open to knowledge the heart of Thy*
*servant.*
*In righteousness, strengthen all his actions, and if it be Thy good will, lift up*
*the son of Thy handmaid,*
*To be among the chosen of mankind, and to stand before Thee for evermore.*

*For, without Thee, no path is perfect, and apart from Thy will, nothing is accomplished.*

*It is Thou who has conceived all knowledge, and everything that shall be is within Thy will.*

*Beside Thee, there is no one who could answer Thy counsels, or think out all Thy designs,*

*Look into the depth of Thy mysteries, or fathom by his thought all Thy miracles and the mightiness of Thy power.*

*Who would be able to comprehend Thy glory? And what is he alone, he, the son of man, among the work of Thy miracles?*

*He who is "born of woman", how could he take his seat before Thee?*

*As to him, out of dust was he kneaded, and as food for worms was he prepared.*

*He, set within bounds, was only formed of clay, and it is to dust that he returns.*

*How can clay make answer, the work that a hand fashioned? And how can it understand the counsels of God?*

This last psalm, of Zadokite inspiration, seems to come from the sect of Baptists, for twice man is said to be "born of woman". This phrase is used in the New Testament to indicate the members of the sect to which John the Forerunner belonged (Matt. 11.11; Luke 7.28, *et passim*). It is true that the expression "Sons of Man" is also found here, but it has not the same connotation as in the preceding psalm. In fact, the scribe has corrected the manuscript, inserting the article "*h-*" between the lines so as to prevent confusion with the expression *without the article* which is found in that psalm.

As in all Zadokite texts, the human being is disparaged. The reminder is given that he is dust and that to dust he returns, to serve as food for the worms of the earth. There is here no vision of the other world, and no conception of life after death. The author hopes to be raised "towards the chosen of mankind"—that is to say, to be rewarded in this world for the acts that God will make just. The same ideas, and even the same expressions, are also found in several *Hymns of Thanksgiving*—again of Zadokite inspiration.

# II

# The "Additions to the Rule"

## I. "RULES"

For a description of this sheet of two columns purchased by the Palestine Archaeological Museum in 1950, see also pp. 132–5. Several translations have appeared since that date, and the present one differs from them to only a slight extent, but the differences are on essential matters, and will be dealt with in the comments which follow.

COLUMN I, LINES 1–5.

And this is the custom for the whole congregation of Israel, when in the last days they shall assemble . . . . . . to act in conformity with the decisions of the Sons of Zadok, that is to say, of the priests (*Kohen*) and of the men of their Covenant, who have withdrawn themselves from walking according to the way of the people. They are the men of His Counsel, those who have maintained His Covenant in the midst of wickedness so that . . . . . . . . . When these days arrive, all who come shall be gathered together, including little children and women, and all the precepts of the Covenant shall be read to them in the hearing of . . . . . . to teach them all their laws lest they should wander in . . . . . . . . .

We find here the preamble of a Constitution prepared for the day when the Zadokites should come into power and form a theocratic government in Israel with the former priests or their descendants who are members of their party.

COLUMN I, LINES 6–18.

And this is the custom for all the soldiers of the Congregation. Every home-born Israelite from the young [man up to . . .] [so as] to be taught in the "Book of Deductions", and in proportion to his age, let him be led to reflect on the laws of the Covenant so as to learn the purpose of the findings given in them. Up to the age of ten years, he will go about amidst the children, and when he is twenty years old . . . . . . . . . . . . . . . the inspectors, to play his part in family life, united to her in the holy congregation.

But if he has not [approached] the woman to know her after the fashion of a man, if he is of the full age of twenty years, and has been recognised [as impotent] and evil, in this case she shall have the right to testify against him, in accordance with the ordinances of the Law, and to be present in the session when the finding is pronounced.

As soon as he has reached the full age of twenty-five years, he will come and present himself to the "Foundation Members" of the Holy Congregation to offer himself to the service of the Congregation. At the age of thirty, he will draw near to play his part in the strife . . . and will present himself to the heads of thousands to be allotted his duties. He may become a commander of a hundred, of fifty, or of ten. He may be made a judge or overseer for his tribe and all its families. But whatever is decided will be according to what is said by the priests, the Sons of Aaron, and by all the commanders, fathers of the Congregation who have been designated as heads of the Congregation, to serve and lead it.

If his conduct has been correct according to his intelligence and gifts, he will receive his place in the army, or for the work he will do in the midst of his brethren—of greater or less importance, and according to his appointment, he may be more honoured than his neighbour.

The Zadokite state was to undertake the education of children. The basis of the instruction was the Law of Moses and the deductions that had been drawn from it. These had been put together in the Sepher HHGW, "the Book of Deductions". A school should gather in children over ten years of age. At twenty years, a young man was to present himself to inspectors so as to be enrolled in his tribe and family as the Law of Moses laid down.

If, at the age of twenty, the young man had not shown himself to be virile, his wife could testify against him, and the law regarding the impotent would be applied. It is thus that the present writer reads this passage, which has generally been translated in an opposite sense. The negation is clearly visible in the manuscript. Moreover, there is no evidence that Jews, whatever their belief, have insisted on the chastity of a youth up to the age of twenty years. He had to enter into marriage at fourteen years, and it is quite understandable that if after six years he had given no sign of virility, he would be considered impotent. On the evidence of his wife, who obtained a divorce, the man was declared unfit for military service. Probably he was excluded from civic duties.

Our text reflects typically Zadokite views on the age of combatants. At the age of twenty, a young man was entered on the civil registers, and at twenty-five received certain responsibilities. But it was only at the age of thirty that a citizen had to present himself for military service, and at once he received the grade of officer or superior official in the administration. Priests and certain "fathers of the congregation" elected as directors were the only persons who decided the position the conscript should take. No Jew could be a mere private soldier (1 Sam. 8.12). Naturally, one can only see in this plan a desire inspired by Holy Scripture.

COLUMN I, LINES 19-29, AND COLUMN II, LINES 1-7.

As a man increases in years, the responsibility given to him in the work of the Congregation shall be in proportion to his ability. A simpleton cannot be elected as a leader in the Congregation of Israel, to decide legal differences, to impose a duty on behalf of the Congregation, or to go into battle to restrain foreign nations. Following the custom of the army, only the name of his family will be entered on the roll, and he himself will do the work of a camp-follower as far as he is able.

The Sons of Levi will each have his post, as directed by the Sons of Aaron. They will have to maintain right behaviour throughout all the Congregation, each with his accustomed task. They will be under the orders of the chief fathers of the Congregation, the commanders and the judges [* and the inspectors],[1] according to the number of their troops, and in conformity with the orders of the Sons of Zadok, the priests, and of the heads of the Congregation.

Wherever all the Congregation shall be called together to give a judgement, to consult together on some matter of common interest, or for a council of war, they shall sanctify themselves three days, so that all of them who come . . . . . . . The following are the persons who shall be called to a Council of the Community, all having attained the age of twenty years. All the . . . of the Congregation, all men of

[1] Inserted between the lines.

learning and those acquainted with the perfect way, the men of valour with . . . . . . of the tribes and all their judges and overseers, the commanders of thousands, of hundreds, of fifties and of tens, along with the Levites in the midst of . . . of His service. These are the men of renown who shall attend the Council of the Community of Israel, in the presence of the priests, the Sons of Zadok.

And any man stricken with any uncleanness that man may have shall not enter these meetings. And no such person can hold a position within the Congregation. Nor can the following hold such a position: a man stricken in his flesh, crippled in legs or hands, lame, blind, deaf, dumb, or disfigured, nor yet a man stumbling through age.

This chapter also forms part of a Zadokite constitution. By "simpletons", we should understand that peasants are referred to. They could only serve in the army as labourers. The Levites, under the orders of the priests and other leaders of the people, fulfilled the rôle of gendarmes, that given them in the Bible. Two kinds of assembly are envisaged, that of the whole people, as in the Pentateuch, and that of the Council of the Community, or in other words, of the Government. Those called to these latter meetings must have been rather numerous, but among the Levites only those engaged in the service of the Temple could attend.

Still influenced by regulations laid down in the Bible, this Zadokite constitution insists that anyone having a physical defect should be debarred from the army or any public service, and the aged and feeble should not attend government meetings.

COLUMN II, LINES 8-11.

Let not those enter, to present themselves in the midst of the Congregation of the MEN OF THE NAME, for holy angels are in their. . . . And should [one of them have anything] to say to the Holy Council, let him be questioned in private, but into the Council that man shall not come, for he is "leprous" (smitten) [and this is the ses]sion of the MEN OF THE NAME . . . meeting for Council of the Community.

It is at once evident that we have here a fragment of a totally different text which has absolutely nothing to do with the Zadokite constitution. The copyist's confusion must be the result of the mention of "men of name" (of renown) in the earlier fragment with the use of "THE NAME" in place of saying "God". A Zealot society might have taken this designation, Men of the NAME, and probably it forbade the entering into its meetings of certain persons who were unclean (not infirm) because the Zealots believed that angels were everywhere present. A similar idea is found in *The War of the Sons of Light* (VII, 5-7). Temporary uncleanness did not deprive a member of his rights. He had to be questioned at the door of the chamber in which the sessions were held, and his observations were presented through his representative.

COLUMN II, LINES 11-17.

If . . . . . . . . . the Messiah is with them, the . . . head of the whole congregation of Israel enters, likewise all the . . . . . . of Aaron, the Cohens [to the . . .] of the convocation of the Men of the NAME and they shall take their seats in his presence each in order of rank. After that the Messiah of Israel [has taken his seat,] then, in his presence, shall seat themselves the heads . . . . . . . . . . each in order of his rank as . . . . . . laid down for their camps and their line of march. Also all the heads [. . . . . . . of the Congre]gation, with the men of learn[ing] . . . . . . in their presence, each according to his rank.

This fragment seems to look forward to an occasion when the Warrior Messiah (the Messiah of Israel) should visit the Zealot society. A gap in the text prevents us from knowing if he would arrive accompanied by the *Nasi* as in other similar passages. The order of precedence to be observed was the same as that in their military camps. The Messiah should take his seat first. Then the (military?) heads followed by the heads (of the civil administration?), and in the last place the rabbis, called here "men of learning", *ḥkmym*, and not "great ones", *rbym*. It is most remarkable that this document does not seem to have made provision for the order of precedence of the descendants of Aaron who should arrive in the company of the Messiah.

COLUMN II, LINES 17-22.

And if [it is at ta]ble that they have come toge[ther,] and if the table of the Community . . . . . . . . . . has been laid, let no one put forth his hand to break the bread or pour the wine before the Cohen, for to him belongs the right to bless the bread and the wine and to be the first to put forth his hand to the bread. After that, it is the Messiah who shall stretch forth his hand to the bread . . . . . . . . . . all the congregation of the Community, each in order of rank. This is what should be done at any meal where there are at least ten persons.

As at all Jewish meals, a blessing should be pronounced over the bread and wine at the moment of sitting down to table. If the Messiah had honoured a banquet of the Zealots by his presence, it was normal to ask a Cohen, descendant of the Aaronite priests, to say the blessing and be the first to take the bread and wine. The Messiah would be the next to partake, and after that the other members in due order. The document deals merely with this question of order, and there is no justification for the attempts to fill up the gaps with directions that a number of persons, including the Messiah, should pronounce successive benedictions. The last sentence is probably an addition by the copyist.

## II. THE BENEDICTIONS

For a detailed description of these thirty-two fragments, some of which are extremely small, see also p. 135. These benedictions were grouped together in series, apparently four in number, each series being called a *maskîl*, or to use the form familiar from English versions of the Bible, *maschil*.

The first series seems to have been a collection of benedictions for the use of all who belonged to the Community of the Covenant, whatever their class or rank. The opening formula is:

Words of benediction to bring success and to bless those who fear God, keep His commandments, strengthen themselves in His Holy Counsel and walk in perfectness of . . . . . . . . . . It is among them that He will choose for His eternal covenant, which shall be established for ever.

The following fifty or so lines are represented by mere fragments, but apparently were a collection of short phrases of benediction suitable for inscribing on small pieces of parchment and carried as amulets.

The latter part of Column II and the greater part of Column III contain fragments of benedictions on behalf of an individual, who may be the Warrior Messiah or the High Priest, but the opening formula which would tell us is missing.

The third series is the best preserved, though there are two long gaps of about twenty lines each, and many other lines are incomplete. It opens:

Words of benediction to bring success and to bless the Sons of Zadok, the priests among whom God has chosen to strengthen His Covenant . . . . . . . . . all His judgements in the midst of His people, and to instruct them, as He has commanded. Indeed, they have maintained their faithfulness, and with righteousness they have watched over all His statutes, and their conduct has been what He has chosen.

May the Lord bless His holy dwelling and place thee as a splendid ornament in the midst of the saints. May He renew for thee the priestly covenant and give thee thy place . . . . . . of holiness. May all doers of good be judged by what they do, and by the sortilege of thy lips may all . . . . . . . .

Some later sentences read:

As for thee, thou shalt be as an Angel of the Presence in the holy dwelling-place for the glory of the God of Hosts . . . . . . and thou shalt be a constant servitor in the Royal Temple. With the Angels of the Presence, thou shalt decide the casting of the lot, and give counsel in concert with . . . . . . . .

The fourth series begins with the formula ". . . . to bring success and to bless the *Nasi* of the Congregation". Among later fragments we find: "May the Lord lift thee up to a universal greatness, as a tower of help on a steep wall . . . . . . . . . with thy sceptre shalt thou lay waste the earth, and destroy the wicked by the breath of thy lips. . . ." "May justice be the girdle of . . . . . . . . . the girdle of thy loins. May He transform thy horns to iron, and thy sandals to brass." "For God has raised thee up to be a rod on the oppressors . . . . . . . . . and they shall serve thee, and by His Holy Name He will give thee power and thou shalt be like . . . . . . . ."

# III

# The Interpretation of the Prophecies of Habakkuk

Many translations of the *Habakkuk Commentary* have been put forward, and there have been numerous studies published on points of detail. As far as possible, these have been taken into account in drawing up the present version, which in its general lines is a reproduction of that published by the present writer in 1951.

Quotations from the Book of Habakkuk do not follow any one of the current versions of the Bible, but take account of what the author of the interpretations wished to read in Habakkuk's words. The quotations are printed in italics in the translation which follows.

COLUMN I

This first column is far too fragmentary for any useful information to be gathered from it. It covered the first four verses of the Prophet's book, with the quotation of most of the fifth verse. These verses cry out to God against violence and lawlessness. In the fragment of the thirteenth line, we have the words *mwrh hṣdq*, Teacher of Righteousness, the personage who is to figure so largely in this series of interpretations.

COLUMN II

As stated on p. 137, this column has a gap in the centre extending all down the sheet, so that we have the first and last parts only of each line. The first line begins with the last word in verse 5 of the Prophet. The comment on that verse, beginning at the end of the line and passing over into the next line speaks of ". . . . traitors with the Man of Lying. For they have not . . . . . . . . the Teacher of the Jus[t] from the mouth of God." Other characteristic expressions found in this column are "the Covenant of God" (line 4) "interpretation of this word" (line 5): "last days" (lines 5-6): "His servants the prophets" (line 9). From lines 9-14 we read: "God has related al¹ that should happen to His people and . . . . . . . . . *For behold, I shall raise up the Chaldaeans, the people fi[erce and has]ty.* Its interpretation applies to the legions which . . . . . . . . . quick and valiant in battle, to destroy the great . . . . . . . . . . in the empire of the legions." The remainder of the column is fragmentary or destroyed.

The commentator is reporting a terrible judgement of God which has fallen on the traitors and the Man of Lying (Eleazar) because they have not had faith in the Teacher of the Just (Menahem). The same prediction applies to a "tyrant" (Agrippa II) who had not believed what had been said by the priest of God (Anan) to whom God had entrusted the authority to explain ancient prophecies. Then the commentator identifies the Chaldaeans with the legions and the empire of the legions (Rome and the Romans).

## Column III

[(*Book of the Prophet,* 1.6) *He marches over the wide extent of the land.* Its interpretation applies to . . . . . . . . . .] and in the plain they advance to destroy and pillage the cities of the country. For this is what he said (1.6-7) *To take possession of dwellings which are not his, he is terrible and formidable. From himself proceed his law and his greatness.* Its interpretation applies to the legions, the terror and fear of whom is heavy on all [* the nations],¹ and deliberately all their plans are to do evil. For with deceit and treachery they behave towards all the nations (1.8-9) *and more swift than tigers is his horse, and more agile than the evening wolves, they spread themselves out. The horsemen of his cavalry come from far, flying as a vulture hastening to devour. All arrive for pillage; driven by greed, their faces poke forward.* [Its interpretation] applies to the legions which have winnowed the country with their horses and beasts. From distant lands they come, from the isles of the sea, to eat up . . . . . . . all the nations, insatiable as the vulture. It is with anger that they . . . . . . . nose inflamed and sullen face, they speak with . . . . . . . For this is what he said, (1.9) *He po[kes his face forward, and like the sand, will he gather] prisoners.*

All that the prophet had said about the Chaldaeans had come true with the arrival of the Roman legions. Their swift cavalry had conquered vast

¹ Added between the lines.

countries, which are given over to systematic pillage. The Romans bear themselves arrogantly, and lead away captives. The "vultures" of which the prophet spoke are the Roman eagles. The "wolves" are those and other animals displayed on the standards of the legions.

COLUMN IV

(1.10) *And he, of kings will he make mock, and princes will be for him an object of scorn.* Its interpretation is that they make mock of rabbis and jeer at respected scholars, as they mock at kings, and laugh at princes making scorn of them, as they do of a numerous nation (1.10). *And he will laugh at every fortress; he will heap up earth and take it.* Its interpretation applies to the commanders of the legions, who treat the fortresses of the nations with contempt, and with jests laugh at them. With (*the help of*) a multitude of people, they surround them so as to take them. Out of fear and terror they are surrendered into their hands, and they utterly destroy those who dwell in them. (1.11) *Thus retaking his breath, he passes on and sets up this his might as his god.* Its interpretation applies to the commanders of the legions who according to the Council of the Temple of Asm[odaeus] retire each before his neighbour. Their commanders, one after the other, come to lay waste the [country and he sets] *up his might to be his god.* Its interpretation . . . . . . . . . . . . . . . all the nations.

The commentator applies the prophet's words to the contempt shown by the Romans for the rabbis (*rbym*) and for the "respected" (*nkbdym*) of their academies: the princes are entitled to no more respect than the common people. Then he calls to mind the capture of fortresses by the Romans and the slaughter of their inhabitants (during the war of A.D. 66-77 and up to the taking of Masada. Verse 11 is given two interpretations: The Roman Senate, here called the Temple of Asmodaeus,[1] nominated the procurators of Judea who followed each other in quick succession, the one aim of all of them being to plunder the country. The second interpretation is lost, as lines 15 onwards are completely destroyed.

COLUMN V

[(1. 12–13) *Art thou not from all eternity, Yahweh, my God, my Holy One. We shall not die, O Yahweh,*] *Thou hast established him for judgement,*

---

[1] Asmodaeus was the evil spirit in the Book of Tobit (3.8, 17), who in quick succession destroyed seven husbands one after another.

*and hast founded him* (to be) *a rock for those who punish in Thy name. Pure eyes revolt at evil, and to look* (unmoved) *on suffering, this they cannot do.* The interpretation of this word is that God will not cause [* His][1] people to be destroyed by the hand of (*foreign*) nations, but it is into the hand of His Elect that God will give (*the authority*) to judge all (*foreign*) nations. And when he shall call them to account, they also shall pay for their errors, the wicked ones of His people who through fear for themselves obeyed the commandments of the foreign oppressor. For this that he said, "*Pure eyes revolt at evil*", its interpretation is that there are those who prostituted themselves by following their eyes (*by covetousness*) right to the limits of wickedness.

(1.13-14) (So) *why have they looked* (unmoved), *the betrayers holding their peace when the wicked swallowed up the man more righteous than he?* Its interpretation applies to the "House of Absalom" and to the men of the council who kept silence when the accusation was levelled against the Teacher of Righteousness, and they did not help him against the Man of Lying.

He who had despised the Law in the midst of all their . . . . . .
(1. vv. 14-16) *And he has treated man like the fish of the sea, like a reptile, to practise his might upon him. [With a hook] he has made him rise up whole, and he has drawn him into his net and destroys him [in its meshes. Therefore he sacrifices] to his net and therefore he rejoices and is full of glee for his meat will be plenteous and his portion will be fat.* Its interpretation . . . . . . .

It is clear that Yahweh will not abandon His people. The commentator sees in the prophet's words the promise of the coming of a Messiah, an "Elect of God" who will judge all foreign nations. He will call to account those who obeyed the oppressor through fear of him. In speaking of those who had not let themselves be drawn into the ways of wickedness, the speaker is thinking of Menahem's followers.

The interpretation of verse 14 calls for a brief remark. Those who remained unmoved while the Man of Lying (Eleazar) made his charges against the Teacher of Righteousness (Menahem) which led to the latter's being put to death, they were the ministers of Menahem, "the House of Absalom and his council"—that is to say, Menahem's chief minister, Absalom. Instead of coming to the help of their leader, they hoped to save themselves by keeping quiet.

[1] An insertion between the lines.

Unfortunately, a considerable gap in the manuscript prevents us from knowing if in the mind of the commentator Eleazar had lured Menahem to Jerusalem. Verses 14-16 also serve for a second interpretation, this time applied to the Romans.

### COLUMN VI

. . . of the legions, and they have increased more and more their riches by their booty, like the abundance of the sea. And that which he said, *It is why he sacrifices to his net and offers incense to its meshes,* its interpretation is that they sacrifice to their insignia. Their instruments of war are for them objects of veneration. *For by them his portion is fat, and his meat plenteous.* Its interpretation is about them, that they divide out the world and that they eat up the product of the forced labour of all the nations, ruining many countries. (1.17) *Therefore he will draw his sword continually to slay the nations, and he will show no pity.* Its interpretation applies to the legions who put many to the sword, the young, the mature, the aged, women and children, and even on the fruit of the womb they have no pity.

The interpreter of Habakkuk comes back to his indictment of the Romans. The worship of the SIGNA, over which so much ink has been spilt, is attested to by the Romans, Moreover the text only speaks of "signs", *'wtwt,* not "standards" *dglim.* All the same, it is recognised that the Romans did offer worship to the weapons. The commentator applies Habakkuk's allegory to the Roman fiscal system and draws the conclusion that Rome would never cease to make war, and massacre men, women and children because for Rome it was a way to acquire wealth.

(2.1) *Standing at my guard-post, and set upon my wall, and attentive to see what He should say and that which He should respond to my complaint, Yahweh*[1] *spoke to me and said, "Write the vision and make it plain upon the tablets, so that he hurries who reads them.* Its interpretation . . . . . . . . .

### COLUMN VII

and God said [* to][1] Habakkuk to write the things to come concerning the last age, though the final end is not known.
    And that which he said, "So that [* he hurries][2] who reads them," its

---

[1] Written in ancient Phoenician characters.
[2] Inserted between the lines.

interpretation applies to the Teacher of Righteousness, who has been taught of God in all the mysteries of the words of His servants the prophets. (2.3.) *For there is yet a prophecy for an appointed day; it is panting towards the end, and it will not be found false.* Its interpretation is that the final end will be long in coming, and the remainder is about all that the prophets have said, for the mysteries of God are marvellous (*or, there are mysteries of God on the subject of Hophlah*).

(2.3) *If it tarries, wait for it: for it will surely come and cannot be avoided.* Its interpretation applies to the "Men of the Truthful One" who practise the Law, and whose hands cease not to serve the Truthful One because to them the final end is long in coming. For all the purposes of God happen in their turn as He has caused it to be inscribed in the secrets of His wisdom.

(2.4) *Behold the presumptuous, it dwells not in his soul.* Its interpretation is that they have made double upon them [ . . . . . . . . . . and have not taken de]light in the Laws [. . . . . . . . .

COLUMN VIII

[(2.4) *But the just, it is in his faith that he will live.*] Its interpretation applies to all those who observe the Law in the House of Judas; them, God will save from the House of Judgement because of their sufferings and their faith in the Teacher of Righteousness.

One of the outstanding features of the *Habakkuk Commentary* is the absence of all apocalyptic visions. This is the more remarkable since other manuscripts from Qumrân have become known. Yet verses 1-3 lend themselves admirably to such a topic. The commentator just says that the date of the Last Day is not known. The Day of Yahweh will be slow in coming, but it will inevitably come. In the uncorrected version of this manuscript the commentator has interpreted a passage of the prophet in the sense that the divine revelations were written for "him who reads them", and that this person, learned in all mysteries of the prophetic books, was the Teacher of Righteousness (Menahem). Yet Menahem was certainly dead at the time when the *Commentary* was written. Was there a belief that he would rise again? One sentence can be read "for there are the mysteries of God on the subject of Hophlah" and we know from Josephus that Menahem "was found in a place called Ophlah" and that there he was publicly executed.

Next, the commentator speaks of certain persons whom he calls "Men of the Truthful One". They had continued to serve God in spite of the fact that they found the last day long in coming. All that the commentator tells us about them is that they belonged to the "House of Judas", adherents to the teaching of Judas of Galilee, that they had faith in the Teacher of Righteousness, and that they were enduring suffering. God would save them from human justice (the House of Judgement), and they would live, whilst the presumptuous would lose their souls. Because of a gap in the manuscript, we do not know who these presumptuous were.

The above gives ground for the supposition that some Zealots were definitely allied with Menahem, as Josephus says. For a time they had been able to form a party with a religious colouring—above all, from the fact that they were already separated from the Temple and had their own priests and rabbis to whom they paid their tithes. Influenced perhaps by the first Christians, who awaited a second coming of Jesus, were they also hoping for a resurrection of Menahem? It would appear that in the mind of his followers, he had already risen again once. The commentator lets it be understood that the second resurrection would take place, but much later than his adherents thought.

At the time when the *Commentary* was written, a number of Zealots were prisoners in the hands of the Romans, and awaited their trial. The commentator gives them the hope that God will save them from human justice.

(2.5–6) *And since riches lead a man away so that he becomes a traitor, even more so shall he become arrogant and restless whose soul is enlarged like Sheol. Like death, he is insatiable. Around him shall gather all the nations, about him shall be heaped all peoples. Have they not, all of them, composed proverbs about him, moral refrains concerning him. And they say, "Woe to him who increases, and yet it does not belong to him. For how long shall the burden of his yoke weigh heavily?"* Its interpretation applies to the Wicked Priest who gave himself the Name of the Truthful One at the beginning of his ministry, but when he had exercised his authority in Israel, his heart was puffed up, and because of the love of riches, he abandoned God, and betrayed the precepts. He plundered: he amassed wealth which came from violent men revolted from God: he accepted the wealth of foreign people, heaping on himself the sin of trespass, and he has prepared the paths of abomination with all filth and covetousness.

Verses 5 and 6 are applied to the Wicked Priest (Ananias), who was very popular at the beginning of his ministry. We should recall that

Ananias had taken the place of Anan, the father (?) of Menahem. It had been considered a happy omen that the new High Priest had a theophorous name, as the commentator said, "he caused himself to be called by the Name of the Truthful One". The expression "called by Thy name" is well known, and "the Truthful One" is an epithet often used to designate God.

The reproaches made against the Wicked Priest agree fully with what Josephus says about Ananias. The commentator above all holds up the fact of his having accepted gifts from apostates and pagans.

> (2.7-8) *But shall they not rise up suddenly? The torturers torment thee and inspire terror. Thou art become a prey to them. For thou, thou hast spoiled peoples* (or corpses) *and so shall all the remaining peoples spoil thee.* [Its interpretation applies to] the priest who revolted [against the . . . . precepts.

COLUMN IX
> and in accordance with wicked laws have they struck him, horrible and terrible tortures they inflicted on him, and deeds of vengeance on his corpse.

A long interpretation of verses 7 and 8 must have had many allusions to historical facts, but unfortunately it has been destroyed. The priest referred to at the beginning, and of whom it is said that he had revolted, should be Eleazar or a member of his party, but certainly not Ananias who is always referred to as the Wicked Priest. One the other hand, the person whose torture is referred to at the top of Column IX does seem to be Ananias, discovered in the sewers of Jerusalem on Saturday, 6th Elûl, A.D. 66. A play on the word *gwy*, which can be translated by either "people" or "corpse", allows the commentator to justify the treatment meted out to the High Priest by the populace.

> And that which he said, "*For thou, thou hast spoiled many peoples, and so shall all the remaining peoples spoil thee*", its interpretation applies to the priests of Jerusalem, the last ones, those who amassed wealth, the proceeds from the plunder of peoples. But in the final days, they had to give up their wealth and their booty into the hands of the army of the legionaries.

The last priests of Jerusalem—it is not here the question of the apocalyptic end of priesthood in general—were those in office on the 9th Ab, A.D. 70.

They had to hand over to the legionaries all the wealth hoarded up in the Temple. The commentator implies that this was only justice as their belongings were in part derived from gifts made by the heathen, and hence coming from the plundering of nations.

> For these are they, "the remaining peoples": (2.8.) *the men bled, and the countries squeezed, the town and all [\*the dwellers]*[1] *in it.* Its interpretation applies to the Wicked Priest who by the . . . of the Teacher of Righteousness and the men of his council, God had given over into the hands of his enemies, so that they humiliated him by punishments that ended in death in the bitterness of the soul, because he had acted wickedly towards His Elect.

In this second interpretation, supported by the close of verse 8, "the remaining people" are the inhabitants of the countryside, the Zealots whom the Wicked Priest (Ananias) had ground down. Thanks to (the help of ?) the Teacher of Righteousness and his ministers (Absalom), they had been able to seize the Wicked Priest and execute him. In the mind of the commentator, it was God who had delivered the Wicked Priest into the hands of his enemies, because he had dealt wickedly (*hršy'*) with the Elect of God, most probably the former High Priest Anan.

> (2.9-11) *Woe to him that getteth an evil gain for his house, so that he may set his nest on high, to be able to despoil [by making use of the wi]ng of the wicked. Thou has taken Shame as the adviser of thy house, the cuttings-off of many nations and the sins of thy soul. For the stone in the wall cries out, and the beam of wood makes [answer. The interpretation of the word]* applies to . . . who . . . . . . . . . . . .

COLUMN X

. . . to become stone by violence and beam of wood by robbery. And that which he said (2.10) *the cuttings-off of many nations, as well as the sins of thy soul,* its interpretation is the Judgement Seat where God will give his judgement in the midst of many nations. And from there He will make him rise up to be judged, and in the midst of them, He will declare him guilty, and condemn him to fire and brimstone.

[1] Inserted between the lines.

Verses 9-11, like those which follow, are not interpreted in relation to Ananias, the Wicked Priest. They are applied to another personage who can be identified with Agrippa II. A play on words, marked also by a difference in writing, has allowed the commentator to accuse Agrippa of having taken for councillors the scum (literally, "the bits cut off", *qswwt*) of many nations and to have given himself over to sin. That is why his palaces built in reliance on the power of the occupant have been a prey to violence, and are no more than beams and broken stones. Agrippa had followed Vespasian, and lived at Rome with his son Monobazus, "in the midst of many nations". It is there that God will judge him, says the commentator, at the same time that He will judge the Romans, and He will condemn him to perish by fire and brimstone.

It may be that we have here an allusion to the eruption of Vesuvius in A.D. 79, which caused the death of a nephew of Agrippa, the son of his sister Drusilla and the procurator Felix. This cataclysm could be considered as a prelude to the Last Judgement. Actually, the destruction of Pompeii had had a great influence on all the apocalyptic literature.

(2.12) *Woe to him who builds a town with blood and founds a city in sin. Is it not from Yahweh[1] of Hosts that the people tire themselves for the fire, and wear themselves out for vanity?*

The interpretation of the word applies to the Orator of Falsehood who has led many persons into error, in bloodshed making them build a city of nothingness, and by the heavy weight of enforced toil, set up a memorial which was an imposture. He wore out many people with their labour that had no worth, and brought about their destruction by works of imposture, with the result that their labour should be a vain thing. This came about that those who insulted and despised the Elect Ones of God should be brought to fiery judgements.

This is still dealing with Agrippa II. He is called the Orator of Falsehood, and as a matter of fact it seems that he often did address the people, exhorting them to submit to the Romans. The City of Nothingness built by him is Caesarea Philippi. He made it into a memorial by naming it Neronias. The Jews who settled there must have been more or less pro-Roman, and in consequence opposed to the Zadokites and to Menahem. On 10th Tishri, A.D. 66, the place was a prey to fire and, according to Josephus, the 20,000 Jews living there were massacred.

[1] Written in Phoenician characters.

(2.14) *For the earth shall be filled with the glory of Yahweh[1] as the waters cover the sea.* The interpretation of the word [applies to . . . . . . . . .

COLUMN XI

. . . of falsehood. Afterwards, knowledge as abundant as the waters of the sea, shall be revealed to them. (2.15) *Woe to him who gives his neighbours drink, mixing fury in it, making them drunk, so as to gaze on their celebrations* (or, on their staggerings; or, on their nakedness). Its application applies to the Wicked Priests who pursued the Teacher of Righteousness right up to the "house of his exile" in order to confuse him by the violence of his anger. But at the close of the feast of quietness, on the Day of Atonement, he appeared to them to confuse them and make them stumble, on the day of fasting, the sabbath of final rest.

The interpretation of verse 14 is too fragmentary for any useful information to be gathered from it. The most that can be said is that the commentator looked forward to a time of *gnôsis* for all the human race.

It is very difficult to grasp what the commentator means in his interpretation of verse 15, and it has been the subject of much controversy. Thanks to the translation of the expression *'byt glwtw* (to the house of his exile) established by Henoch Yalon, we understand that the Wicked Priest (Ananias) had pursued the Teacher of Righteousness (Menahem) right into his exile where he had set up a school. We should recall that *beth (byt)* was the designation of the various schools—Pharisaic, Zadokite, etc. Earlier in this manuscript, the Zealots had been called the Beth-Juda or House of Judas. It may be supposed that Menahem was a son of the former High Priest, Anan, removed from office to make way for Ananias. At any rate, he was a member of his school or house of exile. The *Thanksgiving Hymns* reveal to us similar dissident schools founded in the Diaspora by teachers in exile. It should be remembered that in A.D. 66 Menahem returned from outside Judea—that is to say, from exile.

All the same, it is difficult to be sure of the precise meaning of these lines, for they include more than one play upon words. Menahem signifies "consoler", and *menuḥah* can be translated by "quietness", "consolation", "rest", or even by "death", the final repose. So we do not know what the commentator meant by *mw'd mnwht*, the feast of quietness. Is he referring

[1] Written in Phoenician characters.

to the Saturday after the 9th Ab, the Xylophoria, called the Shabbath Menahem (more usually Shabbath Nahamu) in memory of Menahem? Or was this expression used formerly with the Xylophoria? We know that the Sabbath following the 9th Ab, A.D. 66, marks the beginning of hostilities in Jerusalem, and that on that day Ananias had to seek shelter in the town's sewers.

Must the expression *Yom Kippûr*, day of expiations, be taken to the very letter, and be applied only to the 10th Tishri, or should it be given a more general sense? Menahem was put to death on the 1st Tishri, and the massacre of the Roman garrison took place on the 10th Tishri, definitely the *Yom Kippûr*. Nearly five weeks before, on the 7th Elûl, Ananias had been killed. Can it be supposed that the commentator wanted to regard the 7th Elûl as a day when Ananias made expiation for his crimes? It must be admitted that the 10th Tishri was as bloodstained a "day of expiations" for Eleazar and his followers both at Jerusalem and in the provincial towns, notably at Caesarea Philippi, and at Scythopolis, where the Zadokites, the followers of Menahem, joined with the Gentiles and massacred 13,000 Jews.

If, on the other hand, the term *Yom Kippûr* must be taken in the strict sense, and restricted to 10th Tishri, we are faced with another problem: how could Menahem have appeared to them since he had been dead for more than a week? Already it has been stated that at the time when the *Commentary* was written, there was a belief in his resurrection. Was it believed that he had already risen a first time and been seen in Jerusalem on the 10th Tishri? Did the "appearance" of Menahem take place elsewhere than at Jerusalem? It is difficult to get a clear idea out of the legends around Menahem which have been and still are current. What Rabbinic literature says about his resurrection is very confused and full of contradictions.

(2.16) *Thou art filled with shame more than with glory! Drink thou, then, and stagger! The cup in Yahweh's[1] right hand is turned towards thee, and double shame upon thy glory!*

Its interpretation refers to the priest whose shame is greater than his glory, for he did not circumcise the foreskin of his heart and walked in the ways of excess in the slaking of his thirst. But the cup of God's wrath has made him reel . . . . . . . . . . . and he who has caused suffering . . . . . . . .

[1] Written in Phoenician characters.

I

Although the epithet "wicked" is not used here, yet the priest referred to must still be Ananias. Is the further reproach made that he gave himself to drinking?

## COLUMN XII

(2.17) [*For the violence of Lebanon shall cover him* (?) *and the fury of beasts*] *will blaze forth, because of human blood, and of the oppression of the country, of the town, and all who dwell there.*

The interpretation of the word applies to the Wicked Priest, who has had to pay retribution for what he did to the poor. For "Lebanon", it is the Council of the Community, and the "beasts" are the simple in mind in Judah (*or of Judas*) who observe the Law that God has commanded us to fulfil.

In the same way that he thought to wipe out the poor, so when he (*Habakkuk*) said "*by the blood of the town and the oppression of the country*", its interpretation is that the town is Jerusalem in which the [\* Wicked][1] Priest has committed abominations and defiled the sanctuary of God. And the oppressed of the country are the disciples of Judas, the poor whose patrimony he despoiled.

In this passage, which deals again with the deeds of Ananias, who oppressed the dwellers of the countryside and profaned the Temple, the commentator supplies several details about the curious alliance between the Zealots and the Zadokites which existed at the beginning of the war, and which was re-established a number of times before A.D. 132. The commentator gives the word "Lebanon" of the text of the Prophet, a very definite meaning. For him, it can only refer to the "Council of the Community", those Zadokite lodges which came into being after A.D. 70, and of whose initiation rituals, some fragments are preserved in the *Manual of Discipline*.

As to the "beasts", these are the simple-minded, the poor, who lived in the country and were regarded as cattle. An ambiguous expression ('*ry yhwdh*) can be translated either by "the cities, (fields) of Judah", or by "the disciples of Judas" (of Galilee). This second interpretation seems preferable, as it puts into parallel the Zealot communities and the Zadokite lodges.

(2.18) *What use is an image? As a molten image it has been created, and it is*

---

[1] Inserted between the lines.

*a lying rebellion. For a creature itself has imaged his image on it, to make dumb idols.* The interpretation of the word applies to all images of foreign nations which they create to serve them and fall down before them. But they will not save on the Judgement Day. (2.19) [*Woe to him that says to the w*]*ood "Arise", [. . . to a stone that is*] *dumb* [*Wake up. Will it instruct? Behold it is decked out in gold and silver, but has no breath within it.* Its interpretation . . . . . . . . . . . . . . .

## COLUMN XIII

(2.20) *But Yahweh dwells in His Holy Temple. Keep silence before Him, all the earth!* Its interpretation applies to all the nations which have served stone and wood. And at the Judgement Day, God will destroy all those who serve idols and the wicked who shall be on the earth.

In our Bibles, the Book of the Prophet Habakkuk is followed by a third chapter called, "Prayer of Habakkuk the Prophet". The *Commentary* does not contain this chapter, and it is generally held that it had not yet been added to the book. A further remark, however, may be made. In the middle of line 13 in Column XII, the writing changes, and another hand has continued the manuscript. The first commentator, having exhausted his subject, had merely applied verse 18 to all the images of the nations. This has been amplified by the continuer, who felt a need to speak about the Judgement Day, and it is in this sense that he has interpreted the last two verses.

This observation brings up the questions: Did the Book of Habakkuk interpreted by the first commentator end at verse 18, or has the book been only partly interpreted? Did not the continuer know Chapter III, or was it that he thought it enough to complete an interpretation of the first two chapters? It is hard to say.

# IV

# The Book of the War of the Sons of Light
# against the Sons of Darkness

Many theories have been put forward regarding this manuscript. Father M. Delcor would see in it a Manual for the Perfect Warrior (*Nouvelle Revue Théologique*, LXVII (1955), pp. 5–9). Theodor H. Gaster, like many others, would take it to be a kind of religious drama (see footnote on p. 155 of this present work).

As a matter of fact, this roll manifests no unity of composition. It is a collection of fragments taken from various sources. On this point, as on a number of others, it has not been possible for the present writer to bear in mind every theory that has been put forward. This is especially true in the case of the "*Kittîm* of Egypt", over whom there has been so much discussion. As with the *Habakkuk Commentary*, the name *Kittîm* does not occur in this manuscript.

COLUMN I, LINES 1–3.

[This is the account] of the war before the Sons of Light lifted up their hands to wear down those who are in the portion of the Sons of Darkness, in the army of Belial: (*the account of the war against those who were*) in the regiments of Edom, of Moab and of the Ammonites [and of all the inhabitants] of Palestine, and in the regiments of the legions of Aššûr. And as auxiliaries with these (*the last-named*) were certain of those who had fought against the Sons of Light, being opposed to the Covenant of the Sons of Levi, and of the Sons of Judah, and of the Sons of Benjamin, when these came back from exile in the desert. They were auxiliaries for all their troops when the Sons of Light came back from exile, from the desert of foreign nations, in order to establish themselves in the desert of Jerusalem.

All these passages as far as line 15 should be translated in the past tense, and not in the future, as has been done usually. It is not a prophecy, but a historical introduction such as can be seen in several other writings and collections of the same kind. The events to which allusion is made in this introduction are placed BEFORE the war of extermination of the Sons of Darkness (the Romans). We find here a reminder of events in the reign of Cambyses (529-522 B.C.) when the "legions of Aššûr" crossed Judea on the way to their campaign in Egypt. It is well known that many Jews, descendants of those who had not been deported to Babylon, were opposed to the ideas of their fellow Jews who had returned from exile. The Persian armies found many auxiliaries among the inhabitants of Judea and Samaria.

In the nature of things, this passage cannot be dealing with *Kittîm* (Cypriots). As in the *Habakkuk Commentary,* and in spite of a slight difference in spelling, the *ktyym* are the "legions", the plural of *kt* or *kty'*. Here *'šwr* (Aššûr) denotes the Persian Empire, successor to the Assyrians. In some other passages, *'šwr* denotes the kingdom of the Seleucids, sometimes Rome even.

COLUMN I, LINES 3-5.

And after the war, they (*the Jews in opposition*) helped from there (*Jerusalem*) [the Macedonians and] the legions (*of the Ptolemies*) in Egypt. But eventually, he (*Judas Maccabaeus*) came forth with great zeal to make war on the kings of the North (*the Seleucids*) and his wrath was aimed at breaking the horn [of the wicked. There c]ame an age of deliverance for the people of God, and at last, dominion for all the men of His portion, and the ultimate extermination of all those who were of the portion of Belial.

Very rapidly, the author reviews the Macedonian domination, and that of the Ptolemies of Egypt. Both had had numerous partisans among the Jews. Then, with no transition, the author recalls the Maccabean rising, the freeing of the nation, and the return to orthodoxy under the Hasmonaeans.

COLUMN I, LINES 5-7.

Then was there g[reat] panic [among all] the Sons of Japhet, and Aššûr fell and for him there was no help. But the empire of the legions will cease from subjecting countries to wickedness, so that no remnant (*will remain of him*) and there will be no (*possible*) escape [for the Sons] of Darkness.

In a few words, the expansion of the Roman Empire is recalled, the submission of all Asia Minor (the Sons of Japhet), and the downfall of the Seleucid kingdom, which became a Roman province in 65 B.C. Here, '*šwr* should be translated by "Seleucid kingdom".

COLUMN I, LINES 8-9.

[For the decrees of ju]stice will (*one day*) shine to the ends of the inhabited world, and (*there will be*) light at the end of all the ages determined for (*the rule*) of Darkness. And at the time fixed by God, the display of His greatness will glow forth to all the ends [of the world], to bring peace and blessing, joy and glory, and length of days for all the Sons of Light.

These phrases, which interrupt the narrative, are significant. God Himself will determine the date when "all" the nations under the yoke of Rome will be freed, and an age of felicity open for "all" the Sons of Light, that is to say, not for Israel only, but for all who believe in God.

COLUMN I, LINES 9-10.

And the day when the legions fell on him (*Israel*), there was a hard struggle and "chase" (*nḥšyr*) in the presence of the God of Israel, for this was the day fixed of old for the war of extermination against the Sons of Darkness. In that day they strove against one another as presenting themselves in the arena.

The author makes no mention of the events leading up to the war of A.D. 66-70. The war is presented as a tournament in the presence of the God of Israel. The term *nḥšyr*, a word of Persian origin, is only found in Rabbinic literature under the form *nḥšyrkn*, "expert hunter". It is as well to point out here that the word "chase" was also used for the gladiatorial combats in the arena, called *venatio* in Rome and it is with this connotation that it is used here. At Byzantium, the *kynegion*, or Little Hippodrome, was reserved for these combats against which the Fathers of the Council of Carthage protested. The continuation of this text, and the use further on of the synonym *ṣydh* supports this interpretation.

COLUMN I, LINES 10-17 . . .

Great was the gathering of the gods, and the meeting together of men—Sons of Light and those of the portion of Darkness—struggling against each other for the power of God, with the noise of a great tumult. And the din of the gods and men lasts even up till now. It was an "age of anguish" [. . .] for the people often freed by God. And in all its anguish, there will never be another such people for having suffered, right to the end, in the cause of universal freedom.

And on the day when they made war on the legions, there s[eemed an equal]ness in the war. Three lots fell to strengthen the Sons of Light in their fight against wickedness, and three others fell to encourage the army of Belial, to cancel the fortune [favourable to the com]panies of the "Sons", and to make their hearts to melt. And the power of God, by the force . . . . . . . . . . . But on the seventh lot, the great hand of God lay with its weight.

(The next four lines contain only fragmentary phrases, including ". . . the angels of His empire . . .": "for the exterminations of the Sons of Darkness". The subsequent half-dozen lines, as at the foot of all the columns, are missing.)

This passage is one of the most curious in this manuscript. As at the time of the Trojan War, all the gods were present to help in the struggles of men fighting each other for the glory of their respective divinities. The supreme arbiter was God, the God of Israel, who could sway the balance from one side to the other.

The author has inserted a gloss, "the din of the gods and of the men lasts up till now". Whatever the changing fortunes of the struggle, however serious the defeats, the contest was not lost.

The war in question is called "the age of anguish" ('t ṣrh); and it is well known that this name was given to the war of A.D. 66-70, and more particularly to the siege of Jerusalem. The Maccabean War was called the "war of deliverance" ('t yšw'h), and the war of Bar Kochba carried the name "the hour of peril" (š't sknh). It should be noticed that in the mind of the author, Israel was fighting for universal freedom, the liberation of all nations.

Like the Emperor attending the games in the amphitheatre, God regarded impartially the human struggle. In this war, as in all the circumstances of life, chance played an important part. It appeared that the chances were equally divided and nothing could make God decide to throw into the mêlée the "seventh" lot, which He held in His hand. The text is very fragmentary here, but it seems that God stopped the conflict after having made certain recommendations to the angels and the Jews, the people of His portion. He wished to put His people to a further test before fixing the date for the extermination of the Romans. If the Jews remained "holy", He would finally accord them the victory.

The conclusion of the historical introduction is missing. This passage is a piece on its own, and one of the latest of those forming this composite text. Certain deductions can be drawn which allow an approximate dating of the fragment. One can also form certain ideas concerning the author.

(a) *The Date.* The text was certainly written after A.D. 70, as "the age anguish" is mentioned. One cannot say how this chapter ended as the last lines are missing, but it can be supposed that it was written before the revolt of Bar Kochba. That does not exclude the possibility, as we shall see later, of the author having inserted his own remarks written after A.D. 135.

(b) *The Author.* There are certain indications that the author of this passage was a Jew of the Diaspora. He knew Greek, for he used the Persian equivalent for the Greek expression *kynegion,* which denoted gladiatorial combats—not using the Hebrew term *sydh,* which occurs later on in this manuscript. He knew Greek mythology, and probably the *Iliad.* He had mixed feelings for Syria. So as not to say that Judea was liberated from the Seleucids, he refers to "the kings of the North", and he has an air of regret over Aššûr falling under the Roman yoke. He can therefore be placed in Syria, among Jews influenced by Greek civilisation.

His beliefs, which do not reflect an absolute orthodoxy, seem to be well established. He believes in the superiority of the Jewish religion, and in the mission of the Jewish nation to free the world from the Roman yoke. But he also believes in the powers of "lots" or fates, against which even God supreme is powerless. We do not know what rôle he gave to angels, as the text is here too fragmentary, nor what his conception of Belial was. Another fact worth noting is the magical value he gives to the number "seven". From his beliefs also, it seems therefore that we can place the author in Syria, perhaps even in Dura-Europos. He was certainly of the Jewish faith, but we cannot be sure that he had not recently adopted it.

COLUMN II, LINES 1–6.

The fathers of the Congregation to the number of fifty-two, and the chief priests to the number of twelve will join with the Chief Priest and his assistant chief priests to maintain a constant service before God. And the chief guards to the number of twenty-six shall fulfil their service as guards, and following them, the chief Levites, twelve in number, one for each tribe, shall be on constant service. The chief guards shall serve, each in his post, and the heads of the tribes as well as the fathers of the Congregation will set themselves in their turn to stand continually at the doors of the sanctuary. As to the chiefs of their guards and their overseers, who shall be present at their posts on feast days, new moons, sabbaths and all days of the year, they shall be fifty years of age or more. These are they who shall present themselves to see to the whole burnt offerings, the sacrifices, to the arranging for the burning of incense of a pleasant odour in accordance with God's will and commandment, to make atonement for all the Congregation, and to offer sacrifice of fat before Him continually, at the Table of His Majesty.

The lower part of the preceding page is missing, but it is hardly likely that the beginning of this passage was to be found there. This seems to be an extract from the regulations for the ideal Temple, how it was to be organised when rebuilt. As in the time of the Exodus, the nation should form a Congregation of twelve tribes. Each tribe was to be ruled by its priests arranged in order of rank, under the orders of the Chief Priest for the entire nation. The priests were to have command over the Levites who, according to rank, fulfilled police duties.

For the service of the Temple, the chief priests and the fifty-two "fathers" were to place themselves at the disposition of the High Priest of the Congregation and his twelve assistant chief priests. The number of fifty-two mentioned here suggests that the Roman civil calendar was to be more or less adapted to the religious services, and that the civil year was to be divided into fifty-two weeks. Each week in rota, a "father" was to undertake the service of the Temple, having the oversight of its entrances along with the head guards of the Levites. These would do a fortnight's service, as they only numbered twenty-six. The head guards, aged fifty or more, would naturally be accompaned by their "overseers" under their orders. It was also intended that this civil personnel should see that sacrifices and the burning of incense were regularly practised.

The cult was to include all the ancient sacrificial institutions, but all the same we should notice that the word for altar, *mzbḥ* is replaced by the expression "Table of His Majesty", the *trapeza tou theou* of the Greek temples.

I*

*Date and Author.* This passage, an extract from a dream by an author who perhaps believed himself to be a second Ezekiel, can only have been written after A.D. 70, and at a time when in certain Jewish circles there was a hope that the Temple would be rebuilt, and the cult reorganised on a fresh basis. As with the preceding passage, the author should be looked for among the Jews of the Diaspora, in a region where the civil calendar was generally accepted. His interest in the cult, and his idea of government by men who were literally "elders", lead us to suppose that he was a Zadokite.

E. L. Sukenik thought he could see an indication of date in the expression "chief priest," which disappeared as a title at the end of the Hasmonaean period, giving way to the title "High Priest". We would point out that the "chief priests" in this passage are rather numerous, and the text cannot be dealing with THE Hasmonaean Chief Priest, who was also king, or one of his near relations. Even if we do not know all the aspirations of the Zadokites, we do know that they hoped to re-establish the régime as it was under John Hyrcanus, with the privileges of the priestly caste. The expression "chief priest" is not an indication of date but of the fact that this passage may be attributed to a Zadokite author.

COLUMN II, LINES 6-9.

All this shall be determined during the celebration of the jubilee year, and the remaining thirty-three years of the war, the "Men of the NAME" shall be "readers" to the army. And the fathers-in-chief of the Congregation shall themselves recruit warriors in all foreign countries. From all the tribes of Israel, they shall lead away with them men for the army, to set out in the army year by year, following the regulations of the war. But during the jubilee years they shall not lead them out to enter the army, for there shall be a Sabbath of Rest for Israel.

We owe this passage to the compiler of the manuscript, and it is intended to form the transition to what follows. The idealised organisation of the nation and its cult, as described in the previous passage, obviously does not fall in with the requirements of the war to be carried on for the liberation of Israel and of the rest of the world. The compiler therefore has provided that all these details were to be worked out during the jubilee years which should be observed during the war. This war would be long. Fighting would continue for thirty-three years without counting the years of rest, and the years of preparation for the war. In the compiler's opinion, there would be no question of a sacrificial priesthood while the war lasted and moreover the Temple could only be rebuilt after the victory. The "Men of the NAME"—and by that we must understand the men fulfilling the service of the cult at the time—should carry on the religious observances as they were practised in the synagogues and, so long as the armies were on campaign, should serve as "readers".

In what follows, the compiler appears to criticise a situation which had actually arisen, and which he considered unjust. The recruitment of troops ought to be done by the fathers-in-chief mentioned in the preceding passage. He now says that this recruitment ought to be made in all the countries of the Diaspora, and among all the tribes of Israel. This leads one to understand that the Palestine Jews formed only a feeble minority. It should be recalled that on the eve of Bar Kochba's revolt, Rabbi Aqiba and his colleagues did in fact go to gather funds and arms in Asia Minor and in the countries of the Parthians, and that they even recruited men from among the pagans and so brought up the army of the revolt to nearly half a million men.

Most probably it is these recruitments that the compiler calls to mind here. One feels that he is reproaching the rabbis for having acted unwisely, and above all, not having respected the sabbatical year, an obligation to be observed even while preparing for war. Further on, the reproach of insufficient preparation for the war will be met with again.

COLUMN II, LINES 9-14.

Thirty-five years' work shall go to the preparing for the war. During six years, all the Congregation together shall make preparation. During the remaining twenty-nine years, divisions will carry out local wars. In the first year, war shall be made against the Aramaeans of the Two Rivers: in the second against the Lydians: in the third, against the remaining Aramaean people of Uz, Hûl, Togar, and of Mesha, on the other side of the Euphrates. In the fourth and fifth years, they shall exercise themselves in warfare against the sons of Arpachshad. In the sixth and seventh years, they shall war against all the sons of Aššûr, the Persians and the men of the East as far as the Great Desert. During the eighth year they shall war against the Elamites, and in the ninth against the descendants of Ishmael and of Keturah. During the next ten years, the war shall be carried out successively against all the sons of Ham [to drive them from all] their dwelling-places, and during the ten years

which remain, the war will be spread over all the . . . . . . . . .
their dwelling-places.

Still from the pen of the compiler, we have here a few details about the
preparation for the war of liberation. In the same way that the taking
possession of Palestine only took place after forty years spent in the desert,
the new army of Israel should be hardened to war during forty years of
preparation. There were to be six years spent in warlike exercises, all
preparing together. Then should follow twenty-nine years of minor
warfare, broken only by the five sabbatical years, which are not once more
mentioned. After the six years of united preparation, and the first sabbatical
year, the army was to be divided into sections and should accustom itself
to war in the course of nine campaigns of a year each, and two great wars
of ten years each. The names of the nations against which they were to
war are more or less fanciful, and are taken from the Old Testament, or
from the *Book of Jubilees*.

Certain points should be noted. Countries to the west and south of the
Euphrates are said to be on "the other side of the Euphrates". This would
place the author of the fragment on the left bank of the Middle Euphrates.
Aššûr, Persia and the countries of the East stretch as far as the "Great
Desert"—that is, the plateau of Iran.

The texts forming part of the introduction come to an end here. After a
space left blank, one finds the beginning of a new text, but no precise
information can be gained from it, as only the following disconnected
phrases survive: "the trumpet-calls for all their services in order that. . . ."
". . . to their overseers . . .": ". . . and the riches . . ."

COLUMN III, LINES 1-11.

Regulations for the war and for the trumpets and their calls, when the
gates of war open to allow the light infantry to pass out, and for the
trumpets sounding "At the smitten", and for the trumpets for ambush,
trumpets for pursuit, when the enemy is beaten, and the trumpets for
the re-assembling on the return from the battle.

On the trumpets calling together the Congregation shall be written,
"The Called of God".

On the trumpets calling together the commanders shall be written,
"The Princes of God".

On the trumpets calling together the enlisted men shall be written
"The Bond of God".

On the trumpets of the "Men of the Name" shall be written, "The Fathers-in-chief of the Congregation".

When they shall assemble to go to "the House of Meeting", it shall be written, "Testimonies of God to the Holy Council", and on the trumpets of the camp shall be written, "The Peace of God in the Camps of His Holiness", while on the trumpets for the march shall be written, "Might of God to scatter the Enemy, and to put to flight all who hate Righteousness, turning from Good Deeds through Hatred of God". On the trumpets of the ranks of battle shall be written, "Ranks of the Companies of God to perform the Vengeance of His Wrath upon the Sons of Darkness". On the trumpets for the recall of the light infantry when the gates of war open for the regiments to go forth to do battle with the enemy shall be written, "To bring to mind the Vengeance of God's predestined Day". On the trumpets sounding "At the Smitten", shall be written, "The Hand of God's Might is in the Battle to make fall all the Smitten Profaners". On the trumpets of ambush shall be written, "Secrets of God for the Destroying of Wickedness", and on the trumpets of pursuit shall be written, "God has smitten all the Sons of Darkness. His wrath will not cease till all are wiped out."

And when they return from the battle, as the regiment re-enters shall be written on the trumpets of recall, "God has re-gathered". On the trumpets for the march back from doing battle with the enemy, and for the re-entry into Jerusalem of all the Congregation, there shall be written, "Joys of God for those returning in Peace".

These regulations, presented as a "custom" (srk) are part of a taktikon, or manual of tactics, such as must have existed before the war of A.D. 66, when the Roman trumpets made such an impression on the Jews. In Josephus one finds echoes of the impression produced by the Roman marching formations, and above all by their trumpets. Is it to be wondered at that ordinary people—and perhaps not they alone—thought that they could achieve victory by imitating the external marks of Roman power?

In the mind of the author, who perhaps had never had a trumpet in his hands, each call was made by a separate instrument. It was necessary, therefore, to provide as many trumpets as there were trumpet-calls. We have here fourteen trumpets four parade calls, for general assembly, for officers, for rank and file, and for chaplains; two garrison calls, to the synagogue and to the camp; six combat calls, march, falling-in in order of battle, throwing forward the light infantry or skirmishers, killing off the fallen, ambush, pursuit of the enemy; two calls for after the battle, re-form and return. It is important to notice what the author thought was the part played by the written word, and the magical effect it was supposed to transmit to the trumpet-call.

It should also be remarked that the camps were to be provided with a synagogue, a "house of meeting" corresponding to the "tent of meeting" in the Bible. Religious services were to be assured by kinds of rabbis (?) called in one place "fathers-in-chief" and in another "men of the NAME". Obviously the author is avoiding the use of the word *Kohen* (priest). One also notes that the victorious return to Jerusalem is taken for granted.

*Date and Author.* This passage, probably drawn up by a man of the people before A.D. 66, must have been written in Judea. It may have formed part of one of those Zealot books of military instruction referred to in the *Manual of Discipline* (III, 13-17, IX, 16-21). Other such works must have existed. This one is distinguished by the length of the inscriptions, and by the number of trumpets—fourteen, which is a multiple of seven.

COLUMN III, 13-16 (lines 15 and 16 being fragmentary, and lines 17-23 completely missing).

Regulations for the ensigns of all the Congregation, on their assembling:

On the great ensign at the head of all the people shall be written, "People of God" and also the names of Israel and of Aaron and the names of the Twelve Tribes of Israel according to their genealogies. On the ensigns of the chiefs of the camps formed by the Three Tribes shall be written . . . . . . . . . On the ensign of the tribe shall be written "Signal of God" and also the names of the princes of . . . . . . according to their fami[lies. On the ensign of the auxiliaries shall be written . . . . . . . . . and also] the name of the prince of the auxiliaries and the names of the . . . . . . . . . . .

COLUMN IV, LINES 1-5.

And on the ensigns of the Merari shall be written, "Tribute of God" and also the name of the prince of the Merari and the names of the commanders of his thousands. And on the ensign of the thousand shall be written, "The Wrath of God is seen when it falls upon Belial and all the men of his portion so that none whatsoever survive", and also the name of the commander of the thousand and the names of the commanders of his hundreds. And on the ensign of the hundred shall be written, "In the Name of God the hand of war is upon all sinful flesh", and also the name of the commander of the hundred and the names of the commanders of his tens. And on the ensign of the fifty shall be written, "By the Might of God, the Place of the Wicked has Perished", and also the name of the commander of the fifty, and the names of the commanders of his tens. On the ensign of the ten shall be written, "Songs of Joy to God on the Harp of Ten Strings", and also the name of the commander of the ten and the names of the nine men of his group.

Still under the influence of the Roman model, and convinced of the magical power of the written word, the same author continues by a description of the ensigns which, in place of animal figures, were to carry mottoes and names. From the fact that about half the passage is missing it is difficult to say if two parallel texts have not been united here. It is impossible to know how many ensigns were thought of altogether. The division of the people into twelve tribes would imply a list of their ensigns. Three tribes were covered by a special regulation, the tribes of Juda, Levi and Benjamin, which in popular belief had returned from the Exile while the other nine were lost in the Diaspora. The mention of the Merari, a sub-tribe of Levi, is rather surprising. It appears to figure here at the head of a military division of people arranged in thousands, hundreds, and tens, with the group of fifty which would seem to be a duplication.

COLUMN IV, LINES 6-8.

And when they go forth to battle, on their ensigns shall be written "Truth of God", "Righteousness of God", "Majesty of God", and "Judgement of God", with, after that, the detailed list of their names. And as they draw near to battle, on their ensigns shall be written "The Right Hand of God", "The Destined Day of God", "The Tumult of God", "The Smitten of God", and after that, the details of their names. And when they return from the battle shall be written on their ensigns, "The Loftiness of God", "The Greatness of God", "The Glory of God", "The Majesty of God", and also every detail of their names.

Obviously this passage is not a continuation of the preceding one. It begins after an *alinea*, which would seem a pretty sure sign that the compiler saw in it a separate fragment. One remarks that the number of ensigns is reduced to four, but that their inscriptions are changed according to circumstances. It is noticeable too, that these twelve short inscriptions are limited to the attributes of God. Each attribute is followed by a detailed list of names, but the phrase used by the author (*srk prwš*) is not the same as in the foregoing passage.

There is nothing in this passage to give any clear indication as to date. Following on immediately comes an extract from another text, giving us a third account of the ensigns.

COLUMN IV, LINES 9–14.

Regulations for the ensigns of the Congregation. When they set out to battle, on the first ensign shall be written, "God's Congregation": on the second, "Camps of God": the third, "Tribes of God": the fourth, "Families of God": the fifth, "Companies of God": the sixth, "The Assembly of God": the seventh, "The Callers upon God": and on the eighth, "The Armies of God". The details of their names, shall they write with their complete lists (*srkm*). As they draw near to battle, they shall write on their ensigns "The War of God", "The Vengeance of God", "The Strife of God", "The Retribution of God", "The Power of God", "The Healing of God", "The Might of God", "Extermination by God of all the Nations of Vanity". All the details of their names shall they inscribe on the ensigns. When they shall return from the battle, they shall write on their ensigns "God's Healing", "God's Victory", "God's Help", "God's Support" ". . . . . to God", "Thanks to God", "Praise to God", "Peace of God".

In the third version, the number of ensigns amounts to eight. There are three sets of eight inscriptions, a set for each phase of the war—life in camp, the battle, and the victorious return. We do not know what were considered the right methods under which the division of the people into eight groups should operate, but the first ensign seems to have been more important than the others. The list of names of the combatants is spoken of in a different way from that in the preceding fragments.

*Date and Author.* This fragment obviously belongs to the same period as the foregoing ones, and its author should be looked for among the Zealots who formed the people of the countryside before the fall of Jerusalem. On the seventh ensign there is mention of the Callers upon God, while there is the same avoidance of the term *Kohen*.

Lines 15–17 are fragmentary, but apparently dealt with the length of the flagstaffs of the ensigns, beginning with that of the ensign of the whole Congregation and ending with that of the group of ten. The length of the first is fourteen cubits, and there is a descending scale of one cubit each time, so that the length of the flagstaff of the smallest group is seven cubits. The mention of eight ensigns links these lines with the preceding third fragment.

COLUMN V, LINES 1-2.

And on the shield of the Prince of all the Congregation shall be written his name, the names of Israel, of Levi and of Aaron, the names of the Twelve Tribes of Israel according to their genealogies, and the names of the twelve commanders of their tribes.

This is the conclusion of a paragraph on the inscriptions to be carried on shields, the earlier part of the paragraph having been on the destroyed part of the previous column. It probably formed part of the work from which comes the first set of regulations about ensigns (III, 13ff.) and as there, so we have here, mention of Aaron and the use of the term "genealogies". It should also be noted that the shield of the *Nasi* bore no invocation, and the name of Aaron followed that of Levi.

COLUMN V, LINES 3-14.

Regulations concerning the equipment of the battle units, when their army shall be at full strength, so as to form regiments for the line of battle. A regiment should consist of a thousand men, and each regiment should be arranged in seven ranks one behind the other. All shall have shields of polished copper similar to that used in making mirrors. The ring of the shield shall be in a twisted cord pattern, looking like a combination of gold, silver and copper, and decorated with imitation precious stones resembling the work of a lapidarist. The shields shall be two and a half ells in height, and one and a half in width.

And in their hands they shall have a spear and a cutlass. The length of of the spear shall be seven ells down from the ferrule, and the blade shall be half an ell. The ferrule shall have three bands, engraved like a work of twisted cord, a combination of gold, silver and copper, and giving the impression of a figured pattern. The pattern on either side of the band shall be enclosed in artificial precious stones, looking like the work of a lapidarist. The tang and the ferrule shall be engraved between the bands like the work of a column, which it resembles. The blade of the spear shall be of bright and shining iron, looking like the work of an artist. The tang shall be of pure gold let into the blade of the spear and coming to a long point at the top. The cutlass shall be of pure iron refined in the furnace, shining like a mirror and looking like the work of an artist. The exterior of the tang shall be of pure gold, the two sides joined to each other. Towards the head of the blade, the two cutting edges shall be smooth on either side. The length of the cutlass shall be one and a half ells, and its thickness four fingers. The body of the blade shall be four thumbs wide and shall be reckoned as beginning four palms down. It shall be sharpened on both sides for a length of five palms. The hilt shall be of pure horn, looking like a work of many coloured figures in gold, silver, and precious stones.

After a short statement about the organisation of the regiments of the line, who were to operate in seven ranks, the author gives a detailed description of the idealised equipment of the troops, based on, and inspired by, the Roman model.

In the whole of this passage, the term ell ('mh) means the short ell, the distance between the tip of the fingers and the armpit. Even so, the length of the spear is considerable, about sixteen feet, though less than the Hellenistic *sarissa,* which was over twenty feet in length.

The Roman arms must have been the wonder of the author. To be certain of victory, it was necessary to copy them even to the smallest detail. In spite of its size, over a yard high and three-quarters of a yard wide, the shield had to be entirely of polished copper. The cutlass in polished iron was to be a little more than a yard long, with an average breadth of four inches.

However, it was the decoration of the weapons that struck the author most. All the details were carefully noted as if they possessed magical power, and as if the slightest omission might render the weapon useless. He was at pains to lay down that the ornamental designs in bands, cords, and engravings were to be imitated. As to images, it was necessary to give the impression that they had been reproduced, though in actual fact they were to be avoided. In the same way, it was necessary to avoid the use of precious stones to which pagans attributed magical power. Artificial stones would do equally well. Yet, on the other hand, spears and cutlasses were to be decorated with pure gold.

*Author and Date.* This passage comes from an author who attached no great importance to the written word. There is no mention of any inscription to be engraved on the blade or hilt of the cutlasses. The compiler must have borrowed this passage from a work originating in an entirely different environment—the Syrian Diaspora. Though other expressions do not serve as sign-posts, there is one that does. The ferrule was to be engraven between the bands similarly to the work of a column, which the ferrule resembled. In brief, the author saw in the ferrule a miniature Trajan column, the column *par excellence*, which was not erected till A.D. 112.

COLUMN V, LINES 16-17.

And at the post . . . . . . . . . . . . . . . . . . . the seven regiments will take up their position, one behind another . . . . . . . . . thirty to the ell, which the men of . . . shall raise up there . . . . . . . . . . . . . . . . . . . . . . of the front . . . . . . .

COLUMN VI, LINES 1-6.

. . . . . . seven times, and they shall return to their positions. After them, three companies of light infantry will go out, and place themselves between the (*enemy*) regiments. The first company shall hurl seven projectiles on the enemy regiment, and on the point of the first projectile shall be written, "By the edge of the spear, for the Might of God". On the second shall be written, "Brands of blood to cast down those who are smitten by the Wrath of God". On the third projectile shall be written, "May the point of the sword devour those smitten of sin by the Judgement of God". In all, seven times shall they hurl, and then return to their position. After them, two other companies of light infantry shall go forth and take their stand between the two enemy regiments. The first company shall handle spear and shield, and the second company, shield and cutlass. They shall slay the smitten in accordance with the verdict of God, and humble the regiment of the enemy by the power of God as retribution for the vileness committed by all the people of nothingness. Kingship shall be to the God of Israel, and among the holy ones of His people shall He create strength.

The beginning of this passage, of which nearly half is missing, must have laid down the kind of tactics to be employed by the Jewish legionaries. The legion, composed of seven regiments, each of a thousand men, was to be deployed in seven ranks. The men were to be in such close formation that it should be possible to reckon thirty spears to the ell.

The lower half of the column is missing, and the beginning of the next column refers to something which was to be done seven times by certain persons, who then returned to their former positions. Then the battle is joined. The attack is made by three companies of light infantry, the *'nšy hbynym* (literally "men of the betweens"), who are not necessarily nor uniquely slingers. Those of the first company throw seven times three projectiles (each ?), these projectiles being supplied with inscriptions having power to make the enemy soldier fall. The remaining two companies arrive to kill off the wounded, some with their long spears and some with cutlasses. Thus the victory is won. It will be noticed that in those parts of this passage which have come down to us, there is no mention either of trumpet-calls or of priests.

*Author and Date.* This passage, written in the belief in the magic powers of the numbers seven and three, appears to have come from the author of the "long inscriptions". It may have formed part of the same work as III, 1-12 and IV, 1-5.

COLUMN VI, LINES 8-17 . . .

Seven ranks of cavalry shall place themselves to the right and the left of the regiment; on one side and on the other shall they place themselves in ranks; seven hundred on one flank and seven hundred on the other. Two hundred horsemen shall go out with every thousand men of the regiment of light infantry, and it is thus that they shall be placed in all the exercises of the camp. In all there shall be four thousand six hundred foot soldiers and one thousand four hundred horsemen. As to the "Men of the Bond" (*'nšy srk = ministers*), there shall be fifty to each regiment.

And the horsemen who shall ride forth on the chariots shall be "Men of the Bond" (*'nšy srk=Zadokites*) to the number of six thousand five hundred to each tribe. All the chariots which go out to war with men of the "Sons" shall have male horses, light on their feet, not hard in the mouth, and sound in wind. Fully trained for the war, they shall obey the (*real*) calls that they hear, but take no notice of imitated calls. Charioteers shall be men who are valiant in battle, accustomed to ride in chariots, aged from round about thirty to round about forty-five. The horsemen of the "bond" shall be aged from round about forty to round about fifty. And they . . . . . . . . . and the head-badges and the greaves, and they hold in their hands round shields and the spear of a length of . . . . . . . . . and bow and arrows and projectiles of war, and all shall hold themselves ready . . . . . . . . .

. . . . . . . . . to spill the blood of the smitten because of their guilt; only they . . . . . .

This passage is written between two blank lines, and divides into two parts:

(Lines 8-10): The author of this first part had envisaged there being cavalry, which Jewish armies never possessed. Each regiment of seven thousand men was to include one thousand four hundred horsemen. A copyist who was not strong in arithmetic gave the figure for the infantry as four thousand six hundred instead of five thousand six hundred! In this passage, the expression "Men of the Bond" should be taken in the sense of "ministers". See below, VII, 1.

Lines 11-17. The second part plunges us into a quite different environment. It seems to come from a Zadokite text which insisted that the command of the army should be entrusted to the "Men of the Bond". In this passage the expression means members of Zadokite lodges, reckoned at six thousand five hundred per tribe. Naturally, these privileged persons would all be horsemen or officers of chariots (cf. 1 Kings 9.22). And as the members of Zadokite societies were usually of a ripe age, the author fixed the age for horsemen at between forty and fifty years.

The end of this passage deals with the equipment of the combatants in chariots. They should have helmets, greaves and a round shield. Reference is also made to bows and arrows and the short spear.

*Author and Date.* The Zadokite passage can hardly have been written before A.D. 70. No precise indication as to date can be drawn from this text, unless it is that "the Men of the Bond" were envisaging their joining with "the men of the Sons" in the war for freedom, on condition that they were charioteers. The terms employed for helmets and greaves may be able to supply more precise information (see below).

After leaving a line blank, the compiler seems to have copied a fragment from a Zadokite Constitution of which only the conclusion is preserved at the head of the next column.

COLUMN VII, LINES 1-2.

And the men of "the bond" (*ministers*) shall be aged between forty and fifty, and the ministers of the camps between fifty and sixty. The overseers also shall be between forty and fifty.

One can recognise here the typical Zadokite government by elders, and their form of titles, to which they had just added that of "minister" (*srky'*) (Dan. 6.3-5).

Following straight on at the end of this passage is a Zealot fragment on the organisation of the army and of the military camps:

COLUMN VII, LINES 2-7.

All those who strip the smitten, divide out the spoil, clean up the country, guard the prisoners and arrange for "the chase" shall be between twenty-five and thirty years of age. No inquisitive boy, and no woman, shall come into the camp between the time when they set forth from Jerusalem for the war and the time of their return. No one who is lame, blind, or paralysed shall go to the war, nor anyone with a general defect in his flesh, nor anyone unclean through self-contact. All the warriors shall be men offering themselves like sacrifices because of the war, sound in mind and body, and ready for the day of retribution. No man who shall be sexually impure on the day of battle shall go forth with them. For holy angels will be assembled with their armies, and the Spirit will be amidst all their camps in place of the HAND, as if the angels were many thousands to the ell. Therefore nothing unseemly should be seen in all their camps.

The compiler probably had left out the beginning of this text, which must have laid down the age of the combatants, and replaced it by the Zadokite fragment given above, which deals only with a labour corps composed of men between the ages of twenty-five and thirty. Shock troops would naturally have been younger. These men were responsible for dealing with the wounded, sorting out the spoil taken from the slain, collecting the stragglers, guarding the prisoners, and the organisation of the "chase"—that is to say, of gladiatorial combats. The text here employs the Hebrew term *sydh*, whereas in an earlier passage (I, 9) the equivalent Persian word *nhšyr* had been used. In 1 Sam. 22.10, *sydh* refers to provision for the journey, but the context excludes that interpretation in this case.

Then follows the question of the purity of the camps, where no youth in search of sensations (*z'twt*=Greek *zêtêtês*) and no woman was to enter. After giving the list of those who were precluded from going to the war because of being lame, blind or paralysed, the author comes back to the topic of purity, and demands the sending back from the army of all those who practise self-abuse. These exclusions are justified because of the presence of angels with the army. These were so numerous that they could be reckoned as many thousands to the ell! During the time that the Hand of God was heavy on the enemy, the Spirit would be in the Jewish camp, and naturally anything indecent should not be seen in his presence.

*Author.* It may be noted that the author thought of their prisoners of war being treated in the way the Romans treated their Jewish prisoners, a similar organisation being set up for games in the amphitheatre where prisoners would be thrown to the beasts. The reference to angels and the Spirit places the author in a Zealot environment, whilst the use of the Hebrew term for "chase" and the mention of the army's departure from Jerusalem puts him in Palestine. The writing of this fragment can hardly have been before A.D. 70.

COLUMN VII, LINE 9 TO THE END OF THE SURVIVING LINES OF THIS COLUMN.
And when the regiments are arrayed for battle, and a regiment goes out to meet an enemy regiment, then from between the regiments and through a "gate" chosen by God, shall go forth seven priests, sons of Aaron, clothed in white *byssus,* with shirts and breeches of linen, and girdles of *byssus.* These girdles are to be woven of dark purple, bright purple, and scarlet, and the many-coloured shapes shall give the impression of works of art and of fruits. On their heads they shall have bonnets (*mgb'wt=helmets*) and they shall be clothed with battle garments (*armour*) which shall not be allowed inside the sanctuary.

One of the priests shall march in front of all the men of the regiment to strengthen their hands in the battle. In the hands of six others shall be trumpets for the "fall in", and trumpets for remembrance, clamour, pursuit, and re-form. When the priests go forth to take their place between the regiments, seven Levites shall go forth with them holding in their hands seven rams' horns of jubilation. Three Levite inspectors shall take their place in front of the priests and Levites. The priests shall blow their two trumpets for the "fall-[in" . . . . . . . . . bat]tle, on fifty shields, and fifty light infantrymen shall go forth through one of the "gates" [. . . . . . with] the Levite inspectors and with all the regiment. And the regiment shall go forth like all the [. . . . . . . . . . light] infantry from the [. . . they shall] stand between the two . . . . . . . . . . . .

COLUMN VIII, LINES 1-17 . . .
The trumpets therefore shall continue to sound for the victory of the

slingers until these shall have finished throwing their projectiles seven times. After that, the priests shall blow on their trumpets of re-call, and the slingers shall go to the flank of the first regiment, and take up their position there. Then the priests shall blow their trumpets of "fall-in" and three companies of light infantry shall go out through the "gates" and take their stand between the regiments, with the chariots to their right and left. The priests shall sound a long note on their trumpets for the line of battle to be formed, and the leaders shall go forward to the lines, each to his post. And when the three lines shall have been formed, the priests shall blow a second time on their trumpets, this time a steady, sustained note, the "advance", until the light infantry are near to the enemy regiment and are taking their weapons in hand. The priests shall then sound on their six trumpets the call "At the smitten", a long, shrill note, for success in the fight. And the Levites along with all the people provided with horns shall together make a great noise and din of battle for the purpose of making the heart of the enemy to waver. At the sound of this din, the armoured combatants shall go forth to finish off the fallen. The sound of the horns shall cease, and the priests on their trumpets shall make a long, shrill note for success in the battle now joined until they have hurled their projectiles on the enemy seven times. Then by a steady and sustained note on their trumpets, the priests shall re-call them. This regulation lays down that the priests shall sound the call for the three companies. If those of the first company of assault should give way, the [priests . . . . . . . . . trum]pets a great outburst of noise to bring success in the bat[tle . . . . . . . . . they shall sound] for them, the priests on their trumpets . . . . . . . . . at their posts in the regiment . . . . . . . . . . . . . . .

Two Zadokite texts have been combined here by the compiler. The first, VII, 9, to VIII, 12, begins with a description of the clothing of the priests when the army marches forth from the camps to do battle with the enemy. In spite of certain analogies of style, mostly in terminology, the resemblance of this passage to the Zealot description of arms in V, 3-14 should not be pushed too far.

As in all Zadokite passages—and in this manuscript they are numerous—the priests should be in command. Provided with a number of trumpets, six priests direct the three phases of the fight. First of all, the slingers—not the light infantry—throw their projectiles seven times. Then three companies of light infantry advance, accompanied by chariots and cavalry, and the battle becomes general. Finally, soldiers wearing cuirasses go out to finish off the wounded.

The second text, from VIII, 12 onwards, is very fragmentary, and the end is missing. It gives a parallel version of the battle: seven times the projectiles are hurled at the enemy, three companies of light infantry enter into action. They are here called the *tl*, a word in the Bible hitherto misinterpreted (*vide* the present writer's article, "Melchizedek", in *Z.A.T.W.*, LXIX (1957), pp. 160–70). This version foresees the possibility that the first company of assault might take fright and give way, but the sequel is missing.

Naturally, it is the first and better-preserved version which supplies some interesting information. It appears that the "people" were thought of as watching the battle from afar, shouting and blowing horns to scare the enemy. Signals by rams' horns were given by seven Levites who accompanied the army and who had with them three of their overseers. One of the seven priests had no trumpet, his entire task being to maintain the morale of the troops. It should further be noted that we have here no reference to any inscriptions on trumpets or weapons. Attention may also be drawn to the mention of horsemen, war-chariots, soldiers wearing cuirasses, and of priests with helmet or bonnet and cuirass. There is also a provincialism, *ydy* (=because), which occurs three times in this fragment, in VIII, 5, 7, 12.

*Author and Date.* The two versions of the battle given here seem practically identical. They could come from two slightly differing copies of the same work. The author, most certainly Zadokite, speaks of war-chariots, and that invites identification with the author of the fragment VI, 8-17.

COLUMN IX, LINES 1-9.

. . . . they shall (*not?*) defile their hand by striking down the wounded. All the people shall cease their outcries, but the priests shall make the trumpets to ring out "At the smitten", for victory in the battle, continuing till the enemy is beaten and turns his back. The priests therefore shall blow the trumpets for victory in the battle, and when the enemy is beaten before them, they shall sound the "fall-in" and from between the line regiments all the light infantry shall go forward. To carry out this attack, therefore, there will be six companies, plus the company already in contact with the enemy, a total of seven companies or twenty-eight thousand warriors and six thousand chariots (*or cavalry?*). All these shall pursue the enemy to destroy him utterly in God's war. The priests shall sound the trumpets of pursuit, and they shall themselves . . . over all the enemies who shall be pursued till none is left alive. The chariots (*cavalry?*) shall make the circuit of the field of battle until all the enemies have been given over to utter destruction. And while the smitten are falling, the priests shall keep sounding their trumpets from afar, but they shall not go into the midst of the fallen lest they should make themselves unclean by their blood. For they are holy, and must not defile the oil of their priestly anointing in the blood of a people of nothingness.

It is possible, but by no means certain, that this fragment may have been a continuation of the third version of the battle of which the beginning is seen in VIII, 12-17. That, however, would make the third version very long—thirty-two lines. The present writer would prefer to consider this fragment as belonging to a fourth version, the first few lines of which were written on the lower, the destroyed, part of the preceding column.

The author of this version attached great importance to ceremonial cleanness. At the point where we find the text, the first phase of the battle is over. The slingers have hurled their projectiles, and if, as we may suppose, the negative particle *lw'* had been written at the end of the previous column, they had not soiled their hands in the blood of the enemy because they had only fought from afar off. When the enemy has been thus thrown into confusion by the first company of light-infantry slingers, six other companies throw themselves into the battle to finish off the wounded. At that moment twenty-eight thousand men will be engaged in the fighting, while six thousand chariots or horsemen encircle the field of battle to prevent the flight of the enemy. Last of all, there is the reminder that the priests should keep away from the battlefield and not profane their anointing.

*Author and Date.* This version, also Zadokite, seems to be later than the preceding passages. It is inspired by the same model, but has several significant modifications. The rôle of the chariots or cavalry is clearly presented: a subtle distinction is made between combatants who could soil their hands in the enemy's blood (mercenaries ?) and those who ought not to do so. The passive rôle of the priests is explained by their obligation not to profane their anointing. The mention of large armies, twenty-eight thousand footmen and six thousand chariots or horsemen, would lead one to suppose that this was written well after the fall of Jerusalem. It might be earlier than A.D. 132, but it could be later.

We may recall that in the older Jewish tradition the blood of the enemy brings no defilement.

COLUMN IX, LINES 10-16 . . .

Regulation for the formations of battle units and the arrangements of their lines in accordance with . . . . . . . . . . [or in acc]ordance . . . . . . . . . "hand-circles", "towers", and "bows and towers". Also on "slight curves" when the heads of columns project forward and the wings . . . . . . the flanks of the regiment . . . the enemy.

The shields of the soldiers of the "towers" shall be three cubits long, and their spears eight cubits. And the towers which go out from the regiment shall reckon a hundred shields and a hundred men in front of the tower. [For it is thus that they surround] the tower on three of its sides. The men in front of the shields shall number three hundred. And there are two "gates" to each "tower", [one on the right and the o]ther on the left. And on all the shields of the towers, there shall be inscriptions: on the first "Michael", [on the second, "Gabriel", on the third] "Sariel", and on the fourth, "Raphael". Michael and Gabriel . . . . . . . . . . .

This paragraph deals with certain battle formations copied from the Roman model. The "towers" are square formations, fairly flexible, protected by close ranks of soldiers carrying shields, which were probably rectangular. On three sides of these living citadels were soldiers fighting in the open. These could retire into the "tower" through two "gates", which would open to let them in. The shields of the soldiers in these "towers" were to bear the name of a single angel, different for each of the four sides, though their shape and size would have allowed for much longer inscriptions.

*Author and Date.* Because of the analogy with the "four ensigns", this passage can be assigned to the same Zealot author as the fragment IV, 6-8. The text from which it was taken could be dated before A.D. 68.

COLUMN X, LINES 1-7 . . .

. . . our camps, and we shall not [give way] before the shame of all the things of evil, and this is what had been announced to us. For in our struggle, Thou art the great and terrible God, who canst give over all our foes to . . . These words were taught us of old, so that we should know them in our age: "*And it shall be, when ye draw nigh unto the battle, the priest shall stand and speak to the people, saying, 'Hear, O Israel, ye draw nigh this day unto battle against your enemies. Fear not, nor let your heart be troubled. Tremble not nor be affrighted before them, for your God goes with you to fight against your enemies, to save you*'" (*Deut. 20.2-4*). Our overseers shall therefore speak to all those who, with willing hearts, offer themselves for the battle, to strengthen them by the might of God, sending away those of doubtful courage, and at the same time encouraging the valiant of the army. For it is thus that Thou hast spoken by Moses saying: "*When in your land you go to war against the enemy who fights against you, you shall sound an alarm with the trumpets, and you shall be remembered before your God, and you shall be saved from your enemies*" (*Num. 10.8*).

Who is like unto Thee, O God of Israel, in Heaven or on earth, to perform great works like Thine, and be great in might like Thee? And who is . . . like Thy people, Israel, whom Thou hast chosen from among the peoples of all lands? It is the people of the saints of the Covenant, and of those instructed in the commandments, of those who have insight into . . . . . . . who listen to the voice of the Venerable, and of those who see holy angels, whose ears are open, and who understand deep secrets . . . . . . . . . . who turn the dark clouds of the commandments into clearness, and [who can distinguish between] the deceitful spirits and those which come from Thy [glorious] courts.

[It is Thou who shalt give to the hun]gry the fruits of the land and of its surrounding provinces as far as the desert and the land of Arabia, and all their descendants, it is with the fruits of . . . . . . . . . (*that Thou shalt feed them*). The ocean of the seas, the sources of the rivers, the chasms of the abyss, living creatures and the wingèd race, men with all their tribes, (*it is Thou who hast created them* . . . . . . . . .) of barbarous tongue and it is Thou who dost divide for the nations the habitations of their families, and the heritage of the lands. [It is Thou who dost fix] . . . the holy feasts, the round of the years, and the ends of eternity . . . . . . . . . . All that we have learned by Thy wisdom which [Thou hast placed within us . . . . . . . . Thou hast bent Thine ear] to our cry of distress, for . . . . . . . . .

COLUMN XI, LINES 1-18 . . .

For the war is Thine, and by the might of Thy hand shall their bodies be overwhelmed and find no place of burial. Goliath of Gath, him, a man of great valour, didst Thou deliver into the hand of David Thy servant, because he trusted in Thy great NAME, and not in sword or spear. For the war is Thine, and many a time were the Philistines made to bow down by Thy holy NAME, and even by the hand of our kings. It is Thou who many a time hast delivered us, because of Thy loving-kindness, and not because of our deeds, for we did wickedly, and in spite of our wicked deeds and our sins. For the war is Thine, and might comes from Thee and not from us. It is not our strength, nor the force of our hands which makes might, but it comes from Thy strength and by the help of Thy great power, as Thou hast declared to us of old saying: *"There shall come forth a star out of Jacob, and a sceptre shall arise out of Israel. It shall smite through the corners of Moab, and beat down all the children of Seth. And he shall be of the descendants of Jacob, and he shall destroy him that escapes from the city"* (*Num. 24.17-19*). But he was the enemy of the heritage and of Israel.

Thou who dost create might, it is by the medium of Thine anointed ones, men who saw omens, that Thou hast had related to us the combats of the wars of Thy hand so as to teach us how to fight (*corrected into: to gain the victory over*) our enemies, to beat down the armies of Belial, the seven nations of nothingness by the hand of the poor whom Thou shalt set free in . . . and in peace, to show the greatness of the miracle, and for the love of those whose hearts melt through the disillusions of hope. Do to them, as to Pharaoh and the officers of his chariots in the Red Sea. Set alight, therefore, a destroying breath which, like a flaming torch in straw, will devour wickedness till it is no more, even to the blotting out of guiltiness. For, from of old, Thou hast declared to us [what would be the . . .] might of Thy hand upon the legions, saying: *"And Aššûr shall fall by the sword, not of man; a sword, which is not that of a man, shall devour him"* (*Isa. 31.8*).

For it is by the hand of the poor that the enemies of all the countries shall fall, and it is by the hand of those who kneel in the dust that the heroes of the nations shall be brought low, to bring retribution upon the wicked by . . . . . . and by the verdicts of Thy truth to give judgement to all mankind and to spread Thy renown to the ends of the earth among the peoples of the . . . . . . . . . . . the wars, in order to magnify and make holy in the eyes of the . . . . . . . . . . . . . . . . the verdicts against Gog and against all his company . . . . . . . . . . . . . . for Thou shalt make war against them from the height of heaven . . . . . . . . . . . . . . . to panic . . . . . .

COLUMN XII, LINES 1-5.

For the multitude of the holy . . . in heaven, and the armies of the
angels in Thy holy dwelling-place for that Thou . . . . . . . The
elect of the holy nation, Thou hast placed them for Thee in [. . . . . . .
nor can be coun]ted the names of all their armies which are with Thee
in Thy holy habitation, and who . . . and . . . in Thy glorious
dwelling. The favours of Thy blessings, and the Covenant of Thy
peace, Thou hast inscribed them as with a living chisel so that they
shall reign . . . . . . to all the days determined for eternity to keep
watch over Thy . . . and over Thy . . ., Thou hast . . . their
thousands and their tens of thousands. At the same time as Thy saints,
[Thou hast appointed] Thy angels to have the upper hand in the battle
. . . . . . of the country in the struggles conducted according to
Thy verdicts, and the nation of the elect of heaven . . . . . .

This long piece, of which the beginning is missing, takes the form of a
prayer to God, drawn up in a manner changing very little since the time
of the Psalms.

In the first prayer, the suppliant affirms that he had done everything in
conformity with the commandment of God. The texts of Scripture which
he quotes depart slightly from the Massoretic text. Some inversions and
omissions will have been noticed in the quotation from Deut. 20.2-4.
The name of Yahweh is omitted, and also in Num. 10.9. A verse is left
out from Num. 24.17-19. All these passages are the subject of interpretations. God had commanded that the priest should address the people
before the battle so as to inspire courage. At the time when this text was
written there were no longer any priests, but in addition to that the
writer obviously was opposed to the establishment of the priesthood, and
also according privileges to the Cohens on the ground of the name
they bore. Therefore the "overseers" should fill the rôle of the priests,
and thus the commandment of God would be obeyed in spirit if not
strictly in letter. The order to sound the trumpets would be scrupulously
observed.

In the second part we have alternately the praises of God and the
declaration of the merits of His people. Israel is a holy nation because it
has been instructed in the Commandments, and because its sons listen to
the voice of the "Venerable" and of those who have visions of angels. It
may be taken that this refers to certain prophets going about among the
people, interpreting "sibylline" predictions and offering explanations of

obscure Biblical texts, and giving out that they could distinguish between false and true omens.

The third part begins with a vision of dominion. Israel will not only be master of her own land, but also of vast provinces stretching to the desert of Arabia. After that we find a more equitable outlook, a stereotyped phrase often recurring in our manuscripts, that God had created the different races and tongues with the intention that each nation should have its own land and live there in peace. Each might follow its own particular calendar. . . . The end of this section—about six lines—is missing.

Our text now recalls victories gained through the help of God, the Master of War. Now God had foretold that a Star should go forth from Jacob: the hour of victory therefore had struck. This is a very important item for the purposes of dating. Of all the passages in the Bible which lend themselves to a Messianic interpretation, Num. 24.17-19 was especially popular round about A.D. 130. These words were in everybody's mouth when Rabbi Aqiba recognised Simon ben Kosiba as the Son of the Star, the "Bar Kochba" announced by Scripture. But the revolt came to grief, and it had to be recognised that there had been an error over the person. The prophecy itself could not be false, and after his death Bar Kochba was called Bar Koiba or "the Son of the Lie". There can be no doubt but that the writer was influenced by the events following A.D. 135 when he inserted a gloss which was a paraphrase of a part of verse 18 of Num. 24: "But he was the enemy of the heritage and of Israel."

The author continues by returning to the prophets, who saw omens announcing the coming of the liberator. Some "anointed ones" (false messiahs ?) were moving about among the people. It should be recalled that so as to gain the support of the crowd, Bar Kochba had himself been anointed, though the practice had not been in use since the destruction of the Temple. These visionaries, says the author, recited the history of God's wars. Probably there is an allusion here to a book which related the history of the Maccabees—*The Sepher Milḥamôth ʿAm Yahweh*, (The Book of the Wars of the People of Yahweh), considerable extracts of which are found in the Jewish compilation known as the *Yossipon*. They also gave military instruction to the people, probably making use of such manuals of tactics as those from which numerous extracts have been copied into our manuscript. The invocation of God, calling upon Him to destroy the foe, closes with a quotation from Isa. 31.8, followed by a significant comment: God had said that Aššûr would fall under a sword, which was not of man. This could therefore be the sword in the hands of the "poor", the simple sort of people, who did not merit the name of "man", because they were regarded as mere beasts of burden. Twice the author repeats that the "poor" are designated in this prophecy to set the country free (XI, 9, 13). The simple-minded, the peasants who knelt in the dust, would have the mission of beating down the warriors of the oppressor, and of carrying afar the renown of the God of Israel. The prediction about the Star had been misinterpreted, but could not be false. The destruction of the following half-dozen lines deprives us of the continuation of this argument.

The fifth and last section of this piece gives us a picture of Heaven as conceived by the inhabitants of the countryside. An army of angels and saints hold themselves in readiness for God's orders, prepared to intervene on earth as soon as God should give the word. For God has inscribed in a manner that cannot be effaced, not only the terms of His covenant with His people, but also His decision made in advance of what benefits they should enjoy, and when.

*Author and Date.* The author of this portion of the manuscript—half prayer, half commentary—should be looked for in Palestine on the eve of Bar Kochba's revolt. The text shows that there were poets in that environment, for certain phrases are of real beauty. The ideas that are expressed, however, are not all of an absolute orthodoxy, especially, from a rabbinic point of view, the beliefs in oracles and omens. These must have raised quite a number of objections. Quotations from the Bible are often only approximate, and this was considered a grave crime at a time when the Canon of the Old Testament had been fixed. The interpretations are clearly tendencious. It is noticeable, too, that the author carefully avoids any mention of priests or Cohens. One cannot be far out in dating the first writer of this piece to round about A.D. 130. The style, and certain peculiarities of vocabulary, would suggest the same author as for the fragments found in XIII, 7-16, XVI, 5-XVII, 9.

As already mentioned, this text must have been retouched quite a number of times. The phrase given above—"an enemy of the heritage and of Israel"—seems to be an interpolation on the part of the compiler of this manuscript. The date of this interpolation would be after A.D. 135 and might be as late as A.D. 162.

COLUMN XII, LINES 7-16 . . .

And Thou, O God, in the glory of the Kingship, and in the Congregation of Thy saints, who are among us to give us help without end, (*enable*) us (*to spread abroad*) contempt upon barbarous kings, and derision on the men of war. For the Holy One, my Lord and the King of Glory is with us, accompanied by the saints, and the warriors of the army of angels will watch over us. The Hero of War is in our Congregation, and the army of His spirits accompanies our steps. Our horsemen are as the clouds, and spread over the earth like the dew, and like a shower of hail, in their tens of thousands are they ready to overwhelm with the judgement of God all the sons of the earth.

Arise, O man of valour! Lead forth thy captives, O man of glory. Take thy spoil, thou who dost deeds of bravery. Put thy hand on the nape of thy enemies, thy foot on the high places of profanity. Beat down the peoples who bear thee enmity, and may thy sword devour the flesh of the guilty. Fill thy land with glory and thy heritage with blessings. May there be abundance of riches in thy possessions, [* silver][1] gold and precious stones in thy palaces. Zion, make great thy joy! Shine with jubilation, O Jerusalem, and make jubilee all you towns of Judah! Open for ever your gates that the armies of the nations may come in, and that kings may serve thee. All thy oppressors shall bow down before thee, and the dust (*of thy feet, shall they lick. Break forth into joy, O daughters*) of thy people! Cry out with a voice of joy! Put on your glorious ornaments, and be as lords over all the . . . . . . . . . . . . . . . . . . Israel is called to rule over the whole world.

Here we have a hymn composed of fragments taken from many books of Scripture—Genesis, Judges, Psalms, etc. The date of its composition should be somewhat early, perhaps it goes back even to the times of the Maccabees. Once again, we find the play on the word *ṭl*, which can mean either "dew" or "company of assault". The play on this word is already found in 2 Sam. 17.12 and Isa. 27.19, so it furnishes no evidence of date.

This song must have circulated among all classes of the population, but naturally it frequently had to be modified in accordance with the accepted beliefs in the different circles of society. Here we have a popular version which gave a big place to angels, saints, etc. Note should also be taken of the word *Adonai*—my Lord—written out in full in this text. This word was considered extremely sacred by the Pharisees, and almost unpronounceable by the Zadokites. A parallel version of this hymn has been

---

[1] Inserted between the lines.

K

re-copied further on in XIX, 1-8, and in that version the word *Adonai* does not figure in the corresponding sentence.

This hymn begins after a line left blank, and it is followed at the end by an *alinea*. From the two fragmentary phrases which represent all that has survived of the remainder of this column, one can presume that another popular hymn followed. The phrases are: ". . . . the heroes of the war, O Jerusalem . . .": ". . . upon the Heavens, my Lord (*Adonai*). . . ." The hymn did not take up the whole of the remaining part of the column, for a Zadokite fragment began on it, and is continued in the next column.

COLUMN XIII, LINES 1-5.

and his brothers the Cohens, as well as the Levis and the elders of the Bond who accompany him. Then standing on the dais, they shall bless the God of Israel and all the works of His truth, and from there too shall they pronounce anathemas upon Belial and all the spirits of his portion. They shall therefore begin by saying: "Blessèd be the God of Israel in all His Holy designs, and in all the works of His truth, and blessèd be all those who serve Him in righteousness, and acknowledge Him in sincerity. And cursèd be Belial in his plans for persecution, and detested him who serves him, and cursed be all the spirits who belong to his portion, even in thinking. They are wicked and detestable in all their obscene rituals and their impurities. They belong to the portion of Darkness, whilst those in God's portion are led into the light . . . . ."

This fragment continued from the lower destroyed part of the preceding column resembles the ritual of initiation in a Zadokite lodge. Though much shorter than the text found in the *Manual of Discipline* (II, 1-8), it reveals the same ceremonial, the same type of mind, and the same terminology. In any case, it has nothing to do with the Battle Manual into which the compiler of our roll wished to incorporate it.

All the same, certain differences should be noted. The benediction extends to all who serve God and sincerely acknowledge Him, whilst the anathema applies to those who approve Belial even in thought. Also the authority to pronounce a blessing is not limited to persons of the name of Cohen, but extends also to the Levis and to the elders of the societies.

*Author and Date.* These observations lead one to suppose that we have here a passage from a modified ritual, such as must have been in use at a time when the Zadokites were less exclusive, and more disposed to collaborate with other classes of the population. Perhaps the passage may be dated in the years preceding Bar Kochba's revolt, let us say about A.D. 130.

COLUMN XIII, LINES 7-17.

. . . . And Thou, God of our forefathers, may Thy name be blessed for evermore. As to us, we are the people of peace, and of Thy Covenant, which Thou hast made with our forefathers, and which Thou wilt maintain with their descendants until the times determined in the eternities. In all the manifestations of Thy glory, there was a reminder of the [greatness of] Thy [ways] when Thou didst draw near to help the remnant of Thy people, and the [faithful] survivors of Thy Covenant, those who recite the works of Thy truth, and the verdict which Thou didst execute by the power of Thy miracles. As to Thee, (*Thou hast* . . .) for Thee to be the people for ever, and Thou hast set us apart in the portion of Light, because of Thy Truth. From of old Thou hast confided the oversight of Thy people to the Prince of Lights that he should come to our help and [. . . . . . of just]ice, and all the spirits of truth which are in his empire.

But Thou, Thou hast made Belial for the pit, and Thou hast created the angel of persecution as likewise the chos[en of his guilt]iness, and those in his council, in order to persecute and afflict. And all the spirits of his portion are angels of sufferings. In the realm of Darkness do they walk, and it is towards them that . . . . . . together. We on the other hand, in the portion of Thy truth we shall rejoice, thanks to Thy power, and we shall have gladness because of Thy salvation, and we shall sing aloud because of Thy he[lp which will bring to us Thy] peace. Who is like unto Thee in power, O God of Israel, when the hand of Thy might draws near unto the poor. And what angel or prince can equal the succour by [which Thou wilt set us free? F]or from of old, Thou hast determined, and Thou alone, the day of the struggle . . . . . . . . . . . . . . . in truth, so as to exterminate by a guilt offering, to overturn the Darkness, and to add strength to the Light, and to . . . . . . . . . . . . . . . . . . in a world-wide revelation, to exterminate all the sons of Darkness, and Thy name . . . . . .

The translation of this passage is difficult because of its high-flown style, and because of certain awkward gaps. It is clear that "the Prince of Lights" denotes an angel specially charged with helping Israel. On the other hand, it is hard to say if "Belial" applies to the Romans, as in other texts, or if this term is here the equivalent of "the angel of persecution". It appears that in the mind of the author, the realm of Darkness was peopled by certain demons called "angels of sufferings". They were under the orders of the angel of persecution and came periodically to afflict (persecute) and torment human beings. None of these demons will ever be able to leave the realm of Darkness. Moreover, no angel or prince could bring to the enemy a help comparable with that which God will bring to the "poor", the simple men of the people, when the day comes which God has predestined for the wiping out of the Romans.

*Author.* The mention of the "poor" and all the angelology and demonology which is found in this passage warrant its attribution to a Zealot author. Many similarities of style, and the frequent use of certain terms such as "from of old" (*m'z*), lead one to suppose that this passage comes from the hand of the author of fragment X, 1–XII, 5, but it is impossible to say if this was an immediate continuation of that passage.

After a space left blank, we come across a few words from the middle of the first line of another fragment: ". . . . Thou hast made us to know. . . ." The rest of the column has been destroyed, and in the first line of the following column we have the concluding words of the fragment: ". . . . as the fire of His passage over the idols of Egypt. . . ."

This passage may be a text parallel to XI, 9-10, perhaps even applying to the Romans certain verses from Exodus. The name for Egypt, *Miṣraim,* can be read as the plural of "anguish", and by a play on the word and with the meaning "Country of anguish" the name was frequently given to Rome in Jewish literature of the early centuries A.D. After the fall of Jerusalem in A.D. 70, many Jews were "in bondage" in Rome, and used by the state in building operations.

Following an *alinea,* a totally different kind of text begins and by no degree of probability could it have been the continuation of the last fragment.

COLUMN XIV, LINES 2-17 . . .

And after having retired from the smitten to re-enter the camp, they shall all sing the hymn of return. And the following morning, they shall cleanse their garments and wash themselves of the blood of the corpses of the guilty. Then they shall return to their appointed place, there where the regiment will have been lined up facing the smitten of the enemy who will have been beaten down, and there they shall all bless the God of Israel and in united joy they shall glorify His name, saying,

"Blessèd be the God of Israel who maintains His goodness for the people of His covenant, and the signs of His salvation for those whom He has redeemed. It is He who has called together the weary for . . . and as for the meeting of the (foreign) nations, He has called them together that they may be utterly destroyed, not a remnant remaining. He has done this to lift up the downcast by His judgement, and to open the mouth of the dumb that they may declare His might. [He sends hea]ling to those who learn to fight, to the fainting, He grants the blessing of strength, a firm foot and a stout heart to those whose shoulders are drooping, and whose spirit has been brought low. [He . . . . . . ] to the heart of the crooked, and by those whose ways are straight shall the nations of wickedness be wiped out, not one of their men of valour standing firm.

"And we, the rem[nant of Thy people, we laud and bless] Thy NAME, O God of kindness, faithful to the Covenant of our forefathers, and who through all our ages hast accorded the miracle of Thy benefits to the rem[nant of Thy people who . . . ] in the realm of Belial. In spite of all his plans for persecution, Thou hast not rejected us from Thy Covenant, and to the spirits of nothingness Thou hast forbidden . . . . . . . . . of his dominion. Thou hast preserved the souls of Thy redeemed, and by Thy help hast lifted up the fallen. But the traitor who lifts himself up, Thou hast cut down . . . . . . . . . . . For all their men of valour, there will be no hiding-places, and for all the hordes that they have gathered together, there will be no place of refuge. Those whom they honour, Thou hast reduced to contempt, and likewise, those who exalt themselves, Thou . . . . . . . . . . And we, the people of Thy holiness, we shall glorify Thy NAME for the works of Thy truth, and by Thy mighty deeds, we shall arise.

"[May Thy name be blessed in all] the ages, at the feasts laid down for all eternity, at the coming in of day and of night, at the going out of evening and morning. For great is [ . . . and we shall declare Thy good]ness and the mysteries of Thy miracles in songs of praise, Thou, who canst lift up the humbled out of the dust into Thy presence, and canst bring low the idols.

"Glorify, glorify the God of gods and let one carry in . . . . . . . . . . . . . of Darkness, and the Light of Thy greatness . . . . . . . . . . . . . . set alight to burn . . . . . . . . ."

This column is made up of very dissimilar fragments. A series of hymns is introduced by some phrases which could have formed part of a *taktikon* of the kind seen in IX, 10ff., only here there is no mention of priests, and even their trumpets seem forgotten. It is singing the hymn of return that the soldiers leave the field of battle. It is only on the following morning—and this is very strange—that they wash and clean their garments, but the word "purify" is not used. Then the regiments goes out to line up before the corpses of the enemy, which would involve a new defilement (? cf. IX, 7-8, and comment on p. 282). The hymns sung by the soldiers, never a question of priests, reveal here and there a state of mind which is not found in parallel texts.

These hymns may have formed part of a popular collection. Inspired by Ezek. 39.2-4, the composer of the first hymn thinks that the Romans have been gathered together in Judea simply that they might be exterminated. It is to be noted that the victory would be gained by the weak and humble to whom the art of warfare will have been imparted (cf. XI, 8), though the actual word "poor" does not occur in this passage. On the other hand, one meets with another expression *n'lmym*, "the dumb". It probably refers to certain Zealots of whom Hippolytus writes (*Philosophumena*, IV, 26): "If one of these is tortured in order to make him abjure the Law, or eat what has been offered to idols, with an air of not suffering, and with patience awaiting death, and submitting to martyrdom, he does not transgress his conscience." Other texts mention these "dumb", and it seems that they courted martyrdom in order to give others an example of courage. It is possible, but by no means certain, that this hymn may have been composed at the time of Hadrian's persecutions, and there is in fact in this passage a reference to plans for persecution by Belial.

Of the second hymn only a few phrases remain, and it has no relation to victory, for the praises of God were to be sung on all occasions, and every day, morning and night. This prayer must have formed part of the liturgical texts most current at the time. As one can see, it underwent modification so as to fall in with the different tendencies in Judaism.

The following column is very fragmentary, and begins with three lines which are the conclusion of a text begun in the previous column.

COLUMN XV, LINES 1-3.

For there will be a period of anguish for Israel . . . . . . . . . . . period of war against all the foreign nations. Those of God's portion will be destined to eternal redemption, but extermination will be the lot of all the nations of wickedness because all the na[tions . . . and all the men] of valour must come and set up their camp in the presence of the king of the legions, and of all the armies of Belial confederate with him, for the day [of their extermination] by the sword of God.

This fragment, also an extract from some popular work, refers to "the period of anguish", the war of A.D. 66-70. It may be part of a commentary on Ezekiel. The author foresees that all the nations subjected to Rome will come and fight at the side of the Jews, and this would suggest that the fragment was written about A.D. 130, or even later, about the time of the Parthian advance in A.D. 162.

COLUMN XV, LINES 4-14 . . .
And the Chief Priest stands with his brethren [the priests and the fathers of the "Bond"] and the Levites and all the men of the Bond are close to him. He reads in their ears the prayer for the destined day of the w[ar, and also . . . . . . such as they are written in the bo]ok of the Bond of the age, with all the words of their Thanksgiving Hymns. There he puts all the regiments in their ranks as it is wr[itten in the book . . . . . . of the w]ar. And the diligent priest will act, on the day of vengeance, according to the word of all his brethren, and he will encourage the [men of the Bond, and . . . . . . .] and he begins by saying: "Be strong and of good courage. Be like sons of valour. Fear not and be not aff[righted nor terrified in the presence of men of w]ar. Do not be affrighted nor terrified. Do not be driven back nor [flee before . . .]! As to them, they are members of the congregation of wickedness, and all their deeds are of Darkness. Poured out for him to drink will be [the cup of bitterness . . . . . . . . . . . vanish will] their places of refuge, their might will be dispersed like smoke, and the gathering together [of their hor]des [. . . . . . . a way of escape from the des]truction he will not find, and every living soul amongst them who shall rise up, shall soon have fulfilled [all the meas]ure [of his life] in the battle . . . . . . . Strengthen you for God's war, for today is that day of battle, [the day of retribu]tion to all the . . . .
Upon all flesh will the God of Israel lift up His hand with the might of His miracles . . . . . . all the spirits of wicked[ness . . . . . . the war]riors of the gods gird themselves for war . . . . . their ranks. '

COLUMN XVI, LINE I.
until all the adversaries shall be wiped out. The God of Israel has

called for the sword upon all the presumptuous, and by the saints of His people shall He fulfil His mighty acts.

Two texts have been put together here. The first and larger portion presents a Zadokite version of the ritual for entering into battle, similar to that met with in Column X. Large gaps in the text prevent us from learning all the details, but one notices the use of the term "Chief Priest", and the mention of "the men of the Bond" (the Zadokite lodge). It is probable that the Zadokites of the Diaspora pictured a Chief Priest as being naturally advanced in years. The burden of addressing the congregation should therefore devolve upon a "diligent priest", who should do as directed by the college of priests. The Chief Priest would merely read certain hymns and prayers said to come from an old book dating from "the period of anguish". The compilers of our text probably made use of a recovered manuscript of that kind, containing *Hôdayôth* or Thanksgiving Hymns. The text of the appeal to the warriors owes its inspiration to passages of the Bible, and nothing more definite than that can be said of it.

To this exhortation is added a popular Zealot fragment in which mention is made of the "miracles of God", the "spirits of wickedness", "angels", "warriors of the gods", etc.

*Date and Author.* The special terminology of the former passage, the picture of a future organisation on the lines of a "lodge", and the mention of old books possessed by his group, all lead us to attribute this text to an author living in the Diaspora, as we have already done with Fragments II, 1-6, and XIII, 1-6. As to the additional Zealot passage, there is no means of determining its date and authorship.

COLUMN XVI, LINES 3-9.

They will comply with all these regulations that day, in their positions before the camp of the legions. Following that, the priests shall blow the trumpets of remembrance, the "gates" shall open in the ranks, the light infantry shall march out, and the leaders shall stand between the regiments. The priests shall blow the call for forming line, and the leaders . . . . . . at the sound of the trumpets, until each one is at his post. Then the priests shall blow the second call . . . . . . . . . and as they come alongside the regiments of the legions, as the importance of an assaulting company demands, every man shall raise his "sword-arm" for the struggle. The six [priests . . . . . . shall sound on the] trumpets the call "At the smitten", a shrill, prolonged note, for success in the battle. The Levites and all the people who have horns shall make a great noise [blowing the horns and yelling] at the top of their voices. As soon as this uproar breaks out, their hands shall begin to beat down the smitten of the legions. Then all the people shall stop their noise [of horns and yelling, only the pries]ts shall keep on sounding the call "At the smitten", and the battle over the legion will be won.

We have here a fifth, Zadokite, version of the battle against the Roman legions. The compiler introduces it by saying that the exhortation by the priest, referred to in the preceding fragment, was to be delivered on the destined day, and in the presence of the legions.

This version begins with the formations of the Jewish troops. They are in squares or "towers", not in line seven ranks deep. Only two sorts of trumpets are mentioned. In place of calling the people to prayer, the "trumpets of remembrance" give the signal for the opening of the "gates", and the marching out of the light infantry and their officers. Nothing is said about preliminary attacks by slingers. At the second trumpet-call, everyone should be at his post. Then is sounded another call—actually the third, but called the second—to put in movement the assaulting company which goes forward to attack the enemy already harassed by the light infantry. When the regiment is at grips with the foe, the priests blow the call "At the smitten", the people who are watching and the Levites shout and blow horns till all the army is in contact with the enemy. Then the people stop shouting, leaving the priests to continue blowing "At the smitten" and the battle is won.

Without the shadow of a doubt, we have here a Zadokite fragment, but it is impossible to assign even an approximate date to it.

COLUMN XVI, LINES 11-14.

and if [the warriors who go] to the help of the Sons of Darkness swing round and the wounded among the light infantry begin to be beaten down, in the mysteries of God which include the putting to the test of the valiant in war, then the priests shall sound the "fall in" on their trumpets so that another regiment shall move forward as relief. They shall take their place between the regiments, and to those engaged in the fighting . . . . . . . they shall blow the call to retire. The Chief Priest goes to them and, standing in front of the regiment, he strengthens hearts by . . . . . . . . . . . . in His war.

K*

It is possible that in the missing part of the Fragment XV, 4, to XVI, 1, there was an account of the battle up to the time when the light infantry went out to the attack. This present fragment seems to be a continuation. The author, aware of defeats suffered in previous wars, is much less optimistic than the writer of XVI, 4-9. He foresees that blowing trumpets will probably not be enough to gain the victory. Before the troops of the line march out to beat down the wounded of the fleeing enemy, the light infantry thrown forward to the attack may have suffered a reverse. The priests should then sound for their being relieved. Another regiment of light infantry should be thrown against the enemy lines, and those previously engaged should rally and reform. For it is in the mysteries of God to test brave men.

Although the High Priest plays a more active part, even advancing between the enemy lines, yet the similarity of language allows this fragment to be assigned to the Zadokite writer of Fragments XIII, 1-5, and XV, 4, to XVI, 1.

COLUMN XVI, LINES 15-16 . . .

And he begins by saying . . . . . . the heart of His people, He puts it to the proof by . . . Do not . . . . . . . . . . your smitten, for of old you have heard that in the mysteries of God . . . . . .

COLUMN XVII, LINES 1-3.

And there, they are unharmed in the flames . . . . . . . . . . . those tried in the furnace. Even if they have sharpened their weapons, they shall not strike so long as . . . . . . . . . . the wicked. And you, recall the judge[ments of God by which He put to death] the sons of Aaron whom he had sanctified by His verdicts: it was in the eyes of [all the people that He made Nadab and Abihu to perish, and it was Eleazar] and Ithamar with whom He made an everlasting covenant.

It is certain that this passage which begins after an *alinea* is not connected with the preceding one. Unless these two imperfectly preserved fragments were separated in the missing lower part of Column XVI, they form part of an exhortation to battle by a Zealot author. It would be pronounced by an "overseer" (*vide* X, 2-8), and certainly not by a priest. Quite apart from several allusions to popular beliefs—furnace, flames, etc.—there is a definitely anti-Zadokite sentence: Aaron had been sanctified by God, but the Sons of Aaron were burnt because of their impiety (Lev. 10.1-2), and it is Eleazar and Ithamar that God kept for Himself.

(From this, can it be inferred that in certain Zealot circles there still remained a memory of Eleazar, the opponent to Menahem in A.D. 66? *Vide* the *Habakkuk Commentary*.)

COLUMN XVII, LINES 4-9.

And you, be strong, and fear not [for] it is towards the waste and void that their instincts and their reasonings go because they do not [. . . . . . Has He not ordained, the God of] Israel all that is and is to be, and [has He not allotted the por]tion of all those who will be for all eternity? Today is the day destined by Him to humble and bring low the Prince of the Kingdom of Wickedness. He will send help without measure to those in the portion of His Congregation, sending by the might of the powerful angel who does Him service. To Michael, in the light everlasting, will it be to make radiant with joy [the chosen of] Israel, peace and blessing for those of God's portion, for it is Michael's task to lift them up among the gods. The realm of Israel shall rejoice in the justice for all human beings, and the heavenly heights as well as all the Sons of His Truth shall exult over endless knowledge. And you, sons of His Covenant, be strong in the furnace of God until those who make signs with the hand shall have filled up the furnaces of His mysteries for your strengthening.

The further version of the call to battle which we have here probably comes from those versions circulated by the "venerable who see angels and hear sibylline words" (X, 11). A very curious kind of determinism is seen in these lines. God has ordained everything beforehand, and chosen those who will rise again to everlasting life. Michael already appears as the leader to the celestial regions of those souls in Israel who fell in battle. He was given the duty of taking them up to the abode of the gods—and the use of the plural should be noted. The dead, whom the author calls forth by the formula, "Peace and blessing for those of God's portion", will experience joy in the light everlasting. One should not therefore mourn them, but rejoice in the acts of divine justice, as the angels do who possess knowledge of all things. The image of the refining furnace (Isa. 48.10) occurs again. Those destined for eternity will come forth purified by their sufferings. The lost will remain at the bottom of the furnace. The author anticipates that once the furnace has been filled, its purpose will

have ended. When the adversaries shall have filled it up, there will be no
further testing of Israel.

The expression "those who sign with the hand" is fairly current in
rabbinic literature for the Romans, who, ignorant of Hebrew, expressed
themselves by gestures. The same idea is found in the *Manual of Discipline*,
XI, 2, and in the *Thanksgiving Hymns*.

COLUMN XVII, LINES 10–16 . . .

And after these words, the priests shall blow with the trumpets for the
companies of the regiment to line up, and the officers shall separate
themselves out at the sound of the trumpet until every man is at his post.
The priests shall sound the second time for close action, and when the
men shall have arrived at . . . . . . of the regiment of the legions,
[everywhere] as the importance of an assaulting company demands,
each man shall lift up his "sword-arm". Then the priests shall sound
the call "At the smitten" [and the Levites and all] the people provided
with rams' horns shall raise the clamour of war. Then the light infantry
shall fight hand to hand with the army of the legions. [And as they hear
the noise of the war clam]our, they shall start to beat down the smitten.
Then all the people shall stop the noise of the clamour, the priests alone
continuing to sound with the trumpets . . . . . . . . . to those
fallen before them, and those whose lot it is to be untouched . . . .
. . . . . . the smitten . . . . . . . . . .

Here we have a sixth, Zadokite, version of the battle. Certain expressions
recall the Fragment VII, 9 to VIII, 12, the compiler perhaps having
recopied here a second recension of the same text.

COLUMN XVIII, LINES 1–7.

. . . and in causing to fall the great hand of God upon Belial and upon
all the rulers of his empire in an everlasting extermination . . . . . . .
. . . and the outcry of the saints when Aššûr was overrun and the
sons of Japhet fell to rise no more, and the "crushers", the legions,
crushed the nations till none was [left. But the day will come
when] the God of Israel will lift up His hand upon all the horde of
Belial.

At that time, the priests shall blow [the trum]pets of remembrance,
and all the regiments of war shall gather round them, and they shall
divide them out upon the whole em[pire of the leg]ions, to destroy

them. When the sun rises that day, the Chief Priest and the priests and Levites who shall be near to him, along with the lead[ers of the men of] the Bond, shall stand up and there shall they bless the God of Israel. They shall commence by saying, "Blessèd art Thou, O God of . . . for Thou hast manifested the greatness [of Thy benefits] by performing wonders, and Thou hast preserved Thy Covenant with us of old, and full many a time Thou hast opened for us the gates of salvation because [. . . . . . and of Thy . . .] in us. And Thou, O God of righteousness. Thou hast done it [because of] Thy name."

With this fragment, of which the beginning must have been at the bottom of the preceding column, we come across the opening of a further collection compiled on the same lines as the earlier one. It is rather late in date, and it must be supposed that this was a much shorter collection, the author having avoided the numerous repetitions which we find in the roll of the War.

As introduction to this compilation, we find a very brief historical survey, of which another version has been found at the beginning of the roll in I, 5-6. There are several noteworthy variants. An outcry was made to Heaven by the saints when Rome conquered Asia Minor (the sons of Japhet) and the kingdom of the Seleucids (Aššûr). Then there is the subject of God's destined day of vengeance. The priests will call the people together by trumpet, and in the place of the exhortation to the battle, they recite a blessing to God. The mention of the High Priests recalls the Fragments II, 1-6, and XV, 1 to XVI, 4, but several points of detail suggest that we have here a rather late adaptation of a Zadokite work. In the mind of the adaptor, the trumpets must have been those of silver mentioned in Num. 10.10, which were exclusively used for calling together the people. Once assembled, the Jewish forces were to be portioned out over the entire Roman Empire, and not kept together in camps. Note should be taken of the importance of the hour of prayer, and above all of the play on the word *ktyym* (the legions) associated here with the verb *ktt*, to crush or destroy.

*Author and Date.* Seeing that our fragment comes to us as a readaptation of a copy, it is difficult to assess its date and origin. What we have is mostly a reflection of the environment in which the redactor of this little collection lived. One has the feeling that he is more concerned with the Jews of the Diaspora than with those of Palestine. It was throughout the Roman Empire that the Jews were going to be set free. His sentiments for

Syria (Aššûr) bear no sign of hostility. He speaks of the rulers of the Roman Empire and not of its sole ruler.

After a line left blank, we find another passage of this same compilation.

COLUMN XVIII, LINES 10-14 . . .

. . . . . . . . . miracle, and from of old there had not been the like. For Thou hast made known to us our predestined days, and today there shines forth . . . . . . . . . of our nation, in an everlasting salvation, to drive afar . . . . . . the enemy so that of them there remains not one. With Thy might and with [Thy . . . we shall devote a]ll our enemies to complete and final extermination. But now, today, speed us that we may drive away their horde.

For Thou . . . . . . . . . the heart of the valiant, Thou hast given them over so that no prowess can maintain itself before Thee. War is within Thy hand, and there is not . . . . . . . . . and the feasts according to Thy will, and . . . . . . . . . And Thou shalt make the gathering in among . . . . . . . . .

Two prayers are joined together here, of which the former is the more significant. The author, or the redactor of this re-copied collection, was willing to acknowledge that God had ordained the day of the Romans' final extermination, but that day was in the distant future. What interested him more was immediate freedom.

He wished that God would do something "today", that he might at once begin to drive away the enemy from the countries occupied by him. How he should be destroyed would be seen later.

After that, we find the same prayer that we have met with in a different version in XI, 1-7. It must have been given in a much shorter form and somewhat modified. It may be supposed that it was followed by a description of the battle.

COLUMN XIX, LINES 1-8.

[We shall spread abroad contempt on the] men of war, for the Holy One shall glorify us, and the King of Glory is with us and with our ar[mies. Our horsemen are as the clouds,] and spread over the earth [like the dew,] and as a shower of hail in their tens of thousands are they ready to overwhelm with the judgement of God a[ll the sons of earth.

Arise O man of valour! Lead forth thy captives, O man of glory! Ta]ke thy spoil, thou who dost deeds of bravery! Put thy hand on the nape of thy enemies, and thy foot [on the high places of profanity. Beat down the peoples who bear thee enmity] and may thy sword devour their flesh. Fill thy land with glory, and thy heritage with blessings. May there be ab[undance of riches in thy possessions, silver, gold and precious stones] in thy palaces. Zion, make great thy joy, and make jubilee all you towns of Ju[dah . . . . . . . . . . . Open for ever your gates, so that] the armies of the nations [may come in], and their kings shall serve thee. [All thy oppressors] shall bow down before thee, [and they shall lick the dust of thy feet. Break forth in joy daughters of my people] Cry out with a voice of joy. Put on your glorious ornaments, and [be as lords over all the . . . . . . . . . . . . . .] Israel is called to rule over the whole earth.

With a few slight changes, we have here the two prayers already reproduced in XII, 7-10, 10-16. The first prayer is somewhat abridged. The word *Adonai* does not appear, and there is no mention of the saints and the armies of angels.

The second prayer, on the other hand, must have been longer. For instance, the mention of the towns of Judah was followed by a phrase, now perished, which did not occur in the previous version.

*Author and Date.* These facts warrant the assumption that the fragments copied directly by the compiler of our roll were taken from originals which were older than the small collection added at the end. The author of this small collection avoided writing *Adonai* and intentionally left out the reference to saints and angels. He added to the quotation from Zech. 2.10 by associating the cities of Judah with the joy of Zion. He may have added the names of other towns inhabited by Jews. There are good reasons therefore for supposing that the person who drew up this small collection belonged to a circle of some culture, and was living in the Diaspora.

COLUMN XIX, LINES 9-13 . . .

. . . . . . . that night, so as to rest till morning. And in the morning . . . . . . . . . . . . . . . . . the men of war of the legions and the multitude from Aššûr, and the army of all the nations . . . . . . . . . . . . . . . . . . . . . . are fallen there by the sword of God. The Chief Priest draws near from there . . . . . . . . . . . . . . . the men of war as well as the leaders of the regiments and the overseers of the . . . . . . . . . . . . . . . . . the smitten of the leg[ions . . . . . . . and they glor]ify there the God of [Israel . . . . . . . . . .

This last fragment seems to reproduce a ritual for the day following the battle, another version of which, a Zealot one, was met with in XIV, 2-4. If we understand correctly this most fragmentary text, the army was to rest on the night of the battle, and not take part in a service of thanksgiving till the following morning. In the present text, the army of Israel has been fighting against the legions and the Roman mercenary troops, Syrians and others. The High Priest, who was not mentioned in the Zealot version, arrives on the field of battle—contrary to what the Zadokites laid down—and in front of the enemy dead is met by the army, its officers and overseers. These last-named do not appear in the earlier version.

*Author and Date.* The impression is given that the author of this passage must be the editor of the "small collection", and that he composed this text by combining some Zadokite elements with some Zealot ones, taken from two different rituals.

As already indicated, the author of this "little collection" has to be looked for in a Pharisaic circle somewhere in the Diaspora. He hoped for freedom from the Roman yoke, but obviously was averse to war. Judging from the arrangement of the fragments copied out into our roll, and on the assumption that its compiler was not making a selection, then one is forced to admit that the author of the "little collection" did not make use of the principal parts of the ancient *taktika*, those which dealt with the organisation of the army and the conduct of the battle, etc. Was he hoping that the "sword of God" would smite Rome as the "angel of Yahweh" smote Assyria (2 Kings 19.35)?

One can suppose that this "little collection" was written some time between A.D. 135 and 160, perhaps about the middle of the reign of Antoninus Pius.

★          ★          ★

That is all that remains of the roll *The War of the Sons of Light against the Sons of Darkness*. It is difficult to say even approximately how many pages are missing from this manuscript. There are ten rather small fragments which could not be fitted into any gap in the text, but the few letters or isolated words which are legible on them do not supply any additional information.

# V

# The Thanksgiving Hymns

The translation of these poems presents many difficulties, above all from the fact that a number of passages lend themselves to two or even three different interpretations. The greater part of the phrases are borrowed from Biblical Hebrew. Verses from the Bible are reused, with slight alterations at times. It is thus comparatively easy to "re–discover the Bible" in each sentence of these hymns—which is, in fact, what many translators have tried to do. As a matter of fact, the interesting thing about these poems often lies in the meaning that the different authors wanted to give to certain current phrases, and in the more or less obvious play on words. Of different possible translations, the present writer has kept to that which seemed to conform most with the spirit of each hymn, and wherever there are gaps he has avoided reconstruction of the text as far as possible.

As he has done for other collections, he has tried to distinguish Zadokite poems from those coming from Zealot (popular) and from Christian sources, etc. He has made an effort to date the different parts, and to determine their place of origin (Judea or the Diaspora, Syrian, Roman, etc.). It does not look as if all these compositions in the first place were thought of as thanksgiving hymns. The opening formula, "I give Thee thanks, my Lord", seems to have been an addition on the part of the compiler of the roll.

## FRAGMENT 1

SCRIBE A, COLUMN I, LINES 1–38.
(The first four lines are completely missing, and the next two are only partly preserved. We begin, therefore, near the end of line 6.)

. . . . . *Charity is in all Thine acts, and by Thy wisdom* . . .    . . .
. . . *of the world.*

*Before they were created, Thou didst know their deeds, even to all eternity:*
*[Without Thy command] naught can be done, and nothing can be known*
   *unless Thou dost purpose it.*

*It is Thou who hast created all that breathes, and . . .  . . .  . . . and*
   *Thou dost [pronounce] sentence on all they do.*

*Thou hast spread abroad the heavens for Thy glory,*
      *All the [. . .  . . . Thou hast cre]ated according to Thy will,*
   *And the helping spirits for their appointed bounds.*

*Before they became angels of . . .  . . .  . . . Thou [didst make of them]*
   *spirits for the universe, each in his own sphere,*
*The sun and the moon, each with its hidden meaning, the stars, each in its*
   *own path.*

*For [. . .  . . . Thou hast commanded] to carry to them, balls of fire and*
   *lightnings, as the spirits make them,*
*Collections of visions, as they desire them, [phenomena] . . . each with its*
   *hidden meaning.*

*By Thy might Thou hast made the earth, the seas and the deeps,*
*[. . .  . . .  . . . and all that in them dw]ells, Thou hast called into being*
   *by Thy wisdom.*
*Everything that is in them Thou hast established by Thy will.*

*[And the whole Thou hast made subject] to the breath of man,*
*Whom Thou hast formed in the world, for all the days of the universe, the*
   *ages of eternity,*
*So that [he might have dominion over them.]*

*[To men,] Thou hast allotted their forms of worship, within their borders and*
   *for all ages,*
*But judgement on the destined day [Thou shalt pronounce] on all their empires.*

*[They however think that their empire is firmly fixed] to all eternity*
*And to the enrolling of the complete number, nation by nation, of those they*
   *have conquered [have they proceeded.*
*But their empire will be destroyed] and divided for all the time of their*
   *descendants, all the ages of the universe, and the years of eternity.*

*[Thou, by Thy knowledge] and in the wisdom of Thy understanding, hast*
   *ordained the signs of things before they come to pass,*

And it is according to the word [of Thy mouth] that all things [come to be,]
And without Thee naught shall be done.

All this have I understood, through the understanding that Thou hast given me,
For Thou hast opened my ears to the meanings of miracles.

And I, a creature of clay, and kneaded with water,
Issue of the rock of nakedness and the spring of impurity,
A melting-pot of wickedness, and dwelling-house of sin,
A spirit of abomination, and a trough of stupidity,
I, whom Thou hast made to increase, thanks to Thy righteous verdicts,
What shall I say, that is not already known,
Or what shall I declare, that has not been already told?

All has been judged before Thee, and engraven with the chisel of remembrance,
To endure to all the ends of eternity, the circling numbers of the world's years,
    with all their destined days.
Nor can these things be hidden and concealed from before Thee.

How can a man confess away his sin?
How can he make himself begin again because of his transgression?
And how can the guilty make the judge reverse his just sentence?
To Thee alone is the understanding of the works of righteousness, and of the
    secrets of truth,
But to the sons of man are the works of transgression, and the deeds of deceit.

Thou hast made the spirit which resides in the tongue,
Thou hast known his words, and determined the fruit of his lips before ever
    they were.
The words Thou dost test with Thy line.
And on what gushes forth from the spirit of the lips, Thou dost place Thy
    measuring-rod.

Thou dost bring out lines to test their secrets, rods to measure their designs,
To make known Thy glory, and declare Thy wonders among the works of
    Thy truth and justice,
That Thy name might be glorified in the mouth of all,
And that in proportion to their intelligence they may know Thee, and bless
    Thee for evermore.

For Thou in Thy mercies, and in the greatness of Thy bounties,
Thou hast made strong the spirit of man when he faces the torturer,

*. . . .. . ... in the excess of his sins, that Thy miracles with regard to all Thy creatures might be recited.*

*. . . .. . ... the sentences of the torturers, and to the sons of flesh all Thy miracles by which Thou dost show forth Thy power.*

*They shall hear it, the learned who are restless and eager to declare knowledge, and they shall become steadfast.*

*[For the learned] have heaped up trickery, the "just" have ceased to offer burnt-offerings, and all those "of the right way" have seized up . . . . . . and the "poor" alone are high-minded.*

*Despise not then . . . . . .. . . . .*

*Those whose heart is hardened will not understand this . . . .*

The first hymn is a composite work. The first part (1-20) is made up of fragments derived from popular literature, and in it a rather curious doctrine is set forth which reflects a kind of universal determinism. God, the creator of all that exists, has determined in advance the behaviour of every being, and how he will be judged. There follows a justification for belief in omens. God has created tormenting spirits (?) and helping spirits, but before these had become angels they had been charged with the ordering of the movements of the planets and other heavenly phenomena, so as to make known by omens the fate awaiting the different countries. In the popular interpretation of Genesis, God created the angels on the fifth day at the same time as everything else that flies in the firmament of heaven and He entrusted to these spirits the movements of the stars created the previous day. According to later tradition, however, the angels' bodies were composed half of water and half of fire (or light), elements existing on the first day or created then. Next we have the idea frequently put forward that God had divided out the world so that each nation might practise its own religion within its own borders, and that there it would be judged as to the manner in which it had behaved. But the Romans (there is a gap here, but the reference is undoubtedly to them) believed that their rule over all nations would go on for ever, and they had proceeded to a census of all the conquered peoples. Their Empire was to be destroyed and divided out for ever. Omens had announced this, and all would come to pass as God had said.

It is difficult to fix an exact date for this passage. It may be supposed that some parts of it were written after the census of A.D. 6 and before the war of A.D. 66.

The second passage (21-31) is composed of two fragments and is certainly Zadokite. One finds again a typical attitude of mind, and the use of certain phrases which recur frequently in the writings of this sect. As in Psalm "D" of the *Manual of Discipline* (XI, 15-22) the human being, a creature of water and slime, counts for little because of the taint which he holds from birth. He is congenitally loaded with sins, but although his words have been fore-ordained by God, yet he can redeem himself by proclaiming the miracles of God. There is an echo of the Zadokite presumption when the author says that men understand God in proportion to their intelligence.

This passage contains nothing which could date it.

The last two passages (32ff.) are again from a popular, a Zealot, environment. There is mention of the torturer (*ng'*), a word which has also the sense of "leprous", i.e. smitten of God. In another hymn (II, 7) the Romans are called the "infected", which suggests that by a play on the word the torturers were called lepers. We have here a very clear allusion to those who gave proof of their steadfastness under torture, probably the "dumb" whom we have already come across (see p. 294) and who are frequently mentioned in these hymns. The last fragment has too many gaps for its exact sense to be known. We think we can read in it an attack on the "learned" rabbis, on the priests (?) or the Zadokites here called "the just", and on a party within the latter sect, those "of the right way". The fragment closes with praise for the "poor".

The mention of burnt-offerings suggests that this passage was written before the destruction of the Temple in A.D. 70.


## FRAGMENT 2

SCRIBE A, COLUMN II, LINES 1-19.

(As in Column I, the first few lines are either completely missing, or are preserved only in disconnected phrases. We begin with the latter part of line 5.)

> . . . *joyful news to those in sorrow* . . . . . . . . .
> . . . *to all the villages news* . . . . . . . . .
> *Strength to those whose hearts are melting,*
> *Help to those who waver, as they face the wicked.*
>
> *Thou givest a tongue quick to reply to him whose lips are uncircumcised,*

*Thou dost strengthen my soul under the domination of the infected and of the*
  *men of insolent power*
*And dost perserve my foot from slipping in the haunts of evil.*

*I shall become, therefore, a snare for sinners, and a healing remedy for those*
  *who depart from sin.*
*I shall seem cunning to the simple-minded, and of firm opinions to all whose*
  *hearts are wavering.*
*Appoint me therefore to be a mocking and a shame to renegades, the secret of*
  *truth and understanding to those who seek the right way.*

*For the crimes of the wicked, I shall become a reproach in the tyrants' own tongue,*
*I shall be he whose scorn will make them grind their teeth.*

*And even if I become the object of the sinners' mocking taunts,*
*And if the gathering of the wicked grows wild against me,*
*And even if they roar against me like the surf of the sea,*
*When its waves are wild and they throw up mud and slime,*
*Thou shalt set me as a signal to those who choose righteousness,*
*A symbol of the understanding of the meanings of miracles,*
*For the testing of those [who seek] the truth,*
*And the proving of those who love correction.*

*I shall become a fighter for [those who pour out] mocking songs,*
*A man of peace for those who have visions of justice,*
*And the spirit of zeal in the eyes of all who seek assurance.*
*[And even if all] the men of treachery roar against me with the noise of the*
  *tumult of the mighty waters,*
*And if the tricks of Belial [are in all] their designs,*
*And though they turn again to bring to naught the life of the man whom Thou*
  *hast appointed by the word of Thy mouth,*
*And also that of his disciple,*
*Yet Thou hast placed intelligence in his heart so that he shall open the fountain*
  *of knowledge to all who understand,*
*And they shall translate his knowledge into uncircumcised tongues, and into*
  *the speech of strangers,*
*For the sake of the nations who do not understand, so that they may let fall*
  *their errors.*

After the introduction, the beginning of which is missing, the author,
or the person in whose name this hymn is written, praises God who has

enabled him though not speaking his mother tongue to reply without hesitation to those of a foreign tongue. God has given him firmness to resist the Roman, here called "the infected", the synonym for "leper", and the emphatic expression for the torturer (see p. 309).

Thanks to his knowledge of foreign languages, and the firmness of his faith, he will be looked upon in different ways. The simple-minded will take him for a cunning person, whilst the wavering will find in him an example to follow. He will shame the renegades, and the faithful will see in him the upholder of the truth. In the tyrants' own language (Latin), he will so mock them that they will grind their teeth.

It is not certain if the author was courting martyrdom. In any case, he envisaged it with serenity. Even if his conduct did result in his being put to death, he was convinced that others would translate his teaching into foreign languages, so that people who did not know Hebrew would be able to turn from their errors.

This hymn seems to have been written by or for a Christian coming from Asia Minor, where he had spread "the good news". It could be supposed that he was converted by St. Luke, who also thought that Christianity would bring peace to some, division to others (cf. Luke 2.14 and 34, especially 12.50-1; Acts 14.2-4). He was proud of his ability to speak the language of the pagans, especially Latin, and considered this as a "gift" (cf. Acts 2.4). He felt his life was threatened, as had been the life of "Him whom God had appointed by the word of His mouth", but he was confident about the future of his teaching.

It would seem difficult to date this hymn before A.D. 70. Its composition might be placed at the end of the first or the beginning of the second century A.D. It might be supposed that it was written in Judea.

## FRAGMENT 3

SCRIBE A, COLUMN II, LINES 20-30.

*I give Thee thanks, my Lord, because Thou hast placed my soul in the bundle of life*
*And hast put a fence around me against the snares of the Pit.*

*Tyrants have sought after my soul, because I uphold me by Thy covenant.*
*They, the close friends of Nothingness and the counsellors of the Void have not understood*
*That by Thee is my case established, and that Thy favours preserve my soul.*

*It is Thou who dost direct my steps,*

*And it is by Thy will that they have not seized upon my soul,*
*For it is Thy glory to judge the wicked.*

*Thou wilt manifest in me Thy might, in the eyes of the sons of man,*
*For it is of Thy goodness that I stand upright.*

*As for me, I said,*
*"Let them lay siege to me, the men of power,*
*And let them place around me all their engines of war.*
*Past all hope of repair, their arrows will be broken to pieces,*
*And the point of their spears by the fire that devoureth the trees.*

*Even though the din of their voices is like the tumult of the mighty waters*
*Their race will waste away and perish, and many are they who will burst as*
*   do blisters.*
*The Chimaera and the Void, when they arise, shall chase them away.*

*For me, when my heart melts like water, my soul shall strengthen herself in*
*   Thy Covenant,*
*But for them, the net they stretched for me shall take hold of their feet,*
*And the snare which they have set for my soul, upon them shall it fall.*
*And my foot [\* shall remain upright in righteousness]*
*In the synagogue, I shall bless Thy name.*

This hymn, of a current type and made up stereotyped phrases, could
have been written any time after A.D. 70. The terms of warfare are merely
figures of speech. The words immediately marked with an asterisk are
entered in another handwriting.

The author of this poem should be looked for among the class of
ordinary people, whose beliefs are revealed by the mention of the
Chimaera. A more detailed image of this monster is given in III, 12ff.

## FRAGMENT 4

SCRIBE A, COLUMN II, LINES 31-9.

*I give Thee thanks, my Lord, because Thine eyes [are set] upon my soul,*
*And because Thou hast saved me from the zeal of those who sing lying songs;*
*And from the society of those who seek flatteries, Thou hast saved the soul of*
*   the "poor" whose blood they thought to shed in the spreading of vanity in*
*   Thy worship.*

*For [they did not under]stand that it is from Thee that I keep my feet,*

*And they chose me for contempt and shame by the mouth of those who seek*
*crookedness.*
*But Thou, my God, didst come to the aid of the poor and wretched, [to save*
*him] from the hand of one stronger than he was.*

*Thou hast redeemed my soul from the hand of the powerful,*
*And hast caused me not to sin through their blasphemous doings,*
*In abandoning Thy worship for fear of denunciation to the Ro[man]s,*
*And in turning to folly the steadfast mind that [Thou hast placed within*
*me . . . . . .]*

*. . . . . . the laws, and the evidences which have come to the ears . . .*
*[. . . . . . the destruc]tion to all their descendants . . . . . . . . . . . .*
*by Thy precepts and . . . . . . . . . .*

We probably have here another Christian hymn. It seems to have been
written by a Jewish-Christian who came from the class of the "poor", but
who had departed considerably from popular beliefs. It is worth noticing
that, whilst he once uses the term *'bywn* (Ebiôn) in common use by the
people, he prefers the synonyms *'ny* and *rš*.

The author thanks God for having saved him from the zeal of those—
the Zealots—who propagate lies, and from the society of the others—
the Zadokites—whom he reproaches for being seekers after honours, and
who were wanting to sacrifice the lives of the people in an effort to
establish a worship of no value. He shows himself equally hostile to the
influential Pharisees, who were ready for any compromise, lest they should
be denounced to the Romans. The last lines would suggest that he had had
news of certain omens—evidences—announcing the destruction of Rome.

One will notice that the Romans are here mentioned by name. The
manuscript is difficult to read, but in another passage (III, 29), and on
several fragments, the reading is perfectly clear. Up till now, this is the
only manuscript from Qumrân in which Rome (*rwm*) is written in so
many letters. It is true that the different texts put together in this manuscript come from greatly varying environments, but they have all been
remodelled, if it is only by the addition of the thanksgiving formula at the
head. These details should make it easier to indicate the date of this roll,
and the region where it was drawn up. The author should be looked for in
Jewish-Christian surroundings in Palestine. The mention of "evidences
which have come to the ears", probably an allusion to the eruption of
Mount Vesuvius, should place the work a little after A.D. 79.

## FRAGMENT 5

SCRIBE A, COLUMN III, LINES 1-18.

This passage is a kind of apocalypse. The first three lines have perished, and from the broken phrases of the next few lines one gets the impression that the author has had knowledge of certain signs in the heavens announcing coming disasters. He beseeches God to give his soul a refuge, a boat in the midst of the deeps of the sea.

Then follows a detailed description of the pangs of childbirth and the writer develops the well-known parallel between birth and death which forms part of the esoteric teaching of so many sects. The author wonders what would happen if Sheôl itself should give birth, as the omens have made him understand that the Chimaera (the viper or serpent; cf. Isa. 27.1 and 51.9) was about to bring forth.

*Now the Chimaera is in labour,*
*And the Pit opens her womb to give birth to all the creatures of horror.*

*The walls, they stagger like a boat on the surface of the sea,*
*The clouds toss here and there with the noise of tumult.*

*The dwellers of the dust, and those who go down to the sea, are utterly con-*
  *fused because of the uproar of the waters.*
*The learned are at a loss, and cannot account for it,*
*The mariners are perplexed at the far deeps of the seas.*
*All their knowledge is confounded through the uproar of the oceans,*
*By the seething of the deeps above the turmoil of the waters,*
*And they ask the reason of the towering waves.*

*But the wombs of the waters, in the din of their commotion, and the shakings*
  *into which they have worked themselves,*
*Will open to Sh[eôl, and then shall fly forth a]ll the shafts of the Pit with*
  *their following.*
*Their voices will have been heard through the deeps,*
*And the gates [of Sheôl will give passage to the] creatures of the Chimaera.*

*But the doors of the Pit will shut before the suckling to be born,*
*And the bolts of the world will be pushed home in the face of all the spirits*
  *of the Chimaera.*

The author imagines that the Chimaera lives at the bottom of the deeps, which he identifies with the abode of the dead. By a miracle, it must have become pregnant for all the symptoms of childbirth are seen in Nature, but in an extreme form. Earthquakes and tidal waves are the convulsions of the Chimaera in labour. Human knowledge is helpless, and cannot offer an explanation. It can see the mere fact of mountainous waves and totterings walls, but cannot understand what is happening in the depths. There would be nothing to hinder the opening of the gates of Hell and the Chimaera giving birth, but God will be able to prevent the real world from being swallowed up when those gates open. The brood of the Chimaera would invade the earth, but the gates of Hell would at once be shut, and the human child who is to be born would not immediately fall into the hands of Sheôl.

One might have held that this apocalyptic vision, like so many others, was a result of the eruption of Mount Vesuvius, only the picture drawn here is wholly of earthquake and tidal waves, and not of a shower of ashes and a flow of lava. Moreover, the author is not concerned with distant Rome. He seems to fear for himself, and for his own land, and everything points to the fact that he was not an inhabitant of Italy. In conclusion, at the time of the appearing of these symptoms, a human child was to be born against whom all the doors of the Pit would be closed. It was believed therefore that a miraculous birth had taken place at the time of the earthquake. That would lead us to see in this apocalyptic vision a reminiscence of the earthquake at Antioch in A.D. 115, the earthquake which nearly caused the death of Trajan. It is well known that this cataclysm was followed by a rising—quickly checked—of the Jews of the Diaspora. All the predictions had not yet been realised. The earthquake had opened the gates of Hell and let loose all the ills which the Jews had had to suffer, but at the same time, a Saviour must have been born, the Son of the Star, Bar Kochba, in whom Rabbi Aqiba was about to see Israel's Messiah.

This composition therefore may be attributed to the Syrian Diaspora between the years A.D. 115 and 132—that is to say, during the reign of Hadrian.

## FRAGMENT 6

SCRIBE A, COLUMN III, LINES 19–36.

*I give Thee thanks, my Lord, for that Thou hast redeemed my soul from the Pit;*

*From Sheôl and its depths, Thou hast raised me up to the world above, to make me walk on its unfathomable plains.*

*I shall thus know that for him whom Thou hast formed from the dust, there is
    a hope for the eternity which is beyond our understanding.*

*The mind of the wanderer Thou hast purified from the multitude of his sins,
So that he may take his place in the armies of the saints,
And enter in along with the congregation of the sons of heaven.*

*And if on man falls the eternal lot to have knowledge with the spirits,
And in concert with the Spirit, to glorify Thy name,
And to record Thy wonders before the face of all Thy creations,
Then what of me, a creature of slime,
And what am I, kneaded with water?
Who am I thought to be? And what strength is there in me?
For I take my place within the borders of wickedness,
And the army of the shades is my destiny.
Also, the soul of the "poor" must dwell among torments enormous,
And in my following are the misfortunes of anguish.*

*When open the hatches of hell,
When stretched out are all the nets of wickedness,
When the barbs of the shades are on the surface of the waters,
When all the arrows of the abyss are flying, and turn not back,
When they are destroying utterly, leaving no hope,
When there falls on the abandoned of God, the line of His verdict and the lot
    of His wrath,
On the disinherited of God, the metal glowing and melted,
And on all who accept not God's yoke, His wrath that is final,
When the bonds of death surround, and leave no way of escaping,
Then shall the rivers of Belial rise in flood o'er the banks of Rome,
Like a stream devouring all that drinks of it, till every green tree is no more.*

*Their provinces will be parched, and glowing flames will spread over them,
Till all their springs of water shall run dry.
By burning pitch will they be devoured,
And be as dry as sheets of metal.
The foundations of the mountains will become a consuming fire,
And their roots of flint will turn into floods of mud,
Swallowing everything up as far as the great deep.
The rivers of Belial will split up to the Void,
And in the tumult of what the slime throws up, the phantoms of the abyss will
    raise their clamour.*

*The ground will cry out against the lesson inflicted on the world,*
*And on what has been prepared for it.*
*All upon the earth will lose courage and be mad with fear,*
*And their strength will depart from them after this great lesson,*
*And they will be in fear of God in the commotion caused by His power.*

*Also His holy dwelling-place shall be in a ferment at the truth of His Glory,*
*And the armies of Heaven will lift up their voice.*
*They shall be unnerved and tremble in the presence of the world-wide con-*
*    flagration*
*And the war of the heroes of Heaven shall spread over the earth*
*Nor will it cease till the world is wiped out and for ever destroyed?*
*And the war of the angels will end with the end of the world.*

This hymn, which has been translated in very different ways, falls into two parts. In the first part one of the "poor" is living within the borders of "wickedness" (Rome), and he makes complaint over the tortures which he has to bear. His fate is to be bound up with the country in which he dwells, and the shades (*ḥlk'ym*) form part of this fate. He knows, however, that at the hour of death he will be saved from Sheôl and will present himself in Heaven.

In the second part, the author informs us of the reason for his anguish. A part of what had been foretold (Isa. 34.9) had just come to pass. The Herodian Dynasty drew its power from Rome, but its origin was in Idumea or Edom, and thus Esau. As is well known, this term came to be applied to Rome itself, and the prophecies against Esau would therefore be fulfilled on Rome. Vesuvius had in fact spouted forth lava and covered the ground with a layer as dry as a sheet of metal. A second and more terrible disaster was going to befall Rome—here written out definitely as such. Too late, men would recognise the mightiness of God. Even the angels would tremble at the sight of the universal conflagration. They would set out to do battle with the forces of Belial, and only with the end of the world would the struggle cease.

A number of the author's beliefs are worth noting. Heaven is pictured as a vast plain upon which the elect may walk, presenting themselves from time to time before God along with the armies of the saints and angels, to glorify God, and to recite His miracles to all His creatures. There is a reference to the Spirit, perhaps the Alexandrian *Logos,* who also dwelt in the holy place. The angels could feel fear. On the other hand, the "heroes of Heaven" would go forth and fight on earth against the forces of evil, but would not be able to save the world.

As to Hell, the author puts this below the sea, following an ancient Canaanite belief taken over by the Hebrews. It was the abode of the Rephaim, those ancient heroes now reduced to mere strengthless shades. A corrupt reading in Ps. 10.8, 10, and 14 gave birth to a set of beliefs according to which the shades of the dead let barbed hooks float on the surface of the waters to catch the living. An echo of this is found here.

The author of this apocalypse should probably be looked for among the Jews of Italy. He was one of the ordinary people, and styles himself one of the "poor", and also a "wanderer", and this implies that he had been taken from his native land. The description which he gives of the eruption of Vesuvius seems to come from the pen of a well-informed person.

No plea is made in this hymn for a revolt; the most that one can read in it is an invitation to purify oneself from sin whilst awaiting the con-flagration (*ekpyrosis*) which Hippolytos mentions as one of the Jewish beliefs (*Philosophumena*, IV, 27).

The date for the composition of this apocalypse naturally falls after A.D. 79, but it may be earlier than the end of that century.

## FRAGMENT 7

SCRIBE A, COLUMN III, LINE 37, TO COLUMN IV, LINE 4.

This is a very fragmentary passage which provides no material on which any conclusions could be formed as to date, author, etc.

## FRAGMENT 8A

SCRIBE A, COLUMN IV, LINES 5-29.

> *I give Thee thanks, my Lord, because Thou hast turned my face to the light*
> *of Thy Covenant,*
> *And . . . . . . . . . . . . . . . . . . . . . I shall seek Thee.*
> *Like a true dawn, to give me enlightenment, hast Thou shone upon me.*

> *But as for Thy people, [they make mock of me.*
> *They wish for so]ngs which flatter, and [respon]ses in lying strains.*

> *They shall however stumble through their lack of understanding,*
> *For they persist in the vanity of their deeds.*

> *In themselves, they have despised me;*
> *They have not thought of me as one in whom Thy power is shown.*

*So I have been driven from my country, like a bird from its nest.*
*My friends and my family have fled from me,*
*And as a broken vessel, they consider me.*

*And they who will not bear God's yoke*
*From me have sought for lying songs and visions false,*
*That turning from Thy law, which Thou hast hidden in my heart,*
*I should use flatteries towards Thy people:*

*From the parchèd, they have held back the waters of knowledge,*
*And for those who are athirst, they pour out the purple wine*
*To induce them to walk in their follies,*
*To lose their reason in their festivals,*
*And to be taken in their nets.*

*But Thou, O God, wilt cast away all the designs of Belial,*
*And it is Thy counsel which will arise,*
*And the plans of Thy heart which will remain fixed for ever.*

*And they, the abandoned, they elaborate the plans of Belial;*
*They ask of Thee, but with a double mind,*
*And they have not found in Thy truth the root that puts poison and worm-*
*   wood in their plans,*
*For their searching is with stubborn mind.*

*With amulets they ask of Thee,*
*And the stumbling-block of their sins have they set before their faces.*

*They come and question Thee through the mouth of lying prophets, seducers*
*   full of craft,*
*Who with barbarous speech and a foreign tongue speak to Thy people,*
*Making them senseless by the corruption of all their deeds.*

*For they have not followed Thy law, nor listened to Thy words.*
*When knowledge is revealed, they say, "It is not true."*
*And of the ways of Thy heart, "That shall not be."*

*But Thou, O God, wilt reply to them, and wilt judge them by Thy power,*
*Along with all their amulets and the multitude of their abominations,*
*For they are taken in their own devices, they who turned away from Thy*
*   covenant,*
*And they have not yet discovered that extermination is the fate of all deceitful*
*   men and of all false visionaries.*

*But there is no folly in any of Thy works,*
*Nor any corruption in the purposes of Thy heart.*
*They who conduct themselves in accordance with Thy soul,*
*Shall stand before Thy face for ever,*
*And those who walk in the way of Thy heart,*
*Shall live for evermore.*

*And I, when the griefs which tear my soul are over,*
*I shall rise above my reproach, and my hands will be upon those who despised me.*
*For they had not thought of me [as the serv]ant in whom Thy power was*
*    shown.*

*[They have not believed] that Thou by Thy power didst give me light, so*
*    that I might enlighten them.*
*But Thou hast not plastered with shame the face of all who seek my ruin*
*Who [\* in union] set themselves against Thy Covenant.*

*They shall listen to me, those who walk in the way of Thy heart,*
*And they shall muster themselves in ranks for Thee.*
*The verdict concerning them will be set forth in the council of the saints and for*
*    ever:*
*The promise of the plain of Truth will be for them, and Thou wilt not let*
*    them fall into the hands of the shades who long for them.*
*Thou wilt set their "venerable" over Thy people,*
*And Thou shalt give destruction to all the peoples of foreign lands,*
*Breaking in pieces by a judgement all who transgress the words of Thy mouth.*
*Also by me Thou shalt make the face of many to shine, and thus show Thy*
*    might in a manner unthought-of.*
*For Thou hast taught me the hidden meaning of Thy miracles,*
*And it is with the secret of Thy miracles that Thou wilt show forth by me*
*    Thy power.*
*I shall perform miracles in the eyes of many,*
*For the love of Thy glory, and to make known Thy praise to every living*
*    creature.*

What should one think of this very curious hymn? The author tells us his history. He regards himself as one enlightened by God, and commissioned to preach the true religion, but men do not believe in him. He has been driven out of the country. He is considered as a man no longer of any account, and his family and his friends avoid him. His visions are regarded as delusions, and his prophecies as lies. At the time of writing, he is living far away, but the time will come when his tears will be dried. He will find disciples among his former detractors, who, swallowing their pride, will come and take their stand along with him. They will be destined for everlasting life. Himself, their "venerable" (*mwr'*, which may be a slip in writing for *mwrh* or Teacher), will be advanced to the rank of leader of the people of God, and with the help of divine power which would be revealed in him, he will be able to destroy all foreign nations and perform miracles in the eyes of the crowd.

What can we gather about his detractors? They did not believe in him, had driven him from the country, but apparently had not put him in prison nor tortured him. Leaving aside the epithets which he applied to his opponents, we can see them as persons loving to be flattered, and knowing how to flatter the crowd. They prevented people from acquiring knowledge, and propagated only their own particular teachings, and they themselves fixed the dates of festivals. It can therefore be taken that it is a question of the rabbis of the Pharisees, with whom the author did not agree over their system of drawing up the calendar. Another reproach that he makes is that they are inconsistent in their interpretation of the Law, have an absolute lack of sincerity, and do not perceive that the interpretation of a text might result in "poison and wormwood". This metaphor is taken from a story related further on in VIII, 4-15. He makes the further approach that they use amulets in place of phylacteries (*tephilin*) the use of which, according to the interpretation of Deut. 6.8-9, goes back to remote antiquity. As a matter of fact, the wording of phylacteries had been the subject of very strict legislation, and the rabbis termed "amulets and abominations" any phylacteries which did not absolutely conform with their directions, and, as certain irregular phylacteries found at Qumrân show, they were sometimes seized and consigned to *genizoth*. It will be understood that dissident rabbis took another view. Finally, the author says these rabbis spoke a barbarous and foreign language. This can only mean either Greek, current in Egypt, or Aramaic, the use of which was tolerated in the synagogues of Syria and Mesopotamia.

The last point leads us to place the author of this pamphlet—for it is that more than a hymn—in the Diaspora and not in Palestine. Now, in the period with which we are dealing, the only rabbinic authority in the Diaspora which could fix the date of feasts and, above all, declare someone a false prophet and drive him into exile was the Great Sanhedrin of Babylon. From A.D. 130 to about 150 it sat at Nahar Paqôd, and it was

L

the only recognised Jewish authority. As is well known, after that, Rabbi Simon III, and, following him, Rabbi Yehuda, re-established the Palestinian Sanhedrin, which continued until A.D. 210. Then the Babylonian Sanhedrin was again formed, and till the end of the Middle Ages it exercised its authority over the Jewish world. We can thus find indications as to the date of this curious text. It must have been written shortly after the defeat of Bar Kochba, perhaps early in the reign of Antoninus Pius. About this time there were a number of small risings, all in the Diaspora, where it was believed that Bar Kochba was a false messiah, but that it still remained to discover the true one.

No definitely unorthodox tendency can be recognised in the author of this piece of writing. One can see that he was not just one of the ordinary people, for he never styles himself "poor", and his views of the Beyond are not markedly those of popular belief. No mention is made of angels and demons, and the opposition is centred in false prophets and false interpreters of the Scriptures. Nor can he have been a Zadokite, for he believed in eternal life beyond the grave. In certain respects he appears orthodox, as Palestinian rabbis regarded orthodoxy, when he reproaches rabbis for their studies and sermons in a barbarous tongue. It is known that for a long time Palestinian rabbis allowed only Hebrew to be used in synagogues and academies, whilst in Mesopotamia Aramaic was in current use. This would lead us to suppose that probably the author had originally belonged to rabbinic circles in Palestine, but that after the defeat of A.D. 135 he had settled in Syria or Mesopotamia. A number of practices different from what he had known must have shocked him. Perhaps he had wanted to set up a separatist rabbinic school, and had been excommunicated. Did he think that he himself was the true Messiah? In any case, he hoped to be the leader of the people, to perform miracles, and to avenge himself upon his detractors. For the present, that is as much as can be said about him.

Our author was not the only person who wanted to be the Messiah. It is related in the *Tractate Sanhedrin* (94A) that this wish was expressed by Hiskiya the Pious. The angel ruler of this world was willing that this wish should be realised, but the Voice of Heaven opposed it.

## FRAGMENT 8B

SCRIBE A, COLUMN IV, LINES 29–40 . . .

*To magnify Thy miracles, what is a creature of flesh like this, a creature made of slime?*

*It abides in sin even from the bosom of its mother, and till its old age it commits*
*guilty deeds.*

*I know that in the human being righteousness does not exist,*
*And that with the son of man there is no rightness of way.*

*Acts of righteousness belong to God Most High,*
*And human paths cannot be made straight.*

*It is only by the spirit, which God has made for man,*
*That the paths of the sons of man may be straightened,*
*That they may know His acts performed by the power of His might,*
*And the multitudes of His kindnesses towards the "Sons of His Will".*

*As for me, trembling and fright have taken hold of me,*
*My bones break, and my heart melts like wax before the fire,*
*And my knees are as water, slipping down a slope.*
*For I remembered my sins, and the faithlessness of my fathers,*
*When sinners set themselves against Thy Covenant.*

*In the hour when shadows are upon the pool I said,*
*"In my sins, I departed from Thy Covenant,"*
*But as I remembered the Might of Thy hand and the streams of Thy mercies,*
*I stood once more erect.*

*I will arise, and my spirit will be fortified, as I take my stand and confront*
*the torturer,*
*For I have made Thy graciousness my support, and the streams of Thy mercies.*
*Moreover, Thou wilt pardon sin, and for the im[pure there will be . . .*
*. . .] from his guilt through Thine acts of righteousness.*

*It is not for man whom Thou hast made . . . . . . . . .*
*For Thou didst create the just and the unjust . . . . . . . . .*
*I will strengthen me in Thy Covenant as long as . . . . . . . . .*
*[And I shall bl]ess Thee, for Thou art the Truthful One and righteous are*
*all . . . . . . . . .*

It is at once clear that this passage does not belong to the preceding one, although it is not separated from it by any *alinea*. We are far from the self-styled prophet who vilified his opponents, and who hoped one day to perform miracles. Here we have an apostate who returns from his apostasy. He puts forth an excuse for his sin, his flesh is born in sin, and he cannot know where truth is to be found. But one day he remembered how he had strayed, and his fathers before him, and he returned to God's Covenant. Now he will stand firm even when he faces the torturers, "when the barbs of the shades are floating on the surface of the pools" (cf. III, 26).

It is difficult to place the author of this text. Perhaps we should seek him among the Zadokites, whose ideas he shared. The idea of original sin is clearly expressed. Eternal life is not mentioned in this passage. As to date, it may be placed between the first and third centuries A.D., a period when apostate Jews who returned to their former faith were often persecuted.

## FRAGMENT 9

SCRIBE A, COLUMN V, LINES 1-4.

This fragment, consisting mostly of disconnected words and phrases, could easily be the conclusion of the foregoing prayer. It presents nothing that is new.

## FRAGMENT 10

SCRIBE A, COLUMN V, LINES 5-19.

*I give Thee thanks, my God, that Thou hast not abandoned me during my
    sojourn in a strange land,
And in the midst of a people . . . . . . . . . .*

*According to my transgressions judge me,
    And leave me not to the designs of those who afflict me.
Thou wilt save my life from the Pit,
    And Thou wilt bring me [help in my distress.
For they have pla]ced me in the midst of lions—
    The delight in the festivals for the sons of guiltiness—
And among the lionesses who break the bones of the stalwarts,
    And drink the blood of the valiant.*

*Thou hast put me in a strange land, among a multitude of fishermen who
    stretch their nets upon the waters' face,
And of hunters who serve the sons of iniquity.*

*The secret of the Truth, or at least of Thy Covenant,
    Thou hast strengthened in my heart that I may ask of it.
Therefore Thou wilt stop the mouth of the beasts, whose teeth are as swords,
And whose claws are as spears, sharpened in the dragons' fire.
Their one desire is to tear in pieces,
But though they are many, yet they will not open their jaws upon me,*

*For Thou, my God, wilt hide me from the sons of man, as Thy law is
concealed [within me,
Until the] final moment when Thou shalt show forth that Thou wilt save me.
For in the anguish of my soul Thou hast not abandoned me.
Thou didst hear my crying, forced from the bitterness of my soul,
Whilst the sufferings which they did inflict on me
Thou didst remove as soon as I gave voice to my yearning.*

*Even so wilt Thou save the soul of the poor in the den of lions,
   Whose tongues are sharpened like to swords.
Thou, my God, shalt close their jaws lest their teeth
   Tear in pieces the soul of the poor and the needy,
And Thou shalt reduce to naught their tongue which resembles the sword.
It shall not be made bare, unless [Thou hast given ov]er the soul of Thy
   servant.*

*For it is to show forth Thy power in me before the eyes of the sons of man
That Thou shalt perform a miracle upon the poor.
Thou shalt cause him to enter the refining fur[nace,
   And Thou shalt submit him] to the action of the fire,
And he shall be like silver seven times refined in the smith's furnace.*

*And so the sinners in their might do fling themselves upon me,
   And with their tortures all day long, do they assail my soul.
But Thou, my God, dost change my soul from storm to gentle breeze,
   And the soul of the poor, Thou shalt save it . . . . . . from the torment
      of tearing by lions.*

This prayer, one of the most beautiful of the collection, appears to be
the work of a prisoner in the hands of the Romans, who, in his cell, is
waiting to be thrown to the beasts in the arena. As he says, these "games"
were the delight of the Romans. Around him he can only see gladiators,
the *retiarii* and the *bestiarii*. The former fought with nets like fishermen,
and the words "upon the waters' face" are probably an interpolation due
to confusion with the shades who fished for living souls (cf. III, 26, IV,
35). The *bestiarii* were reserved for the chase, the *venatio* (see p. 263), the
combat with wild beasts. He hopes that God will perform a miracle and
save him for in the depths of his heart he has maintained his faithfulness
to the Covenant, to the Jewish law.

But the prisoner also thinks of those in the country living in the midst of people whose tongues are as sharp as lions' teeth, and who with them can cause much harm. Even as God will perform a miracle on his behalf, so He will preserve the poor exposed to these calumnies. The poem ends with the metaphor of the refiner's furnace.

In spite of the mention of the "poor", for whom he is concerned, one cannot be sure that the author came from a Zealot environment. In this poem there is no mention of the Beyond, nor are other phrases used which are typical of some well-defined circle. The author probably was not a Christian, and it would seem in all likelihood that he was a native of Palestine. The date of the composition can be put down to any time under the Roman domination after A.D. 70, when many Jewish prisoners were thrown to the beasts, "to make a Roman holiday".

## FRAGMENT 11

SCRIBE A, COLUMN V, LINES 19-39 . . .
Blessèd be Thou.

I give Thee thanks my Lord, for Thou hast not abandoned the orphan and hast not despised the needy.
For Thy might is . . . and Thy glory is beyond measure.
Marvellous heroes serve Thee, and the people of lowly origin are in the dust of Thy feet.

[However] those people, the crazed about "Justice", [go on] making deceitful burnt-offerings
In company with all the destroyers of the poor who keep faith.

In the eyes of the C[ouncil of the Presump]tuous, I have become a person of discord,
To "The Friends of Zeal", a stumbling-block,
And even to those who pledged themselves with me, a cause of murmuring,
And to those who flocked and [. . . who had ea]ten my bread, a source of agitation.

They kick at me, and with their wicked lips they blaspheme me.
All those who were attached to my secrets, and the men of my [party]
They revolt and spread murmurs around.

Because with me the cake is plain, they go with their scandals to the "sons of ambition",
And because they love to be big, [they depart from] my way.

*Yet because of their guiltiness, from their eyes is hidden the understanding and
   meaning of truth,*
*For the longings of their hearts are like the . . . of Belial.*
*They have put out a lying tongue which, like to the poison of dragons, increases
   to infinite limits,*
*And like the reptiles of dust, they pour out hiss[ings and behave like] vipers
   which nothing can charm from their stinging.*

*If the human being is destined to pain and to tortures,*
   *I shall bear them in myself.*
*I will serve Thee in making [the wicked] to stumble, and in putting an end to
   violence, taking all its strength from its foundations.*
*And even if they deport me to the "land of anguish" so that no way of escaping
   remains,*
*And though there was only slavery in the exile which they impose,*
*Though with their discordant citherns they raise uproar,*
*And accompany their instruments with howlings,*
*Though the wasting and wrecking of the sand-storm [pursues me]*
*And pains like the labours of childbirth assail me,*
*I shall clothe my heart in black, and my tongue shall cleave to the roof of my
   mouth,*
*[All the time that they blas]pheme, [in the falseness] of their hearts*
*And whilst their fabrication makes me blush with bitterness*
*And shadows darken the light of my face,*
*And my renown is o'erthrown so that it may come to an end.*

*Thou, my God, didst place great comfort in my heart,*
   *And by anxiety, they have brought it to naught.*
*They have shut and fenced me in with a deadly anguish.*
*They feed me with the bread of lying,*
*And give as drink, my tears which never cease.*
*Mine eyes are dim with grief, and with the bitterness of the days my soul is
   sick.*
*Cares surround me, for detestation is seen in their faces.*
*They make of me the f[oo]d of discord and the drink of dissension for the
   "Lord of Strife".*
*He has entered into their councils to make the spirit falter, and take away all
   strength.*

*By their guiltiness, the mystery of sin redoubles the power of deeds of vanity.*

*They have imprisoned me in chains that cannot be broken and in fetters that
    cannot be smashed.*
*Mighty walls [surround me,] with iron bolts and gates . . . . .*
*. . . . . . . . . like the deep from which no one can escape . . . . . .*
*. . . . . . . . . of Belial, they have put around my soul . . . . . . . . .*
*. . . . . . . . .*

The text found here comes from a heretic, and is contrary to all the
chief currents of Judaism. The writer has a special grudge against the
Zadokites, "those crazy about 'Justice' " and filled with presumption, but
neither did he reckon among his friends "the Friends of Zeal" (Zealots)
nor the rabbis with their schools and alliances. Perhaps he himself had
wanted to form a school, but his disciples, "who had eaten his bread",
left him because "the cake was plain". They had therefore joined the
"sons of ambition" (Zadokites) and spoken calumnies against him. The
author gives the impression of being imprisoned at the hands of the
Zadokites, and of an attempt being made to convert him by certain
mysteries which he considers abominable. Rather than being in the power
of the Lord of Strife, he prefers to be handed over to the Romans and
deported to the "country of anguish", where he would be able to give
an example of stoicism under his sufferings. (The phrase about his
tongue cleaving to the roof of his mouth indicates that he would become
"dumb".)

Naturally, we should avoid seeing an allusion to Egypt in the word
*mṣrym,* which at this period was translated "country of anguish" and
meant Rome.

The author of this prayer should be looked for in the Diaspora perhaps
at Damascus, where the Zadokites seem to have been fairly influential.
The text would come from the years following Bar Kochba's defeat.

## FRAGMENT 12

SCRIBE A, COLUMN VI, LINES 1–36 . . .

(The first few lines are missing or are very fragmentary. We commence
with line 5.)

*. . . Thou hast [kept me apart] from the congregation of the [wick]ed, and
    from the council of the violent,*
*And Thou hast made me to enter into the covenant of the . . . . . . . . .*
    *[who flee from the] . . . and guilt.*

I shall know therefore that there is hope for those who turn from sin and
abandon crime,
Making themselves to . . . . . . . . . to walk in the way of Thine heart
wherein is no iniquity.
And I shall comfort myself from the tumult of the people and the blarings
of roy[al]ty and its "pick-ups".

I shall know also who those are whom Thou shalt lift up from their lowliness,
From among the living of Thy people and the remnant of Thy heritage,
In order that Thou shalt re-cast them, and refine them from their guilt.

All their doings conform to Thy truth, and it is by Thy kindnesses that Thou
wilt judge them,
With streams of mercy and abundance of pardon.
According to Thy sayings, they should be instructed,
And in consequence of the integrity of Thy truth, they should be placed in
Thy council.

It is for Thy glory, and for Thine own sake, that Thou hast caused . . . the
Law, and that . . . . . . . . . .
. . . men of Thy council in the midst of the Sons of Man to relate for ever
Thy miracles,
And that they . . . Thy mighty acts which cannot be denied.
Thus shall all peoples know Thy truth, and all nations Thy glory.

Thou shalt bring into [the presence] of Thy glory, all the men of Thy council,
Whose lot is to be united with the Angels of the Presence.
But not one of the sons of flattery shall draw [near . . . . . . . . . .] dug,
because . . . . . . .
They have turned away from the word of Thy glory, shall become the leavings
in the portion of . . .

[They are the bush] which grows like the thorn . . . . [for ever] and ever,
Sending out branches to bring darkness on all the world's planting,
And to cover with shade all that [which is seeking the light.
It will grow] so far that . . . . . . . its roots reach down to the deeps, and to
all the rivers of Eden.

It will become . . . . . . which digs . . . . . . on the earth without
stopping, and even as far as to Sheôl . . .
But there will be a source of light, near the everlasting fountain which runs not dry.
Glowing flames shall burn all B[elial . . . . . . . . . .] in the burning fire,
Along with all the men of guilt till all shall be destroyed.

L*

*But those attached to my testimonies, by their de[eds] shall persuade . . .*
*. . . . . . to worship of righteousness.*

*Thou, O God, hast commanded them to profit by their paths in the ways of*
*hol[iness,*
*To avoid the apos]tate, the uncircumcised, the impure and the violent,*
*Lest they turn themselves back, and depart from the way of Thine heart,*
*For it is in covetousness that . . . . . . . languish, and the counsels of*
*Belial are in their hearts.*
*[They invent] plans of wickedness and wallow in guiltiness.*

*[But I am full of ca]re, like the pilot in a bark*
    *When the seas and their waves are wild,*
*And all their breakers growl at me [with] wind that makes me stagger.*
*[Change the storm to] gentle breeze, and rescue the soul of him, adrift on the*
*face of the waters,*
*For the deep growls in reply to my sighs, and I am arrived at the gateways of*
*death.*

*But though I am only some refuse in the city of anguish (Maṣôr)*
*I shall be set in safety, with a wall made high to protect me,*
*And I shall be sa[ved by] Thy truth, my God.*
*Thou dost place a footing on the rock, a beam on the line of judgement, and a*
*buttress . . . . . . . . . .*
*[But Thou dost also set] a stumbling-block for those whom Thou wouldst*
*pr[ove,*
*Giving] strength to those who should not tremble, and to all those who enter*
*that they waver not.*

*But a stranger shall not enter . . . . . . . . .*
*[It is closed] with gates like bucklers, so there is no way of entry,*
*And with bolts, strong past all breaking,*
*Lest a band should break in with its weapons of war, and all the wasting*
*accompaniments of sinful strife.*

*Should that happen, then God's sword will hasten to the final judgement,*
*And all the sons of His truth shall wake, to . . . and to put an end to evil,*
*While the sons of guilt will be no more.*
*The hero shall direct his bow, and the city of anguish shall open.*
*[Anguish will give way] to a fulness without measure,*
*And through the gates of the world will be brought out the weapons of war.*

*[Angels] shall take counsel together at the farthest borders of Eden,*
*. . . . the idol of abomination to exterminate it*
*They shall tread it under foot, so that naught remains.*
*[There shall be no] hope [whatever] in the crowd [of warriors,]*
*And for all the mighty men of war there will be no way of flight.*
*Because it is to God Most High that belongs the [victory . . . .]*

*Those asleep in the dust shall lift themselves up like a flagstaff,*
*And the risen from the dead shall raise up a signal . . . .. . . ...*
*In the wars of the faithless and renegade, scourge shall spread so that into the*
  *citadel there shall not enter . . . . .. . ...*
*. . . .. . . to plaster, and like a beam which does not . . . . . .*

In spite of its length and the diversity of the subjects with which it treats, this is a single work of writing from the hand of one author. It consists of fragments, but these are skilfully put together to form a single whole.

The author begins by thanking God for having caused him to avoid certain "congregations" and "councils", probably Zadokite lodges and rabbinic schools, and, further for having led him to join the society of the "Sons of Man". This sect, as removed from the ordinary people as from royalty and its "pick-ups" (procurators), taught that God would choose His elect among the humble when they had been instructed by the sect's preachers. The mission of these extended to all peoples, in spite of the recommendation to avoid apostates and heathen. It does not say how these two conflicting conditions can be reconciled, but it may be that the second condition was an interpolation by the copyist.

An attack against the "flatterers", the Pharisees, is embellished by a pretty legend, but unfortunately only fragments of it have survived. There have already been several allusions to it (IV, 14), and further on in Column VIII another and more developed version is given. The legend seems to have been based partly on the fable of the trees seeking a king (Judges 9.8-15), and partly on the parable in Ezekiel (17.3-10, 31.3-15). Here the word for thorn (ṣyn) is taken from Prov. 22.5. Echoes of this legend are also found in *1 Enoch*. It deals with trees growing in the Garden of Eden. The author compares the opportunists (mlyṣ bnym) with the thorn whose branches keep out the light instead of only providing an agreeable coolness. The roots of their plants reach as far as Sheôl, threatening to dry up all the rivers of Eden. Near the fountain of life, however, there is also a spring which ejects flames, and these will consume all those (the Belials) who do not submit to the yoke of God.

Then the author takes up the simile of the pilot in his boat, with the soul in the midst of tempests, but he does not use it to recall a recent cataclysm (cf. III, 6). He concludes by calling to mind the Last Judgement: the dead will come forth from their tombs to join God's host, which will destroy the infidels and their idol; plague will rage in the army of the blasphemers and renegades; and the gates of the universe will open so that all the weapons of war may be driven away.

The picture which the author draws for himself of the Beyond is worthy of notice. His paradise is somewhere in the extreme parts of Eden. It is there that are found "The Angels of the Presence" (cf. Isa. 63.9). Allusions to this belief are found in apocryphal books (*Jubilees* 1.27, 2.1ff.; *Testament of Judah* 25; *1 Enoch* 40.2), and in rabbinic literature. The author believes in the resurrection of the body and thinks that the dead will come forth from their graves to join with the host of angels who will go out to fight at the Last Judgement.

The author seems more concerned with the fellow members of his religion who lives as "refuse" in *Maṣôr* (Rome) than with those who dwell elsewhere in God's heritage. Above all, he anticipates that God and the angels will direct their shafts against Rome, and the anguish (*maṣôr*) will come to an end. One concludes that he was living in the Diaspora, probably in Rome itself. In any case, there is nothing to suggest that this text was written in Palestine. The author may have been born there, and may have emigrated voluntarily before A.D. 66. The mention of royalty and the "pick-ups" would suggest that the hymn dates from the time of Agrippa II (cf. *Manual of Discipline*, X, 1). It may be neccessary to regard this hymn as the work of a Jewish-Christian, but it is hard to say if the writer was already converted to Christianity before he arrived in Italy. The fact that the Zadokites and the Pharisees had tried to win him over to their parties shows that he could only have left Palestine after he was of an age to choose for himself. That would also suggest that his conversion took place after he had arrived in Rome. He may have escaped the Neronian persecution.

## FRAGMENT 13

SCRIBE A, COLUMN VII, LINES 1-5.

  . . . . . . . . . *I myself have become dumb* . . . . . . . . .
[. . . *my arm*] *gives way in its socket,*
*My feet sink into the mire,*
*My eyes are blinded by the sight of evil,*

*My ears are deafened by the news of bloodshed,*
*And my heart is terrified by the projects they proclaim.*

*For in the radiance of the statue of their beasts is Belial,*
*And they bellow, all those who assail my firm foundation.*
*My bones fall apart, and shake within me*
*Like a boat caught in the fury of an eastern gale.*
*My heart longs for death, and my head turns,*
*And makes me totter before their insatiable sins.*

This fragment can hardly have any connection with the preceding passage. It must be supposed that we have here the ending of a hymn of which the beginning is missing.

Except for the picture, so frequently employed, of the storm-tossed vessel, and the reference to Roman ensigns, "the statues of their beasts", this fragment supplies nothing to indicate its date. The context is missing of the word *n'lmty* ("I have become dumb"), so one cannot assume that the author was a Zealot who bore his tortures in silence. The hymn appears to refer to threats of persecution, the date of which cannot be ascertained. It is possible that the author lived in Italy.

## FRAGMENT 14

SCRIBE A, COLUMN VII, LINES 6-25.

*I give Thee thanks, my Lord, for Thou hast upheld me by Thy power,*
*And hast breathed into me Thy holy spirit, so that I should not waver.*

*Thou dost make me strong to meet the warring of the wicked,*
*And in spite of all their evil desires, Thou hast not disowned Thy covenant.*

*Thou hast placed me to be a strong tower, and a steep wall,*
*And on a rock my building Thou hast fixed.*

*The pillars of the universe serve me for foundations,*
*And all my walls are tested ramparts,*
*So I have no cause to tremble.*

*Thou, my God, hast set me to be a branch in Thy holy Council (=tree),*
*Thou hast . . . me . . . to . . . of Thy Covenant,*
*And, moreover, my tongue conforms to Thy Precepts.*

*In me therefore is no mouth to reply to the spirit of covetousness,*

*No tongue to reply to the sons of guilt,*
*And my lips must be dumb, nor speak in lying tongues.*

*For those who drag to judgement, Thou dost declare them guilty,*
*To mark me out clearly, the just from the unjust.*
*For Thou, who knowest all the works of Creation,*
*Thou hast destroyed every tongue that makes answer,*
*But Thou dost establish my heart.*

*Following in Thy teaching and in Thy truth, towards uprightness go my*
    *steps,*
*Steps made for the paths of righteousness and to walk before Thee,*
*Within the circle of the world, and in the ways of glory, [* and of life],*[1]
*And of that infinite peace, which ends not for ever and ever.*

*Thou who dost know Thy servant's frame,*
*Dost know that not [on sons of man do I re]ly to lift me up*
*Nor seek for strength in their brute force.*
*The refuges of flesh do not exist for me,*
*[For I know . . . and that] there is no justice which can save*
*When be[fore him who has n]o pardon.*

*I stay me therefore on [Thy mercy and on the multitude] of Thy favours*
*Grant that they may be apportioned for the protection and greatness of the*
    *Branch*
*So that he may be made strong by the power . . . . . . . . .*
*[In] Thy righteousness, lift me towards Thy Covenant,*
*And I shall comply with Thy Truth.*

*And Thou, . . . . . . . . . set me up as father for the "Sons of Good*
    *Deeds",*
*And as foster-parent for the men who serve the sign.*
*Others will open their mouths like a suckling [who is dumbfounded]*
*And will wonder like a little child in the lap of his nurse.*

*Thus wilt Thou lift up my horn above those who blaspheme me,*
*They will be . . . . . . . . . . by my footmen and archers,*
*And like the chaff before the wind.*

*Thou wilt make me to reign over the s[ons of Thy people . . . . . . .]*
*Thou wilt succour my soul, and lift up my horn on high.*
*Sevenfold will be the light of Thy truth upon me*

[1] Erased, but still faintly legible.

*Be[cause of . . . that Thou wilt have . . .] for Thy glory.*
*Thou art for me the Light eternal,*
*And Thou wilt make firm my foot in . . . . . .*

Like the author of Hymn 8A, the writer of this hymn considers himself a man inspired. Like him, he desires to reign, and though up to the present he has put no confidence in man, yet he certainly hopes that having attained power he will be able to destroy his detractors with the help of his troops.

He declares that he is attached to his own language, Hebrew, but it is a poor play on words that he makes on "council", '*ṣt,* and "tree", '*ṣ.* In any case, he affirms that his lips are silent when he has to make use of "tongues of lying" in replying to wrongdoers. Although he is certainly not a Zealot, yet he becomes a "mute", for he knows that his uprightness has no chance of being recognised before human justice which lacked clemency. God, however, can recognise His own, and He will declare guilty those who excuse themselves in a foreign tongue, so that all those who speak foreign languages will in the end be destroyed.

The author should be sought for in a Zadokite environment in Palestine. Nowhere is there any mention of the Beyond. What he hoped for was glory, life and power on earth. (The word "life" was afterwards erased.) He belonged to a lodge named "The Sons of Good Deeds" (*bny ḥsd*). He hoped to be named "father" in this society, and to astonish everybody— by his miracles? Perhaps he even thought of himself as The Branch, *nṣr,* foretold in Isa. 11.1, as Israel's Messiah.

The date of this hymn falls certainly after A.D. 70, and probably after A.D. 135, like Hymn 8A, with which it presents certain resemblances.

## FRAGMENT 15

SCRIBE A, COLUMN VII, LINES 26-32 . . .

*I [give Thee thanks, my Lord,] because Thou hast instructed me in Thy truth*
*And hast made known to me the secrets of Thy miracles.*

*By Thy acts of kindness towards the man . . . . . .*
*And by Thy mercies towards him whose heart is shaking.*

*Who is like to Thee among the divinities, my Lord?*
*And what can be compared to Thy truth?*
*And who can appear [just] before Thee when he is judged?*

*There is no going back on Thy decisions about any inspiration [\* and
    commandment],*[1]
*And no one can take his stand before Thy wrath.*

*But all the sons of Thy truth (or of Thy handmaid) [\* Thou dost make
    enter]*[1] *with pardons before Thy face*
*[To absolve them] from their sin through the multitudes of Thy favours and the
    streams of Thy mercies,*
*So that they may stand before Thee through all eternity.*

*For Thou art the God of the Universe.*
*All Thy ways have been fixed for ever and ever,*
*And there is none beside Thee.*

*What is man, shapeless and master of nothing,*
*To be able to understand the works of Thy wonders . . . . . .*

This prayer seems to come from the same sect, "Sons of Truth" (or
"of the Truthful"), to which the author of Hymn 12 belonged. This
Christian sect had members in the Diaspora, most probably in Italy. The
author seems to be a recent convert, but the fact must never be overlooked
that a number of hymns were written for use by certain persons, and that,
like the Psalms, they might be attributed to certain authors who would
have composed them under the given circumstances and situations. The
person presented as the author of a text is not necessarily the one who
wrote it.

Apart from a degree of determinism, frequent in these poems, one notes
that the emphasis is on God's Judgement. The "Sons of Truth" will profit
from divine clemency: their sins will be absolved and for eternity. Our text
does not say whether the Abode of the Blessèd is in Eden or in Heaven.

The date and place of origin of this hymn cannot be established, except
within very wide limits. It can be supposed that the author lived towards
the end of the first century A.D. and perhaps in Italy.

## FRAGMENT 16

Scribe A, Column VII, Lines 34-6.

*[I give Thee th]anks, my Lord,*

*For Thou hast not made my lot to fall within the Congregation of nothingness*
` (or, of vanity)`

---

[1] Words inserted between the lines.

*Nor placed my destiny within the Council of those who act in secret* (or, of the
cunning).
*Thou wilt . . . by Thy goodness and by Thy pardon,*
*And by the streams of Thy mercies towards those who will be judged by . . .*
*. . . . . . iniquity, and in the bosom . . . . .*

COLUMN VIII, LINE 2.

*. . . . . . . . . Thy righteousness is fixed for ever, for Thou hast*
*not . . . . . . . . .*

A note of determinism can be seen in these small fragments, which are
clearly anti-Zadokite. They are too fragmentary to supply any information as to date and place of origin.

## FRAGMENT 17

SCRIBE A, COLUMN VIII, LINES 4-41.

*I [give Thee thanks my Lord,*
*For Thou] hast placed me near the spring of waters flowing in the dry plain,*
*Near to the fountain from which flows water for the parchèd earth,*
*And [hast made me to see] the streams which water the Garden of Eden.*

*[And there, there is a] plantation of yews,*
*Of pines and cypresses also, and solely for Thy glory.*

*The trees of life, at a spring of mystery, are hidden in the midst of all aquatic trees.*
*They had been destined to send forth a shoot for the plantation of the world,*
*And to take root there, before flowering.*

*Their roots should have grown forth until they reached the channel*
*Which should have opened out for the living waters,*
*And the stock of the shoot should have become the fountain for the world.*
*The shoots of its branches should have fed the [beasts] of the forest,*
*The fallings from its trunk, which are trodden underfoot,*
*Should have been eaten by the creatures which pass by,*
*And its boughs should have been food for the fowls of the air.*

*But all aquatic trees, they rose against this plan.*
*They wished in their plantation to make the shoot to grow,*
*And towards the water-channel, no roots have they sent forth.*
*Thus hidden is the shoot which flowered for the planting of truth.*
*No one now may see it, and its secret is sealed beyond man's understanding.*

*All has been enclosed because of its fruits, by "the mighty in power", by "the spirits of holiness".*
*A glowing fire throws flames around, for fear [that someone might approach the] source of life,*
*For if eternal trees drink not of holy water, there is fear that their fruit will be hollow, and [their seeds turn] to dust.*

*Likewise he who sees, but does not understand,*
*He who believes in the source of life, but is not convinced,*
*He shall be given over . . . . . . . eternal.*
*But I, I have been right to the secret rivers which flow abundantly,*
*And behold, they spilt on me their slime.*

*Thou, my God, hast placed in the mouth of man,*
*What is like the early rain for every . . .*
*And like a spring of living waters.*

*And men should not become deceivers, and open the . . . which give not way,*
*If it is not to become an overflowing river, the . . . of water and seas without . . . .*
*Suddenly the streams pour out what they keep hidden in the secret of . . .*
*. . . . . . .*
*They become [torrents of fire, devouring each] green tree,*
*So that there dries out—an abyss for every living thing,*
*And a . . . . . . . . . . of lead, by the mighty waters.*
*[The plants of the fields] wither in the fire, and the orchards . . . . . . . . .*
*. . . universal, because of Eden, a glory of . . .*

*And by the hand with which Thou wilt have opened all their springs, the people of their provinces,*
*Thou, the . . . . . . . to present itself before the destined measuring line of judgement,*
*And the plantations of their trees upon the balances of the sun so that . . . . . .*
*[For its trees have provided the leaves] for their garlands of glory,*
*(Plaited) by those who make signs with the hand.*
*To undermine its provinces (Italy) its roots will strike the granite rocks,*
*And their trunks . . . . . . . . . . . . upon the ground.*

*In the age of darkness, divine help will be held back,*
*And if I stretch out my hand, it will be like a m[ist.*
*The] . . . of its trunk will be as thorns in a desert of salt,*

*And its provinces will be covered with brambles and thorns.*
*[The fruit] of his lips will turn to sour grapes,*
*Before the heat, his branches shall wither,*
*And it will not open with . . . . . . . . .*

*[But I have] my dwelling with the afflicted,*
*And the . . . has been fixed for me in the midst of the ills which shall strike*
  *them.*
*I have to live like a man abandoned in . . . . . . . . .*
*There is no help for me, for my . . . lies open to the tribulations.*
*Man suffers, and there can be no holding back.*
*. . . . . . . . . over me like over those who go down to Sheôl?*
*And the people of the dead lie in wait on my breath,*
*For they have worn out, even to the grave . . . . . . . . .*
*My soul droops day and night, and finds no comforter.*

*And should an eruption come to pass like glowing fires held in . . .*
*. . . . . . it will devour to the end of all time.*
*Thou hast decided to destroy violence completely,*
*And make an end of flesh until appointed ages.*
*The [shafts] will fly from the openings of death,*
*And my soul shall bow itself down before it ceases to be.*
*For my body, all help is at an end,*
*My heart flows away like water,*
*Any my flesh melts like to wax.*

*The fortress in which I was placed,*
*Is devoted to utter destruction.*
*My arm lies shattered in its joint,*
*[And I am captive] of those who sign with the hand.*
*In prison and in fetters have they put me.*
*My knees are weak as water,*
*In no way can I stretch out my foot,*
*Nor take a step to ease my legs.*
*. . . . . . . now shakes within its chains,*
*And the tongue in my mouth, by which Thou hast shown Thy power,*
*Is on the point of perishing.*
*There is no way to lift up my voice,*
*. . . . . . . . . to revive the spirits of the shaken,*
*And at the right moment, to let fly the word.*

*. . . . . . . . .*

(The following few lines are very fragmentary, and their meaning is uncertain.)

This long poem begins with a curious recital obviously inspired by the parable of Ezek. 31.3-18.ᐟ Similar fables are found in Hebrew literature (see p. 331). As in 1 Enoch 17.18, the author states that he has himself seen what he relates.

In the Garden of Eden, the source of living water and of mighty rivers, grow also trees of life. It had been intended that the trees should send out far their roots, and that a "shoot" should issue from them. One asks by whom it was intended, for on principle the purposes of God must be fulfilled. A channel was to make possible the passage of living waters to water the shoot which should have blossomed and given its fruits to the rest of the world. The beasts of the field were to feed on its leaves and buds, insects and creeping animals were to eat of the pieces of bark which came from its trunk, and in its branches the birds were to have found their food. But the trees whose roots plunged into the water revolted against this design, and desired to keep in their own midst the shoot which should have flowered, and it could not make its roots reach as far as the channel. Thus the tree of truth remains concealed in this garden, and cannot be found, for the jinns ("the mighty in power") and the angels ("spirits of holiness") have enclosed this garden with a curtain of fire.

This story serves the author as a preamble to remarks on wisdom and knowledge. If the trees of the Garden of Eden are not watered by living water, their fruit becomes hollow. In the same way, anyone who sees without understanding or believes without conviction can only propagate empty ideas.

After having stated that he had been as far as the abundantly flowing and mysterious rivers, the author changes the picture and says he is speaking about the streams of speech. He adds, moreover, that these streams have covered him with their slime. He develops this further. God has given man the gift of speech, which ought to be as a beneficent rain, but it is also possible to open the sluice-gates, which should regulate the flow, and then the words spit out what should have been kept hidden in the depths. For words can cause such disasters as the author has himself witnessed.

We are then given a description of another calamity which had actually occurred when God opened the sluice-gates of the river of fire on the (Roman) people and on the provinces. It is always the eruption of

Vesuvius which seems to have supplied the subject of these visions. As in the description given in Hymn 6, III, 19–36, there is reference to trees withered by the fire which came out of the earth, but, as in Hymn 12, we are told of trees undermining the country, their roots having dug down into the granite earth. If the trees perish, it is because God will judge them as He judges men. Men are measured by His line, and the trees will be weighed on the scales of the sun, and condemned because they had supplied the leaves in the garlands of victory for "those who make signs with the hand" (the Romans: see *Manual of Discipline*, XI, 2; *The War*, XVII, 9, etc.). Not only will the land become a desert of thorns and brambles, but even the prayers that are made, the fruit of the lips, will taste like sour grapes which never ripen. In this apocalyptic vision recalling the catastrophe of A.D. 79, even the rain of ashes and the darkness are mentioned.

The author then informs us of his despair. He will have to share in the punishment of his torturers, for he is a prisoner in the hands of the Romans. If God has decided to exterminate violence the captive will perish along with his gaolers. Here he gives us some facts about his life past and present.

In spite of the stereotyped phrases which he uses, one gets the impression that he is supplying details which are facts. He had been made responsible for the defence of some fortress, but it had been taken, and now he was a prisoner. Having been deported, he now languishes in a dungeon. He is in chains, and unable to make the least movement. He has even lost the power of speech at a time when it would have been most useful to him for encouraging his fellow prisoners.

Obviously, it is not easy to see what connection there can be between the parable and fable of the first part, and the account of his sad fate given us in the latter part. After his statement that the rivers had poured out their slime over him, we should have expected him to speak about the calumnies to which he had been subjected, as the writers of several others of these hymns had done. All the earlier part, with its reasons for the faith which should accompany all search for knowledge, would lead us to suppose that the author belonged to a circle where there was a doctrine to be maintained, not to a group of officers responsible for the defence of a fortress and now a prisoner in the hands of the Romans. Perhaps the redactor has put together two different pieces, thanks to the description of the catastrophe that can be caused by careless talk. It may equally well be that the author himself lost the thread of his thought, and came back to his own situation after calling up the picture of the eruption of Vesuvius and of the final catastrophe.

If this work is to be considered a unity, its author must be looked for among the defenders of the fortresses of Judea during the war of A.D. 66–70. Although led away to Italy, he does not seem to have been chosen for the combats in the arena, like the author of Hymn 10. Perhaps he was too old to provide an interesting exhibition.

Not only does the author present beliefs which are far from orthodox upon the Garden of Eden, and upon certain "mighty in power" and "spirits of holiness", who seem to act more or less as they like. It has also to be noted that to a certain degree he limits the divine power, for even the trees in Eden can refuse to obey the orders given them. Moreover, he thinks trees will be judged in the same way as men will be. The judgement of God will fall upon man, beast, and plant, and will be followed by the destruction of all that lives—until an age determined in advance (?). That does not mean that the author believed in a resurrection of the body, and in any case he never mentions it. He rather suggests that God will create another world, having destroyed this one in which violence reigns.

Nowhere in this piece of writing is there any mention of the Beyond, of Heaven, or of survival after death. Like the Jewish-Christian writer of Hymn 12, the author of this work had the idea that the Garden of Eden was on this earth—he had even been there! There is no sign of Christianity in this poem, which is supposed to have been written in prison, some-where in Italy, a little after the eruption of Vesuvius in A.D. 79.

## FRAGMENT 18

Scribe A, Column IX, Lines 1-36.
(As in preceding hymns, the first lines have perished or only survive in fragments.)

> . . . . . *so that wrath has no mercy and zeal is laid bare to exter-*
> *minate . . . . . . . . . . .*
> *The womb of Death and Sheôl shares with me my couch,*
> *And the wailing of the dead mounts up . . . in the sound of my sighs.*
>
> *My eyes burn like the metals' furnace,*
> *My tears which are rivers of water, no longer soothe my eyes.*
> *Afar off stands my soul, and my life has turned aside.*
>
> *I cry out in my desolation,*

*My pains are like those inflicted by the torturer,*
*Like those of the opening of the womb in childbirth.*

*Yet will my soul recover, because of Thy miracles,*
*And in Thy goodness Thou wilt not utterly forsake me.*

*Let my soul find help through the streams of Thy mercies,*
*And I shall make answer to those whose words bring confusion.*

*Thou shalt cause me to judge him who made me to stoop:*
*I shall belittle his law, and justify Thy judgements.*

*For I have been taught in Thy truth,*
*And I shall distinguish between judgement and the pains which I wished to*
*  inflict.*

*For I made my hope in Thy benefits,*
*And Thou dost place pity in the mouth of Thy servant.*

*Thou wilt not therefore threaten my life,*
*And Thou wilt not destroy my health.*

*Thou wilt not forsake my hope,*
*And Thou wilt uphold my spirit when faced with torture.*

*Thou hast laid the foundations of my mind, and knowest my thoughts;*
*And in my anguish Thou hast consoled me.*

*Therefore because of Thy pardons, I make myself ready to help,*
*And I shall show pity on him who is the first of sinners.*

*I know now that one can hope in Thy goodness,*
*That there is hope in the greatness of Thy power.*

*Hence one must not execute judgement on everybody as if it was Thy judgement,*
*For it is not as in Thy contentions that man may judge man.*

*A man, [it is by another man] that he gets instruction.*
*The flesh, it is by a creature (also of flesh) that it can get itself glory.*
*And the mind, it is by the minds of others that it gains strength.*

*Like to Thy might, there is nothing equal in power,*
*As to Thy glory, there is not any . . . . . . .*
*And as to Thy wisdom, it is beyond measure.*

*Therefore they . . . . . . . . . . . . . . not*
*And for those who have been forsaken by it . . .*

(Here follow four lines surviving only in very fragmentary condition.)

For Thou, my God, . . . . . . . . . Thou dost conduct my fight,
And in the secret of Thy wisdom, Thou hast justified me.
And the desire for truth . . . . . . . . . to its appointed end.

May that which Thou hast decided for me, be for joy and gladness,
And may the pains be trans[formed] into healing . . . . . . eternal!

May contempt be changed to perfect glory,
And may the fall into which I was led, become everlasting might!

For it is in . . . . . . . . . and in Thy glory that my light shines,
And in the darkness it is a torch which Thou hast set alight . . .
. . . . . . . . . . . . . . . . . . . . . . . . . . . . . . . . .
. . . . . . .

[Thou art] my shelter, my rock and my refuge,
My strength and my stronghold, they both are in Thee.

He who mourns, I shall protect against all the . . . . . . . .
. . . to me, that he may evermore be in safety.

Better than my father did, Thou hast known me.
From the bosom . . . . . . . . . of my mother Thou hast protected me.

From the breasts of her who bore me, Thy mercies have been upon me,
And from the lap of my nurse . . . . . . . . .
And since my youth, Thou hast enlightened me through Thy wise decisions.

In established truth, Thou hast made me to rejoice,
And by the spirit of Thy holiness Thou wilt gladden me.

And even till this day, [the . . . . . .] and the instruction of Thy justice
   is near to me,
The watch-tower of Thy peace to protect my soul.

Many pardons and streams of mercies accompany my steps
Whilst Thou dost display Thy justice in me.

Even to old age, I beseech Thee, provide my food,
For my father has not known me, and my mother has left me in Thy
   hands.

*Thou art the father of all the [Sons of] Thy truth* (or, of Thy handmaid),
*And Thou dost rejoice in them.*

*Like a man of mercy to a little child, and as a nurse to the babe in her lap,*
*Thou givest food to all Thy creatures.*

This hymn is certainly the work of a Christian, and it gives the impression that the author, a Jewish-Christian, had only recently been converted to Christianity. It would appear that formerly he had been in a position of some authority, but that now he was wounded and ill, though not a prisoner, and lying deserted on his bed of suffering and hoping for healing by God. As soon as he will have recovered, he will put himself to the service of the cause, and he will know how to answer those causing confusion. He hopes once more to exercise judgement, and make right to triumph. His sufferings have taught him much. He had hoped in God, and God had had pity on his soul. He will no more seek to inflict penalties, but will show himself full of pity and ready to help. He now knows that he must not judge men with God's rigour. God's arraignments are not to be used in human contentions, for men are bound up one with another, and learning, honour, and power are only obtainable through human co-operation.

Unfortunately, this text has many gaps, but in spite of these we believe we can see that the author intended to share with the weak and oppressed what he called his shelter and stronghold, and to protect anyone who mourned, and place him in safety. The hymn concludes with a prayer that God will assure him his daily bread right to old age.

In this hymn, where one meets with no picture of the Beyond, and no reference to resurrection, one is rather surprised to come across so many Christian ideas. From forgiveness of one's enemies (Matt. 6.12) to the prayer for daily bread, (Matt. 6.11) we have here the principles of Christianity of the first generation. A gap in the text prevents us from knowing if the author had belonged to the sect, "The Sons of Thy Truth". The hymns which can be attributed to this Christianised sect are all late, and appear to have been written in the Roman Diaspora. It is possible that this phrase is an interpolation by the copyist, for none of the typical popular beliefs of this sect is found in the hymn. It could also be that the phrase should be read as "The Sons of Thy Handmaid", an expression of humility.

Before his conversion, the author could have belonged to Zadokite circles. The hymn may date from the middle of the first century A.D., and in all likelihood was composed in Judea.

## FRAGMENT 19

SCRIBE A, COLUMN IX, LINES 38-41; COLUMN X, LINES 1-21.
The very fragmentary state of the first part of this hymn (the lower part of Column IX and the upper part of Column X) makes it impossible to know the purpose for which it was written. The subsequent lines deal with the weakness of man and the foreknowledge of God.

*What is man if not a thing of earth?*

*[What is he who of the clay] was formed and unto dust returns*

*That Thou shouldst make him understand Thy wonders such as these?*
*And that Thou shouldst instruct him in the secrets of [Thy truth?]*

*And I, dust and ashes, what can I propose didst Thou not will it?*
*And what can I conceive apart from Thy consent?*

*To what may I lay hold, if Thou dost not uphold me?*
*What reasons should I form, hadst Thou not formed me?*

*What should I say, didst Thou not open my mouth?*
*And what should I reply, but that Thou didst teach me?*

*Behold Thou art the Prince of Gods, of honoured ones the King,*
*The Lord of everything that breathes and Ruler of Creation.*

*Without Thee nothing can be done,*
*And nothing known apart from Thy consent.*

*Outside of Thee is nothing,*
*And nothing is like Thee in power.*

*Nothing can oppose Thy glory,*
*Nothing is equal to Thee in might.*

*Among all the great works of Thy wonders,*
*Who can keep strength enough to stand before Thy glory?*

*What then is he, who unto dust returns,*
*And how can he maintain . . . . . . . .?*

*Only for Thy glory has everything been made.*

Apart from the fact that this is unquestionably a Zadokite hymn, there is nothing to indicate its date and place of origin. The poem seems to be a string of phrases taken from a commonplace book.

## FRAGMENT 20

Scribe A, Column X, Line 14 to Column XI, Line 2.

This passage has suffered very much damage, and there are only two lines, 33 and 34, which have survived in a complete state. Line 33 and the beginning of line 34 read as follows:

*When my heart is pierced with terror,*
*And my reins are seized with trembling,*
*And my sighs reach down to the abyss,*
*Even in the halls of Sheôl, Thou wilt set free "the only one"* (the soul).

This passage shows that the author believed in the resurrection of the dead. For the use of "the only one" as an equivalent or parallel for "the soul", see Ps. 22.21 and 35.17.

The remainder of line 34 with the surviving parts of lines 35 and 36 reads:

*And even if I become fearful at the news*
*That Thou judgest the people mighty in power,*
*And of the struggle which Thou leadest with the army of Thy holy ones*
*against . . . . . . . . .*
*And of the judgement on all Thy creatures,*
*And of the righteousness . . . . . . . . . .*

The author says he is taken with terror at the news which had come to him of the Judgement of God already begun along with the army of His "holy ones". The news probably was that of the eruption of Vesuvius.

The earlier and incomplete lines begin with the usual form of benediction. There are then references to the frequently treated themes of God having given varying degrees of intelligence to men with different forms of service and degrees of responsibility, and of God also having given to man the work of making the ground yield fruit for his nourishment. The author feels it unjust that the legions should come and take the corn, wine, and oil, and pour them out on the Roman provinces like a fertilising rain. This part of the hymn reads:

*Thou hast created me and Thou hast not placed my reliance in a profit and*
*in . . . . . . . . . .*
*And for me, a creature of flesh, Thou hast not put my strength in an army more*
*valiant*

*Than the crowd that fight in ranks* ('dr–) . . . . . . . . .
*[And who take the gre]ater part of the corn, the wine and the oil,*
*And who boast about their buying.*
*And these goods* . . . . . . . . .
*[Like] a cloud upon the province, pouring forth rain upon it and multiplying
   the shoots.*

The mention of those "who boast about their buying" brings up an
interesting point. The text of Ps. 68 is very corrupt and has been given
some strange translations. Verse 30 should not be read as "the wild beast
of the reeds". The reference is to the plunderer, "the being who buys
by the right of the strongest", which is the boast here. In Cave I of
Qumrân a number of fragments of an "interpretation" of Ps. 68 have been
found. One of these lets it clearly be understood that "the being who
buys by the right of the strongest" refers to the "legions", the *kty'ym*, as
in the *Habakkuk Commentary*.

The author of this prayer probably belonged to the Jewish-Christian
sect, "The Sons of Truth", and lived in Judea, where he received news of
the cataclysm of Vesuvius. The date of the composition of the hymn
must be a little after A.D. 79.

## FRAGMENT 21

SCRIBE A, COLUMN XI, LINES 3-14.

*I give Thee thanks, my God,*
*Because Thou hast made distinction among that which is dust,*
*And in the creature of slime, Thou hast manifested Thy power by quality.*

*But what am I [\* what is my quality],*
*That Thou hast put within me the secret of Thy truth,*
*And hast instructed me in the works of Thy wonders?*

*Thou wilt endue my mouth with praises,*
*And my tongue* . . . . . . .

*My circumcised lips shall make proclamation with constancy,*
*They shall sing, by favour of Thy kindness.*

*Before Thy majesty, I will bow myself to the earth all the day long,*
*And always will I bless Thy* NAME.

*I shall tell of Thy glory in the midst of the sons of man,*
*And through the multitude of Thy kindnesses, my soul shall rejoice.*

*I have understood,*
*That Thy mouth is truth,*
*That in Thy hands is righteousness,*
*That in Thy designs is complete knowledge,*
*That in Thy power is all might,*
*And that all glory is with Thee.*

*In Thy wrath is the judgement of every torturer,*
*And in Thy kindness is a multitude of pardons,*
*And Thy mercies towards all the Sons of Thy Will.*

*For Thou hast instructed them in the secret of Thy truth,*
*And hast made them to understand the secrets of Thy wonders.*

*It is because of Thy glory, that Thou hast purified the human being from sin,*
*So that for Thee he may sanctify himself from all the lust of sex, and from the*
  *guilt of apostasy.*
*To join himself to . . . of the Sons of Thy Truth,*
*And to the lot of the people of Thy holy ones,*
*So that he shall arise from the dust of the worms which consume the dead,*
*And take part in the Council of the . . . . . . .*
*That from being of a changeful mind, [he shall be changed] to prudence,*
*To take his place before Thee with the eternal army and the spirits of . . . . . . .*
*To renew himself along with all that shall be,*
*And to shout with joy in concert with all who know.*

A slight variation in the opening formula, "My God", in place of "My Lord", suggests that this hymn, and also the following one, was taken from another such collection as this roll of the *Thanksgiving Hymns*. The author, in all likelihood a former Zadokite, must have joined the sect of the Sons of Truth rather than belong to a Baptist sect. Because of this, he feels that he has been purified from original sin (sexual desire) and from the sin of apostasy. He had probably opposed the sect which he had just joined. He now knows that it is in this sect that God will choose His elect. He is sure of rising from the dead and of taking part with angels and heavenly spirits in the creation of a new universe, for he now forms part of an élite and has been instructed in the secrets of the truth.

The belief that the elect will work together with God in the creation of a new universe is found in a number of popular writings (cf. *Manual of Discipline*, XI, 2-5), but it is rarely associated with the idea that the human being must first return to the dust and from there be brought back to life again. It would seem that this Christian sect of the Sons of Truth gathered together a number of trends all more or less unorthodox and influenced by the surroundings from which the members came.

The author was of Hebrew ("circumcised") speech, and doubtless lived in Palestine. Although the hymn bears no indication of date, one may imagine that it had been composed fairly late, and after A.D. 70.

## FRAGMENT 22A

SCRIBE A, COLUMN XI, LINES 15-22.

. . . *I give Thee thanks, my God,*
*I magnify Thee, my rock, and in wondrous manner . . . . . . .*
*. . . . . . . . . . . . . . . . . . . . . . . . . . . . . . . . .*
*For Thou hast caused me to know the secret of truth.*

*. . . . . . . . . . . . . . . . . . . . . . . . . . . . . . . . . . . . . . . . . . . . . .*
*Thou hast laid them bare for me, and I can meditate . . . . . . . . . . of*
  *the kindness.*

*I understand that justice is Thine, and that in all Thy kindnesses there*
  *is . . . . . . . . . .*
*And extermination in the absence of Thy mercies.*

*As for me, the spring of bitter griefs is open, . . . . . . .*
*Suffering is not hidden from my eyes since I have learned the nature of man,*
*And the tendency to apostasy by the human being.*

*. . . . . . . . . . . . [They dream] of sin, and their thoughts run to abomi-*
  *nations*
*They pierce my heart, and torture my bones,*
*And on the making of deductions, they keep harping,*
*And the number of bitter things (increases) until the end of injustice*
*And I . . . . . . . . . .*

It is difficult to attribute this fragment to any of the major trends in Judaism, and it seems impossible to give it a date, even within very wide limits. The one thing that can be gathered from it is the reproach made concerning certain unspecified persons that they are obsessed by religious problems which they resolve by means of "deductions". The repetition of the same root *hgw* in the phrase *wlhgwt hgw ygwn* suggests that these unspecified persons possessed a *Book of Deductions*, a *sepher ha-hagû*, but such books were in current use and mention of them is found among the

Qaraites in the Middle Ages. The attacks by our author could have been directed against some sect which had arisen within the Zadokite movement, but on the other hand, they could equally well have been aimed at certain unorthodox rabbis.

★     ★     ★

At this point the handwriting of Scribe A comes to an end. At first sight one has the impression that Scribe B continued the hymn which clearly had not been completed, but this impression is deceptive. As a matter of fact, Scribe B appears to have copied out as a continuation a totally different hymn, which to him seemed to link up through a similarity of language. In the inter-line, and above the last words of Scribe A, "and the number of bitter things (*increases*) until the end of injustice", Scribe B has added: "And I shall calm, etc." Apparently he misread the word for "number", *mspr*, as *mspd*, "lamentation".

## FRAGMENT 22B

SCRIBE B, COLUMN XI, LINES 22-7.

*[And the lamentation of those in bitterness (will last) until the end of injustice,]*
*And I shall calm with the lyre the dirge of those who mourn,*
*And I . . . . . . . . . for there is no punishment for the profanations.*

*Moreover upon the lyre I shall sing of help,*
*And on the harp of eigh[t strings] . . . . . . . . . .*
*And the flute shall make a joyful noise without ceasing.*

*For who then among the works of Thy hand will be able to recite Thy*
  *wonders?*
*By the mouth of all shall Thy* NAME *be acclaimed.*
*For ever and ever Thou shalt be blessed by the mouth of . . . . . .*

*[These praises] will be heard at the same time as the voice of those who*
  *acclaim,*
*But no one will think of appeasing, and crime [will not cease . . .]*
*Thy truth however shall shine forth for eternal glory and universal peace.*

This fragment, like the preceding one, supplies no indication of date. What is more, this text gives the impression that the author or the copyist had had to translate from a foreign language. It is rather difficult to get the exact sense of this passage.

## FRAGMENT 22C

SCRIBE B, COLUMN XI, LINES 27-35 . . .

*Blessèd be Thou . . . . . . . . . who hast given to [Thy servant] insight
into knowledge allowing him to understand Thy wonders?
. . . . . . . . . so as to recite the multitude of Thy mercies.*

*Blessèd be Thou, O God of compassion. Spare me, in the great[ness of
Thy . . .]
And the abundance of Thy truth, and the streams of Thy mercies towards
Thy creatures
Will rejoice the soul of Thy servant through Thy truth.*

*Purify me by Thy righteousness for I have waited for Thy goodness,
And I have hoped for Thy mercies.*

*Because of Thy pardons Thou hast opened my apertures* (!),
*Thou hast consoled me for I made my support on Thy compassions.*

*Blessèd be Thou, my Lord, for Thou hast performed all this,
And in the mouth of Thy servant, Thou wilt place . . . . . . . . . and
pity.*

*Thou hast put within me a tongue ready to make answer,*

. . . . . . . . . . . . . . . . . . . . . . . . . . . . . .

These three benedictions, at the end of which there may have been
others, must have formed part of a collection of *Berachoth*. One notes
that the author calls himself "the servant of God", an everyday expression
which however is found only rarely in this roll.

Whilst the prayers may have undergone some slight modification, yet
they give the impression of being part of the ordinary prayers of the
Jewish liturgy used in all circles and by Jews of all trends. Because of this,
it is difficult to assign any precise date to this passage, but it is not the less
significant that it should have been the second scribe who copied the
passage into this collection.

## FRAGMENT 23

SCRIBE B, COLUMN XII, LINES 1-37 . . .

In this column at least four texts have been put together by the second
scribe, but the fact that he did not make use of *alineas* renders the task of
separation difficult.

Only a few words remain of the first text which seems to have dealt with the life of the elect in the Beyond. That suggests that it is a text of Zealot origin.

The second text reads:

I shall glorify Thy NAME amidst those who fear Thee [. . . for all ages,]
And the prayer when one bows down and implores, at all times,
From end to end (=from birth to death),

As soon as light comes in the E[ast] with the circuit of the days,
In accord with what is fixed by the laws of that great light.

When evening appears and the light fades away by order of the dominion of
    darkness
For the appointed time of the night with its circuit meeting the morning;
And at the end, it is gathered to its dwelling-place.

Because the light is there for night to go and day to come,
And that for ever, so long as the ages, foundations of eternity, come to birth,
And for the round of feast, as they have been fixed with their dates for all their
    dominions,
By the decision ever true of the mouth of God.

The revelation of what is now, of what has been and what shall ever be,
Outside of that was nothing, and nothing else will be,
For the God of knowledge fixed it, and there is none apart from Him.

This second text reproduces a prayer which must have been current at the time and in common use by all Jews, to whatsoever school they belonged. An echo of it is even found in the *Epistle of Clement to the Corinthians* (20.1-3). A paraphrase of this prayer supplied the material for a political pamphlet against the government of Agrippa II which is reproduced in the *Manual of Discipline* (X, 1-8). Very different interpretations have been given of this passage, in which the greater part of the words are used with a double sense. If we have not here the original text of the prayer, we have a version but slightly modified which in general preserves the original meaning. As in a number of similar prayers, some still in use, there is the reminder that prayer should be made to God every day, morning and night (cf. *The War*, XIV, 13-14), for it is He who created the miracle of the days with their regular sequence. The succession of the days marks the time, and renews the cycles of the festivals as God fixed them for all the empires of

M

the world. It may be that this version brings out more the triumph of light over darkness.

The third text begins:

> And, my God, I reflected on Thy knowledge, with the mind Thou hast placed
> within me,
> And with the faith in what I heard of the secret of Thy wonders.
> By the spirit of Thy holiness, Thou hast opened in me the knowledge of the
> hidden meaning of Thy wisdom, and a mighty fountain . . .

The text then becomes very fragmentary, but the rare phrases which have survived suggest that the writer was a Christian who looked forward to the conversion of foreign nations and their coming to God. They will have been influenced by the divine chastisements of their empires, and also by God's goodness. They will serve Him in proportion to their intelligence—an idea often expressed in the hymns of this collection. It may be remarked that the writer gives no evidence of any desire on his own part to propagate the faith.

Following this comes the fourth text, which is also fragmentary, though less so than the third text. It is clearly Zadokite. In extremely crude terms, the author disparages the human being, made of dust and destined to return to dust. Conception and birth are presented as defilements, and the parallel between birth and death is pushed much further than in any text already met. These descriptions are also found in rabbinic literature. For example, we read in *Pirqe Aboth*, III, 1: "Know whence thou camest and whither thou art going and before whom thou wilt in future have to give account and reckoning. Whence thou camest—from a putrefying drop; whither thou art going—to a place of dust, worms, and maggots; and before whom thou wilt in future have to give account and reckoning —before the Supreme King of kings, the Holy One, Blessèd is He." In our text there is no reference to a resurrection or a judgement after death. It is in his own lifetime that man is judged by God. Yet man's actions are determined beforehand by God. Prayer, therefore, is summed up in the asking from God the intelligence not to go against His precepts.

★          ★          ★

Here we come to the end of the texts of the bundle, which, as already said, consisted of three separate sheets, each of four columns.

The second bundle provided five columns in the handwriting of Scribe

A. The three columns numbered XIV, XV, and XVI are on one sheet, and continuous, and have no signs of stitching either on the right side or the left. They therefore come from the middle part of some sheet. The fragment with the column here called XIII has signs of stitching to the right. The remaining column, here called XVII, has on the left holes made by a needle. These two columns, therefore, were respectively the first and the last on a sheet or sheets, but it cannot be said that they must have formed one sheet with the middle portion mentioned above.

Three fragments from the hand of the second scribe have been put together to form Column XVIII. One column at least preceded the upper part, for the endings of twelve of its lines have survived.

## FRAGMENT 24

SCRIBE A, COLUMN XIII, LINES 1-21.

This fragment also is composed of a number of texts joined together. The beginning (lines 1-6) is separated from the rest by a space left blank. It is far from complete, but appears to be a hymn praising the works of God, and promising eternal peace for the elect and the Pit for the wicked.

The second passage reads:

*And those which [Thou . . . . . . . . . . .] of all Thy works,*
*Before Thou hadst created them with the host of Thy spirits, and the con-*
  *gregations of . . .*
*. . . . . . . its hosts, the people of the earth and all that grows in it,*
*In the seas and in the deeps . . . . .*
*. . . . . . . to watch over them for ever.*

*For Thou didst establish them before the world, and the works of . . . . . . .*
*They shall relate Thy glory throughout Thy dominion,*
*For Thou wilt show them that which was not . . . . . . . before*
*So as to create new things, destroy the things set up before, and . . . the*
  *things which shall be for evermore.*
*For Thou . . . . . . . . . . Thou wilt be through everlasting ages.*

*In the secrets of Thy wisdom, Thou hast . . . all that to declare Thy glory.*
*[But] the spirit of flesh [is n]ot made to understand it all,*
*Nor reason on the se[crets of Thy] great . . .*

This passage seems to speak of the destruction of the present world and the building of the world to come (cf. XI, 13-14). It would seem to mean

that God had prepared the plans of all that exists, and that before Genesis
He had set certain spirits as guardians over all that was about to come
into existence. In the same way, God had initiated certain elect into His
designs for the world to come. It would be these who would have to
undertake the destruction of what is, and the building up of what is to be.
God alone is eternal.

The third passage reads:

*What is he, therefore, the being born of woman, amongst all the terrible* . . .
*If not a construction of dust kneaded with water?*

. . . . . . . . *his foundation is a shameful nakedness* . . . . . .
*And a straying spirit has been sent within him.*

*If he becomes evil and it happens that* . . . . . . *of the world,*
*The marvel of the ages* . . . . . . *the flesh.*

*It is only through Thy goodness that man can become righteous,*
*And by the multitude of* [*Thy compassions that he* . . . . . . . . .]

*By Thine adorning, adorn us, and grant us a multitude of joys, unending*
*    peace, and length of days,*
*For* . . . . . . . . . *Thy word shall not be recalled.*

In this third passage there is no reference to the Beyond, nor to the
world to come. The author prays that he may be adorned with God's
adorning, and be granted long life on this earth. The work is therefore
Zadokite, and the expression "the being born of woman" suggests that it
comes from a Baptist sect.

*And I, Thy servant, have understood through the spirit which Thou hast*
*    placed within me,*
. . . . . . . . . . *and that all Thy deeds are righteous,*
*And that Thy words will not be recalled.*

. . . *Thy ends fi*[*xed for* . . . . . . *or for bit*]*ter things, according to Thy*
*    good pleasure.*
*And I shall know* . . . . . . . . . . *and the wicked* . . . . . . . . .

The fourth passage comes from an author who uses the formula "Thy
servant" as in the *Berachoth* in Fragment 22. In spite of the similarity of
certain expressions, this passage cannot be attached to the preceding one.

There the Zadokite author treats the human spirit as straying: here it comes from God and enables man to understand divine truth.

The texts in this fragment may date from the first half of the first century A.D. The last passage may be even earlier.

## FRAGMENT 25

SCRIBE A, COLUMN XIV, LINES 1-7.

This text is most fragmentary. The following phrases call for notice: "The Men of Truth"; "the powers of the spirit of the purified"; "stoical even to . . ."; "the men who prostitute Thee". The text seems to have come from a Christian sect called "The Men of Truth" (cf. X, 14, XI, 12, etc.). Those who had been "purified" were those who had been through the refining furnace of suffering or persecution. A reproach is made against certain opponents that they profane God.

## FRAGMENT 26

SCRIBE A, COLUMN XIV, LINES 8-22.

[Blessèd be Thou], my Lord, who dost give understanding to the heart of
    Thy serv[ant, . . . . . . . . .]
To show himself stoical before the slaughters . . . by the wicked,
To bless . . . . . . . . . those whom Thou hast loved,
And to detest all those whom Thou . . . . . . . . . of the human being.

For it is following the word of the [ever]lasting spirits, that between the good
    and the evil,
. . . . . . . . . . . . . . . . . . . . . . . . Thou hast formed them.
But I have learned through the understanding which Thou hast given me
That it is in following Thy good pleasure . . . . . . [. . . the spirit],
    of Thy holiness.

Thus, Thou wilt direct me towards Thy knowledge, and following the
    instructions of those near to me,
Wilt direct my zeal against all who do evil, and against men of falsity.

For all those who draw near to Thee, change not the utterance of Thy mouth,
And all those who know Thee, hate not Thy words,
For Thou art just, and truthful are all Thy elect.

Every crime [of the wick]ed shall be destroyed for ever,
And Thou wilt unfold Thy acts of justice in the eyes of all Thy creatures.

And I, I have understood the greatness of Thy goodness,

*By an oath upon my soul, I have sworn to be without sin towards Thee,*
*And to do naught that is evil in Thy eyes.*

*Thus it is that I have been in touch with all the men of my Society,*
*And following the instructions of . . . we have drawn near to his "scandal" (rkl).*
*And we have offered adoration to the Cherub of his fatherland.*

*Yet I shall not lift up an evil and a hate[ful] face . . . . . . .*
*I shall not dig . . . . . . . . . . . . . . . . . . . . . . . . summit,*
*Because of the riches of Thy truth, and the ransom of all Thy judgements.*
*For if . . . . . . . . . and he who departs from Thee,*
*That one shall we despise.*
*And I shall not bring into the Society . . . . . . . . .*

This text, which begins with a benediction, is certainly one of the most curious in the whole collection. The author appears to be a Zealot who first of all asks God for strength to remain stoical under torture should he be taken prisoner. In the meantime, he wished to be exonerated for certain actions he was in the process of performing in his attacks upon the wicked. His companions have induced him to act like this, but he assures God that his actions are really only feints. All who really know God can neither hate His laws nor change the sense of His precepts.

As a matter of fact, the author belonged to one of those militant secret societies which had decided to feign conversion to the Roman religion. At the moment of writing, he was in good standing with the oppressor, but—if we understand him correctly—he will not use this favour to his own advancement and go to the height of really sacrificing his faith. It is true that he has had to offer adoration to idols, but he will always despise real apostates, those who are not, like himself, playing a double game, and he will not bring into his Society any person of whom he is not absolutely sure (?).

The situation depicted here must frequently have arisen before A.D. 66, when the *sicarii*, sometimes disguised as legionaries, committed assassinations in the full light of day. The Romans were often more afraid of Jewish apostates than of those who openly showed their enmity. There were Jews who arranged to efface, more or less, the marks of their circumcision, which in that age consisted of a simple incision (cf. 1 Cor. 7.18). They were called *epispastes,* and several passages in the Talmud speak of them. These imitation converts were numerous on the eve of Bar Kochba's revolt. Rabbinic literature relates numerous cases of *epispastes* being re-circumcised.

At the same time that these "converts" removed the traces of their circumcision, they offered adoration to the Roman gods, and, naturally, left off wearing phylacteries. The rabbis held that these two infringements of the law were not serious, as obviously they were not genuine.

The most noteworthy detail in this text is the existence of secret societies of Zealots who obeyed certain watchwords. This organisation had its fullest development about A.D. 130, the period to which this text should be assigned.

## FRAGMENT 27

SCRIBE A, COLUMN XIV, LINES 23-8 . . .

I give Thee [thanks], my Lord,
Because Thy power is great, and Thy wonders [manifest themselves] from eternity to eternity,
. . . . . . and great are [Thy . . . . . . Thou] who dost pardon him who repents of his transgressions,
But who dost keep in mind the crime of the wicked.

. . . . . . by the free-will offering of . . . . . .
And Thou dost hate crime for ever and ever.

Me, Thy servant, Thou hast adorned by the spirit of knowledge,
. . . . . . . . . . so as to detest all the ways of crime.

I will love Thee therefore with a free-will offering (of myself)
And of all my heart . . . . . .

. . . . . . to understand Thee, for it is by Thy hand that all this has come to be,
And without . . . . . . . . .

This very ambiguous text makes use of the expression "Thy servant" already met with in the *Berachoth*. One wonders if this is a prayer by a recently converted pagan.

## FRAGMENT 28

SCRIBE A, COLUMN XV, LINES 9-26.
(Only a letter or two at the beginning of each line has survived of the first eight lines of this column:)

. . . . . . . . . They will . . . Thee all the days and . . . . .
. . . . . . and I shall show forth my love for Thee in offerings.

*With all my heart and soul I have purified . . . . . .*
*. . . . . . . . . and not to waver from all that Thou hast commanded.*

*And I shall strengthen myself by the multitude of . . . . . .*
*[So as not] to depart from any of Thy laws.*

*And I, through the intelligence which Thou hast supplied, have learned*
*That it is not given to the flesh [to be righteous,*
*And that] man [cannot make straight] his way,*
*Nor the human being order his steps.*

*I also know that the nature of every spirit is within Thy hands,*
*. . . . . . . . . . . . Thou hast ordained it, before ever it was created.*

*How then would it be possible for anyone to reply to Thy words?*
*Thou alone, Thou . . . . . . . . . . . . the righteous,*
*From the womb hast formed him for what Thy good pleasure has fixed;*
*That he may be kept in Thy covenant, walking rightly in all things,*
*That on him may be showered the streams of Thy mercies,*
*That there may open for him all that makes the soul firm for everlasting healing*
*    and peace.*
*Likewise that glory shall not be lacking for his flesh,*
*And that he may not be taken in default.*

*But as for the wicked, Thou hast created them for . . . . . . . . . . . .*
*And from the womb Thou hast set them aside for the day of slaughter.*
*For they have walked in a way which was not good,*
*They have despised Thy . . . [by following the wa]y of their covetous souls;*
*They have found no pleasure in all that which Thou hast commanded,*
*They have chosen all that which Thou dost hate,*
*[They have departed from the wa]y which Thou hadst fixed for them,*
*So that Thou dost perform upon them great judgements in the sight of all Thy*
*    creatures,*
*That they may become a sign that is . . . . . . . worldwide making known*
*    that great is Thy glory and power.*

*And the flesh, by itself, how can that reason . . . . . . . . . .*
*And the dust, how can that order its steps?*

*It is Thou who hast formed the spirit, and for what Thou hast created, Thou*
*    hast laid down . . . . . . .*
*And it is from Thee that the way of every living creature proceeds.*

*As for me, I know that no wealth can compare with Thy truth,*
*And . . . .. . .. . .. . Thy holiness.*

*I know therefore that those who shall serve Thee, and for all eternity,*
*Are in the midst of those whom Thou didst choose from amongst all,*
*And that Thou wilt not take . . . .. . .. .*

*Thou wilt not accept atonement for evil deeds of wickedness*
*For Thou art a God of Truth, and every misdeed Thou . . . . .. . it.*
*I know it cannot be before Thy face, for to Thee . . . .. . .. .*

Although the word "priest" does not occur in this text—or, for that matter, in any of these hymns—yet the author seems to be a Zadokite priest: he formed part of the "righteous" chosen by God to conform to His precepts. That is why God grants them all His mercies, frees them from anguish, and sees that their dignity does not suffer. God has also predestined the wicked who depart from the right way to be slain by His judgement, and to be a warning in the eyes of all who survive. It is among the Zadokites—a name that is not found in any hymn—that God has chosen His elect. They alone must serve Him as priests to all eternity. He will accept from no other priest an atonement for sin, the *kpwr*, which was offered on the 10th Tishri.

The mention of offerings and purification, along with some other elements in this text, suggest that this prayer was written before the destruction of the Temple, at a time when Agrippa II nominated High Priests even from among recently converted Gentiles. The re-modelling of the text by the compilers of the roll led, however, to the omission of all references to Kohen, and Sons of Aaron, as well as to the Sons of Zadok.

## FRAGMENT 29

SCRIBE A, COLUMN XVI, LINES 1-7.

This passage has survived in too fragmentary a condition for any consecutive translation to be made, but certain terms and phrases show that it is of Zadokite origin.

## FRAGMENT 30

SCRIBE A, COLUMN XVI, LINES 8-20.

This passage also has survived in a fragmentary condition. It takes the form of a "benediction", and may be the work of a man of the people recently admitted into a Zadokite society. The author blesses God who has allowed him to join those who keep His commandments, and he himself

M*

has chosen to become a member of this group whose aim was to drive all the Romans from the country: "Every torturer shall be driven from the territories of Thy Covenant." A gap makes it impossible to decide if the author is speaking of "the Sons of Thy handmaid" or praying to be kept from all contact with the Christian sect, "the Sons of the Truth".

This prayer must have been written in Palestine at a time when the Zadokites enlarged their ranks by admitting members who came from the less privileged circles of society, that is to say, about the beginning of the second century A.D.

## FRAGMENT 31

SCRIBE A, COLUMN XVII, LINES 1-15.

This text also has only survived in a very fragmentary condition. From the earlier part of it one would gather that the author had been deported and was living in a foreign land. The second part seems to have been written to glorify the Zadokites. The incomplete sentence, "Thou hast caused them to be broken by the hand of Moses", is probably a reference to the first tablets of stone which God caused Moses to break because of the unfaithfulness of the people (Exod. 32.19). The justice of the princes, *qṣyn*, is contrasted with the justice of the brethren. The text concludes with a reminder of the priestly rôle which has devolved upon the Zadokites for evermore—in spite of the fact that the actual word "priest" does not figure in this text. After the expulsion of the Romans, all human glory will return to them, and they will be assured of long life.

> . . . . . . . . . *to serve Thee eternally,*
> *So that their descendants may be before Thee days without end.*
>
> *And the . . . Thou hast raised up . . . . . . . [wi]cked, and to drive out all the . . .*
> *And to give them as inheritance, all human glory, and the multitude of days.*

This piece may have been written by a Zadokite of the Diaspora at the beginning of the second century A.D.

## FRAGMENT 32

SCRIBE A, COLUMN XVII, LINES 17-28.

While this lower part of Column XVII is better preserved than the upper part, yet it has no complete sentences. Among the longer phrases which have come down to us are the following:

. . . . . . . *by the spirits which Thou hast placed in me, I . . . an answering tongue to relate Thy acts of justice, and the slowness of . . . .*

*For it was in the impurity of sex that I was kneaded and from the bottom of . . . . . . . . .*

*Thou art justice, and Thy name shall be blessed for e[ver . . . .]*

*I have been led to understand how he whom Thou hast chosen . . . . . . .*

*. . . . And for the . . . of his sufferings at the time of Thy penances and Thy trials . . . . . .*

*. . . Thy servant from sinning against Thee, and from wavering over anything which Thou dost desire, . . . . . .*

*. . . to walk in all the things which Thou dost love, and depart from everything that Thou dost hate . . . .*

*. . . . . . . . . . Thou hast inbreathed a holy spirit . . . upon Thy servant*

*. . . . . . . . . . . . . . . . and upon every covenant of man, I perceive . . .*

This is another Zadokite fragment. There is reference to penances and trials which God puts upon man, but He also gives to the author, who twice calls himself God's servant, a spirit of discernment so that his conduct may be in accordance with God's will. The phrase about human covenants or alliances may have reference to Zadokite societies.

This text was probably written in Palestine, and may be dated about the end of the first century A.D.

## FRAGMENT 33

SCRIBE B, COLUMN XVIII, LINES 1-32.

As indicated on pp. 157, 355, three pieces of manuscript in the handwriting of the scribe B have been pieced together to form Column XVIII. If however, the piece "b" (the upper part on the left supplying the ends of lines 5-16) seems to fit in well with the piece "c" (lines 16 onwards), the same cannot be said about the piece "a" (the beginnings of lines 1-15). The fitting together of lines 6 and 7 and of lines 13 and 14 may seem to justify the joining together of these two pieces of manuscript, but it may easily be pure coincidence that in these two cases the words do fit together. Lines 11 and 12 certainly do not fit in with each other.

If we really have here one and the same column, the text we read in it seems rather disconcerting. The author says he belonged to the Baptist sect "born of woman". That is about all that these three pieces have in common. At the most we may notice that in piece "b" (line 10) there is a reference to the tongue of God's servant, and of his mouth being "open", while in piece "c" (line 20) to his "non-circumcised" ears the word is "open". This would lead us to suppose that the author was of foreign speech. Must it therefore be accepted that the Baptist sect made proselytes among the Gentiles? That cannot be ruled out (cf. Acts 19.3-4), but the members of this sect were recruited mostly among the Jews (cf. Acts 18.25).

One may note also that there is frequent reference to "light", a characteristic of the Gospel according to St. John, but not very frequent in this manuscript.

As in all Zadokite and Baptist texts, there is no mention in these pieces of the Resurrection, and Heaven, angels, and the Beyond are not mentioned. It may be supposed therefore that the author or authors of these pieces were Zadokite. Two passages would lead one to think that their author was a convert from paganism and wished himself to make proselytes.

As stated on p. 157, within the second bundle were found not only the portions forming Columns XIII-XVIII but also some sixty other fragments, nine of them of fair size, with remains of lines varying in number from six to sixteen. Most of them, however, were very small, bearing only a few words, and in some cases only an odd letter or two.

There is not a great deal of information that can be gained from these fragments. In Nos. 4 and 45 there is mention of Satan the Destroyer, an expression found nowhere else in these texts. In Fragment 5 there is mention of Wicked Rome, unmistakably written *rwm rš'h*. This expression or its equivalent, "the empire of wickedness" is found frequently in Rabbinic literature. Of all the rolls from Cave I, that of the *Thanksgiving Hymns* is the only one to speak of Rome under its proper name. It has already been met with in *Thanksgiving Hymns,* Column III, and it is also found on No. 7 of these smaller fragments.

Attention may also be drawn to the expression "bastards", which is found on Nos. 6 and 9 of these smaller pieces of manuscript. The term was not limited to children of illegitimate birth, but was also applied to children of converts to Judaism, to those of the first generation, according to some, but even to those of the second, according to others. Degrees of bastardy were recognised, and although the contexts are missing, we may suppose that here the allusion is made only to that degree which disqualified anyone from the priesthood.

On the Fragment 15 we come across the words, "and instruct the poor in spirit in the power of Thy might". The expression "poor in spirit" (*pt'ym*) (which is thought to be the source etymologically from which the French word *petit* is derived) is here found for the first time in these manuscripts. In rabbinic literature the term is often applied to country people, but it is found also in Matt. 5.3, and not used in that way. Elsewhere the expression *'bywnym* (Ebionim) is often found.

# VI

# The Book of Mysteries

Only those passages made up of more or less complete sentences are translated here.

PAGE A, LINES 3-12.
. . . But they do not know the mystery of the future,
And they are not instructed by the teachings of the past.

They therefore will not know that which will happen to them,
And their souls cannot escape from the mystery of the future.

Behold, I give you a sign [* that that shall be]:
In the way that the creatures of wickedness will be imprisoned,
And that evil will be driven away before righteousness,
As darkness is driven away before the light,
And as smoke comes to nothing and exists no longer,
So shall evil be destroyed for ever.

As the sun is made for the world, so shall righteousness show itself,
And all those, who by the miraculous mystery should perish, shall be no more.

Knowledge shall fill the earth,
And in it there shall be no more . . . of iniquities.

The word shall certainly come to pass, and the prophecy is true;
By this is it made known to you that it is irrevocable:
Do not all peoples hate iniquity?
And yet the hand of everyone practises it.
Is not the praise of truth in the mouth of all people?
But does there exist a lip or a tongue that is devoted to it?

*What nation wants a stronger nation to oppress it?*
*Who wishes to be wickedly despoiled of his wealth?*
*Yet, which is the nation that does not oppress its neighbour?*
*Where is the people which does not despoil* (another) *of its wealth? . . .*
. . . . . .

PAGE B.

*if not he who does what is good;*
*And he who does what is evil, if he . . . . he shall succeed in nothing.*

*Thus the money which is always of value is in . . .*
*without riches, and sold without price.*

*For . . . that . . . . . . if not all . . . of blood,*
*And no [pri]ce will be sufficient . . .*

. . . . . . . . . . . . . . . . . . . . . . . . . . . . . . . . .

*God knows all.*

These fragments seem to come from a Jewish-Christian writing, perhaps of the first generation even. The style itself, with its rhetorical questions, is in sharp contrast with that of other texts found at Qumrân.

The author announces the coming of a better world. Iniquity will come to an end and righteousness shall reign. The author sees the proof of what he foretells in the fact that those who hate iniquity, untruth, oppression and pillage, are the first to be iniquitous, untruthful, and spoilers of other people's goods. The continuation is too fragmentary to decide if the author is alluding to the Romans, who bought by the right of the strongest, without money and without price (cf. *Thanksgiving Hymns*, X, 24-6), or if he is giving us in this passage some moral teaching on the lines of the parable of the lilies of the field (Matt. 6.19, 34).

# VII

# The Genesis Apocryphon

For general introduction see pp. 173–8. In the following commentaries, linguistic points are only taken up if they give some indication as to date.

★       ★       ★

The beginning of this manuscript is lost. Only a few letters at the end of a few lines of Column I have survived, and these do not lend themselves to any consecutive reading.

COLUMN I, LINES 1-13.

And behold at that moment I thought in my heart that she had become pregnant by the "Watchers", and by the "holy ones" she . . . . . . . . . and my heart within me was changed concerning this boy. At that moment, I, Lamech, hastened and rose up to visit Bath-Enosh, my wif[e, and I said to her] ". . . . . . and swear by the Most High, by the Lord of Glory, by the King of the Universe . . . . . . . . Sons of Heaven, until you have told me all, in sincerity . . . . . . . . . [In sincerity] tell it to me, and not by lying . . . . . . . by the King of all the worlds, until you have spoken sincerely to me, and with no lying." . . . Thereupon Bath-Enosh spoke to me and with a naked vigour and a . . . . . . . . and she said, "O my brother, and O my lord, recall my pleasure . . . . . . . . . . . we knew each other, and my soul right to the middle of its sheath: and I, in all sincerity . . . . . . ." and upon that, my wandering heart was changed within me.

And as soon as Bath-Enosh, my wife, saw that my face was changed . . . . . . . . . At that moment, she controlled her spirit, and speaking to me she said, "O my lord, and O [my husband, recall my

368

pleasure. Should I have sworn by the Great and Holy, by the King of H[eaven and of all the earth] that yours is this seed, yours the pregnancy, yours the planting of this fruit . . .   . . . and not of some stranger or other, not of one or another of the Watchers, not from one or another of the Sons of Hea[ven] . . .  . . . so that your face should be changed and cast down, and your mind be tormented . . .  . . . . . . It is with sincerity that I am speaking to you."

At the point where we take up this recital, Noah must have been born. Apparently (cf. *Enoch,* 106.1ff.), Lamech had been astonished at this strange child, who, as soon as born, could converse with God. This is the epoch of which the beginning of Chapter 6 of the Book of Genesis speaks: "When men began to multiply on the face of the earth, and daughters were born to them. . . ." Our text gives to the wife of Lamech the name of "Bath-Enosh", which means "Daughter of Man". Under the form *Bêtênos,* the name is given again in *Jubilees,* 4.28. According to our text, she was also the sister of Lamech. The passage in Genesis continues: "the Sons of God saw that the daughters of men were fair, and they took wives of all that they chose". Lamech therefore could have doubts as to the faithfulness of his wife.

The rather crude arguments appealed to by Bath-Enosh to clear herself of her husband's suspicions reflect certain popular beliefs on the circumstances favourable to conception. The context of the term *ndnh'* (its sheath) does not fit the current idea that the body is a sheath protecting an immortal soul. Obviously the author has translated literally the Latin *vagina* in place of using an Aramaic equivalent. Further on a similar euphemism is used (XX, 5).

Some partly effaced letters at the end of the first line allow the supposition that there was a question of Nephilim, that Lamech was afraid that his son was one of these fallen giants referred to in Gen. 6.

COLUMN I, LINES 19-25.

At that moment, I, Lamech, ran to Methuselah my father, and [I told him] all that [so that he should question] his father (*Enoch*) and he would surely learn everything because Enoch is a favourite and a . . . . . . . . . . and because all this would be made known to him. As soon as Methuselah heard . . .  . . .  . . .  . . . towards Enoch, his father, to learn from him the truth of it all . . . . . . . . his good will. He went away therefore to the country of death, to the outer courts and there he met with . . . . . . . . . . And he said to Enoch, his father, "O my father and O my lord, behold I on purpose to . . . . . . . . . . . . . . . and I am saying to you not to be angry with me because I have come even as far as here on purpose to . . . . .

The continuation of the recital seems to follow pretty faithfully the version in the Book of Noah (*Jubilees* 106). According to Biblical tradition, Enoch had been a favourite with God, and "God took him" (Gen. 5.24). So as to learn the truth about the child Noah, Lamech thought it necessary to consult Enoch, but in order to do so he had to have recourse to the good offices of his father, Methuselah. In the *Book of Enoch,* Methuselah went to find his father "at the ends of the world". Our text, however, though difficult to read, lets us understand that Methuselah went to the outer courts of the land of death. According to Genesis, when Noah was born sixty-nine years had passed since Enoch "was not", but it was believed that he enjoyed an everlasting life in some distant region. If our reading of the text is correct, we have here an image taken from pagan mythologies, and that would allow certain conclusions to be drawn as to the region in which our text must have been written.

★          ★          ★

Of Columns III and IV very few words remain. Avigad and Yadin, with reason, suppose that they contained the continuation of the interview between Methuselah and Enoch, and probably an announcement of the Flood. Occasional phrases from Columns V-XVIII are given and discussed in Avigad and Yadin, pp. 18-25. They present numerous analogies with the corresponding passages in the *Book of Jubilees.*

The last surviving columns—XIX-XXII—are published in photographic reproduction and in transcription. There we read:

COLUMN XIX, LINES 7-13 (the first six lines being lost).
. . . . and I said: "It is Thou who . . . . . . . . . so far you have not reached the Holy Mountain!" I set out therefore . . . . . . . . . . . and I kept going towards the south . . . . . . . . . . until I came as far as Hebron. [It was at this time that] Hebron was built, and I dwelt . . . . . . Now there was famine in all the land, and I heard that there was corn . . . in Eygpt. I set out therefore for . . . in the country of

Egypt . . . .. . . . .. at the River Karmona, one of the [four]
rivers which . . .. . . . .. It is there that we . .. . . . .. . ..
our country, and I crossed the seven heads of this river which . . .. . ..
. . . There we left our land and we went up to the land of the sons of
Ham, to the land of Egypt.

When we again take up our text, Abram is relating how he went to
Hebron, on the command of God. After having stayed there (two years)
he decided to go to Egypt to escape the famine (Gen. 12.10ff.).

According to a tradition reported in the Talmud, four rivers bordered
Palestine, the Jordan, the Yarmuk, the Qirmyôn (crimson), and the
Pigah (source, from the Greek *pêgê*). As can be easily seen, these four
rivers, thought of after the pattern of the four rivers bordering Eden, are
partly mythical. According to the *Mishna,* the Pigah and the Qirmyôn
were only marshes whose waters could not be used for ablutions. Moreover, further on our author seems to have overlooked the Qirmyôn. He
gives the name of Gihon to the river fixing the southern limit of the lands
promised to the descendants of Abram.

The "seven heads" of the river crossed by Abram are doubtless the
mythical sources of the Karmona.

COLUMN XIX, LINES 14-28.

And I, Abram, I dreamed a dream in the course of the night of our
entering into Egypt, and I saw in my dream, and behold a cedar and a
palm-tree . . . . . . . .. and some men came and sought to cut
down and uproot the cedar and leave the palm-tree by itself. And the
palm-tree cried out and said: "Do not cut down the cedar for doing
that will bring evil on him who does so." And the cedar was spared
for the sake of the palm-tree, and the cedar was not . . .
And I awoke in the night from my sleep, and I said to Sarai my
wife, "I have dreamed a dream . . . . . . and I am frightened by this
dream." And she said to me, "Tell me your dream and I shall know it."
I began therefore to relate this dream . . . and [I gave her the inter-
pretation] of the dream . . . . . . . .. that they will seek to slay
me and not touch you. That day, all the good . . . . . . . . . in
everything . . . that [. . . . . . . and that you may say] this about me,
"He is my brother." In this way you will frustrate their designs, and
my soul will be preserved because of you . . . . . . . .. from me
and to kill me." And Sarai wept at what I said that night . . . . . ..

. . . wounded . . . . . . . . . . . and Sarai to be given to Zoan . . .
. . . . . . on her soul that no one should see her . . . . . . . . .
until these five years had rolled by.

. . . three men of the princes of Egypt . . . . . . . . . . . on behalf
of the Pharaoh Zoan concerning . . . and concerning my wife, and
these rendered . . . . . . . . . kindness, good sense and honesty.
And I cried out before them . . . . . . . . . . . . . during the
famine which . . . . . . . . . But they did not . . . . . . and
they came as far as the place where . . . . . . . . . . . . . . . by a
wonderful banquet and by a carousal . . . . . . . .

Abram's dream is probably an addition by the author of our roll to the
already amplified legends which were current in his day. If we understand rightly this incomplete text, Abram made his wife swear that she
would live hidden from view so long as they remained in Egypt, lest an
attempt should be made on his life and Sarai taken into Pharaoh's harem.
The continuation of this account is an amplification of a short sentence in
Gen. 12.14: *Jubilees*, 13.11.

After having spent five years in Egypt, Abram received a visit from three
princes charged by Pharaoh to find out about him and his wife. We
imagine that, in spite of everything that Abram did to stop them from
coming to his home, the Egyptian princes managed to reach the place
where, probably, Sarai was taking her bath. It appears as if the princes,
dazzled by her beauty, arranged a wonderful banquet, and, judging by
what follows, one can suppose that it was only her presence of mind
which saved Sarai at that moment from being carried off.

The name Zoan (*ṣ'n*=Tanis) here given to Pharaoh probably comes
from an interpretation of Num. 13.22: "Now Hebron was built seven
years before Zoan in Egypt." In the mind of our author, a town should
bear the name of the monarch reigning at the time of its foundation, and
thus, it would seem, he came to give the name Zoan to Pharaoh who was
contemporary with the events which he relates.

COLUMN XX, LINES 2B-11 (the first one and a half lines having been lost).
. . . . . . . how . . . . . . . . . . . and pleasing the shape of her
face, and how . . . . . . . and how fine were the hairs of her head, how
beautiful looked her eyes, and desirable her nose, and all the flower of
her face (*her mouth*). How lovely was her breast, and pleasant the
whiteness of her arms, and how comely were her hands. How round

and . . . the look of her hips, how beautiful her palm. How pleasing and perfectly shaped her thighs. Of all the maids and brides who go up to the wedding canopy, none is more delightful than she is. Her beauty exceeds that of all women, and it is greater than all their beauty put together. Along with this beauty, she has most wonderful good sense and she is gracious to the tips of her fingers.

As soon as the King heard the words of Hyrcanus and his companions, for as with one mouth had the three of them spoken, he fell madly in love, and sent to bring her at once. He saw her and was astonished at such loveliness. He took her to be his wife and sought to slay me. And Sarai said to the king, "He is my brother." Instead of being thrown into prison . . . because of her, I was set free, and because of her I was not slain. I, Abram, wept bitter tears, and so did Lot, my brother's son, that night when Sarai was carried off from me by force.

A number of points in this description of Sarai are worth noting. Except for the whiteness of her arms, no colour is mentioned. Her shapely hips and her slender fingers are remarked on, but the adjectives are simply laudatory, and so it is impossible to form an idea as to what constituted the ideal of feminine beauty in the author's mind.

In the fifth line we have *kpyh*, her palm, a euphemism for her pubis. This was a current euphemism comparable with the use of the term "hand" for the male organ, as in the *Manual of Discipline*, VII, 13.

The name Hyrcanus given to one of the Egyptian princes is an indication of date. Even after the death of Hyrcanus of the Tobias family, it may be ruled out that this name would be given to an unusual character so long as there was a prince of this name still living, as was the case till A.D. 30. In the opinion of the present writer, another century would have to go by before such a name lost all historical associations.

COLUMN XX, LINES 12-21.

Throughout that night I prayed, implored and besought God, and in grief and with flowing tears I said, "Blessed be Thou, God Most High, Lord of all worlds, for Thou art Lord and Ruler of all. Thou art the Ruler of all the kings of the earth, to perform Thy judgement on them all. Now I raise my voice to Thee concerning the Pharaoh Zoan, King of Egypt, for my wife has been taken away from me by force. Exercise judgement upon him for my sake, and I shall see Thy right hand upon him and upon all his household. Take from him the power this night to defile my wife. So the lords, they shall know Thee, that Thou art the Lord of all the kings of the earth." I wept and was dumb. That night God Most High sent a pestilential wind to strike him with a plague, and to every man of his household did He send an evil wind. The plague fell on him, and on all the men of his household, and he could not come near her nor know her, and he was with her two years. And at the end of two years, the plague and affliction increased in violence and force upon him and upon all the men of his household. He therefore sent out and called all the wise men of Egypt, all the wizards and all the healers of Egypt, to see if they could cure him and the men of his household. And all the healers and wizards and wise men could not rise up and cure him, for that wind struck them too with plague, and they fled.

In this passage, which is an amplification of Gen. 12.17 and *Jubilees*, 13.13, there is no mention of the great wealth received by Abram and Lot while Sarai was living in Pharaoh's harem. That fact is an indication of a definite development of the moral sense, and it allows one more easily to set the text in its age and environment.

Abram's propensity for giving way to tears will have been noticed, and this theme of Abram's sorrow over the carrying away of his wife is also a new element, which could only have been introduced at a late date.

Column XX, Lines 21BB-34.

At this moment, Hyrcanus came and begged me to come and pray for the King, and lay my hand upon him, so that he might live, seeing that in a dream . . . . . . . . . And Lot said, "Abram, my uncle, cannot pray for the King so long as Sarai, his wife, is with him. Now, go, tell that to the King, and when he shall have sent back the wife to her husband, Abram will pray for him, and he shall live."

And as soon as Hyrcanus heard what Lot said, he returned and said to the King, "This plague and affliction which afflict my lord and make him ill are because of Sarai, Abram's wife. Let Sarai be given to her husband, Abram, if it is your pleasure, so that this plague departs and the wind ceases." The Pharaoh therefore called me before him and said to me, "What have you done to me because of Sarai? You said this, 'She is my sister,' and she is found to be your wife, and I have taken her to be my wife. Behold your wife who is with me. Go back, and keep afar from the land of Egypt! But for the present pray for me and for all my household that this evil wind may depart from us." I therefore prayed that this might be, and I placed my hand on his head. The evil wind departed and he recovered.

And the King rose up . . . . . . . . . . . and the King swore to me with an oath that cannot be . . . . . . . . . . . And the King gave (*to Sarai*) . . . . . . most wonderful, marvellous garments in *byssus* and purple . . . . . . before her, and even to Hagar . . . . . . and he appointed men to go with me and to see that I departed.

So I, Abram, came back with flocks enough to make one madly happy, and also with silver and gold. So did I return from Egypt, and Lot, my brother's son, was with me. And Lot also had acquired flocks beyond count, and he took for himself a wife from among . . . . . . . . .

Here we have a further amplification of passages found in Genesis and the *Book of Jubilees*. Apart from the fact that Pharaoh gave wealth to Abram at the moment of his leaving the country, and not because he had married Sarai, this text presents few new elements that are significant. It is impossible to know the circumstances under which Hagar is found in Abram's household. On the other hand, it would appear that in the author's mind Lot took for his wife one of the daughters of Egypt.

COLUMN XXI, LINES 1-7.

. . . . in all places where I had encamped until I reached Beth-El, the same place in which I had built an altar. I rebuilt it, therefore, and I sacrificed on it a whole burnt-offering and an offering to the Most High God. And there I called upon the NAME of the Lord of the Universe, and I praised the NAME of God for all the flock and for all the good that He had given me, and for all the goodness He had shown me, and for having brought me back safe and sound to this country.

After that day, Lot separated from me because of the conduct of our herdsmen. And he turned back, and went to live in the Valley of the Jordan, and he took away all his flock with him. And beyond all measure I also added to what he already had. And he, pasturing his flock, finally reached Sodom, where he built himself a house and dwelt in it. As to myself, I kept myself to the mountain of Beth-El, and unhappiness was upon me because Lot, my brother's son, had separated himself from me.

Once again we come across the theme of Abram's sadness, this time over his nephew's departure. This note of affection, like the mention of presents from the uncle to his nephew, are indications of a definite growth in manners.

## COLUMN XXI, LINES 8-22.

And God appeared to me in a vision of the night and He said to me, "Go up to the summit of Hazor which is to the left of Beth-El, where you are living, and judge with your eyes, looking towards the east and the west, and towards the south and the north. Look upon all this land which I do give to you and to your seed for evermore." And when morning came, I went up to the summit of Hazor, and I saw the land, looking on it from this height, the land from the river of Egypt as far as Lebanon and the Senir (*Hermon*), and from the Great Sea as far as the Hauran, and all the land of Gebal as far as Kadesh, and all the great desert to the east of Hauran and the Senir as far as the Euphrates. And He said to me, "To your seed shall I give all this land, and they shall inherit it, even for ever. And I shall make your seed a great multitude beyond all thought. As no man can number the dust of the earth, neither shall it be possible for your seed to be numbered. Arise, go to and fro, and see its length and its breadth, for to you and your seed do I give this land for all eternity."

Then did I, Abram, go about to make the circuit of the land and to see it. Starting out from the River Gihon, did I make the circuit, and I came along the sea-coast until I had reached the Mount of the Ox, and I turned from the coast of this Great Sea which is salty, and I went along the edge of the Mount of the Ox towards the east, following the breadth of the land, and so I reached the River Euphrates. Then I made a turn, and went along the bank of the Euphrates till I reached the Red Sea in the east. And in this manner I came along the coast of the Red Sea until I reached the tongue (*peninsula*) of the Sea of Reeds, which projects into the Red Sea. I then turned round by the south until I reached the River Gihon, and I returned to my house safe and sound. I found all my men safe and sound, and I moved and dwelt at the oaks of Mamre, which are at Hebron, to the north-east of the town. I built an altar, and on it I made a whole burnt-offering and an offering to the Most High God, and I ate and drank there, I and the men of my household, and I invited Mamre, Aner ('*rnm*) and Eshcol, the three Amorite brothers, my chief friends, and they ate and drank together with me.

This passage gives a double amplification of Gen. 13.14-18. For a study of place-names and personal names, see Avigad and Yadin, pp. 28-33. The points which seem to have particular importance for the dating of our text are found in the lack of agreement between the view of the country from Mount Hazor and the journey made by Abram. It is to be noted that the view southward stretched as far as the river of Egypt (the Nile), whilst the journey starts from the Gihon, one of the four rivers of Paradise, according to Gen. 2.13., and not from the Karmona (see above, XIX, II), which supposedly extended along the frontier of Egypt. Abram's journey led him far beyond the Lebanon and Hermon: following the sea coast, he arrives at the Mount of the Ox, obviously the Amanus Range and not that of the Taurus (see Avigad and Yadin, *op. cit.*). From there, he cuts across the country to reach the Euphrates, the right bank of which he follows till he reaches the Persian Gulf, here called the Red Sea. He then follows the eastern edge of the Arabian Peninsula—this peninsula which projects into the Indian Ocean from the "Sea of Reeds", which translations from the Hebrew call the "Red Sea". Then, following the southern coast, he arrives at his starting-out point, the Gihon. Thus in the mind of the author of our text the Jewish world lies within very curious limits. Deliberately, the Jewish colonies in Egypt are excluded from the lands destined to return to Abram's descendants. The Jewish kingdom of Adiabene on the upper Tigris seems to have been overlooked. There is no remembrance of the Jewish proselytising in Cilicia (Josephus, *Antiquities of the Jews*, XX, vii, 1-3). Even the great centres of Judaism in Mesopotamia are passed over in silence. On the other hand, the Jewish influence along the Euphrates seems to be an indication of Jewish expansion into the Arabian Peninsula, which he incorporates entirely within the promised land of the Jewish people.

It is evident that this journey can only have been conceived well after the fall of Jerusalem in A.D. 70, when many Jews settled in central and southern Arabia and won many adherents to the religion of Yahweh. Is it necessary to set our text as late as the time when small Jewish kingdoms were formed in Arabia, kingdoms which fell before the Ethiopian invaders? Perhaps that would be going too far, but in any case this curious delimitation of the idealised Jewish world can hardly allow our text to be dated before the latter half of the second century A.D.

Column XXI, Line 23 to Column XXII, Line 1.

Before these days, Chedorlaomer, King of Elam, Amraphel, King of Babylon, Arioch, King of Cappadocia, and Tidal, King of "The

Nations", which is between the two rivers, came and made war against Bera, King of Sodom, Birsha, King of Gomorrah ('*mwrm*), Shineab, King of Admah, and "Lost-my-name" (*šmy'bd*), King of Zeboiim, and against King Bela. All these joined together to fight in the Plain of Siddim (*sdy'*). The King of Elam and the other kings with him were stronger than the king of Sodom and all his companions, and they forced them to pay tribute. During twelve years they brought their tribute to the King of Elam, and in the thirteenth year they rebelled against him. In the fourteenth year, the King of Elam spoke to all his companions, and they went up by the way of the desert, and they kept attacking and taking spoil from as far as the Euphrates. They smote the Rephaim, who were in Ashteroth Karnaim, the Zamzumim, who were in Ammon ('*mn*), the Emim in Shaveh Kirioth, the Horites in their mountains of Gebal, and so finally they came to the oak of Paran, which is in the wilderness. Then they turned back . . . . . . . . . in Hazazon-Tamar. And there went out to meet them the King of Sodom, the King of . . . . . . . . . . the King of Admah, the King of Zeboiim and the King Bela . . . . . . battle in the plain . . . face to face with Chedorlaomer . . . . . . . . . who were with him. And the King of Sodom was utterly beaten, and fled, while the King of Gomorrah fell into the pits . . . . . . . . . . The King of Elam took all the flocks of Sodom and of . . . . . . . . . . and they took together with them, among the spoil, Lot, Abram's brother's son, for he was living in Sodom, and all his flocks.

There has been much discussion over the fourteenth chapter of Genesis, which, from its style and language, seems to be a little moralising tale introduced into the history of Abram at a fairly late date. The prevailing opinion is that this *Aggada* was invented in the time of the Maccabees, although some writers hold that it has a basis in history. Even if one could find the names of real persons behind the deformed names transmitted in the Bible, yet such fanciful elements as the mention of antediluvian giants, the anachronisms and the geographical impossibilities should be sufficient to throw serious doubts on the historicity of these recorded events. All medieval legends bring in historical persons under deformed names, so that, in the *Nibelungs,* for instance, Attila becomes Etzel, Theodoric of Verona becomes Dietrich von Bern, etc., but this does not mean that such epics may therefore claim to be history.

In our text, this chapter comes in as an interruption to the recital made by Abram in the first person. The third person is used throughout, and we may therefore consider it as a late addition to some *Book of the Patriarchs* which probably linked up directly the thirteenth with the sixteenth chapter of Genesis. As Avigad and Yadin point out, names, both of places and persons, have undergone further deformation in this tale. In the *Book of Jubilees,* no names are given to the five kings of the Dead Sea, and in this roll the King of Zeboiim is called *šmy'bd* (my-name-is-lost).

These are indications that our roll may be a reproduction of some *Book of the Patriarchs* rewritten by the author of our manuscript, and enriched by this episode, which most probably was not found in the original version.

COLUMN XXII, LINES 1B-12A.

One of the herdsmen of the cattle that Abram had given to Lot, and who had escaped capture, came to Abram. Now Abram at that moment was living in Hebron. The man related how Lot his nephew had been taken along with all his flocks, but not slain, how the kings had left for their own lands along the road of the great hive, taking prisoners, looting, wounding, and killing as they went, and how they had turned by way of the country of Damascus. Abram wept for Lot, his brother's son.

Abram pulled himself together, rose up, and from among his servants chose three hundred and eighteen men of valour, tried in war. Aner, Eshcol and Mamre set out with him, and he organised the pursuit behind them as far as Dan. He found them encamped in the plain of Dan, and threw himself upon them during the night, attacking from all four quarters. He made a slaughter of them in the night, beating them utterly. He pursued them, and they all fled before him as far as Helbôn, which is situated to the left of Damascus. He rescued from them all that they had captured, all their booty, and all their possessions. Even Lot, his brother's son, he set free with all his flock. All the prisoners also, which they had taken, he brought back.

The theme of Abram's sadness, which comes in like a *leitmotiv,* sufficiently shows that this passage too has undergone a considerable remodelling by the author of our roll. It may be remarked that the recapture of the booty carried off by the four kings is here justified by the fact that the cattle taken from Lot came originally from a present of Abram's to his nephew. Our text allows us to presume that Abram intended to take over himself all the captured goods and all the prisoners retaken from the enemy.

COLUMN XXII, LINES 12B-26.

The King of Sodom heard that Abram was bringing back all the prisoners and all the booty. He therefore went up (*as to war*) to meet him (*to fight with him*), and he came to Salem, which is Jerusalem. Now Abram was encamped in the plain of Shaveh, which is the King's Plain, the valley of Beth-Kerem. And Melchizedek, the King of Salem, brought out food and drink for Abram and all the men who were with him. Now he was a priest of the Most High God. He therefore blessed Abram and said, "Blessed be Abram of the Most High God, Lord of Heaven and Earth, and blessed be the Most High God who has delivered your enemies into your hands." And he (*Abram*) gave him the tithe of all that the King of Elam and his companions had amassed (*knsy'*).

At that moment, the King of Sodom drew nigh, and he said to Abram, "My Lord Abram! Give me the souls (*persons*), for they are mine, those which you have with you and which you have rescued from the King of Elam, and the flocks, (*nksy'*) all of them, they shall be left to you."

At that moment, Abram said to the King of Sodom, "I lift up my hand this day towards the Most High God, Lord of Heaven and Earth, (*swearing*) that from a thread to the lacing of a shoe I will take nothing of all that which is with me but belongs to you, so that you may not say, 'It is from my flock that all the wealth of Abram comes,' with the the exception of what these young men with me have already eaten and with the exception also concerning these three valiant men who went out with me, and who are masters in their own right to make any gift to you." And Abram restored all the flocks and all the prisoners, and gave them to the King of Sodom. And all the prisoners with him who were inhabitants of this country he released and let them all go home.

The present writer's interpretation of this passage, which explains the moral of the anecdote, has already been mentioned. In the original version of this tale, the King of Sodom must have insisted that Abram should cede to him the three hundred and eighteen men who had taken part in the expedition (*vide* the Septuagint), so that Abram might be considered as his vassal with a right to a share in the booty. It is quite certain that in the mind of the first writer of this story Abram had never wanted to keep as slaves the persons who had been freed, particularly his nephew, Lot, and it is certain that there could have been no question of considering these captives as the property of the King of Sodom. As already pointed out, it is due to a mistaken reading that the description of the King of Sodom as a "righteous and peace-loving king" has become "Melchizedek, King of Salem". Of the original version, our text has preserved the mention that the King of Sodom had set out with the intention of fighting Abram so as to recover his property. It is clear that our author in no way connects the institution of the tithe with the benediction of Melchizedek (*vide Jubilees*, 13.25-7).

Summing up, if one excludes the personalisation of Melchizedek and the attempted identification of Salem with Jerusalem, the principal point of difference between the present version and the original version of the legend lies in the remitting to the King of Sodom of the prisoners, and the freeing of the captives who were inhabitants "of this country". In the last episode, Lot is not mentioned. That should be sufficient to demonstrate the perplexity of the author in the face of a text which he feels he must put into his recital, but of which he clearly cannot see the purpose.

The personalisation of Melchizedek and the identification of Salem with Jerusalem cannot be earlier than the latter half of the first century A.D. But the underlying text of the incident which the author of our roll used may be older, for it puts the accent on the originally hostile intentions of the King of Sodom which the Biblical version has removed.

## Column XXII, Lines 27-34.

After these events, God appeared to Abram in a vision and said to him, "Behold, ten years have rolled by since the day when you set out from Haran; two years were spent in wandering to and fro; seven years were spent in Egypt; and it is a year since you came back from there. Now examine and reckon up all that you possess. See how often and how wonderfully everything you brought out has doubled since the day you left Haran. And now, fear not! I am with you, and I shall be your support and strength. As a protection over you and over all that you have amassed, I shall keep watch, with a might greater than yours, keeping secure your wealth and your flock, to your exceeding great joy."

And Abram said, "My Lord God, I have riches and flocks beyond all reason. But what shall that profit me seeing that when I die, I shall be naked (*as he is*) who has no son. One of the sons of my household will be my heir: Eliezer, the son of . . . . . . . . . . . . will inherit from me." And God said, "It is not he who shall be your heir, for there shall come forth . . .

This passage, which continues the interruption which breaks into the autobiographies of the patriarchs, most probably included all Chapter 15 of the Book of Genesis (*Jubilees* 14.1-18). From the part that has come down to us we notice a displacement of the moral accent. God is not offering Abram a great "recompense" to compensate him for the renunciation he had made in the conflict with the King of Sodom, as in Genesis and Jubilees. Here the accent is placed on the wealth which Abram had already accumulated and which he is not strong enough by himself to defend. In all probability the scene of the covenant with God and the predictions contained in this fifteenth chapter of Genesis would form the subject of lengthy developments.

The part of the roll that has been discovered stops here in the middle of a sentence. As already pointed out, the following sheet seems to have been cut off with a knife before the roll was placed in Cave I at Qumrân. It may be presumed that Abram's recital in the first person was taken up again and gave the events of Chapter 16 of the Book of Genesis.

# PART THREE

# The Damascus Document

Since the publication of photographic reproductions of the medieval fragments found in the *geniza* of the Qaraite synagogue in Cairo, which are sometimes called the *Zadokite Fragments* and at other times the *Damascus Document*, there have been several fresh translations of these texts including that by G. Vermès (*Les Manuscrits du Désert de Juda*, pp. 159–84; English edition, *Discovery in the Judean Desert*, pp. 157–185) and by Thedor H. Gaster (*The Scriptures of the Dead Sea Sect*, London, 1957, pp. 71–94). The divergences from the translation published by R. H. Charles (*Apocrypha and Pseudepigrapha of the Old Testament*, Oxford, 1913, Vol. II, pp. 785-834) are frequently considerable. The translation here offered is based on the photographs published by S. Zeitlin (*The Zadokite Fragments*, Philadelphia, 1952). It does not take into account the different suggested emendations to the text, and follows the text as closely as possible.

The Cairo fragments seem to come from four books. Usually two versions are recognised, the version "A" and the parallel version "B". In reality, the fragments of version "A" divide out between three books here called "A1", "A2" and "A3". These are translated one after the other, with the parallel version "B" inserted after "A1".

## THE FRAGMENTS "A1"

The eight columns of this text seem to be part of a discourse read in the course of the ceremonies of Confirmation (*Bar Miṣvah*) to which the Qaraites attached especial importance. This sermon is rather long, and must have been frequently touched-up, as comparison with the parallel text "B" shows. It outlines the somewhat mythical history of Qaraitism, and emphasises the superiority of the Qaraite sect over all the other schools of Judaism. It appears to be an extract from a work which was probably entitled *The Book of the Division of the Ages* (see below XVI, 3).

PAGE I, LINES 1-8A.
And now listen, all you who know righteousness, and be instructed by

God's doings. For He has a controversy with all human flesh, and He will perform his judgement upon all those who despise Him. Because of the faithless who abandoned Him, He hid His face from Israel and from His sanctuary, and He gave them over to the sword. But because He remembered the Covenant with the "first ones", He caused a remnant to be preserved from out of Israel, and gave them not over to extermination. And when His wrath ended, 390 years after delivering them into the hands of Nebuchadnezzar, King of Babylon, He looked upon them. He made a branch to spring forth from Israel and from Aaron, that it might have His land as an inheritance, and be nourished by the good things of the earth.

This historical introduction was usual with the Jews, and is frequent in all medieval literature. Here it serves as a preamble to what was to be presented as a history of the Qaraite movement. In a few sentences, the author quickly runs through Jewish history up to the Babylonian Exile. The 390 years referred to here are taken from Ezek. 4.5. It is because God remembered the "first ones" (Abraham, Isaac and Jacob) that He allowed a remnant of Israel to survive and allowed them to return to Palestine.

PAGE I, LINES 8B-11A.

Then they understood their crimes and knew that they were guilty men, and were like to the blind and those who grope after the way. During twenty years God took notice of their deeds, for they sought after Him with all their heart, and He raised up for them a Teacher of Righteousness that he might lead them in the way of His heart.

In these lines, the prayer of Ezra (9.6-15) is recalled, and also, by a faulty interpretation of the text, the twenty years mentioned in Neh. 1.1.

PAGE I, LINES 11B-17A.

And he made known, for the ages of those who should come after, what He did at the later time to the Council of the Apostates. They (the apostates) are those who turned aside from the way, and the later time is the age concerning which it was written "Israel hath behaved himself stubbornly like a stubborn heifer" (Hos. 4.16), when arose the Man of Lying who poured out for Israel the waters of falsehood. And "he caused them to wander in a chaos where there is no way" (Job 12.14; Ps. 107.46), to bring low the everlasting hills, to cause men to depart from the paths of righteousness, and to displace the frontiers which the "first ones" had fixed for their inheritance so that within them, they were bound to the power of His Covenant.

The "later" time in which God took action against the Council of the Apostates is that which preceded the fall of Jerusalem and the end of the Jewish State. In the period in which this text was written, it is probable that to one and the same "Man of Lying" were attributed all the misfortunes which fell upon the Jews, and which Nehemiah (or Ezra) was said to have foretold. Even "he who removes the frontiers" (a quotation from Mic. 7, 11, and generally interpreted as an allusion to Agrippa II), to the author of this text, does not seem to have been a very well defined personage.

PAGE I, LINES 17B-PAGE II, LINE 1.

(That came about) so that they might be given over to the sword of vengeance, the avenger of the Covenant, because they sought flatteries, nursed delusions, and desired revellings. They decided for what was convenient and declared the wicked to be righteous, and slandered the righteous. They infringed the Covenant, they committed injustice and sought the soul of the righteous. In their souls they hated all those who walked in the way of what was right, and they pursued them so as to give them over to the sword, and they took joy in the dissensions of the nation. But the wrath of God flamed out against their Councils to cause all their multitude to perish, and their actions were filthiness in His eyes.

In the eyes of the historian, the destruction of the Jewish State was the result of Divine wrath caused by the behaviour of the Pharisaic rabbis and their opposition to the "righteous", to the Zadokites with whom the Qaraites recognised that they had many points in common.

PAGE II, LINES 2-10.

And now, listen to me, all of you who are entering into the Covenant, and I shall lay bare your ears by the recital of the ways of the wicked. God loves knowledge. He hath set up before him wisdom and intelligence, and quickness of mind and knowledge are for His service. Long-suffering is His, and abundance of pardons with remission of sins for those who repent. But power and might and the great heat of flaming fire are His also, announcing the destruction of all who turn aside from the way and hate what is right a total destruction against which nothing can help them. From before the world was, it is not among them that God has chosen His elect, and even before their actions had been decided, He knew them, and He had the periods of their customs in abomination. He hid His face therefore from the country from then until they had been brought to naught. For he knows how long they are allowed to continue, the date of their end, and the reason for it. He knows, not only for the present worlds but also for all the worlds to come, and even what will befall them all through all the years of eternity.

It is not at all necessary to suppose that this discourse was addressed to proselytes, even if it is allowed that at certain times in the Middle Ages the Qaraite movement may have taken in new members. The historical introduction was intended for the Qaraite community, for all those who "knew righteousness", and who are thus called upon to witness to the truthfulness of what follows. The discourse, or rather, the text about to be read, is addressed to young people of the age of thirteen who are becoming *Bar Miṣvah* and who "are entering into the Covenant", as is done in all Jewish communities.

This second introduction develops the current ideas about the succession of worlds destined to come to an end one after the other. The Qaraites' hatred of the rabbinists shows itself by the idea that God had in abomination the period during which the rabbis imposed their customs, and that it was for this reason that He decided to put an end to all the worlds ruled by the rabbis.

PAGE II, LINES 11–13.

And in all (*these worlds*) He has raised up for Himself "callers upon the NAME" so that there should be preserved a remnant on earth to replenish the face of the world with their offspring. And by His Messiah, He has made them to know His Holy Spirit. For it is He who is the Truthful One, and in accordance with the meaning of His NAME are also theirs. But those whom He hates, He causes to go astray.

From this passage it can be seen that the Qaraites placed the origin of their sect in the most far-off ages. In all the worlds gone by, there had been "callers upon the NAME" (*qry'y šm*—really "priests", but, by a play on words, "Qaraites") and at the destruction of each world, a remnant was preserved. A Messiah, doubtless Anan, had impressed upon them later the spirit of God called "the Truthful One", and they can be recognised by their theophorous names.

We should remember that the NAME of God could not be pronounced. It was not allowed even to say *El* (God) or *Adonai* (my Lord) and it was accounted blasphemy to swear by *aleph lamedh* (*El* or *Elohim*) or by *aleph daleth* (*Adonai*)—see XV, 1. One said *ha-Shêm*, "the Name", or *'Emeth* "the Truthful", a word which was made up of the first, middle and last letters of the alphabet. This word was looked upon as God's seal.

In this medieval text, the expression "the interpretation of His NAME" does not apply only to strictly theophorous names in *Jah* and *iah,* or *El* and *-el*. Names like *Zadok* (righteous), *Japheh* (beautiful), *Tob* (good), etc., could be considered as "interpretations" of the NAME of God, as it is done among Moslems, and it is well known that such names figure largely in Qaraite family names.

PAGE II, LINES 14-17A.

And now, sons, listen to me and I shall lay bare your eyes to see and understand the works of God, so that you may choose what He desires, detest what He hates, walk straightly in all His ways, and not go astray through the inclinations of guilty flesh and the instincts of lewdness. For from of old until now, these inclinations have made the Great (*rbym*) to totter and the brave of the army to stumble.

The exordium ends here. The name "son", given to the young Qaraites who had made their first reading in the Synagogue, is a clear indication of the meaning to be given the whole of this discourse. It has nothing to do with the initiation into a monastic order, post-Essene or any other, but belongs to the confirmation ceremony of *Bar Miṣvah.*

The word *rbym* found frequently in this text cannot signify "the many" for it is put in apposition with "the brave". It could signify "the Great" or "the princes", but it is well to remember that in post-Biblical periods a "Great" in Hebrew has never referred to anyone other than a scholar versed in religious knowledge or in other words, a "rabbi". To translate "rabbi" deliberately by "great" in other passages would be to change entirely the nature of the text, as one would be doing to a Christian document if "bishop" was rendered "overseer".

PAGE II, LINE 17B to PAGE III, LINE 12.

By walking in the stubbornness of their hearts, the heavenly Watchers fell, for through it they allowed themselves to be caught and they kept not the commandments of God and also their sons who had bodies which were tall as cedars and of a height like that of mountains. So they fell, as did all flesh that was on the firm earth, and they perished, and became as though they had not been, for having followed their own wilfulness and because they had not kept the commandments of their Creator, so that in the end, His avenging wrath was kindled. By it (*stubbornness*) the sons of Noah and their families were made to stumble, and by it were they destroyed. Abraham did not walk so. He d[id what was right and observed] the commandments of God. He did not choose to do according to the wilfulness of his spirit. He handed on the tradition to Isaac and to Jacob, who observed it, and it was written of them that they were loved of God and were always guardians of the Covenant.

The sons of Jacob stumbled because of them (*inclinations and instincts*) and they were punished because of their errors. Their sons, in Egypt, walked in the stubbornness of their hearts so that they took evil counsel regarding the commandments of God, and each one did what was right in his own eyes. They ate blood, and He wiped out the remembrance of them in the desert [* when He said] to them, at Kadesh, "Go up", and they hardened their hearts and listened not to the voice of their Creator, nor to the commands of their leaders, and they murmured in their tents. And the wrath of God was kindled against their congregation. Also their sons perished because of it, and through it their kings were brought to naught, their heroes perished, and their country became a desert. It is by it that the "first ones" who had entered into the Covenant were rendered guilty, and they were given over to the sword for having abandoned the Covenant of God, for they chose to do as they desired following the stubbornness of their hearts, so that they might each do as he wished.

This further historical introduction addressed to the young man who became *Bar Miṣvah* took the form of a résumé of sacred history. From the time when "there were giants in the earth . . . . . . after the sons of God had gone in to the daughters of men, and these had borne them children" (Gen. 6.4) till the destruction of the whole generation of men who had come forth from Egypt, and till the death of Moses (Deut. 32.51), God had always punished those who had wanted to go their own way, and one of the most serious crimes was that of not respecting food taboos.

This is the history of the "first ones" with whom God had made a Covenant, and of whom a remnant survived to take possession of the land of Canaan. All the teachings of the past had served for nothing. There has always been the stubborn, and that is why the land of Israel had been lost and had become a desert.

## PAGE III, LINES 12B-20A.

And among those who had held fast to His commandments, and who had survived of them, God re-established for ever His Covenant with Israel, revealing those hidden things because of which all Israel had stumbled: His holy sabbaths, His glorious festivals, His righteous testimonies, His true ways, and the desires of His will which a man should fulfil so as to live by them. (*All that*) He had inscribed before them, and they dug a well from which to draw abundant waters, and he who despises them (*the abundant waters—that is to say, the revelations of His Law*) shall not live. But they (*the people of Israel*) let themselves be dragged into the sin of human nature, and into the ways of defilement, and they said, "May we have it as we like it!" However, God, in the mystery of His miracle, forgave them their faults and took away their sins. And He built for them the "House of the Truthful" in Israel, like to which there had not been in the past, nor until this day.

In the mind of the author, God re-established His Covenant with the Israelites (Joshua, 1.7-9, 5.2-8). He raised up wise men to interpret the Law ("dig the wells") and make known the rules about the observance of sabbaths and of festivals, etc., rules which the generation which came out of Egypt had not observed. Still the people did not observe these rules, yet God forgave them and even consented to fix His dwelling in Israel, where the Temple (the "House of the Truthful") was built.

## PAGE III, LINE 20B to PAGE IV, LINE 6.

Those who hold fast (*to the Temple, are destined*) to eternal life, and all human glory will be theirs, as God has established it for them, saying through Ezekiel the prophet, "The priest (*Kohen*), the Levite (*Levi*) and the sons of Zadok who kept the charge of My sanctuary when the children of Israel went astray from Me in their unfaithfulness, they shall offer unto Me the fat and the blood."

The Cohens are those who have repented in Israel, and who have left the land of Judah, and (*the Levis are*) those who have joined them, and the Sons of Zadok are the elect of Israel, who "call upon the NAME" and who shall be standing to the last days. That is the interpretation of their names, according to their families and to the end of their ministries, whatever the number of their tribulations and the years of their exile.

The purpose of the whole of this historical introduction is to explain why the Qaraites alone are promised glory and eternal life. Ezekiel had said (44.15), that the descendants of the priests, of the Levites and the Sons of Zadok alone should have the right of priesthood. The author makes a subtle distinction. The privileges attached to these names are limited to those Qaraites ("callers upon the NAME") who live in the Diaspora ("who have left the land of Judah") and these privileges will remain theirs "whatever the number of their tribulations and the years of their exile".

It should be remembered that among the Jews of the Diaspora, persons with the names of Cohen and Levi, however spelt, always enjoy certain prerogatives and have certain duties with respect to the community. In the synagogue it is always someone of this descent who is called upon to read the first lesson taken from the roll of the Law. And it is a Levi who has to read the second lesson. It is always the persons who claim descent from the priests who have the responsibility to pronounce the benediction of the congregation, and it is always one of them who is asked to receive the gift of the first-born son, who is then redeemed by a sum of money destined to be used as alms, etc. In a word, the ancestral name of a Jew counts for much in religious life even in these days. Anyone of such descent must not get defiled by being present at funerals, and must not marry a widow or a divorced person, etc.

But the author of this writing makes a sharp distinction on this subject. These rules only apply to the Qaraites, for the prophet had also spoken of the Sons of Zadok, and according to the author's interpretation, those who "call upon the NAME" (*qry'y hšm*) must mean the Qaraites.

## PAGE IV, LINES 6–12A.

This is the interpretation of their various sacred actions, for the sake of which God granted them forgiveness, because they had rendered justice to the righteous and had made accusation against the wicked. All who come after them must act according to the interpretation of the Law by which the "first ones" allowed themselves to be admonished, until the end of this present age. They must conform to the Covenant which God established with "the first ones" to grant them forgiveness for their faults. So shall God give forgiveness to them for their sake. And when the number of the years of present age shall be fulfilled, one shall no longer have to join the house of Judah, but everyone shall take his stand on his citadel. The wall is built, the boundaries far removed.

If God pardons the Qaraites, it is because the Cohens have always conformed to the interpretations of the Law which had been laid down by the "first ones" (patriarchs). It must always be so at least so long as the laws then in force confused the Qaraites with the rabbinic Jews who had "built the wall". When the existing period was over, they would no longer have to join "the house of Judah", the separation between the Qaraites and the rabbinists being final (free interpretation of Mic. 7.11).

It should be remembered here that the authorities in Moslem countries did not wish to distinguish between rabbinic Jews and Qaraites, and recognised only one rabbinate. Intolerance, however, was intense within the Jewish communities. In towns where Jews were not shut up in Ghettoes, the Qaraites lived in "camps" surrounded with walls, less for protection from members of other religions than from their rabbinic co–religionists. The case of Constantinople, where in the nineteenth century Jews lived in freedom, is well known. M. Franco (*Essai sur l'histoire des Israélites de l'Empire ottoman*, Paris, 1897, p. 171 and note 2) gives an account of serious incidents which occurred there in November 1866: "The Qaraites were penned up, so to speak, in an area enclosed on all sides by walls so as to escape from the intolerance of the Jewish population. Each evening, the gates of the ghetto were carefully closed by the Qaraites. By day, they dared not go into places frequented by orthodox Jews. Had they done so, they would most certainly have been stoned." It may be supposed that in earlier times, the position of Qaraites in Moslem countries could not have been much easier.

PAGE IV, LINES 12B-20A.

During all these years, Belial will be let loose in Israel, as God said by the mouth of Isaiah, the son of Amoz, saying, "Fear and the pit and the snare, are upon thee, O inhabitant of the earth" (24.17). This means the three snares of Belial spoken of by Levi, the son of Jacob, snares by which he caught some Israelites, setting out as right three things, sensuality, wealth and the profaning of the sanctuary. He who avoids the first is taken by the second, and he who escapes from that will be taken by the third. As to the builder of the wall (Ezek. 13.10) and those who follow the command (Hos. 5.11), their commander is the prattling orator of whom it has been said, "*They shall make a prophet of a little child*" (*Mic. 2.6*).

Referring to an apocryphal work which has not come down to us, perhaps another version of the *Testament of Levi*, the author tells us that so long as the separation between the Qaraites and the rabbinists is not complete, Belial will be let loose in Israel.

The word "Belial" means literally "without yoke", and denotes all those who break loose from the yoke of God, of their father, of their master, etc., that is to say, rebels. The name was applied to the rebel angel, the diabolic tempter, Satan.

In the passage which follows, the author sets out the reasons for considering the orthodox Jews as impious. In the present passage, the phrase "builder of the wall" in all likelihood refers to the redactors of the Mishna and the Talmud. As to the "prattling orator" it could have denoted any rabbi in any community whatsoever. At the time when this text was drawn up, the Jewish community may have elected a chief rabbi who was exceptionally young. The Qaraites seem to be reproaching the orthodox for allowing themselves to be directed by a "mere child".

PAGE IV, LINE 20B TO PAGE V, LINE 6A.

They have allowed themselves to be doubly taken by sensuality, by taking two wives in their lifetime, wheras the principle of the creation is, "*A male and a female, He created them*" (*Gen. 1.27*).

Those who entered into the ark, entered it two by two. As regards the prince it is written, "*he shall not multiply wives to himself*" (*Deut. 17.17*). But David had not read the Book of the Law, which was sealed and in the Ark, and this was not opened in Israel from the day of the death of Eliezer and of Joshua and of the Saviour. And as the venerable who sacrificed to Ashtoreth were rendered unclean, it was hidden until Zadok arose. And the deeds of David were beneficient apart from the blood of Uriah, and God therefore pardoned him.

The first reproach that the Qaraites levelled against orthodox Jews was aimed at their marriage laws. Not only did the rabbis authorise remarriage after divorce, but in certain cases they even allowed a man to have two wives, notably in the case where the man had to undertake long journeys and have two homes in two different towns far away from each other. The Qaraites insisted on strict monogamy. David could have sinned through ignorance, as the Book of the Law had not yet been re-found and read. He therefore took two (?) wives (2 Sam. 12.9-14), but God pardoned him because of his other good deeds. The mention in this passage of the "Saviour" (*ywš[w]‘*) crossed out and then written in again is very difficult to explain.

## PAGE V, LINES 6B TO IIA.

And, moreover, they pollute the sanctuary, for amongst them there is not anyone who makes the distinction laid down in the Law. They lie with her who sees the blood of her menstruation, and they take to wife, one, the daughter of his brother, and another, the daughter of his sister. Yet Moses had said, *"Thou shalt not go into the sister of thy mother, for she is thy mother's flesh"* (*Lev. 18.13*). And if the Law of nakednesses was written for males, it is the same for women. If, for instance, a brother's daughter uncovers the nakedness of her father's brother, she is also of the same blood.

Among the taboos laid down by the Jewish religion, those regarding sex and food are the most numerous and the most severe. The impurity of a menstruous woman extends even to the seat on which she sits. This rule was not always observed, but the Qaraites attached great importance to it. Because of this, it was recommended not to sit down in the house of a rabbinist Jew, as it was impossible to know if the divans were ceremonially clean (see below, V, 15).

The Jewish law, which forbade marriage between aunt and nephew, allowed that between uncle and niece. The Qaraites held that these unions were of an incestuous nature, whether the niece was on the father's or the mother's side. Their point of view was explained by the analogy with "what is forbidden to the boy should also be forbidden to the girl". Through not having observed this principle, the rabbis "profaned the santuary". In the mind of the author, the priests of Jerusalem had been guilty of the same kind of offences before the destruction of the Temple.

These two reproaches made against orthodox Jews are typically Qaraite, and cannot be attributed to any other Jewish sect. (The words "they lie with" should be taken in the sense of "they share the same bed".)

## PAGE V, LINES IIB-I5A.

They have also defiled the holy spirit within them, and in the language of mockers, they have opened their mouth about the statutes of God's Covenant and said, "They are not correct." They utter abominations about them. They are all kindlers of fire, firebrands shooting their arrows (Isa. 50.11). They spin spiders' webs, and the adder's eggs are theirs (Isa. 59.5). He who draws near to them, will not be able to make himself clean, the covering in their houses imparts guilt, unless one has been forced there.

Here it is the opportunism of the orthodox rabbis which is attacked. As they had to have contacts with non-Jews, they had come to say, "in the language of the mockers"—that is to say, in Greek or Arabic—that the Biblical regulations were not to be taken absolutely literally. They had directed arrows against the Qaraites, whom they treated as fanatics, and may thus have been the cause of some persecutions. As they received visits from unbelievers, the uncleanness of their visitors was communicated to the coverings of their divans, *khr bytw* doubtless being another spelling for *kr bytw*. It was therefore forbidden to the Qaraites to sit down on the divan of a rabbinist Jew, "unless forced to do so" (cf. V, 7, above).

PAGE V, LINE 15B to PAGE VI, LINE 2A.
For from of old, God has watched their works, and His wrath has been kindled because of their evil doings. For it is people of no understanding (Isa. 27.11), a foreign nation void of counsel because they have no understanding in them (Deut. 32.28). For, in the beginning, Moses and Aaron stood on the side of the Prince of Light, and in his malice, Belial stirred up Jannes and his brother, when Israel was saved the first time.

   But in the last age of the destruction of the country, displacers of frontiers arose, and led Israel astray. The country was laid waste, for they spoke of rebellion against the commandments of God, given by Moses and by the holy one, His anointed. They prophesied lying, so that Israel should turn from the truth of God.

The author attributes the destruction of the Jewish state to the wrath of God against those who had not kept the commandments promulgated through the mediation of Moses and of His anointed one (Aaron). The names of the magicians called for by Pharaoh (Exod. 7.11) are not reported in the Old Testament, nor in the Apocrypha of the Old Testament, but are mentioned, however, in 2 Tim. 3.8. It may very well be that this epistle of St. Paul borrowed this detail from some Jewish tradition which happened to be known to the Qaraites in the Middle Ages.

PAGE VI, LINES 2B-11A.

And God remembered the Covenant of the "first ones", and He took understanding ones from Aaron, and wise ones from Israel, and He made them to swear that they would dig the well, *"The well which the princes dug, which the nobles of the people delved with the sceptre"* (Num. 21.28). The well, that is the Law, and those who dug are the penitents of Israel who left the land of Judah, and went and established themselves as strangers in the land of Damascus, those whom God has called, every one of them, princes. For they sought Him, though their glory was appreciated in the mouth of no one. And the sceptre (*a play upon the word*) is the study of the Law, as Isaiah said, *"He bringeth forth the instrument for his work"* (54.16). And the nobles of the people are those who come to dig the well with sceptres, following the (*commandments*) set forth by the commander, that they should walk in accordance with them at all times, until the period of wickedness comes to an end. And without these (*commandments*) the nobles would not know how to stand fast until the last days, when the Teacher of Righteousness arrives.

Remembering the Covenant with the "first ones" (Abraham, Isaac and Jacob), God has caused the most intelligent of the sons of Aaron and the wisest of the people of Israel to leave the land of Judah, and He has saved them from destruction. The author tells us that this was the beginning of the Jewish Diaspora in Damascus. It is known that a Jewish colony was living there in the first century A.D., and that its members were not always in agreement with the rabbinic authorities in Judea (cf. Acts 9.1-2). It is also known that in its earlier stages, the Qaraite movement found many of its followers in Syria. It was in Damascus that Anan founded a school, and several learned Qaraites made a name there. Rabbi Mokha and his son Rabbi Mosheh, inventors of the system of vocalisation called "Palestinian" were Qaraites. The author of this text regrets that not all the learned Qaraite Massoretes had been as highly honoured as they deserved, and that in quite a number of cases their names had been forgotten.

It is not at all surprising that the Qaraites of Egypt put back the origin of their community to the Jewish community in Damascus. We do not know how far back the community at Fustât (Cairo) went, nor in fact where its first members came from. After all, it is quite possible that they did come from Damascus. In any case by the beginning of the tenth century, the Qaraite community in Cairo was already firmly established. In A.D. 915 it was violently attacked by Rabbi Saadya ben Joseph of the Fayûm, but this did not prevent it from growing in importance, nor from gaining many proselytes from among the rabbinist Jews, especially in the eleventh century.

In the last sentence we find expression of a messianic hope. A new "Teacher of Righteousness" was to appear at the end of the Jewish Dispersion, and, as a second Ezra, lead back the Qaraites to Judea (see above I, 11).

PAGE VI, LINE 11B TO PAGE VII, 6A.

None of those brought into the Covenant should enter the sanctuary to kindle fire upon His altar in vain. They shall be appointed for the closing of the door, in accordance with what God has said, "*Who among you will shut his door?*" and "*Do not kindle fire on my altar in vain*" (*Mal. 1.10*), if you do not take heed to behave till the end of wickedness, according to the interpretation of the Law, to keep apart from the sons of the pit, to reject the wealth of the wicked by a vow and a curse, swearing by the Treasure of the Sanctuary; and (*if you do not take heed to keep apart*) from him who robs the poor of his people, and from those who make widows their prey, and who murder the orphans; and (*if you do not take heed*) to make distinction between the pure and the impure, and to recognise the sacred from the profane, and to observe the Sabbath day as it has been interpreted, as well as the feasts and the Day of Fasting according to the commandments of those who entered into the New Covenant in the land of Damascus; and (*if you do not take heed*) to deduct the holy things (*the terûmah*) as they are interpreted, to love each one his brother as himself, to stretch out the hand to the sorrowful, the poor and the stranger, and to seek, everyone, the well-being of his brother. Let no one make himself guilty with the flesh of his flesh. Let a vow be made to keep away from harlots in conformity with the Law, to reprove each one his brother, as it has been commanded, and not to maintain ill-feeling from one day to another, and to avoid all forms of uncleanness according to the laws respecting them. Let no one make abominable the holy spirit which God has apportioned out to them. All those who walk in this way, in holy integrity, observing all the prohibitions imposed by God's Covenant, are assured of living a thousand ages.

It is difficult to know if the beginning of this passage, which has to be taken in an allegorical sense, refers to what was an ancient practice. In the early centuries of this era, the Jews gave the name of "proselytes of the door", as opposed to "proselytes of righteousness", to certain Gentiles who adopted a part only of the Jewish practices. Probably this expression is interpreted here in a quite different sense. In the Orient, Qaraite synagogues are in fact closed while services are being conducted. It may be that the young members were charged with the closing of the gates of the Ghetto so that the Qaraites might be safe from the attacks of the orthodox Jews when they celebrated their feasts, which did not always coincide with the dates fixed by the rabbinate.

The other ordinances are: (1) To accept the interpretation of the Law as it has been formulated by the Qaraites. (2) To keep apart from those destined to the Pit—that is to say, the rabbinist Jews. (3) Not to let oneself be corrupted by unbelievers. (4) To avoid contact with the rabbis who "rob the poor of their people". (5) To observe the Qaraite rules as to the clean and the unclean, the sacred and the profane. (6) To observe the regulations regarding the Sabbath. (7) To keep the dates for feasts and the Day of Fasting as laid down in the Qaraite calendar. (8) To deduct the *terûmah* according to the Qaraite rules. (9) To practise charity. (10) To avoid incest as that was understood by the Qaraites. (11) To keep away from prostitutes. (12) Not to harbour ill-feeling. (13) To avoid contact with everything unclean.

A few of these regulations demand further explanation:

(1) A connection has frequently been made between the Qaraites and the Zadokites of the first century A.D., yet there are very noticeable differences between these two movements. It is possible that the Zadokite movement, which survived into the Middle Ages in the Syrian Diaspora, may have evolved in the course of the centuries, and that at the time when Anan separated from rabbinism, the Zadokites had given up many of their earlier doctrines. Like the Zadokites, the Qaraites did not acknowledge the interpretations of the Law codified in the Mishna and in the Talmudim. On the other hand, they recognised the authority of the prophetical books of the Old Testament, and even accepted a number of deutero-canonical and apocryphal books to which the rabbis allowed no authority. The Qaraites had their own exegetes, who were often in opposition to the rabbinist interpreters.

(2) "Those who are destined to the Pit"—that is to say, those for whom there will be no resurrection from the dead—is an expression

which sufficiently marks off the Qaraites from the Zadokites, who had no belief in life after death. Here it is applied to all those who have not observed the Qaraite laws, and who will therefore not partake of eternal life in the world to come.

(3) "The wicked" always denotes the ruling nation—in this case the Egyptian Moslems. The recommendation was given not to allow oneself to be tempted by the riches owned by the rulers. It was necessary to regard them as "a devoted thing" coveting or partaking of which was the greatest of all crimes. Nothing was to be accepted from the Moslems, even as a present, for long experience had shown that wealth possessed by Jews periodically led to pogroms. The Qaraite oath not to defile oneself with the riches of the "wicked" had to be made in a threefold manner: by a vow, by a curse, and by swearing "by the Treasure of the Temple" (see, above, p. 190).

(4) "He who robs the poor of his people." This can only denote the orthodox rabbis whom the Qaraites reproached for covetousness. The other reproaches made against them of plundering widows and murdering orphans suggests that the orthodox rabbis did not carry out charitable duties like those laid by the Qaraites on their judges (see below, page XIV).

(5) The Qaraite regulations concerning purity, especially that of food, differ considerably from those of the rabbinists. This will be dealt with below.

(6) In the same way, the rules concerning the Sabbath rest are most strict among the Qaraites. They are dealt with in Fragment "A2".

(7) The Qaraites do not follow the calendar of feasts as established by the orthodox rabbis. For instance, they insist that Pentecost shall always fall on a Sunday. There are also differences in the way they celebrate some of the feasts—not sounding the horn, for instance, on 1st Tishri. They do not keep the fast of Esther, the feast of *Purim* lasts two days, they ignore *Chanukkah,* and fast on the 10th Ab instead of the 9th. Many traditional prayers are not recited in their synagogues.

(8) After the destruction of the Temple of Jerusalem and the ending of the sacrifices, the rabbis had taken over the right to certain dues which formerly belonged to the priests (see above, pp. 61, 219 and 220). It is easy to understand that the Qaraites insisted that these "pure things of the rabbis" (*toharôth harabbîm*) or "holy things," should be levied exclusively for the benefit of their own rabbis.

(9) The commandment to exercise charity seems to be limited to the

"brother"—that is to say, a Qaraite who is poor, or who is a stranger and on a journey.

(10) The prohibition of incest was aimed specially at marriages between uncle and niece, which were allowed in orthodox Judaism.

(11) For a long time the Qaraites laid it down that a youth should marry at the age of eighteen, so as not to be tempted to frequent prostitutes.

(12) The direction not to harbour ill-will (Lev. 19.18) was interpreted by the Qaraites, as by the orthodox Jews, in the sense that a misunderstanding should be cleared up the same day, and not carried on to the morrow.

(13) Like other Jews, the Qaraites recognised many degrees of uncleanness, which had to be distinguished one from another in accordance with their laws. Thus meat from a butcher's shop was to be regarded as the corpse of an animal unless it had been slaughtered according to traditional rites. Orthodox Jews saw no objection to eating a fish a short time after it had come out of the water, but the Qaraites looked upon a dead fish as an unclean corpse, mere contact with which brought defilement.

The Qaraites believed themselves possessors of some holiness which God had specially reserved for them. They required their fellow members to observe all the restrictions on conduct imposed by this "New Covenant" made with God in the land of Damascus (by Anan). There were certain penalties (*yswryn*) which were inflicted on delinquents, such as the tearing of the clothes of an unfaithful wife, but also prohibitions ('*yswryn*) with which every branch of Judaism encumbered religion. It was said that rabbinic law only contained prohibitions, whereas that of Moses had prohibitions, but also permissions and accommodations. As can be expected, the Zadokites drew up a number of prohibitions not known to rabbinic law, and in their turn, the Qaraites observed a large number of taboos unknown to other Jews. There is reference to these in the Fragments "A2".

PAGE VII, LINES 6B-12A.

And if they dwell in the camps, according to the custom of the country, and if they take a wife and beget sons, and if they walk according to the Law and follow the rules about the prohibitions which conform to the custom of the Law, (*it will be*) as He said, "*Between a man and his wife, and between a father and his son*" (Num. 30.17 ?). And for all who reject

o

them (*the prohibitions*), there will be the retribution of the wicked, when God examines the earth, and when that happens which is written in the words of the Prophet Isaiah, the son of Amoz, saying, "*There will come for thee and for thy people, and for thy father's house, days (like those) which came from the day Ephraim departed from Judah*" (7.17).

Mention is made here of the "camps" (*mahanoth*) in which the Qaraites dwelt in Moslem countries. This name *mahanoth* has come down to our time, for in many towns in the Orient the Jewish quarter still carries the name of "*Mahane-*". We may recall that the Qaraites surrounded their quarters with walls, and made them into veritable Ghettoes. As the Qaraites practised very strict laws as to marriage, they must have thought that it was only amongst them that the word "family" had any meaning. On the Day of Judgement, God would look upon them as His sons, whilst all the Jews who had not observed their "prohibitions" would be given over to extermination. In this text, the quotations from the Bible are frequently only approximate and lend themselves to different readings. They are here translated with a view to what the author wished to make them say.

PAGE VII, LINES 12B-21A.
When the two houses of Israel divided and Ephraim departed from Judah, and all the faithless were given over to the sword, whilst those who remained steadfast escaped to the land of the North, as He said, "*I will reveal (that which was enclosed in) the tents of your king, and the pedestal of your statues, starting with the tents of Damascus*" (*Amos 5.26*). The Books of the Law are the tent of the king, as He said, "*I will raise up the tent of David which is fallen down*" (*Amos 9.11*). The king, that is the community, and his pedestals for the statues, and the pedestal of the statues, these are the Books of the Prophets whose words Israel has despised. And the Star, that is he who studies the Law and has come to Damascus, as it is written, "*A star has come forth out of Jacob and a sceptre has arisen out of Israel*". The sceptre, that is the prince of all the Congregation, and when he arises, he will break to pieces all the sons of pride (*or of Seth*)".

In this passage, which gives an interpretation of Isa. 7.17, the author carries back the schism between the Qaraites and the rabbinists to the death of Solomon, and to the beginning of the community in Damascus!

He paraphrases Biblical passages to show that the revelation of the Law, the true interpretation of the Biblical texts, must come from Damascus. But the Law is not in the Pentateuch alone, as the Zadokites claimed who denied the authority of the books of the Prophets. The Star foretold in Num. 24.17, is held to be distinct from the sceptre mentioned in the same passage. For the Qaraites, the "Star" was Anan, the founder of the movement, and who did, as a matter of fact, live for some time in Damascus. As to the "Sceptre", they awaited his coming when he should destroy the rabbinist Jews, the sons of Seth (or of pride).

PAGE VII, LINE 21B to PAGE VIII, LINE 12A.

Those (*they of Damascus*) escaped at the end of the first examination by God, whilst the renegades were given over to the sword. And such will also be the sentence for all those who enter into His Covenant, and do not keep to these (*ordinances*). Their examination (*will end*) in utter destruction at the hand of Belial. That will happen on the day that God makes examination, and it will be upon the princes of Judah that His wrath will be poured forth. For they begged for a remedy, yet they crushed all the revolted, among those who had turned away from the way of traitors, and from the way of those given over to robbery, to sensuality and wicked wealth, to revenge and resentment, each towards his brother and each one hating his neighbour. They hid themselves, each from his own flesh (*so as not to help his neighbour*), but they came together to commit incest. They were banded together in their search for wealth and lucre, and each one did what was right in his own eyes. They chose to act each according to the stubbornness of his heart, and have not kept themselves apart from the people (*the unbelievers*). They insolently set themselves free to walk in the way of the wicked, concerning whom God had said, "*Their wine is the poison of dragons, and the deadly venom of asps*" (*Deut. 32.33*). The dragons are the kings of the peoples, and their wine is their ways. The poison of asps is the poison (=*the head*) of the kings of Yawan, come to carry out vengeance upon them.

The reproaches levelled at the rabbinists are here clearly stated. It is on the "princes" of Judah that the wrath of God will be poured out, because they persecuted those who revolted against their doings (the Qaraites) and because they acted contrary to the Qaraite principles stated above. The chief reproach was to have consorted with "the people", the Arabs, the "wicked". By a play upon words (r's signifying either "poison" or "head"), the author foresees that the chief of the kings of Yawan will make the rabbinists pay for their collaboration with the Arabs. Yawan originally meant Ionia (see above p. 104), but here, however, it refers to the Byzantine Empire, and to the campaigns of Nicephorus Phocas, and to the persecutions of the Jews to which they gave rise.

PAGE VIII, LINES 12B-21.

And in spite of this, those who build the wall and plaster it with plaster. have not learned that "he who weighs the wind and pours out lies" pours these out on them, with the result that the wrath of God is kindled against all His Congregation. This is what Moses said, "*It is not because of thy righteousness, nor for the uprightness of thine heart, that thou art come to rule over these peoples, but because He loved thy forefathers, and because He keeps His oath*" (*Deut. 9.5*). Such is also the decision for the penitents in Israel, who have departed from the ways of the "people". With the same love which God had for the "first ones" who were zealous for Him, He has loved those who came after them, and the Covenant made with the forefathers is theirs. But in hatred of the builders of the wall, His anger is kindled. This then is the verdict for all those who despise the commandments of God: He will abandon them and He will . . . them in the stubbornness of their heart.

This is the word that Jeremiah said to Baruch the son of Neriah and Elisha to Gehazi his servant. All the men who entered into the New Covenant, in the land of Damascus . . . . . . . . . .

The parallel passage (Fragment "B") allows us to see more clearly what the author means here. In this passage it is the head of the community, the Chief Rabbi of the orthodox Jews, who is attacked. The rabbinists, the builders of the wall, have not realised to what extent their Chief Rabbi has led them into error, and that is the reason for the persecutions which the Jews in general are suffering. Yet the Chief Rabbi ought to have known that he did not owe his position to his own merit, but to the fact that God remained faithful to His Covenant with the forefathers of the people of Israel. Naturally, His wrath is kindled against the rabbinists, who have not shown the same zeal for God that their ancestors did, and all the orthodox Jews would be abandoned to their fate for having despised the commandments of God. The same punishment awaits the apostates.

The version "A1" of the so-called *Damascus Document* stops here.

## FRAGMENT "B"

This fragment gives a parallel version to "A1" from VII, 6, onwards, and then continues the text, perhaps to its conclusion. It offers some oustanding variants to the "A1" version. It was discovered on a large sheet of thirty-five lines, which is inscribed on both sides.[1]

RECTO, LINES 1-13A.

. . . . . . are assured of living a thousand ages, even as it is written, *"He who keeps the Covenant will find grace with those who love and observe My commandments, during a thousand ages"* (*Deut. 7.9*). And if they dwell in the camps, according to the custom of the country as it was formerly, and if they take a wife according to the rule of the Law, and beget sons, let them walk according to the Law and in conformity with the rule concerning the prohibitions applying the Law, as He has said, *"Between a man and his wife, and between a father and his son"*. And all those who reject the commandments and the precepts (*are destined*) to that which will be rendered to the wicked as their retribution, when God examines the earth, and when that thing comes to pass which was written by the hand of Zechariah the Prophet, *"Awake, O sword, against my shepherd and against the hero, my companion, oracle of God. Smite the shepherd and the flock will be scattered, but I shall stretch out my hand over the young"*. Those who are joined to Him, are the poor of the flock. Those will be saved at the end of the examination, and those who remain will be given over to the sword when the Messiah of Aaron and of Israel comes, as it was at the end of the first examination of which He speaks [* Ezekiel], by the medium of Ezekiel, *"Sound the assembly and set a mark on the forehead of those who sigh and of those who groan, and let the others be given over to the avenging sword which takes vengeance for the Covenant"*.

If the spirit of this passage is obviously the same as that of the parallel passage, VII, 6-VIII, 1, yet the differences are sufficiently important to call for attention on a few points.

Dwelling in "camps" (Ghettoes) is here presented as something which has fallen into disuse, and is only envisaged for the case when the country returned to a custom "such as existed formerly". The quotations from Zech. 13.7 and Ezek. 9.4 give the impression that at the time of the redaction of this text, the Qaraites were subjected to the jurisdiction of the Chief

[1]S. Zeitlin, *The Zadokite Fragments*, Philadelphia, 1952, Plates XVII-XX.

Rabbi of the orthodox Jews. But they had no cause to show themselves satisfied over it. They looked upon themselves as the "young of the flock", the "poor", "those who sighed and who groaned", and they were hoping for the destruction of their rabbinist co-religionists.

RECTO, LINES 13B-24A.

Such will also be the sentence for all those who enter into the Covenant and do not remain faithful to those precepts: to be examined for utter destruction at the hand of Belial. That will be on the day when God will make examination in conformity with the word, "*The princes of Judah have been those who remove the landmark: I will pour out upon them the [. . .] of wrath*". For they entered into the "Covenant of the Return", but they have not avoided the way of the apostates and have allowed themselves to be drawn away by the habits of sensuality and the wealth of the wicked. Each one is vindictive and spiteful towards his brother, and each one hates his neighbour. They have defiled themselves, each one with flesh of his flesh, and have come together to commit incest. They have been bold for riches and lucre, and each has done that which was right in his own eyes. Each has chosen the stubbornness of his heart, and they have not kept themselves apart from the "people" (*of the unbelievers*) and its sins. [They insolently set themselves free] to walk in the ways of the wicked concerning whom God had said, "*Their wine is the poison of dragons and the deadly venom of asps*". The dragons are the kings of the peoples, and their wine is their way. The poison of asps is the poison (=*head*) of the kings of Yawan, come against them to carry out vengeance upon them.

The differences from the version "A1" touch mostly upon two points. The mention of the "Covenant of the Return" (*bryt tšwbh*) will be noted—doubtless the Covenant entered into with God on the return from the Babylonian Exile. According to this text, the "New Covenant" entered into at Damascus would therefore be the fourth. The slight variation in the interpretation of Deut. 32.33 will also be noted. The text as given here suggests that the persecutions of the Jews by Nicephorus Phocas have ended, and that many orthodox Jews from Asia Minor and from Syria have come to swell the community in Egypt. It is well known that many Jews from the Byzantine Empire took refuge in the more tolerant countries of Islam.

RECTO, LINES 24B-33A.

And in spite of all this, they have not learned that the builder of the wall and the plasterer with plaster is he whom the wind drives, and who pays with the whirlwind, and that the preacher is a man given to lying, and because of whom the wrath of God is kindled against all His Congregation. And that which Moses said to Israel, "*It is not because of thy righteousness, nor for the uprightness of thine heart that thou art come to rule over these peoples, but because He loved thy forefathers, and because He keeps His oath*", that also is the decision for the penitents in Israel, who have departed from the way of the people. With the love that God had for the "first ones", who led the people to follow God, He has loved those who came after them, and the Covenant made with the forefathers is theirs. But God hates and abominates the builders of the wall, and His wrath is kindled against them and against all who follow them. And [it is written] in the verdict of [. . .] against all who despise the commandments of God and the ordinances of the "first ones", and who are turned aside in the stubbornness of their hearts.

Here ends the passage where the versions "A1" and "B" are parallel. According to our author, the rabbinist Jews and their "preacher" have no right in "God's Covenant"—that is to say, they should not even be looked upon as Jews.

RECTO, LINES 33B-35.

Thus all the men [who entered] into the New Covenant in the land of Damascus, but who have become apostates and turned away from the well of living water, shall not be reckoned in the Congregation of the people, and they will not be inscribed on His list, from the day of the "gathering"[1] of

VERSO, LINES 1-8A.

the Teacher of the Congregation, until the coming of the Messiah of Aaron and of Israel. Such also is the judgement for each of those who join the Congregation of the men of perfect holiness and loathe the doings of those who have the oversight of the just. This is the man who "*is melted in the midst of the furnace*" (*Ezek. 22.22*), and when his deeds are made clear, let him be expelled from the Congregation as one

[1] "Gathering". The word was very frequently used in the Old Testament for "death" (Gen. 25.8, etc.).

expels anyone whose lot is not in the midst of those to whom God gives life. According to his fault, let him be recorded among the men of sin until the day when he comes back to take his place in the gathering of the men of perfect holiness, and his actions appear to conform with that interpretation of the Law by which the men of perfect holiness order their ways. Let no one have dealings with him about money or work, for all the Holy Ones of the Most High have cursed him.

The text continues by extending to the Qaraite apostate who had joined the rabbinist Jews the same maledictions as applied to these. The name of the apostate is removed from God's register until the coming of the Messiah of Aaron and Israel. It must be supposed therefore that in the belief of the Qaraites of that period, the coming of a new Messiah would be accompanied by the resurrection of the dead. The same fate awaited the Qaraite rabbi who contravened the customs of the community. If he refused to acknowledge the competence of his judges, he was excommunicated. If, however, he amended his ways, he could be reinstated and even become once more one of the Qaraite rabbis.

VERSO, LINES 8B-13A.

This shall be the rule in regard to all who treat the "former" and the "latter" (*prophets*) with contempt, who put "things rolled" over their hearts, and who persist in the stubbornness of their hearts. They have no part in the "House of the Law". This is in agreement with the judgement on their companions who will be judged for having turned back to be with false men. For they have uttered falsehoods about the precepts of righteousness, and have treated with contempt the True Covenant which was made in the land of Damascus, which is the New Covenant. Neither for them nor for their families shall there be any part in the House of the Law.

Among Jews, especially at the end of the thirteenth century, there was a widespread use of amulets, "things rolled", brought about by the spread of cabbalistic writings. The books of Abraham Abulafia, and especially the Zohar attributed to Moses of Leon (about 1300), made a great sensation among the Jews of the Orient. It must be understood that the Qaraites who gave themselves to the wearing of amulets and such practices were placed in the same category as those who went over to Christianity or to Islam, and were excommunicated. In the same way, the Qaraites punished with excommunication all those who held strictly to the requirements of the Pentateuch and gave little regard to the books of the "Former Prophets" (Joshua, Judges, Samuel and Kings), and to those of the "Later Prophets" (Greater and Minor Prophets). This can only have to do with some particularly fanatic sect of Zadokites, which implies that the Zadokite movement, to which the Qaraites are here seen to be opposed, had continued for a long time in Egypt as in certain other countries of the Diaspora.

VERSO, LINES 13B-34.
The whole of this passage is very fragmentary, and scholars have filled in the many gaps in various ways. It does not teach us a great deal. In the first two lines we have reference to a period:

> since the day when it was gathered together by the Teacher of the Community until all the men of war may be exterminated who . . . . . . .

It is doubtful if the text is alluding to some definite event. At all times, the rabbinist Jews seem to have persecuted the Qaraites, and it may be that they called in the armed police of the Fatimides. Very often in the Orient, quarrels between different non-Moslem communities, and even those within the communities themselves, were settled by the intervention of Turkish police.

After a short break come the words:

> with the man of lying since forty years. At the end of this, the wrath of God will be kindled against Israel, as He has said, There is neither king nor prince nor judge who renders justice.

The following sixteen lines are all fragmentary, and then the passage ends with:

> They shall rejoice, and their heart will be strong, and they shall become powerful more than all the sons of earth. God will grant them forgiveness, and they . . . for they trusted in the NAME of His holiness.

The Qaraites were thus to become more powerful than all men living in the world.

It may be noted that the whole of this passage is in the form of prediction, and that there is a complete absence of curses and blessings. It is a repetition of the reasons given to a young Qaraite to remain faithful to the tenets of the sect, and not to abandon the teachers of Anan, the Teacher of Righteousness. It is in fact, the conclusion of a discourse to be read in the course of the *Bar Miṣvah* ceremony.

## FRAGMENTS "A2"

The Fragments "A2" are in a different handwriting from that of "A1" and the arrangement of the pages is not the same. They form part of a Qaraite book setting out certain regulations relating to the religious life and the administration of the community in Egypt.

### PAGE IX, LINES 1-8A.

Anyone who causes an anathema to be pronounced against a man from among men, according to the ways of the "peoples" (*unbelievers*), is to be put to death. As to what has been said, "*Thou shalt not take vengeance nor bear any grudge against the children of thy people*", any man from among those who enter into the Covenant who relates a thing concerning a neighbour which is not among the things which can be rebuked before witnesses, if he relates it in anger or tells it to the "elders" in order that they should treat the neighbour with contempt, that man is avenging himself and bearing a grudge. Is it not written, "*If he takes vengeance, let it be of the adversaries, and if he bears a grudge, let it be against the 'enemies'*" (*Nahum 1.2*)? If he kept silence on the subject from one day till the next, and then spoke in his anger, it is a deadly sin that he has committed, from the fact that he has not kept the commandments of God which said to him, "*With a rebuke thou shalt rebuke thy neighbour, and thou shalt not charge him with sin.*"

Like all the religious communities of the Fatimid Empire, and later of the Ottoman Empire, the Jewish community in Cairo had the right to have its own courts of justice. It was therefore recommended not to have recourse to the courts of the ruling power. Anyone who had a co-religionist condemned by Arab tribunals deserved death. As might be expected, a religious community did not possess the authority to carry out a capital sentence, and in all probability a condemnation of this kind only took the form of an anathema.

The rule of not allowing ill-will to be carried over to the following day is here set forth in more detail (cf. above, VII, 2-3). The slanderer who could not repeat his accusation before witnesses is likened to a spiteful person. When it was a matter of the "enemies" or unbelievers, ill-will was allowed. It was a mortal sin not to rebuke a fellow member, and then later charge him with a crime which he would have been able to avoid. It would seem to be in this sense that the author has interpreted the text of Lev. 19.17-19.

PAGE IX, LINES 8B-16A.

Concerning oaths, He has said, "*Let not thy hand be thy saviour*". The man who takes an oath in place of a witness who has not appeared before the judges, it is of him that it is said that his hand is his saviour. As regards anything that is lost when the thief of the money within the camp is not known, the owner shall swear an oath of execration. Anyone who hears it and who knows the thief, but does not denounce him, becomes guilty. As regards the restitution of something for which no claim of ownership is made, the person restoring it shall make confession to the Cohen, and the "ram of the atonement" will be the only charge that he will have to meet. When anything stolen or lost is found, and there is not an owner, the finder shall hand it over to the Cohens, because he does not know what will be decided about it. So long as no owner is known, the Cohens shall have it in their keeping.

According to rabbinic rules, in certain cases an accused person could clear himself by an oath. The Qaraites only recognised the oath made by witnesses, no one having the right "to save himself by his hand". Only one exception was allowed to this rule, and that was concerned exclusively with the oath of execration. If something had been stolen within the "camp", the Ghetto, then it must have been stolen by a co-religionist. The person robbed solemnly pronounced a curse against the thief, and this curse was considered as passing over to all who became accomplices in the crime by their silence. The thief, smitten by the curse, might implore pardon from his victim. In the Orient, it is frequently the case that the person robbed is so touched by the misery of the thief that he refuses to take his property back, especially when it is perishable food. In this case, the thief makes confession of his crime to someone named Cohen, saying that he had restored what he had taken. He then offers an alms for the poor, and this is called "the ram of the atonement", and the curse is lifted.

In the case of something that has been found, it was to be handed over to someone named Cohen, who should have it in his keeping so long as the owner did not make himself known.

The whole of this writing gives considerable importance to the ancestral name of Cohen. Among the Qaraites, anyone with this name receives far more respect than in other Jewish communities.

PAGE IX, LINES 16B–22A.

If a neighbour sees a man committing an offence against the Law, and if it is a mortal sin, and yet he keeps silence, then it becomes the crime of him who sees it. But if he informs the overseer, the latter shall write it down with his hand until the delinquent shall have been guilty a second time and in the sight of another person who shall have come and informed the overseer. If he repeats the offence, and he is taken before another witness, judgement upon him shall be carried out. If the witnesses are two, but they give evidence to different matters, the man shall only be excluded from the ceremony of purification, but on condition that the witnesses are sincere, and that they had informed the overseer the same day that they had seen the man.

Though the text itself is not quoted, we here again come across the classical interpretation of Lev. 19.17, which insists that denunciation should be made of offences against the Law. In principle, two simultaneous witnesses were necessary, but the Qaraites allowed two successive witnesses of the same offence, on condition that each witness certified that the offence had been committed in the course of the day—that is to say, that there had been a repetition of the same offence. If, on the other hand, two simultaneous witnesses were not in agreement, or if two successive witnesses accused a delinquent of two different offences, then the "overseer", the person responsible for the religious policing of the Ghetto, could only inflict the lesser excommunication, that of exclusion from ceremonies of purification.

PAGE IX, LINE 22B TO PAGE X, LINE 3.

There are two breaks in the earlier part of this passage, so a complete translation is not possible. After saying that in matters touching finance two trustworthy witnesses were necessary, the text, here defective, treats of excommunication and possibly of capital offences. It then continues:

Fear God! Let no one be considered truthful and a witness against his neighbour, if by means of falseness he has in some points transgressed commandments.

To say that no one who had transgressed the precepts of religion could be accepted as a witness amounted to saying that no rabbinist Jew could serve as witness against a Qaraite. The deduction can be drawn that when the fragments of "A2" were drawn up the Qaraites were no longer under the jurisdiction of the orthodox Chief Rabbinate, which was not the case with the fragment "B".

PAGE X, LINES 4-10A.

This is the custom regarding the judges of the Congregation. Periodically, up to ten men shall be chosen from out of the Congregation, four from the tribe of Levi and Aaron and six out of Israel, to be taken from those who are well acquainted with the *Book of Deductions* and with the "prohibitions" of the Covenant. Their ages shall be between twenty-five and sixty years. Let no one function as judge in the Congregation if he is sixty or more, for, because of the unfaithfulness of man, his days have been diminished, and in His wrath against the inhabitants of the earth God has said that He would take away their reason even before they have completed their days.

The Qaraite tribunal was constituted from time to time as cases required it. It comprised a maximum of ten judges, whereas the rabbinic tribunals consisted of a great number of rabbis, the Sanhedrin having as many as seventy-one. The Qaraite judges, chosen from among the well known members of the community, were obliged to include a certain proportion of those who, by their names, could claim to be descendants of a Cohen or a Levi. The judges were not to have more than sixty years of age, whereas among the rabbinists it was not until the age of seventy that anyone could become a *zaqên*. There is here a malicious allusion to the rabbinist judges, with the suggestion that, owing to their great age, they were lacking in reason.

According to the opinion of S. Zeitlin (*op. cit.*) the *Book of Deductions* (*HHGW*) referred to here may not have been in existence at the time that this text was written. It is here associated with the "penalties" and "prohibitions" (see p. 401) of the Qaraites, and these seem to have been put down in writing, perhaps in a work of which we have some columns under our eyes at this moment.

PAGE X, LINES 10B-13.

As regards purification by water. Let no one wash in dirty water, or in a quantity less than one *mar'il* per man. Let no one purify himself in any vessel or cavity in a rock which has not the capacity of a *mar'il*. He who touched these would render himself impure and the water of the vessel would bring defilement on any other water.

The directions for ritual ablutions do not noticeably differ from those laid down by the orthodox rabbis. Running water purified. A stream could serve for purifications, even if an unclean person had bathed in it. A waterfall purified, even if a snake had drunk from it. On the other hand, a spring which dried up once every seven years could not serve for ablutions. Stagnant water in a pool did not purify. A basin for bathing had to have more than forty *seah* of running water. If its capacity was less, it had to have a conduit bringing supplementary water. A basin which was drying up and in which less than a quarter of a *log* of water remained, was unclean even when running water afterwards returned to it. Three *log* of stagnant water poured into a basin fed with running water was sufficient to make it completely unclean. In the absence of running water, the required amount of nine *kab* could be brought in three vessels. If the vessels were so small that it needed four to carry this amount of water, the water could not be used for ablutions. In John 2.6 mention is made of six vessels intended for purifications, and each containing two or three measures. It is probably the last quantity which is correct.[1]

In the present text, the ancient measures of capacity are replaced by the *mar'il*, a kind of water-skin which was fastened on each side of the saddle of an ass. Qaraites were forbidden to make up the required quantity by drawing from a smaller pool.

PAGE X, LINE 14 to PAGE XI, LINE 18A.

The following are the rules for the observance of the sabbath. On the sixth day, let no one do any work from the time that the full disk of the sun touches the horizon, for the Law has said, "*Observe the Sabbath day to keep it holy*". On the Sabbath day, let no one speak vain or useless words. A neighbour shall not be asked for any repayment; money and lucre shall not be discussed. Let no one talk about work or the task to be done the next day. Let no one walk about the field in which he wants work to be done. No one should walk more than 2,000 cubits

---

[1] The following are the approximate equivalents for the measures referred to in this commentary. *Log*=1 pint; *kab*=4 pints; *seah*=3 gallons; *bath*=9 gallons. The measures (*metrêtas*) of John 2.6 were the Hebrew *baths*. The Douay Version keeps to the word "measures", while the A.V. and R.V. give "firkins".

outside the town on the Sabbath day. On the Sabbath day, one should only eat what has been already prepared, and what would perish. [. . .] and eat and drink only if one is inside the "camp". On the road, if anyone steps down to wash, he may drink where he stands, but must not draw up any water in any receptacle. The son of the foreigner is not to be sent to do what one wants done on the Sabbath day. Let no one put on soiled or moth-eaten garments, even if washed in water and rubbed with incense. Let no one on the Sabbath follow his desire and have intercourse. Let no one walk behind an animal so as to make it graze more than 2,000 cubits away from the town. Let no one raise the hand and strike it with the fist: if it is stubborn, do not let it out of its building.

Let no one carry anything in or out of the house, or, if living in a tent, in or out of the tent. No sealed jar is to be opened on the Sabbath day. Let no one put on spices when he walks about on the Sabbath. In the dwelling-house, do not remove stone or dust. Let not the nurse carry the sucking-child about on the Sabbath. No one shall give orders to his servant, maidservant, or workman on the Sabbath.

Let no one make an animal to engender on the Sabbath day, and if a beast falls into a well or ditch on the Sabbath day, do not lift it out. Let no one spend the day near to the "peoples" (*the unbelievers*). Let no one profane the Sabbath because of the wealth and lucre of a Saturday. If a human being should fall into a place where there is water, or into any other place, let no one lift him out with a ladder, rope, or any instrument. Let no one offer anything on the altar on the Sabbath beyond the "Sabbath-offering", for it is written, "*Excepting your Sabbaths*".

This long list of *isûrin* (see p. 401), or taboos, is quite in keeping with the Qaraite spirit. There is evidence elsewhere of the Qaraite prohibition against even the smallest piece of activity on the Saturday, going so far as to refuse help to a drowning person. A sick person was not to use ointments on the Sabbath, although the rabbis allowed the use of pomade except on the Day of Fasting. For that day too, the rabbis prohibited intercourse, but the Qaraites extended the prohibition to every Saturday.

Offerings in the synagogue, here called "the sacrifices of the altar", are forbidden on Saturdays if they are in fulfilment of a vow, etc. On the other hand, as with all Jews, spontaneous gifts are allowed and even encouraged so long as they are not immediately settled by some financial arrangement.

PAGE XI, LINES 18B-23.

Let no one send to the altar a sacrifice, or an offering of incense or of wood, by an unclean person or by a heretic, the use of whom as proxy would be a defilement, and would defile the altar. For it is written, *"The sacrifice of the wicked is an abomination, but the prayer of the upright is an acceptable offering"* (Prov. 15.8). Let no one enter the "House of Prostration" in a state of uncleanness, even if washed. And as to the sounding of the trumpets of the assembly, let it be before or after, but not to make a break anywhere in the service.

The different metaphors used here, sacrifices, offering of wood, etc., refer to gifts made to the synagogue, as they do with orthodox Jews. These gifts were not to be taken there by a heretic (*mn*), which amounts to saying that entrance to the Qaraite synagogues was forbidden to the rabbinists.

As S. Zeitlin points out (*op. cit.*, p. 10) the expression "House of Prostration" is a translation of the Arabic *masjid*, or mosque. The recommendation regarding the trumpets was that a service should not be interrupted by the late arrival of some important person.

PAGE XII, LINES 1-2A.

. . . . . . . is holy. Let no one lie with a woman in the "city of the sanctuary" to defile the city of the sanctuary by their nakedness.

This regulation is typically Qaraite. As is well-known, sexual abstinence has always be regarded by Jews as a sin, and the fact of having no children as malediction by God. It was only on the Day of Atonement, and during the month following the death of a near relative, that sexual abstinence had to be observed. Thus, among Jews, no monastic movement is to be found, and in the whole of Jewish literature there is never any mention of a person taking upon himself the vow of celibacy. There is only one known exception to this rule, and it is found among the Qaraites.

In the ninth century a few Qaraites formed the sect of the 'Abele-Ṣion, the Mourners of Zion. They established themselves in Jerusalem to weep for the destruction of the Temple, and, as if they were really bereaved, they followed an ascetic life, with all the rites of Jewish mourning. The present text suggests that no Qaraite could have dwelt in Jerusalem without joining the 'Abele-Ṣion and observing abstinence. But it would be absurd to imagine that any school of Judaism whatsoever could have insisted on the chastity of all the inhabitants of Jerusalem. The regulation given here could only have applied to pilgrims making the journey to the Holy Land to mourn before the Weeping Wall.

PAGE XII, LINES 2B-6A.

Whosoever shall come under the sway of the spirits of Belial and shall talk about rebellion shall be judged by the ruling concerning sorcerers and necromancers. However, any man who falls into error about profaning the Sabbath and the feasts shall not be put to death, but shall be put under the oversight of the sons of man. If he gets better, and after he has been under observation for seven years, he shall be allowed to enter the synagogue.

As a matter of fact, the Qaraite community had no authority to punish an apostate with death. The latter simply left the community, accompanied by the curses of his former co-religionists. Obviously, if he showed himself within the Qaraite quarter, he could expect to have stones thrown at him. As to offences against religion, such as the non-observance of Sabbaths and feasts, these were punished by exclusion from the synagogue for seven years. The phrase used here, "the sons of man", probably denoted the Qaraites in opposition to the other Jews who, without doubt, were considered as not being worthy of this description. The synagogue is here called the qhl, the assembly, a name still in current use. It is also the word used of the trumpets in XI, 22, which are called the trumpets of the qhl.

PAGE XII, LINES 6B-11A.

Let no one through love of money and lucre stretch forth his hand and spill the blood of a man from among the "peoples" (unbelievers). Also let him not carry off any of their wealth, lest they should blaspheme, unless it be by the advice of the Congregation of Israel. Let no one sell a clean animal or bird to the "peoples" lest they should offer it in sacrifice. For all their money, he shall sell them nothing from his barn or press. He shall not sell them his slave or bondwoman if these have entered with him into the Covenant of Abraham.

Obviously the first rule was due to the fear of collective reprisals in the case where an unbeliever should have been wounded in the course of a scuffle. It was therefore wise not to enter into business relations with the

Moslems, the "peoples", except when the community judged that there was no way to avoid doing so. These regulations reflect very clearly the fear in which Jewish communities lived in the Middle Ages. As to the prohibition against selling clean animals to the unbelievers, this can only refer to Moslems, who were the only people, other than the Jews, both to offer sacrifices of blood and to insist on certain rules about "clean" foods.

There is evidence coming down to the eighteenth century of the right of Jews in Egypt to own slaves. This present text is probably referring to Nubian slaves, some of whom had themselves circumcised and entered into the "Covenant of Abraham".

PAGE XII, LINES 11B-15A.

Let no man defile himself through the eating of any animal or reptile, from bees' cakes to any living thing which moves in the water. As to fish, they should not be eaten unless they have been split open while alive, and drained of their blood. All locusts, according to their kind, should either be passed through the fire or through the water, whilst still alive, as this conforms to the law of their creation.

The Qaraites have food taboos which are far more strict than those of other Jews. Thus they do not eat chickens, because these birds were not named in the Bible in the list of animals which were clean. By "bees' cakes" ('gly hdbwrym), honey was most certainly meant. The rabbis who had declared wild honey to be unclean had authorised the consumption of bees' honey. The Qaraites, on the other hand, insist that anything which comes from an unclean creature is itself unclean. They make the ritual slaughter of fish compulsory. The fish has to be drained of blood before it can be eaten. To touch a dead fish is to incur serious defilement. According to their species, edible locusts are to be grilled or boiled alive. These rules only exist among the Qaraites.

PAGE XII, LINES 15B-18.

All wood, stones, and ashes which have been polluted by the unclean-ness of man shall be placed along with other unclean things. Anyone who touches them partakes of their defilement. And every tool, even a nail or peg in the wall, which is found with the dead in a house shall have the same uncleanness as the worked pot.

The Qaraite had already been forbidden to sit down in the house of an orthodox Jew lest he should render himself unclean by the covering of a divan on which some woman who was unclean might have been sitting. Here it is laid down that contact with any object rendered unclean by man brings defilement. The degree of this depends upon the nature of the defilement of the object. In the main, the same rule is observed by certain orthodox Jews. The most serious of all defilements is that imparted by contact with a corpse. A number of rabbinic rules exist concerning pots and receptacles found in the house of the dead. The Qaraites extended these rules to cover nails and pegs in the walls of a house in which there had been a dead body.

PAGE XII, LINES 19-23.

The rule for the inhabitant of the cities of Israel regarding the above-mentioned judgements, to distinguish between the clean and the unclean, and to recognise the holy from the profane. These have been laid down to be known and followed with regard to every living creature, according to the laws, and from age to age. The seed of Israel shall walk according to this law, and it will not be cursed. And this is the rule of the inhabitants of [. . . . . . .] and they will walk according to this till the end of (*the reign*) of wickedness, until the arrival of the Messiah of Aaron.

The fragment ends there. It is possible that there we have the conclusion of a treatise on uncleanness, but it is also possible that a further list of taboos followed on from this column, but has been lost.

## FRAGMENTS "A3"

The pages of "A3" are very fragmentary, and their original format cannot be established with any certainty. Photography has brought out that they were written by another hand, and with a different ink, which was more pale. It is possible that they were joined to the preceding pages to form a single small volume, but it is certain that page XIII did not follow on immediately from page XII of the fragments "A2".

PAGE XIII, LINES 1-7A.

Israel goes as far as ten persons, in thousands, hundreds, fifties and tens. And in the place where there are ten, let there not be lacking a man named Cohen, versed in the *Book of Deductions,* and to whose words all will be obedient. And if he is not well versed in all these things, but a man named Levi is expert in them, then the decision as to the conduct to be followed by all who enter into the camp shall be according to his words. But if judgement should be given concerning someone according to the law of leprosy, let the Cohen come and stand in the camp, and after the overseer has explained to him the meaning of the Law, even if he is simple-minded, it is for him to order him to be kept shut up, for to them (*the Cohens*) is it to declare judgement.

According to an old tradition, the presence of ten adult Jews (a *minyân*) was necessary for God to reveal His presence. However important a community might be, a gathering of ten men was representative of Israel. Among the Qaraites, one person named Cohen was indispensable, but this was not so with the rabbinist Jews. Naturally, in all this passage, *Kohen* cannot be translated by *priest*, for the priesthood had ceased to exist long before. Moreover, so as to avoid all possible confusion, the text says clearly, '*ys khn*, "a man Cohen", and, further on, '*ys mhlwym*, "a man from those who are Levi". Attention has already been drawn to the importance attached to personal names. Here the case is anticipated where the person named Cohen is rather indifferent to religious matters, and when another member of the community, someone called Levi, is better versed in the Qaraite laws. In this case it belonged to the man named Levi to dictate to the inhabitants of the "camp"—that is to say, the Ghetto—what their conduct should be. In certain special cases, however, the privileges of the Cohen could not be touched. Even if the person named Cohen, who had been brought in for the occasion, was simple-minded, yet he alone could order a sick person suspected of leprosy to be put into quarantine. The overseer of the community had to explain to him all that was expected of him, and what he had to do and say, but all the same, a Cohen had to be called in to pronounce the words authorising the enclosure for long months of a person suffering from eczema.

PAGE XIII, LINES 7B-15 . . .

This is the custom for the overseer of the camp. It is for him to instruct the rabbis in the works of God, to explain to them the might of His miracles, and to relate to them in detail what has taken place in the world. He shall care for them as a father cares for his sons and he [. . . . . .] all their anxieties. Like a shepherd with his flock, he shall untie all the knots which bind them, so that there will be no one in the Congregation who is oppressed or crushed.

And he shall examine all those who join his congregation as to their deeds, knowledge, strength, ability and wealth. Each one shall be inscribed in his position, according to what he is, in the portion of [. . .]. Let no one from among the sons of the camp take upon himself to bring anyone into the Congregation without speaking to the overseer of the camp. Let no one among those who enter into the Covenant of God give or take anything from the sons of the Pit, unless it be from hand to hand.

The "overseer" of the Ghetto had the responsibility of instructing the rabbis in the history of the community, for as a rule candidates for the rabbinate came from some other town. He had to recount to them the miracles which had allowed the community to survive, and afterwards he was to look after them like a shepherd does his flock (see also below, XIV, 12ff).

The overseer had to keep up-to-date the register of the members of the community, and conduct an enquiry as to any persons who came to join it. This present text does not mention it, but he had to make sure if those who called themselves Cohen really had a right to that name. In allotting responsibilities, the overseer had to take account of the financial and intellectual capacity of newcomers for the posts to be assigned to them. The reminder is also given that no one was to bring anyone into the Ghetto without consulting the overseer, or to have business dealings with rabbinist Jews except by direct exchange.

The lower part of this page is in a ruinous condition, and not a single complete sentence can be read there.

PAGE XIV, LINES 1–6A.

[. . . . . .] which have not come from the day that Ephraim departed from Judah. And to all who walk according to these, the Covenant of God is faithful to deliver them at once from all the snares of the Pit, and from sufferings.

And this is the custom for those who are established in each camp: let all be examined in order of their names, the Cohens first, the Levis second, the Sons of Israel third, and the stranger fourth. They shall be inscribed in order of their names, each one after his brother, the Cohens first, the Levis second, the Sons of Israel third, and the stranger fourth.

In this order shall they take their seats, and ask questions on any subject.

The rules for precedence, which were also in use among the rabbinist Jews, took account of ancestral names. Those persons named Cohen always had the right to speak first in meetings of the Community. Next came the turn of the Levis, and it was only after that that the other members of the community had the right to speak. There is nothing specifically Qaraite in this arrangement. It will be noticed that the stranger had a right to express his opinion, but naturally after all the others.

PAGE XIV, LINES 6B-16 . . .

The Cohen who examines a man rabbi shall be between thirty and sixty years of age, versed in the Book of [. . .] and in all the decisions of the Law, so as to be able to speak to him about their decisions.

In each camp will be an overseer who shall be between thirty and fifty years of age. He shall be a man of affairs and proficient in languages. It will be in accordance with his word that members shall enter the Congregation, each in his turn. And for any matter [. . . . . . . . .] the man, it is to the overseer that he shall speak for every lawsuit or process.

(And this is) the custom for the rabbis, so as to provide for their needs. (The members of the community), they shall give to the overseer and the judges at least two days' income per month. From this, they shall give for the [. . . . . . .] and from this they shall support [. . .] the poor, the needy and the old who [. . .] and for the man who is wounded, for the [. . .] captive of an enemy people, for virgins who [. . . . . . . . .

It is someone named Cohen who finally carries out an examination of the new Qaraite rabbi, the "man rabbi" (*'yš hrbym*) already approved by the "overseer" of the Ghetto. Naturally, so as to make this examination, the Cohen himself had to be well versed in the Law and the customs. The "overseer", responsible for relations with the non-Jewish authorities, on principle had to be acquainted with foreign languages. He had to watch over matters of precedence, and it was to him that application had to be made for the calling together of religious tribunals to deal with lawsuits between co-religionists.

It was arranged to pay the rabbis a stipend, for small town communities could not have provided much by way of the *terûmah*. The members of the community were to pay into the hands of the judges and the overseer a worship tax, the amount left to the discretion of each member, except that it was not to be less than the equivalent of two days' income each month, or about 8 per cent. From this revenue, the community paid its rabbis and gave help to the poor and the sick. One important charge on this fund was the redemption of captives taken by plunderers of caravans or by pirates.

The imperfect nature of the text prevents us from learning if from this fund dowries were provided for poor brides, as in other Jewish communities.

PAGE XV, LINES 1-13 . . .

. . . .] as much by *aleph* and *lamedh* as also by *aleph* and *daleth*, but by the oath of the Covenant and by the curses of the Covenant. And let him not refer to "the Law of Moses" [. . . . . .]. If he takes an oath and trangresses, and if he profanes the NAME, if it is by the oaths of the Covenant that he has sworn, let him be judged [as someone who] has transgressed. He is guilty. And if he [. . . . . .], he will not take upon himself [. . .] of death.

And for him who enters into the Covenant, for all Israel, this shall be an everlasting ordinance that its sons who [. . . . . .] must present themselves before the overseer so that the oath of the Covenant may be administered to them. Such shall be the law until the final end of wickedness for all those who turn back from their perverse ways. The day when he (*the young man*) shall speak with the overseer appointed by the rabbis, he shall be examined by the oath of the Covenant, as Moses announced it to the people of Israel. It is the Covenant [. . . . . .] Moses, with all his heart and with all his soul, to him who has been found (*fit*) to make [. . . . . .]. Let no one make known to him the provisions which have been laid down until he shall have been before the overseer, lest in studying them he should go astray. But when there has been administered to him the oath to return to the Covenant of Moses, with all his heart and with all his soul, . . . . . . . . . .

Like all Jews, the Qaraites were forbidden to swear by God, whether by *Elohim* (of which the first two letters were *aleph* and *lamedh*) or by *Adonai* (of which the first two letters were *aleph* and *daleth*). Nor were they to swear by the "Law of Moses". He who took a false oath by "the Covenant" was a perjurer, and in consequence had to be punished, but he was not a blasphemer, so that it was not necessary to punish by death.

It was recommended to all members of the Qaraite sect to present their sons for confirmation. When a boy reached the age of thirteen, (the text here is defective) he was to be presented to the overseer, who would put him through an examination. He then took the oath to remain faithful to the Law of Moses, and it was only then that he was informed of the Qaraite law. In brief, the young man had to be able to read the Bible before he was authorised to read Qaraite works.

PAGE XVI, LINES 1-13 . . .

. . . . . .   ". . .] a Covenant with you and with all Israel." That is why the man should promise upon his soul to return to the Covenant of Moses, for there everything is explained. The interpretation of the destructions which came upon them because of their blindness in the face of all these (*the Laws of Moses*), behold, it is given in the Book of the Division of the Ages, according to their jubilees and weeks of years. And the day when the man engages on his soul, to return to the Law of Moses, the Angel of Hostility will turn away from him, if he keeps to his word. That is why Abraham circumcised himself the day that he learned about it. As to that which He said, "*That which has gone out of thy lips, thou shalt observe and do*" (*Deut. 23.23*), even under threat of death, let not a man release himself from any binding oath that he has taken upon his soul to do the things according to the Law. On the other hand, any oath that a man has taken upon his soul to infringe the Law, let him not keep that, even under threat of death.

As regards an oath taken by a woman who has been told by her husband to cancel the oath, let a man not cancel an oath which [. . . . . .]. It is to be kept. As to cancelling, if it is contrary to the Covenant, let him cancel that, for it is not to be kept. And the same law applies to her father . . . . . . . . . .

Here it is still the question of the confirmation of a young Qaraite. In the course of his examination by the overseer of the rabbis, it was said that all is explained in the Bible, but the "interpretation" of historical events, the reasons for the occasions when God was angry with His people, that he would learn by reading the *Book of the Division of the Ages*. Some scholars have seen here a connection with the apocryphal book known as *Book of Jubilees* or the *Little Genesis,* because in that work, Jewish history is interpreted by "jubilees and weeks". Some scholars have gone further, and thought that they could draw conclusions about the calendar of "the sect". Nothing of that kind can be read in this fragment. It is simply the question of the oath of fidelity to the Covenant of Moses which a young man took at his confirmation. In all probability, the *Book of the Division of the Ages* which was read to him, was precisely that writing of which a part has been preserved in the fragments "A1".

There is one other remark to make on this subject. Jewish girls do not have a Confirmation. The text we have here anticipated a case where a woman who was adult had taken an oath. Normally, she should have been married at the age of twelve. In that case, her husband could have released her from her oath if what she had sworn was contrary to Qaraite law. Had she not been married, her father could have annulled the oath. On the other hand, if the oath was not in opposition to the religious laws, it had to be kept in the same way as that taken by a young man at his Confirmation.

It is not necessary to remind the reader that there is no connection at all between the *Damascus Document* and the manuscripts found in Cave I at Qumrân. There would have been no need to include a translation of these fragments had it not been that some authors continue to insert them into their translations of the Dead Sea Scrolls, as if they belonged to the same age and the same place of origin. These medieval pages may be most interesting, but it should be acknowledged that they offer no help in the solving of the riddle of the Dead Sea Scrolls.

# Index